Excavations at Roughground Farm, Lechlade, Gloucestershire: a prehistoric and Roman landscape

Frontispiece: Aerial view of the whole site from the north-west photographed by J K St. Joseph in 1957 (Cambridge University Collection No. VM 5, copyright reserved)

The Oxford Archaeological Unit
Thames Valley Landscapes: The Cotswold Water Park, Volume 1
(Series Editor: Ellen McAdam)

Excavations at Roughground Farm, Lechlade, Gloucestershire: a prehistoric and Roman landscape

by
Tim Allen, Timothy Darvill,
Sarah Green and Margaret Jones

with contributions by
Justine Bayley, Paul Booth, Robin Brunner-Ellis, Sarnia Butcher,
Cecily Cropper, Mary Harman, Kay Hartley, Richard Hingley,
Gillian Jones, Cathy King, John Letts, Bruce Levitan,
Liz MacRobert, Alan Palmer, Mark Robinson, Chris Salter,
John Shepherd, Grace Simpson, and David Williams.

Published for
The Oxford Archaeological Unit
by
The Oxford University Committee for Archaeology
1993

Published by the Oxford University Committee for Archaeology
Institute of Archaeology, Beaumont Street, Oxford

Distributed by Oxbow Books
Park End Place, Oxford, OX1 1HN

© Oxford Archaeological Unit 1993

ISBN 0 947816 83 6

The publishers wish to acknowledge with gratitude
a grant from English Heritage towards the publication costs.

Origination and layout by ArchaeoInformatica
12 Cygnet Street, York YO2 1AG

Printed in Great Britain by
The Short Run Press, Exeter

Contents

Except in Chapter II and microfiche Chapter 2, unattributed parts of the report were written by Tim Allen.

Preface *by David Miles*	xix
Summary	xxi
Acknowledgements	xxii

I Introduction — 1

I.1	The background to the 1957–65 excavations *by Margaret Jones*	1
I.2	The 1981–82 and 1990 excavations *by Tim Allen*	3
I.3	Geology and topography	3
I.4	Excavation methodology *by Margaret Jones*	4
I.5	Post-excavation methodology *by Tim Allen*	5
I.6	The Archive	5
I.7	Preparation of the report	5
I.8	Organisation of the report	5
I.8.a	Conventions used in this report	5
I.9	The Cotswold Water Park series	6

II The early prehistoric period — 9

by Timothy Darvill

II.A	**The Grooved Ware occupation**	**9**
II.A.1	Description of the features	9
II.A.2	Pottery	9
II.A.2.a	Introduction	9
II.A.2.b	Fabrics	9
II.A.2.c	Forms and decoration	9
II.A.2.d	Discussion	10
II.A.3	Flintwork	10
II.A.4	Stone object	12
II.A.5	Bone objects	12
II.A.6	Animal bones *by Gillian Jones*	12
II.A.7	Freshwater mollusca remains *by Mark Robinson*	15
II.A.8	Radiocarbon dates	15
II.B	**Beaker period occupation**	**15**
II.B.1	Description of excavated features	15
II.B.2	Pottery	15
II.B.2.a	Introduction	15
II.B.2.b	Fabrics	15
II.B.2.c	Catalogue of illustrated sherds	15
II.B.3	Ceramic objects and daub	17
II.B.4	Flintwork	18
II.B.5	Stone objects	18
II.B.6	Animal bones *by Gillian Jones*	21
II.B.7	Radiocarbon date	21

II.C Early Bronze Age   21
- II.C.1 Pottery ... 21
- II.C.2 Discussion ... 21

II.D Undated prehistoric features   21
- II.D.1 Description of the features ... 21
- II.D.2 Flintwork ... 22

II.E Flints from later features   22
- II.E.1 General ... 22
- II.E.2 Composition ... 22

II.F Discussion   22

III The later prehistoric period   27

III.A Later Bronze Age occupation   27
- III.A.1 Description of the features ... 27
- III.A.2 Bronze Age pottery *by Richard Hingley* ... 28
  - III.A.2.a Catalogue of the illustrated sherds ... 28
  - III.A.2.b Discussion ... 31
- III.A.3 Flints from Bronze Age features *by Timothy Darvill* ... 31
- III.A.4 Other finds ... 34
  - III.A.4.a Worked bone ... 34
  - III.A.4.b Fired clay ... 34
  - III.A.4.c Stone ... 34
- III.A.5 Animal bones *by Gillian Jones* ... 34
- III.A.6 Mollusca and charcoal from pit 879 *by Mark Robinson* ... 35
- III.A.7 Radiocarbon dates ... 35
- III.A.8 Discussion ... 35

III.B The Early Iron Age occupation   36
- III.B.1 Description of the features ... 36
  - III.B.1.a The major land boundaries ... 36
  - III.B.1.b The main occupation area ... 36
  - III.B.1.c Pit scatters ... 36
  - III.B.1.d The roundhouse ... 40
  - III.B.1.e Other features ... 40
- III.B.2 Early Iron Age pottery *by Richard Hingley* ... 40
  - III.B.2.a Summary ... 40
  - III.B.2.b Fabrics ... 40
  - III.B.2.c Forms ... 40
  - III.B.2.d Catalogue of illustrated sherds ... 43
  - III.B.2.e Decoration ... 44
  - III.B.2.f Discussion ... 44
- III.B.3 Other finds ... 44
  - III.B.3.a Stone ... 44
    Thin-sections by Timothy Darvill
  - III.B.3.b Fired clay ... 44
- III.B.4 Contracted or crouched burials ... 45
- III.B.5 Animal bones *by Gillian Jones* ... 45
- III.B.6 Charcoal from Iron Age features *by Mark Robinson* ... 46
- III.B.7 Radiocarbon dates ... 46
- III.B.8 Discussion ... 46
  - III.B.8.a The major land boundaries ... 46
  - III.B.8.b Pits and pit-alignments ... 47

	III.B.8.c Structures	47

IV The Roman occupation — 49

IV.A Introduction — 49
IV.A.1 Excavation and post-excavation methodology — 49

IV.B The Early Roman occupation — 51
IV.B.1 Introduction — 51
IV.B.2 A ditched compound containing House-enclosure 56, pits and pen — 51
IV.B.3 'Well' 54 and adjacent features — 51
IV.B.4 Pits, postholes and gullies to the west — 51
IV.B.5 Features below the villa buildings and courtyard — 52
IV.B.6 Features east of the main settlement — 52
IV.B.7 Early Roman cremation within square ditched enclosure — 52

IV.C The villa buildings and courtyard — 53
IV.C.1 Introduction — 53
IV.C.2 Building I — 53
IV.C.3 Building II — 53
IV.C.4 Building 'B' — 58
IV.C.5 Quarry hollows 190–193 east of the villa buildings — 58
IV.C.6 Building IV — 58
    IV.C.6.a Pre-building deposits — 58
    IV.C.6.b Phase 1 — 63
    IV.C.6.c Phase 2 — 63
    IV.C.6.d Phase 3 — 66
    IV.C.6.e Phase 4 — 69
    IV.C.6.f Phase 5 — 71
    IV.C.6.g Phase 6 — 71
IV.C.7 Building V — 73
IV.C.8 Building III — 73
    IV.C.8.a Introduction — 73
    IV.C.8.b The hypocausted rooms on the west: Rooms 1, 2, 3, 9 and 10 — 73
    IV.C.8.c The rooms on the east side: Rooms 5, 6, 7 & 8 — 77
    IV.C.8.d The yard east of the building and the boundary ditches to the south — 77
    IV.C.8.e The verandah on the west — 81
    IV.C.8.f Pre-building features — 81
    IV.C.8.g Dating — 81
IV.C.9 The villa courtyard — 83

IV.D The enclosures west of the villa — 83
IV.D.1 Introduction — 83
IV.D.2 Development — 84

IV.E The enclosures north and immediately east of the villa — 89

IV.F The Later Roman enclosures and droveways east of the villa — 89
IV.F.1 Introduction — 89
IV.F.2 'Corndrier' and ovens — 90
IV.F.3 Pits and hollows — 92
    IV.F.3.a The silt-filled pits — 92
    IV.F.3.b Deep pits — 95
IV.F.4 Later Roman burials — 95
    IV.F.4.a Distribution — 95
    IV.F.4.b Burials in the villa — 95

	IV.F.4.c	Burials in the northern enclosure group	95
	IV.F.4.d	Burials in the southern enclosure group and alongside the boundary ditch	101
	IV.F.4.e	Other burials	101
	IV.F.4.f	Points of interest	101
IV.F.5		The northern enclosure group	101
	IV.F.5.a	Introduction	101
	IV.F.5.b	The enclosure ditches	101
	IV.F.5.c	Features behind the enclosures	103
IV.F.6		The southern enclosure group	103
	IV.F.6.a	Introduction	103
	IV.F.6.b	The enclosure ditches	103
	IV.F.6.c	Features behind the enclosures	106
IV.F.7		Circular enclosure 481 and adjacent features	106
IV.F.8		The gravel-pit area	109
IV.F.9		The timber building, Building VI	110
IV.F.10		Post-Roman use of the site	110

V The finds of the Roman and post-Roman periods — 113

V.1		The organisation and phasing of the finds reports	113
V.2		The Roman pottery *by Sarah Green and Paul Booth*	113
	V.2.a	Introduction to the pottery recovered between 1957 and 1982 *by Sarah Green*	113
	V.2.b	Fabrics (for pottery recovered between 1957 and 1982)	114

Amphorae by David Williams
Mortaria by Kay Hartley
Samian ware by Grace Simpson

	V.2.c	Forms (for pottery recovered between 1957 and 1982)	119
	V.2.d	Discussion of pottery recovered between 1957 and 1982	133
	V.2.e	Conclusions from the pottery recovered between 1957 and 1982	134
	V.2.f	Introduction to the pottery from the 1990 excavation *by Paul Booth*	135
	V.2.g	Fabrics of the pottery recovered in 1990	137
	V.2.h	Vessel types of the pottery recovered in 1990	138
	V.2.i	Chronology derived from the pottery recovered in 1990	139
	V.2.j	Discussion	141
V.3		Roman and later coins *by Cathy King*	142
V.4		Copper alloy objects *by Tim Allen, Sarnia Butcher, & Robin Brunner-Ellis*	144
	V.4.a	Summary catalogue	144
	V.4.b	Discussion	149
V.5		Lead objects *by Tim Allen and Robin Brunner-Ellis*	149
V.6		Iron objects *by Tim Allen and Robin Brunner-Ellis*	150
	V.6.a	Discussion	152
V.7		Glass objects *by John Shepherd and Cecily Cropper*	156
	V.7.a	Analysis	156
	V.7.b	Catalogue of illustrated glass fragments	156
	V.7.c	Discussion	156
	V.7.d	Faience and other glass beads	158
V.8		Worked bone and ivory objects *by Tim Allen and Robin Brunner-Ellis*	158
V.9		Jet and shale objects *by Tim Allen*	158
V.10		Stone objects *by Tim Allen*	160
V.11		Fired clay objects *by Alan Palmer and Tim Allen*	165
V.12		Building materials: flooring	166
	V.12.a	Mosaic fragments *by Elizabeth MacRobert and Tim Allen*	166
	V.12.b	*Opus signinum* and mortar flooring *by Tim Allen*	167
V.13		Building materials: walls and ceilings	167
	V.13.a	Painted plaster *by Elizabeth MacRobert (1990 report by Robin Brunner-Ellis)*	167
	V.13.b	Other plaster and Tufa *by Tim Allen*	168

V.14	Building materials: roofing slates and roofing and other tiles *by Tim Allen*	168
V.14.a	Ceramic tiles *by Tim Allen (with comments by Mike Stone)*	168
V.15	Metalworking debris *by Tim Allen (with comments by Chris Salter)*	168
V.16	Human bones *by Mary Harman*	169
V.16.a	Introduction	169
V.16.b	Methodology	169
V.16.c	Decapitation	169
V.16.d	Conclusions	171
V.17	Animal bones *by Gillian Jones and Bruce Levitan*	171
V.17.a	The nature of the assemblage recovered between 1957 and 1982 *by Gillian Jones*	171
V.17.b	Overall results (bones recovered between 1957 and 1982)	171
V.17.c	Cattle bones (recovered between 1957 and 1982)	172
V.17.d	Sheep/goat bones (recovered between 1957 and 1982)	172
V.17.e	Pig bones (recovered between 1957 and 1982)	173
V.17.f	Horse bones (recovered between 1957 and 1982)	173
V.17.g	Bones of other species (recovered between 1957 and 1982)	173
V.17.h	Introduction to the bones recovered in 1990 *by Bruce Levitan*	173
V.17.i	Taxa represented in the bones from 1990	174
V.17.j	Lateral variation in the bones from 1990	174
V.17.k	Cattle bones from the 1990 excavation	174
V.17.l	Sheep/goat bones from the 1990 excavation	175
V.17.m	Pig bones from the 1990 excavation	175
V.18	Charred plant and molluscan remains *by John Letts and Mark Robinson*	175
V.18.a	Introduction	175
V.18.b	Results	175
V.18.c	Discussion and conclusions	176
V.18.d	Molluscan and other charred remains	176
V.19	Coal *by Tim Allen, with identifications by R Neves and G Clayton*	176

VI Discussion of the Romano-British occupation   179

VI.1	The Early Roman occupation	179
VI.2	The villa buildings	181
VI.2.a	The aisled buildings	181
VI.2.b	Dating of the villa buildings	183
VI.3	The field system and enclosures around the villa	187
VI.4	The villa economy	191
VI.5	Burials	192
VI.5.a	Early Roman burials	192
VI.5.b	Later Roman burials	192

VII The site in the landscape   195

Bibliography   201

Contents of Microfiche 1

The numbering of the sections of the Microfiche mirrors that of the printed text and some section numbers are therefore omitted in the microfiche.

1 Introduction — Fiche 1#2
    1.3   List of air photographs consulted . . . . Fiche 1#2

2 The early prehistoric period — Fiche 1#3
by Timothy Darvill

2.A   The Grooved Ware pits . . . . Fiche 1#3
    2.A.1   Description of the excavated features . . . . Fiche 1#3
    2.A.2   Pottery . . . . Fiche 1#5
        2.A.2.a   Catalogue of Grooved Ware sherds . . . . Fiche 1#5
        2.A.2.b   Early prehistoric pottery fabrics and thin-section results . . . . . . Fiche 1#6
        2.A.2.d   Discussion . . . . Fiche 1#8
    2.A.3   Flintwork . . . . Fiche 1#8
        2.A.3.a   Catalogue of the Grooved Ware flint types . . . . Fiche 1#8
    2.A.6   Additional notes on the animal bones *by Gillian Jones* . . . . Fiche 1#9

2.B   Beaker period pits . . . . Fiche 1#10
    2.B.1   Description of excavated features . . . . Fiche 1#10
    2.B.2   Beaker pottery . . . . Fiche 1#11
        2.B.2.b   Fabrics . . . . Fiche 1#11
        2.B.2.c   Catalogue of Beaker pottery . . . . Fiche 1#12
    2.B.3   Ceramic objects and daub . . . . Fiche 1#14
    2.B.4   Flintwork . . . . Fiche 1#14
        2.B.4.a   Catalogue of Beaker flint types . . . . Fiche 1#14
    2.B.5   Stone objects . . . . Fiche 1#15
        2.B.5.a   Catalogue of stone objects . . . . Fiche 1#15

2.D   Undated prehistoric features . . . . Fiche 1#16
    2.D.2   Flintwork . . . . Fiche 1#16

2.E   **Flints from later features** . . . . **Fiche 1#17**
    2.E.1   Catalogue of residual flintwork by type . . . . Fiche 1#17

3 The later prehistoric occupation — Fiche 1#19

3   The Later Bronze Age and Iron Age occupation . . . . Fiche 1#19
    3.1   Sections of the features . . . . Fiche 1#19
    3.2   The Later Bronze Age and Iron Age pottery *by Richard Hingley* . . . . Fiche 1#21
        3.2.a   Introduction . . . . Fiche 1#21
        3.2.b   Fabric . . . . Fiche 1#21
        3.2.c   Decoration and Surface Treatment . . . . Fiche 1#23
        3.2.d   Form . . . . Fiche 1#23
        3.2.e   Discussion . . . . Fiche 1#24
    3.3   Flints from Bronze Age features *by Timothy Darvill* . . . . Fiche 1#25
        3.3.a   Catalogue of Bronze Age flint types . . . . Fiche 1#25
    3.4   Other Finds of Bronze Age or Iron Age date . . . . Fiche 1#25
        3.4.a   Fired Clay . . . . Fiche 1#25
        3.4.b   Stone *by Thin-sections by Timothy Darvill* . . . . Fiche 1#26

3.6	Environmental evidence *by Mark Robinson*	Fiche 1#26
3.6.a	Mollusca from pit 879	Fiche 1#26
3.6.b	Charcoal from Bronze and Iron Age features	Fiche 1#27

4 The Roman occupation   Fiche 1#28

4.A	Introduction	Fiche 1#28
4.B	The Early Roman occupation	Fiche 1#28
4.C	The villa buildings and courtyard	Fiche 1#31
4.D	The enclosures west of the villa	Fiche 1#35
4.F	The Later Roman enclosures and droveways east of the villa	Fiche 1#40
4.F.8	The gravel-pit area	Fiche 1#51

Contents of Microfiche 2

5 The finds of the Roman and post-Roman periods   Fiche 2#2

5.2	The Romano-British pottery *by Sarah Green*	Fiche 2#2
5.2.a	The archive	Fiche 2#2
5.2.b	Catalogue of samian ware *by Grace Simpson*	Fiche 2#2
5.2.c	Catalogue of amphorae sherds *by David Williams*	Fiche 2#8
5.2.d	Mortarium Fabrics *by Kay Hartley and Sarah Green*	Fiche 2#8
5.2.e	Other fabrics	Fiche 2#9
5.2.f	Major form definitions	Fiche 2#18
5.2.g	Pottery from the 1990 excavation: tables *by Paul Booth*	Fiche 2#24
5.4	Copper alloy objects	Fiche 2#27
5.4.a	Catalogue of copper alloy objects	Fiche 2#27
5.4.b	Analytical results for some copper alloy objects *by Justine Bayley*	Fiche 2#34
5.5	Lead objects *by Tim Allen and Robin Brunner-Ellis*	Fiche 2#36
5.5.a	Catalogue of Lead Objects	Fiche 2#36
5.6	Iron objects *by Tim Allen and Robin Brunner-Ellis*	Fiche 2#38
5.6.a	Catalogue of iron objects	Fiche 2#38
5.6.b	Nails	Fiche 2#47
5.7	Glass objects *by John Shepherd and Cecily Cropper*	Fiche 2#47
5.7.a	Catalogue of glass objects	Fiche 2#48
5.7.b	Catalogue of glass objects from the 1990 excavation	Fiche 2#50
5.8	Worked bone and ivory objects	Fiche 2#52
5.8.a	Catalogue of worked bone and ivory objects	Fiche 2#52
5.9	Jet and shale objects	Fiche 2#54
5.10	Stone objects	Fiche 2#54
5.10.a	Summary	Fiche 2#54
5.10.b	Catalogue of querns and 'rubbers' or pestles	Fiche 2#55
5.10.c	Full catalogue of stone objects	Fiche 2#58
5.11	Fired clay objects *by Alan Palmer and Tim Allen*	Fiche 2#62
5.11.a	Introduction	Fiche 2#62
5.11.b	Fabrics	Fiche 2#63
5.11.c	Types of object	Fiche 2#65
5.11.d	Spindle whorls	Fiche 2#66
5.11.e	Sling pellets	Fiche 2#66
5.11.f	Loomweights	Fiche 2#67

	5.11.g	Crucible	Fiche 2#67
	5.11.h	Moulds	Fiche 2#67
	5.11.i	Possible flute	Fiche 2#67
	5.11.j	Ovens	Fiche 2#68
	5.11.k	Wall or oven daubing materials	Fiche 2#68
	5.11.l	General conclusions	Fiche 2#69
5.12		Building materials: floors *by Tim Allen and Elizabeth MacRobert*	Fiche 2#69
	5.12.a	Mosaic and tessellated fragments *by Elizabeth MacRobert*	Fiche 2#69
	5.12.b	*Opus signinum* and mortar	Fiche 2#70
5.13		Building materials: walls and ceilings	Fiche 2#73
	5.13.a	Painted plaster from the 1957–82 excavations *by Elizabeth MacRobert*	Fiche 2#73
	5.13.b	Painted plaster from the 1990 excavations *by Robin Brunner-Ellis*	Fiche 2#77
	5.13.c	Undecorated Plaster and Tufa *by Tim Allen*	Fiche 2#78
5.14		Building materials: roofing slates and roofing and other tiles	Fiche 2#79
	5.14.a	Stone slates and stone ridge-tile	Fiche 2#79
	5.14.b	Ceramic tiles from the 1957–65 excavations	Fiche 2#80
	5.14.c	Ceramic tiles from the 1990 excavation *by Tim Allen, with comments by Mike Stone*	Fiche 2#81
5.15		Metalworking slag *by Chris Salter*	Fiche 2#82
	5.15.a	Sample SF 1419 from context 2413	Fiche 2#82
	5.15.b	Sample SF 1495 from context 2030	Fiche 2#83
	5.15.c	Other slag	Fiche 2#84
5.16		Human bones *by Mary Harman*	Fiche 2#84
5.17		Animal bones *by Gillian Jones and Bruce Levitan*	Fiche 2#89
	5.17.a	Animal bones from the 1957–82 excavations	Fiche 2#89
	5.17.b	Animal bones from the 1990 excavation	Fiche 2#91
5.18		Plant and Invertebrate Remains *by John Letts and Mark Robinson*	Fiche 2#92
	5.18.a	Introduction	Fiche 2#93
	5.18.b	Mollusca	Fiche 2#93
	5.18.c	Carbonised plant remains	Fiche 2#94
	5.18.d	Charcoal	Fiche 2#94
5.19		Coal *by Tim Allen (with identifications by R Neves and G Clayton)*	Fiche 2#96

Contents of Microfiche 3

Table 76: Pits and hollows from the 1957–65 excavations	Fiche 3#2
Table 77: Postholes (or small pits) from the 1957–65 excavations	Fiche 3#10
Table 78: Contexts and their dimensions from the 1990 excavations	Fiche 3#12
Table 79: Concordance of contexts and pottery from 1957–65 and 1981–82 excavations.	Fiche 3#16

Contents of Microfiche 4

Figure 153: Site plan illustrated in 30 × 40 m gridded areas	Fiche 4#2

List of Figures

	Frontispiece: Aerial view of the whole site from the north-west	ii
1	Overall site plan	xx
2	Aerial view of the villa from the north-west, showing the regular enclosure system north and east of the villa buildings. Riley 1942 (Cambridge Air Photograph No. CD 044)	2
3	Aerial view of the villa and Early Roman occupation from the north-west, taken after stripping in 1957 just before excavation began. (Cambridge Air Photograph No. VQ29)	2
4	Site location and geology	3
5	Key to conventions used on section drawings	5
6	Overall site plan gridded to show the layout of plans as illustrated on Fiche 4. The numbers refer to individual frames on the microfiche.	7
7	Plan of the distribution of prehistoric features identified by period	8
8	Grooved Ware pottery	10
9	Flints from Grooved Ware features	11
10	Drawing conventions used for flintwork	12
11	Flints and hammerstone from Grooved Ware pit 785 (photograph by T C Darvill)	13
12	Bone points from pit 784	13
13	Hammerstone from pit 785	13
14	Deposit of antlers in Grooved Ware pit 962	14
15	Beaker pottery	16
16	Graph showing the size distribution of Grooved Ware and Beaker scrapers	18
17	Flints from Beaker features	19
18	Cushion stones and hammerstones from Beaker pit 1260	20
19	Pottery and flintwork from residual and unstratified contexts	23
20	Late Neolithic and Early Bronze Age sites and monuments in the Lechlade area	24
21	Bronze Age pit 879, over-excavated to show undercut	27
22	Later Bronze Age pottery No. 0	29
23	Later Bronze Age pottery Nos. 1–20	30
24	Later Bronze Age pottery Nos. 21–33	32
25	Flints from Later Bronze Age pits	33
26	Plan of Early Iron Age settlement at the east of the site	37
27	Early Iron Age settlement: sections	38
28	Early Iron Age four-post structure 1201–1204 taken from the south-east	39
29	Iron Age roundhouse taken from the north-east (photographed by W T Jones)	39
30	Iron Age roundhouse and Early Roman burial	41
31	Early Iron Age pottery	42
32	Later prehistoric burials: 1157 Bronze Age; 1275 & 1215 Iron Age	45
33	Early Roman settlement plan: overall distribution of features	48
34	Early Roman occupation: plan of House-enclosure 56, pits and ditches	50
35	Early Roman square-ditched cremation burial 1137, from the east (photographed by W T Jones)	52
36	Plan of layout of trenches and villa buildings	54
37	Plan of Buildings I and II	55
38	Building I: sections	56
39	Building I: Trench 7a from the south-east	57
40	Building II: Wall 153 and trenches from the east	57
41	Building II and courtyard: sections	59
42	Plan of Building III and Building IV	61
43	Building IV: phases 1 and 2	62
44	Building IV: N–S sections	64
45	Building IV from the north-west showing the apsidal west end	65
46	Building IV machine-cut trench: N–S section drawn in 1982.	67

47	Building IV: phases 3 and 4	68
48	Building IV: NW–SE section	70
49	Building IV: phases 5 and 6	72
50	Building III: sections of west wall at the south end, of Box I, and of features below the west wall	74
51	Building III: Rooms 1 and 2 showing the channeled hypocaust from the south-west	75
52	Building III: sections across ditch 2029 and wall 2028	76
53	Building III: sections of Boxes L, T, U and W	78
54	Building III: Room 9 showing sub-floor and hypocaust piers	79
55	Building III: section to south across boundary ditches	80
56	Building III: verandah from the east-south-east with ranging rods in the first phase postholes	82
57	Building III: verandah from the north-east alongside the west wall 240, showing the second phase dry-stone wall sitting upon the first phase floor	82
58	Trenches north-west of Building III: sections	83
59	Phased plan of the development of the western enclosures (2nd–4th centuries)	85
60	Enclosures west of the villa: Pit 409 from the north-west	86
61	Enclosures west of the villa: 'Corndrier' 469 from the north-east	87
62	Enclosures west of the villa: Culvert 468 and 'Corndrier' 469 from the west, showing how 468 was cut away by recutting ditches 402 and 416	88
63	Enclosures west of the villa: Culvert 468 and 'Corndrier' 469 from the north-east, showing the channel running from 469 into 468 and the south wall of 468 cut away by the recut of ditch 418	90
64	Late Roman enclosures: distribution plan of ovens and 'corndrier' east of the villa	91
65	Enclosures east of the villa: oven-base of Stonesfield slate in 647 from the south	93
66	Distribution of wells and Late Roman silt-filled features	94
67	Enclosures east of the villa: Silt-filled pit 550 from the south-east	96
68	Late Roman silt-filled pits: plans and sections	97
69	Distribution plan of Romano-British burials	98
70	Late Roman burial 206 found in the middle of the villa courtyard, taken from the east	99
71	Late Roman double burial 584 in the northern enclosures, viewed from the south-west	100
72	Late Roman decapitated burial 894 from the north-east. Skeleton damaged by scraper	100
73	Development plan of northern enclosure group (2nd–4th centuries)	102
74	Development plan of southern enclosure group (2nd–4th centuries)	104
75	Northern enclosure group after machine stripping, photographed by W A Baker in 1961	105
76	Circular enclosure 481: plan and sections	107
77	Circular enclosure 481 in the middle of the open area east of the villa, taken from the west	108
78	Plan of pit alignments and Building VI	111
79	Roman pottery: histogram showing number of mortaria present on site	115
80	Roman pottery: illustrated samian Nos. 1–4	117
81	Roman pottery: illustrated samian Nos. 5–20	118
82	Roman pottery: pie diagram showing proportions of major forms	120
83	Roman pottery: Form Corpus Types 1 to 3.2	121
84	Roman pottery: Form Corpus Type 3.3 to 3.4	123
85	Roman pottery: Form Corpus Types 3.4 (cont.) to 3.6	125
86	Roman pottery: Form Corpus Types 3.7 to 5	126
87	Roman pottery: Form Corpus Type 6.1	128
88	Roman pottery: Form Corpus Types 6.2 to 6.11	129
89	Roman pottery: Form Corpus Types 6–7 to 10.11	131
90	Roman pottery: Form Corpus Types 11 to 13	133
91	Roman pottery: illustrated vessels from the 1990 excavations. Samian and 'early' groups.	140
92	Roman pottery: illustrated vessels from the 1990 excavations. 'Late' groups.	141
93	Copper alloy objects: Nos. 1–12	146
94	Copper alloy objects: Nos. 13–26	147
95	Copper alloy objects: Nos. 1016, 1020, 1408, 1412, 1417, 1445, 1564, 1565, and 1568	148
96	Copper alloy and lead objects: Nos. 27–33.	149
97	Iron objects: Nos. 34–44	152
98	Iron objects: Nos. 45–55	153

99	Iron objects: Nos. 56–67	154
100	Iron objects: Nos. 1027, 1425, 1441, 1447, 1462, 1535	155
101	Glass vessels: Nos. 68–91, 1435, & 1448; and faience melon bead: No. 92	157
102	Bone and ivory objects: Nos. 93–102, 1437, and 1560	159
103	Jet and shale objects: Nos. 103–105, 1567	160
104	Stone objects: querns Nos. 106–114	162
105	Stone objects: Nos. 115–123	163
106	Stone objects: Nos. 124–131	164
107	Stone objects: Nos. 132–135	165
108	Fired clay: Nos. 136–142	166
109	Tile: No. 143	169
110	Vertical aerial view of Roughground Farm and the area to the south	180
111	Possible reconstructions of Building IV	184
112	Roman field system showing standard measurements of layout	188
113	Phase plan of the late 2nd/early 3rd century villa	190
114	Phase plan of the late 3rd/4th century villa	190
115	Interpretation of the organisation of the Late Roman villa	198

List of Microfiche Figures

116	Plan and section of Grooved Ware pit 962 and posthole 983	Fiche 1#4
117	Plan and section of Beaker pit 1260	Fiche 1#11
118	Flint from undated prehistoric features 1209, 1145 and 1288	Fiche 1#17
119	Later Bronze Age settlement: sections	Fiche 1#19
120	Sections of Early Iron Age ditch 2602 and pit 2611	Fiche 1#20
121	Early Iron Age: sections of scattered pit groups	Fiche 1#20
122	Early Iron Age quernstone from pit 1257	Fiche 1#26
123	Early Roman House Enclosure 56 — sections	Fiche 1#28
124	Early Roman pits and ditches — sections	Fiche 1#29
125	Early Roman occupation: sections of pits, postholes and gullies in western area	Fiche 1#29
126	Early Roman occupation: sections of ditches, pits and postholes adjacent to droveway boundary 959/960	Fiche 1#30
127	Roman villa: plan of features underlying Buildings I and II	Fiche 1#31
128	Plan of 2600s area excavated SE of Building IV, including Building V	Fiche 1#32
129	Roman villa: Building IV assorted sections	Fiche 1#33
130	Roman villa: plan of features underlying Building III	Fiche 1#34
131	Plan of western enclosures showing excavated trenches and drawn sections	Fiche 1#35
132	Western enclosures: sections of trackway ditches	Fiche 1#36
133	Western enclosures: sections of small enclosures W of villa	Fiche 1#37
134	Western enclosures: sections of later Roman ditches	Fiche 1#38
135	Western enclosures: plan of 'corndrier' 468 and culvert 469	Fiche 1#39
136	'Corndrier' 590: plan and section	Fiche 1#40
137	Late Roman ovens: plan and sections	Fiche 1#41
138	Plan of northern enclosure group showing excavated trenches and drawn sections	Fiche 1#44
139	Northern enclosure group: sections of large pits and ovens	Fiche 1#45
140	Northern enclosures: sections of ditches	Fiche 1#46
141	Northern enclosures: sections of ditches and silt-filled pits	Fiche 1#47
142	Plan of southern enclosure group showing excavated trenches and drawn sections	Fiche 1#48
143	Southern enclosures: sections of ditches and silt-filled pits	Fiche 1#49
144	Southern enclosures: sections of large pits and ovens	Fiche 1#50
145	Roman gravel-pit 660: section	Fiche 1#51
146	Roman pottery: diagram showing the major vessel forms present in the fabrics	Fiche 2#19
147	Roman pottery: Vessel Types I	Fiche 2#20
148	Roman pottery: Vessel Types II	Fiche 2#21

149	Roman pottery: rim forms	Fiche 2#22
150	Roman pottery: pie diagrams showing proportions of fabric by period	Fiche 2#23
151	Mosaic fragments	Fiche 2#71
152	Romano-British animal bones: sheep mandible wear stages	Fiche 2#90
153	Site plan illustrated in 30 × 40 m gridded areas (see Fig. 6 for key)	Fiche 4#2

List of Tables

1	Grooved Ware and Beaker features and their finds	9
2	Summary of flintwork from Grooved Ware features	12
3	Animal bones found in the Grooved Ware pits (by fragment count)	14
4	Radiocarbon dates obtained from bone from features containing Grooved Ware pottery	15
5	Flintwork from Beaker features	18
6	Radiocarbon date obtained from bone from pit 1260	21
7	Summary of the residual flintwork assemblage	22
8	Pottery fabric proportions in Later Bronze Age features	29
9	Occurrence of vessel types in Bronze Age contexts (giving absolute number and percentage as a proportion of all types	29
10	Summary of flintwork from Later Bronze Age features	33
11	Animal bones: percentages of species from Bronze Age features	34
12	Radiocarbon dates obtained from bone from Bronze Age features	35
13	Early Iron Age Pottery: Fabric Proportions by context groups	43
14	Summary of Occurrence of Vessel Types (giving absolute number and percentage as a proportion of all types)	43
15	Animal Bones: Percentages of species in Early Iron Age contexts	46
16	Radiocarbon dates obtained from bone from Iron Age features	46
17	Proportions of amphora sherds by fabric	115
18	Quantity of samian by site period (excluding 1990 finds)	116
19	Fabric sherd totals of Roman pottery from the 1990 excavation	135
20	Fabric by vessel types (EVEs) for Roman pottery from the 1990 excavation	136
21	Coin List	143
22	Copper alloy objects	144
23	Iron objects	150
24	Querns by source and date	160
25	Stone objects: types and distribution	161
26	Summary of details of human burials of Roman date	170
27	Animal bones from the 1957–82 excavations	172
28	Vertebrate remains from the 1990 excavation	174

List of Microfiche Tables

29	Summary of Grooved Ware pottery by context	Fiche 1#5
30	Summary of early prehistoric pottery samples examined in thin-section	Fiche 1#6
31	Measurements of Late Neolithic antlers from 962	Fiche 1#10
32	Summary of the Beaker pottery by context	Fiche 1#12
33	Summary of flintwork from undated features	Fiche 1#16
34	Incidence of Later Bronze Age pottery by context	Fiche 1#21
35	Proportions of Early Iron Age sherds from contexts across the site	Fiche 1#21
36	Decorative motifs on Bronze Age and Iron Age pottery	Fiche 1#23
37	The incidence of vessel types by feature including type of decoration for Later Bronze Age pottery	Fiche 1#23
38	Occurrence of vessel types in Bronze Age and Early Iron Age contexts	Fiche 1#24
39	Mollusca from pit 879	Fiche 1#26
40	Charcoal identifications of hand-picked samples from Bronze Age and Iron Age contexts	Fiche 1#27
41	Ovens in the eastern enclosures giving type and dimensions in metres	Fiche 1#42
42	Samian by context and type	Fiche 2#2

43	Roman pottery: codes for handles	Fiche 2#18
44	Roman pottery: codes for bases	Fiche 2#18
45	Roman pottery: codes for decoration types	Fiche 2#18
46	Roman pottery: correlation of fabric codes	Fiche 2#24
47	Roman pottery from the 1990 excavations: numbers and percentages of fabrics in 'early' group of features.	Fiche 2#25
48	Roman pottery from the 1990 excavations: numbers and percentages of fabrics in later Roman features.	Fiche 2#26
49	Results of analyses of copper alloy objects	Fiche 2#36
50	Stone objects by type and area	Fiche 2#55
51	Catalogue of stone objects	Fiche 2#58
52	Fired clay: weight by fabric and type of object for all periods	Fiche 2#64
53	Fired clay: types of object and fabrics	Fiche 2#66
54	Fired clay: distribution and date of sling pellets	Fiche 2#67
55	Numbers of tesserae of different colours and sizes	Fiche 2#69
56	Distribution of types of tile by fabric from the 1957–65 and 1981–82 excavations	Fiche 2#81
57	Numbers and percentages of different tile types from the 1990 excavation	Fiche 2#81
58	Weights and percentages of Roman tiles of different fabrics from the 1990 excavation	Fiche 2#81
59	Analyses of slag samples RGF 1–6 from SF 1419 from context 2413	Fiche 2#82
60	Analyses of slag samples RGF 13–15 from SF 1419 from context 2413. Standardless analysis, element weight and % oxide by stoichiometry.	Fiche 2#83
61	Analyses of slag samples RGF 7–12 from sample SF 1495 from context 2030. Weight concentration of metal/sulphide.	Fiche 2#83
62	Analyses of slag samples RGF 16–18 from sample SF 1495 from context 2030. Standardless analysis, element weight and % oxide by stoichiometry.	Fiche 2#84
63	Distribution of slag in the northern and southern groups of enclosures	Fiche 2#84
64	Sex, age and height of each individual with other comments	Fiche 2#84
65	Dental formulae and condition of teeth (see Table 64 on Fiche 2#84)	Fiche 2#87
66	Animal bones from 1982: percentages of species from Building IV and the Courtyard by phase	Fiche 2#89
67	Animal bones: age data from Romano-British cattle.	Fiche 2#90
68	Animal bones from 1957–82: percentages of species for all periods	Fiche 2#90
69	Animal bones from the 1990 excavation: comparison of assemblages from Building III and Building IV areas	Fiche 2#91
70	Charred cereal and weed seeds from the 1990 excavation	Fiche 2#92
71	Molluscs from Early Roman Well 320	Fiche 2#94
72	Carbonised plant remains from Roman contexts	Fiche 2#94
73	Charcoal identifications from Roman contexts	Fiche 2#95
74	Charcoal identifications of hand-picked samples from Roman contexts	Fiche 2#95
75	Analyses of coal samples from Roman contexts	Fiche 2#96
76	Pits and hollows from the 1957–65 excavations giving dimensions, profile and date	Fiche 3#2
77	Postholes (or small pits) from the 1957–65 excavations giving dimensions and date	Fiche 3#10
78	Contexts and their dimensions from the 1990 excavations	Fiche 3#12
79	Concordance of contexts and pottery from the 1957–65 and 1981–82 excavations	Fiche 3#16

Preface
Thames Valley Landscapes

Since its formation in 1973 the Oxford Archaeological Unit has carried out major excavations on sites in the Thames Valley ranging in date from the Neolithic to the Early Modern Period. Several of these, for example the excavations at Ashville and Barton Court Farm, Abingdon, and the Farmoor Reservoir, were published by the Council for British Archaeology.

As the scope of our investigations increased it was decided to launch a new series, *Thames Valley Landscapes*, in co-operation with English Heritage and the Oxford University Committee for Archaeology. In this way it is hoped that the complex story of human activity in the Thames Valley will emerge.

The reports are grouped into various sub-regions. The first to be published was Tim Allen's Watkins Farm site (Northmoor), near the Thames/Windrush confluence. For many years archaeologists from Oxford have salvaged archaeology from the huge gravel pits around Northmoor and Stanton Harcourt in the Windrush Valley, and in the near future the OAU will publish the results of work in this area at the Devil's Quoits henge monument, the Iron Age enclosure at Mingies Ditch, and the Gravelly Guy prehistoric and Roman settlement.

In 1978 the main area of unrecorded destruction of archaeology in the Upper Thames Valley was in the Cotswold Water Park in Gloucestershire. With the financial help of ARC, the main gravel company working in the area, and then major support from the Department of the Environment (now English Heritage), the OAU began a ten year programme of investigation into a block of landscape centred on the Late Prehistoric and Romano-British settlements at Claydon Pike and Thornhill Farm (Lechlade and Fairford). Two kilometres to the east was Roughground Farm. This site was part of the mythology of Thames Valley archaeology. It was here that, between 1957 and 1965, Margaret Jones had undertaken what was, in 1978, still the largest rescue excavation in the region. As usually happened in the 1960s, no sooner had Margaret Jones finished battling the bulldozers of Lechlade than she was called elsewhere. Her destination was Mucking in Essex, and what became one of the classic rescue excavations of the 1960s and 1970s.

As a result Roughground Farm remained unpublished — a major gap in the archaeological record of the Upper Thames Valley.

When the OAU's new project began in the Cotswold Water Park we suggested to Margaret Jones that we should co-operate in publishing her site. She was immediately enthusiastic and, thanks to English Heritage's commitment to publish 'backlog' sites, their financial support was forthcoming. In 1990, just as the report was finished, the last part of the site was redeveloped and the OAU carried out a final season of excavation on the villa, 23 years after work began. The results of all these investigations are published in this volume.

I am very pleased that thanks to the energy of Tim Allen and his co-authors Roughground Farm has at last entered the ranks of the fully published. It should soon be joined by its neighbours, Thornhill Farm, Claydon Pike and the Butler's Field Anglo-Saxon cemetery, to form one of the most thoroughly investigated archaeological areas in Britain.

David Miles
Director
Oxford Archaeological Unit

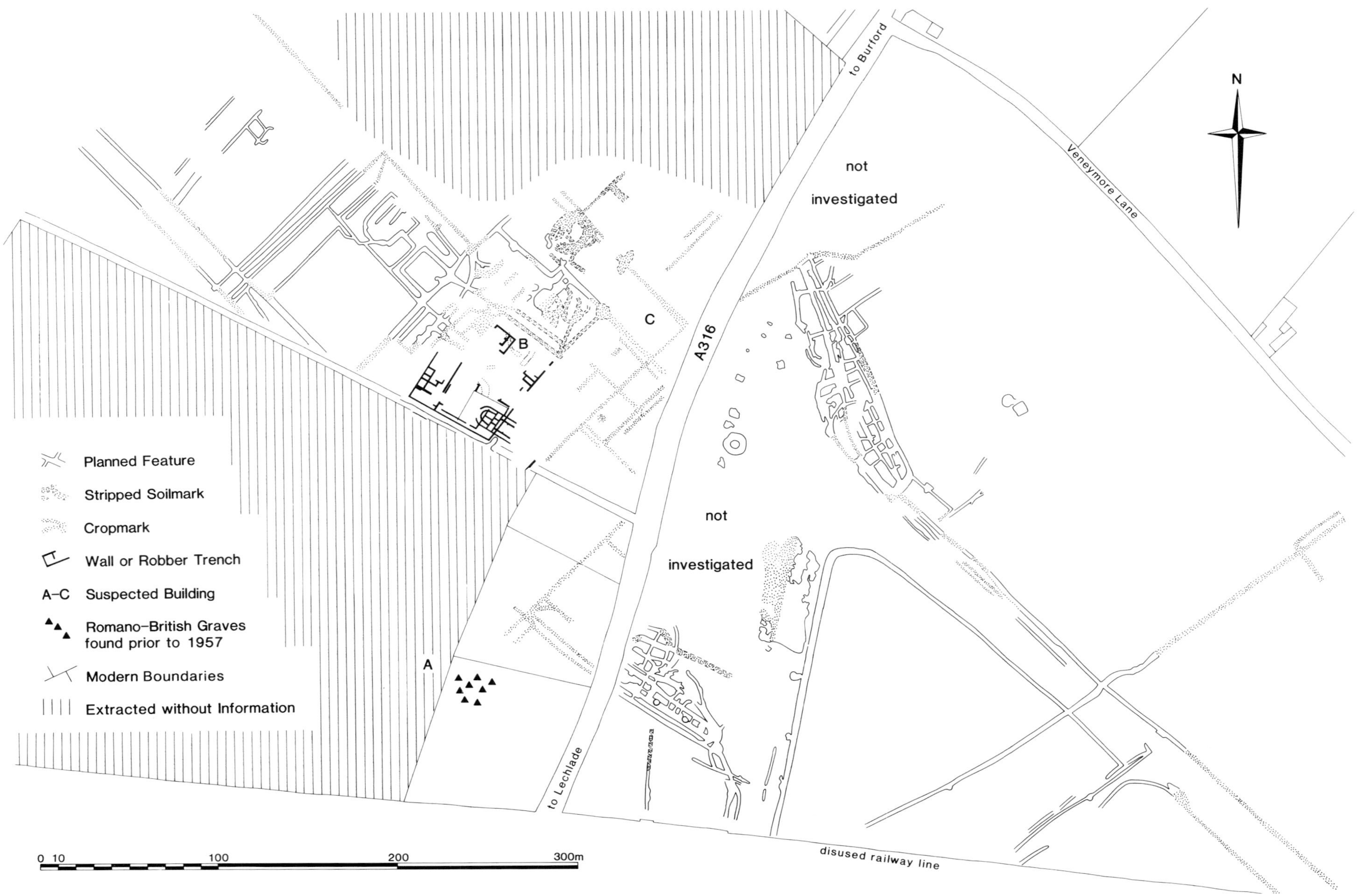

Figure 1 Overall site plan

Summary

The archaeological remains at Roughground Farm cover an area of *c* 8 hectares on the second gravel terrace just north of Lechlade between the rivers Leach and Thames (SP 216/009 to 221/005). The site was investigated by Margaret Jones in advance of gravel extraction between 1957 and 1965. These excavations revealed evidence of occupation from the Late Neolithic to the end of the Roman period and represent one of the first landscape studies undertaken in this country. The work was stimulated by the discovery of a Roman villa, whose buildings were partly investigated in 1957 and 1959. Further excavations on the villa buildings were carried out by Tim Allen in 1981–2 and in 1990 prior to a housing development.

The Neolithic occupation consists of a small cluster of pits containing Grooved Ware, contrasting with a dispersed scatter of pits with Beaker pottery. The Earlier Bronze Age is only represented by a stray sherd, but there is a wide scatter of Later Bronze Age pits, which tend to congregate in small groups. In the Early Iron Age the landscape was divided by large boundary ditches, roughly parallel to one another and at right angles to the river Leach, with smaller ditched subdivisions. This land-division appears to respect established trackways, which met within the excavated area. Pit groups indicate an arable economy and occupation, including posthole groups and burials, was concentrated at the east edge of the site.

The Middle and Late Iron Ages are hardly represented, but an Early Roman native settlement was established just west of the trackways. This included an oval house-enclosure with accompanying pit-group, small stock enclosures, and pens, lying within a larger rectilinear enclosure. Between the trackways and the settlement was an open 'green'-like area. The economy was similar to that of the Iron Age and this settlement persisted until the early 2nd century AD, when it was replaced by the building of a villa.

At least two masonry buildings were put up in the mid 2nd century and were surrounded by an enclosure ditch. One of these was an aisled building, with an apsidal end unique in Roman Britain. Outside this was a regular system of paddocks and larger fields laid out to a standard unit of length. The villa occupation area, however, kept within the limits of the preceding native settlement. Trackways and droveways approaching the villa were delineated by boundary ditches.

In the 3rd century another large domestic building was constructed, while the ends of the trackways east of the villa were overlaid by two groups of enclosures facing each other across the 'green', which were used for various agricultural and semi-industrial activities and may also have been occupied. These may represent centralisation of the villa's estate management. Small groups of late Roman burials were found in and around these enclosures. In the 4th century, if not before, another domestic building was added to the villa. Occupation of the villa and adjacent enclosures continued beyond 360 AD, but possibly not as late as the end of the 4th century.

There was very little evidence of Saxon activity, although the villa buildings were robbed for stone for graves in this period. The east part of the site was overlaid by ridge and furrow in the medieval period and the west appears to have been pasture; both parts remained open fields until gravel extraction began in the 1930s. Virtually the whole site has now been destroyed.

Acknowledgements

The 1957–65 excavations

by Margaret Jones

The excavations and watching briefs were initiated, financed and administered by the then Ministry of Works through Assistant Inspector Sarnia Butcher. The Ancient Monuments Laboratory handled some finds and some drawings were produced by the Inspectorate Drawing Office. The Ashmolean Museum, which received the finds, contributed finds conservation and other post-excavation support.

Throughout the years during which their gravel pit was being investigated the management of Amey's Aggregates Ltd through H T Lucy and the late W A Richardson co-operated fully, especially in permitting archaeological supervision of topsoil stripping and in allowing time for planning and excavation.

Practical help in providing storage for finds, local information and in digging is acknowledged from the late Mrs Helen O'Neil, the late Mr and Mrs F C Innocent, A J Baxter (also for animal bone identification). Dorothy, Sarah, Patrick and Mark Wise and Richard Reece helped in the crucial first watching brief.

W T Jones gave much background support, especially with photographic processing of more than a thousand exposures, with transport and on watching briefs. He was responsible for the excavation of the roundhouse and cremation (Fig. 30). Christine Mahany was responsible for the excavation of Feature 481 (Fig. 76). Ernest Greenfield deputised for the writer, when abroad in 1963, directing the excavation of the eastern half of the northern enclosure group (Fig. 73 and Fig. 138 on Fiche 1#44).

The following museums are thanked for their co-operation: Ashmolean Museum (H J Case, D Sturdy, P D C Brown), British Museum (I H Longworth) and Filkins Museum (G Swinford). These visitors gave advice and/or support: the late Professor D Atkinson, the late Mrs E M Clifford, Professor G W Dimbleby, the late Professor I A Richmond, D Roe, the late Dr K Sandford, G A Webster.

Thanks are due to the following specialists for their initial work on finds: the late D Charlesworth (glass), the late M R Hull (bronzes), and the late Professor F W Shotton (stone). Help with air cover is acknowledged from: W A Baker (especially from his dramatic near vertical shot of excavation in progress), Professor J K St Joseph, D Sturdy (for studying the Allen Collection in the Ashmolean Museum), and B Carter from Cirencester.

The 1981–90 excavations

by Tim Allen

For permission to undertake the 1981 and 1982 trenching I would like to thank ARC Estates and Mrs Nightingale, the former occupant of 'Woodlands', the modern house which overlay Building IV. The work was carried out at weekends by members of the Oxford University Archaeological Society. I am grateful to all who gave their free time.

The 1990 excavation was only made possible by the enlightened interest and financial support of the developer Venymore Homes, a joint venture by ARC and Westbury Homes plc. In this connection I would like to thank Chris Hall and Roger Hart for their prompt support in enabling the excavation to take place and Paul Wood for his ready assistance with machinery on site. I am also grateful to Tony Fleming of English Heritage for augmenting the excavation budget and for funding the post-excavation work.

The excavation was supervised by Mick Parsons, assisted by John Hiller, and thanks are due to all of the team for their hard work when facing a tight time deadline.

Post-excavation work

by Tim Allen, Timothy Darvill and Sarah Green

Leigh Turner and Elinor Beard drew the plans for the printed publication and Wendy Page most of the finds. Jane Timby drew the illustrations for Ch. II and the Later Bronze Age flintwork, Richard Hingley the later prehistoric pottery and Maggie Sasanow some of the copper alloy and iron Roman finds. Danyon Rey compiled the detailed site plans in the microfiche. Many people contributed to the section drawings, chief among whom were Rachel Brak, Elizabeth MacRobert and Tim Allen. Elinor Beard made the final alterations to the drawings and paged-up.

Thanks are also due to the following for information and advice: Humphrey Case (Beaker pottery), Leslie Cram (animal prints), Martin Henig (copper alloy finds), Maureen Mellor (pottery), Wendy Page (draughtsmanship), Philip Powell (stone identification), Janet Richardson (pottery), Chris Salter (slag), Alan Saville (flints), Mike Stone (tile), and Chris Young (Roman pottery).

Jackie Wilson deserves special thanks for typing and editing the whole report on computer. Betty Green typed the Roman pottery report, and Sebastian Rahtz gave up much of his time to help with computing and photography during the analysis of the finds, as well as undertaking the typesetting of the final publication and microfiche; Professor Sheppard Frere very kindly read and edited the report in draft, and George Lambrick, David Miles, and Simon Palmer also contributed ideas or gave encouragement at various times. Erica Hemming undertook the laborious task of pasting in all the figures.

The preparation of the report was funded by HBMC and by ARC.

For the 1990 excavation the plans, sections, and finds were mostly drawn by Simon Chew. Danyon Rey drew the reconstruction drawings of Building IV. The cover illustration was drawn by Karen Nichols.

Some of the original drawings have been amended to incorporate new information. This work was carried out by Tim Allen and Danny Hacker.

The whole publication report was streamlined in the final editing stages by Michael Roaf.

Chapter I

Introduction

I.1 The background to the 1957–65 excavations

by Margaret Jones

Quarrying had been part of the farming enterprise in field OS 73 since 1930. Known as Roughground, this field gave its name to the farm; Mr B F Poole, who then farmed it, observed that his plough brought stone to the surface. Quarrying took place also in the adjacent field to the south known as Iles' and/or Stratton's pit.

Cropmarks of ancient features around Lechlade had been photographed by Major Allen, but this site was first photographed by D N Riley (Riley 1942, 112–3; Riley 1942, 73 and ff.) (Fig. 2). Several local people had observed sections of pits and ditches exposed in quarry faces, and had rescued finds: notably the late Mrs E D Atkinson, the late Mr and Mrs F C Innocent and A J Baxter. Some finds made their way to the Ashmolean, British, Cirencester, Filkins and Stroud museums, and site visits were made by the staff of Pitt Rivers and Stroud museums.

In 1957 Mr Poole sold the rights for gravel to Amey Aggregates Ltd of Oxford, who began extraction on a large scale. Graders were used for the first time to clear large areas of topsoil. Mr and Mrs Innocent and A J Baxter made further finds in the topsoil dumps, realised the implications and informed the county correspondent of the Ministry of Works, the late Mrs H E O'Neil. Air photographs of the newly stripped gravel and adjacent cropmarks were taken by St. Joseph (Fig. 3), and the writer was asked to hold a watching brief.

Despite dumping and lorry tracks, some soilmarks were still visible in the cemented oolitic gravel. This was aided by the comparatively small-tracked scrapers in use. With the help of local volunteers an early Roman area was sampled (Fig. 34). On the south-east of the fields still under cultivation topsoil removal had exposed large, pitched oolite blocks, and to the east Romano-British tile fragments, including tubuli, had survived.

The prospect of a substantial Romano-British building was held to justify an excavation with labour supplied by a gang of MoW mobile excavators, and it now became feasible to trench likely sites. The plan of the exposed building indicated a corner, or the end of a wing running west (Fig. 37); three trenches into the arable (112, 115, 116) confirmed this. Since this area was still under cultivation further trenching was restricted to the south-east of the exposed building (Fig. 36).

Another Romano-British building was discovered by lines of trial trenches to the east, but since spoil had to be dumped alongside few trenches could be extended, and thus only a partial plan was obtained (Fig. 37). An excavation of the building under crop was arranged for 1958, but when the writer visited the site a few days before the start of excavation, the 'building' was a pool of water. It had been quarried away.

Amey's management granted permission to excavate the surviving south edge of the building site and agreed to make more land to the west available for investigation, the topsoil stripping to take place under archaeological supervision. This new area — some 200 by 100 m — provided what was, in the 1950s, a novel opportunity to plan on landscape dimensions, albeit imperfectly, the buildings and fields of a Roman villa (Fig. 59). A third building complex was found at the south edge of the quarried area (Fig. 42), which was tackled in 1959. The gravel quarry spoil heap however overlay the north part of this building, so that only a part of the building was excavated.

By 1950s standards, Roughground Farm had by now received a good share of official funding. The original justification for excavation had been the rescue of Romano-British villa buildings; the landscape element had come about by chance following the unforeseen destruction of the centre of the villa. This explains why the area first extracted east of the Burford road, which contained no apparent cropmarks, was not examined. However, the writer had by now no doubts about the value of landscape rescue, both for itself and as an aid to the incipient study of cropmark interpretation. Quarrying east of the Burford road was due to extend into areas where cropmarks of ditches which lined up with those already investigated were visible, and where the distinct cropmark of a round ditched feature was evident (Frontispiece). Moreover, field walking had indicated a rise in the ground just north of the station, and stone had been picked up there.

It was therefore decided to excavate two further areas of dense cropmarks adjacent to Burford Road (the area between to be abandoned), and to carry out a watching brief on any subsequent stripping. The same strategy was followed: rescue of the entire plan, sampling of linear features particularly for stratigraphic relationships, half-sectioning of discrete features and verification of blank areas.

Figure 2 Aerial view of the villa from the north-west, showing the regular enclosure system north and east of the villa buildings. Riley 1942 (Cambridge Air Photograph No. CD 044, Crown copyright reserved)

Figure 3 Aerial view of the villa and Early Roman occupation from the north-west, taken after stripping in 1957 just before excavation began. (Cambridge Air Photograph No. VQ29, copyright reserved)

The area excavations were carried out in 1961, and a watching brief in 1962. A further season of excavation on the south-east half of the northern cropmark complex was directed by Ernest Greenfield in 1963 during the writer's absence. Recording of the final most easterly areas was less adequately tackled due to increasing involvement in excavations at Mucking, Essex.

I.2 The 1981–82 and 1990 excavations

by Tim Allen

In 1981 Tim Allen returned to the site and began excavations at weekends with the Oxford University Archaeological Society, picking up the continuation of the west wall of Building III. In 1982 trenches were dug around a modern house adjacent to the track and recovered a small part of Building IV east of Building III and yard surfaces outside Building III (Fig. 36).

During the summer of 1990, when the report on Margaret Jones' excavations had just been completed, it was discovered that the remaining part of the villa, which lay beneath the track to Roughground Farm and the modern house adjacent, was under threat from housing development. Although building had already commenced adjacent to the site it proved possible to carry out a 4-week salvage excavation, directed by Tim Allen for the Oxford Archaeological Unit, which uncovered the south end of Building III, most of Building IV and the enclosure ditches surrounding the villa on the south side.

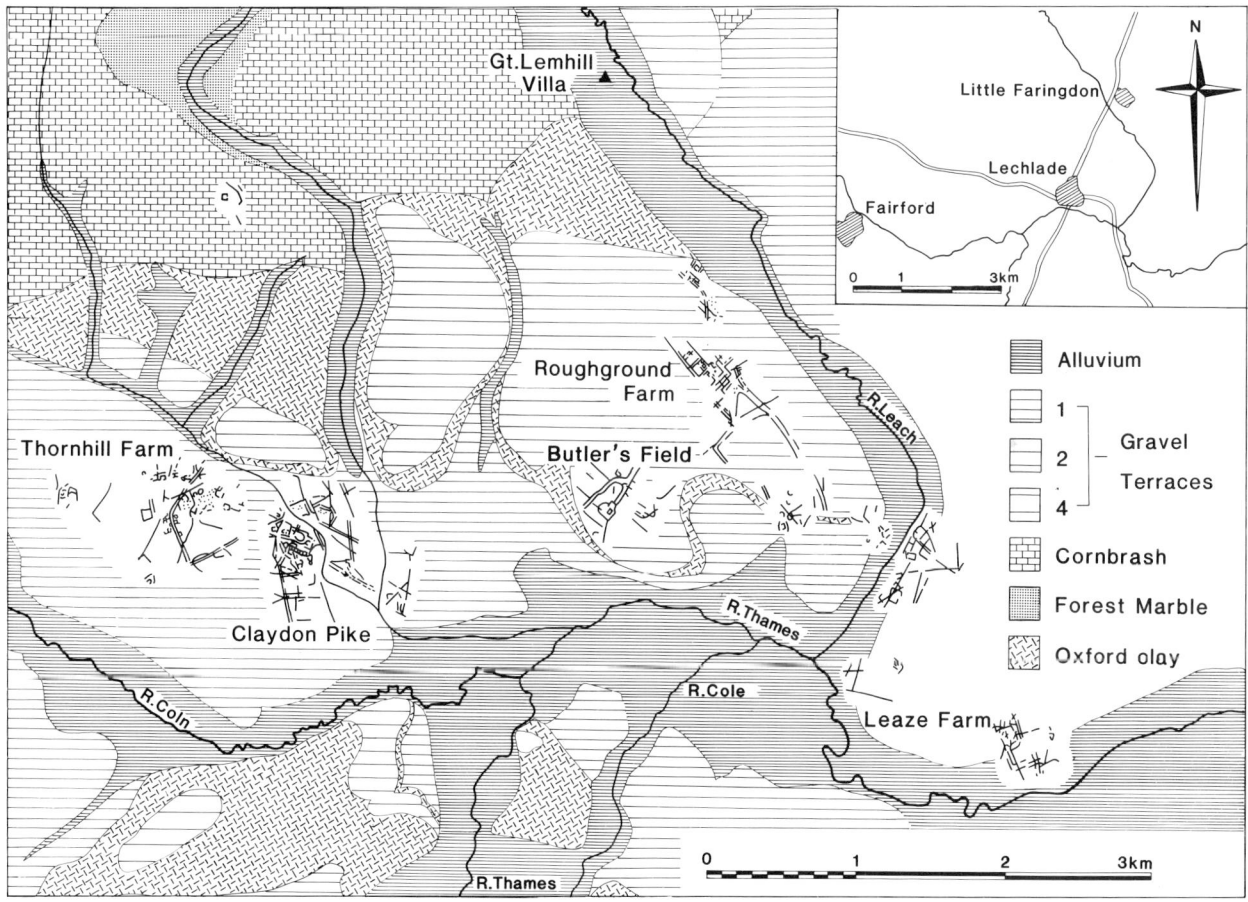

Figure 4 Site location and geology

I.3 Geology and topography

Roughground Farm lies upon an area of well-drained second terrace gravel between the rivers Leach and Thames just north of Lechlade. This area of gravel is adjacent to the confluence of several rivers, the Coln and the Leach running into the Thames from the Cotswolds to the north, the river Cole from the Corallian Ridge to the south. Upstream of the site the closest of these, the river Leach, cuts through the successive exposures of the Cotswold dipslope: Cornbrash (less than 2 km away), Forest Marble (3–4 km distant) and the Great Oolite, which is visible alongside the river only 4–5 km to the north, but only outcrops extensively

9 km or so away. All these types of rock were used in buildings on the site. South of the Thames the floodplain gives way to a broad expanse of Oxford Clay, upon which are small deposits of sand and gravel which may have been the source for the quartzite pebbles used by the Neolithic inhabitants of the site. The sand and Ragstone deposits of the Corallian Ridge are 8–9 km distant, and beyond these lie the Kimmeridge and Gault clays, which were used to make some of the later prehistoric pottery found around Lechlade. The river Cole rises on the edge of the chalk of the Wessex downland some 15 km away, from which came the chalkland flint used on the site.

The tributary valleys of the Upper Thames provided easy routes of communication between the valley bottom and the higher ground either side, and the rivers were perhaps used for transporting materials downstream. The Lechlade confluence was thus an important meeting point for the products of different geological resources, hence its significance from the Neolithic onwards.

The second terrace gravel upon which the site lies is bounded on the north and north-east by the floodplain of the river Leach only a few hundred metres away, and on the south gives way to the lower-lying first terrace gravels which slope down to the floodplain of the Thames. On the north a band of Oxford Clay separates the gravels from the Cornbrash foothills of the Cotswolds, and on the west the gravel terrace is bounded by a minor tributary, beyond which the second terrace gravel peters out and Oxford Clay reappears. The Oxford Clay is poorly-drained and was probably marginal land for agriculture in the prehistoric and Romano-British periods.

These natural constraints define an area of c 5 square kilometres. The alluvial channel of another former tributary divided the western part of the second terrace here from the main portion upon which the site sat (see Fig. 4); this latter area was between 3.5 and 4.0 square kilometres in extent. The settlement lay approximately at the centre of this, and it may represent the area of potential arable available. The first terrace and floodplain to the south is today mostly under grass, and excavations at Claydon Pike and Thornhill Farm, Fairford, nearby show that this was also true in the Iron Age and Roman periods (Miles and Palmer pers. comm.). Additional grazing would have been available along the narrow floodplain of the river Leach.

I.4 Excavation methodology

by Margaret Jones

During the period in which Roughground Farm was first investigated (1957–1965), the writer was concerned also with a Roman landscape at Stanton Low, Bucks., (Woodfield & Johnson 1989, 135 & ff). There, a loose sodden gravel in the valley bottom and the absence of air photographs showing cropmarks made area planning impossible. In contrast the cemented gravel at Roughground Farm made possible the recording of the landscape, with the plan the prime aim, following by the rescue of as many features and their finds as possible. This was not quite in accord with current practice which advocated the selection of 'typical' features for more intensive excavation rather than extensive studies. A survey of gravel archaeology which was then being compiled makes this point (Royal Commission on Historical Monuments 1960).

Even though there was insufficient labour to clear the ground after the scrapers had left, most features were at least partly visible and could be handled individually. The site conditions are well-recorded in W A Baker's near-vertical shot showing one of the cropmark areas as left by the scraper (Fig. 75). An important aspect of landscape archaeology — the mapping of blank areas — was not usually a problem. Another hazard of planning gravel sites — the recognition of periglacial features — was luckily confined to one small area. Field work at Roughground Farm enjoyed two major advantages: the full co-operation of Amey's Aggregates Ltd and the nature of the gravel. Features as shallow as ridge and furrow could be recognised, and this was the first excavation to plan them.

Originally the site was planned with a 50 foot linen tape, ranging poles and six inch nails. A drill developed for the larger areas in which six steel 100 foot tapes were laid out at 10 foot intervals. Features within the 100 by 50 foot rectangle were then plotted systematically within each 10 foot square by offset, using ranging poles. According to circumstances, scales ranged from 1:120 to 1:12. Scaled paper was used. At first features were numbered serially; however in the larger areas numbered and lettered grid squares gave identity (and also location). Planning thereafter continued to be based upon a grid, with points measured in by offset. Because of the difficulty of maintaining fixed points however each new area had a fresh grid origin; field gates, hedge junctions, and railway fencing had to serve as fixed points.

To support the plans a full photographic archive of more than 1,000 negatives was produced. Colour films were available only in the final years. Near-vertical air photographs of the areas stripped in 1961 were taken during excavation by W A Baker, which have as expected proved very helpful in post-excavation analysis. (A full list of the air photographs consulted will be found in the microfiche Ch. 1.3 on Fiche 1#2).

Since most of the labour was (archaeologically) unskilled and there was at best only one assistant, digging strategy also had to be simple. Where stratigraphy was difficult — as in soil filled features — excavation was by levels ('spits'). Plans of the principal finds at each level were drawn. The aim was to record all informative sections, with layers shown with continuous or broken lines.

Storage and transport of finds were major problems. After discussion with the Ashmolean museum staff in

1959 and with Graham Webster, unstratified coarse pottery found up to that date was discarded, fragmented animal bones and the bulk of building materials, unless of intrinsic interest, were not kept. Categories of finds for which specialists could be found to report on them were kept entire: prehistoric pottery, flints, glass, metalwork, coins.

Although the Ancient Monuments Laboratory was then in existence, staff and resources were limited. Samples for identification and environmental evidence were taken rather as an act of faith.

I.5 Post-excavation methodology

by Tim Allen

For the post-excavation analysis of the 1957–65 excavations the decision was taken to provide an unique context number for each stratigraphic deposit, in order to facilitate description and to provide a coherent system of cross-referencing between the original paper records, the photographs and the finds. This unique numbering system is that used to refer to contexts in the report. The context record sheets will be found with the original site records in the Archive. The 1981–82 and 1990 excavations were recorded in the field by unique context numbers starting at 1400 and 2000 respectively.

The partial nature of the excavations and the character and the variety of the excavation and recording techniques used have left an incomplete picture of the site. In ordering this for publication a choice had to be made between full description, often involving lengthy discussion of the doubtful validity of particular pieces of evidence, or more summary description, based around whichever interpretative framework best fitted the available data. The second approach has been adopted here, and for reasons both of brevity and clarity much of the information is presented through an interpretative rather than a purely descriptive framework. This is drawn from a fuller description of the stratigraphy, which can be found in the Archive.

I.6 The Archive

The original site notebooks, drawings and photographs from the 1957–65, 1981–2 and 1990 excavations, together with the context numbers and secondary data generated during post-excavation, have been deposited with the finds at the Ashmolean Museum, Beaumont Street, Oxford. A copy of the paper archive is also held on microfilm by the National Monuments Record.

I.7 Preparation of the report

Some draft reports on the finds and the stratigraphy were prepared in the 1960s. Post-excavation resumed in 1980 at the Oxford Archaeological Unit, and the various specialist reports and the text sections dealing with the stratigraphy were completed at different times between 1980 and 1986, by which time the report was substantially complete.

Following the 1990 excavation some of the original finds reports were amended to incorporate the new material, but in other cases separate reports were written for this to stand alongside the unmodified existing reports. The original specialist reports were not updated to take account of information published since completion in or before 1986. Except for those aspects of the discussion directly affected by the results of the 1990 excavation, the same is true of the discussion sections in Chapters II, III, VI and VII.

I.8 Organisation of the report

This report is divided between Print and Fiche. The printed part provides a characterisation of the stratigraphy and summaries of the finds, followed by a discussion of the discoveries. Most of the illustrations have been included in the Print section for ease of reference. The Fiche contains detailed plans of the site, a key to which will be found in Fig. 6 in print, and supplementary section drawings of the areas around the villa. The bulk of the Fiche comprises full reports on the finds with supporting Tables and Catalogues.

I.8.a Conventions used in this report

A variety of styles will be found among the illustrations, as different groups of finds have been drawn at different times over the last 30 years.

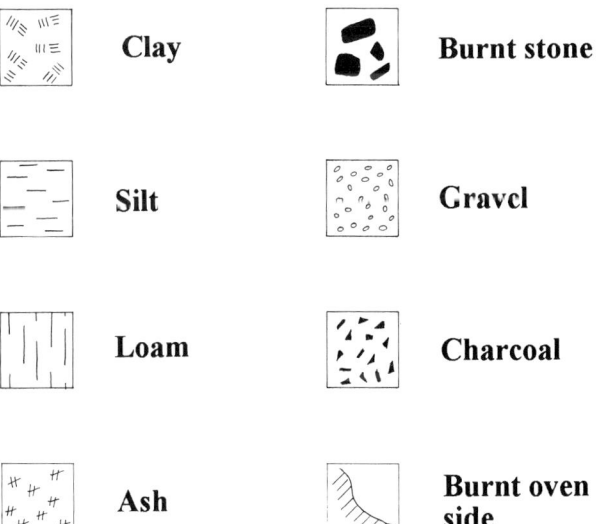

Figure 5 Key to conventions used on section drawings

I.8.a.1 Sections

The standard conventions used for soil descriptions are illustrated in Fig. 5. Where conventions vary they are given in a key on the relevant drawing. No levels were taken during the excavations between 1957 and 1982, but gravel was found at between 78.60 m and 78.65 m OD beneath Building IV in the 1990 excavation. Most of the site was however fairly flat, and the level of undisturbed gravel in adjacent trenches is therefore likely to be very similar.

I.8.a.2 Plans

A simplified version of the actual site plan is used in the reduced figures in print; a detailed plan will be found on Fiche 4, for which Fig. 6 provides a key. Wherever possible hachures are shown in the excavated features, but these were not always drawn and have therefore sometimes been extrapolated from the sections and photographs.

I.8.a.3 Radiocarbon dates

Uncalibrated dates are quoted in the form BP or uncal. BP, calibrated dates are given as cal. BC. Where periods of time are mentioned, eg the third millenium BC, these are always given in calendar years.

I.9 The Cotswold Water Park series

The publication of this report was undertaken by the Oxford Archaeological Unit on behalf of Margaret Jones because of the intrinsic value of the site and because it forms the first stage of a major landscape study of the Lechlade–Fairford area. This study has centred on the excavation of Iron Age and Roman settlements at Claydon Pike and Thornhill Farm and of a Bronze Age ring ditch, Early Iron Age features and an Anglo-Saxon cemetery at Butler's Field (see Fig. 4). A series of reports about these and other excavations is now in preparation, and the Roughground Farm report is intended as the first volume in this series.

The interpretation of the landscape at Roughground Farm is intimately bound-up with these more recent excavations and, although some of the results from them are mentioned in this report, the details of the evidence will be presented in future volumes in the series.

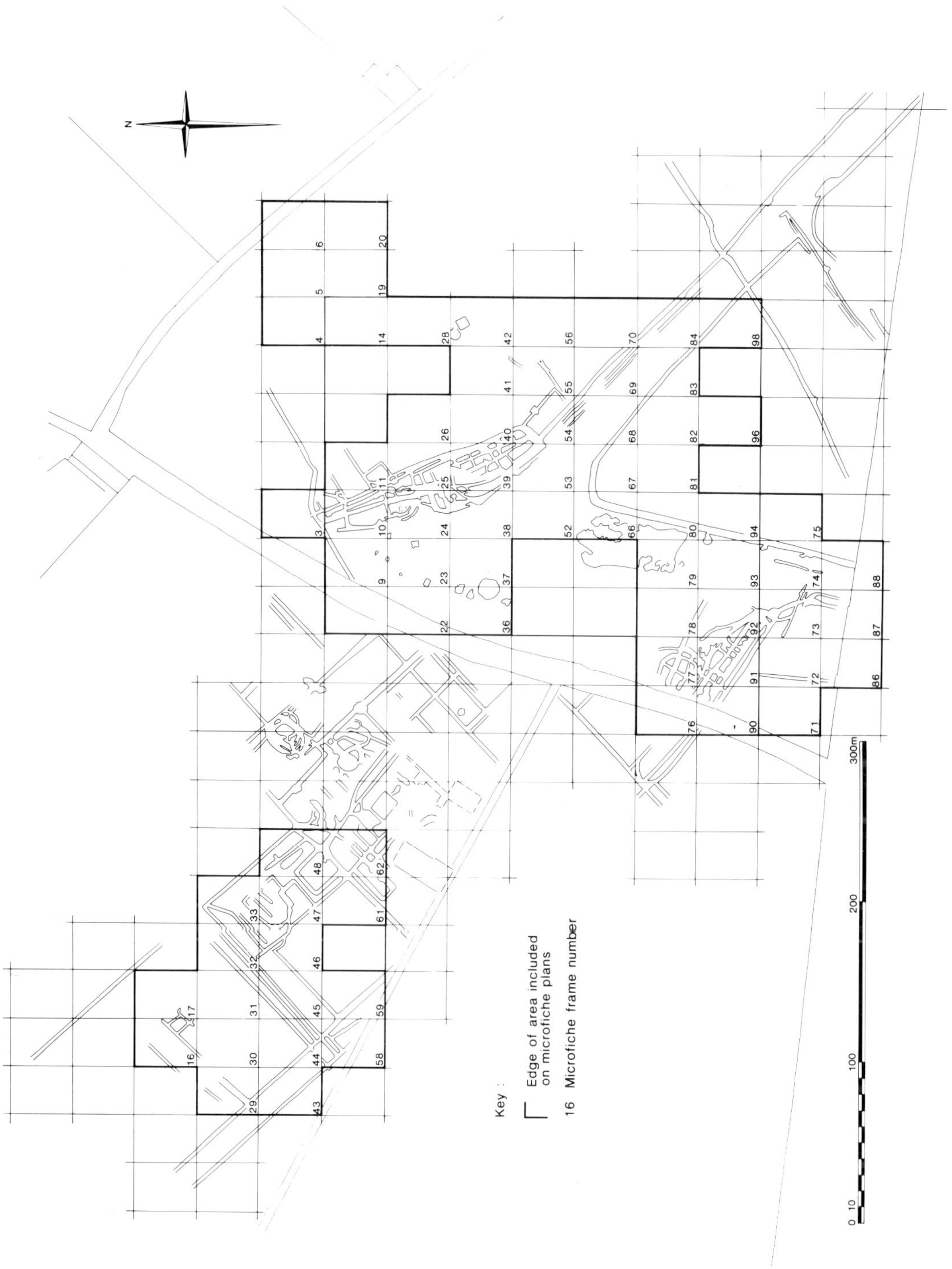

Figure 6 Overall site plan gridded to show the layout of plans as illustrated on Fiche 4. The numbers refer to individual frames on the microfiche.

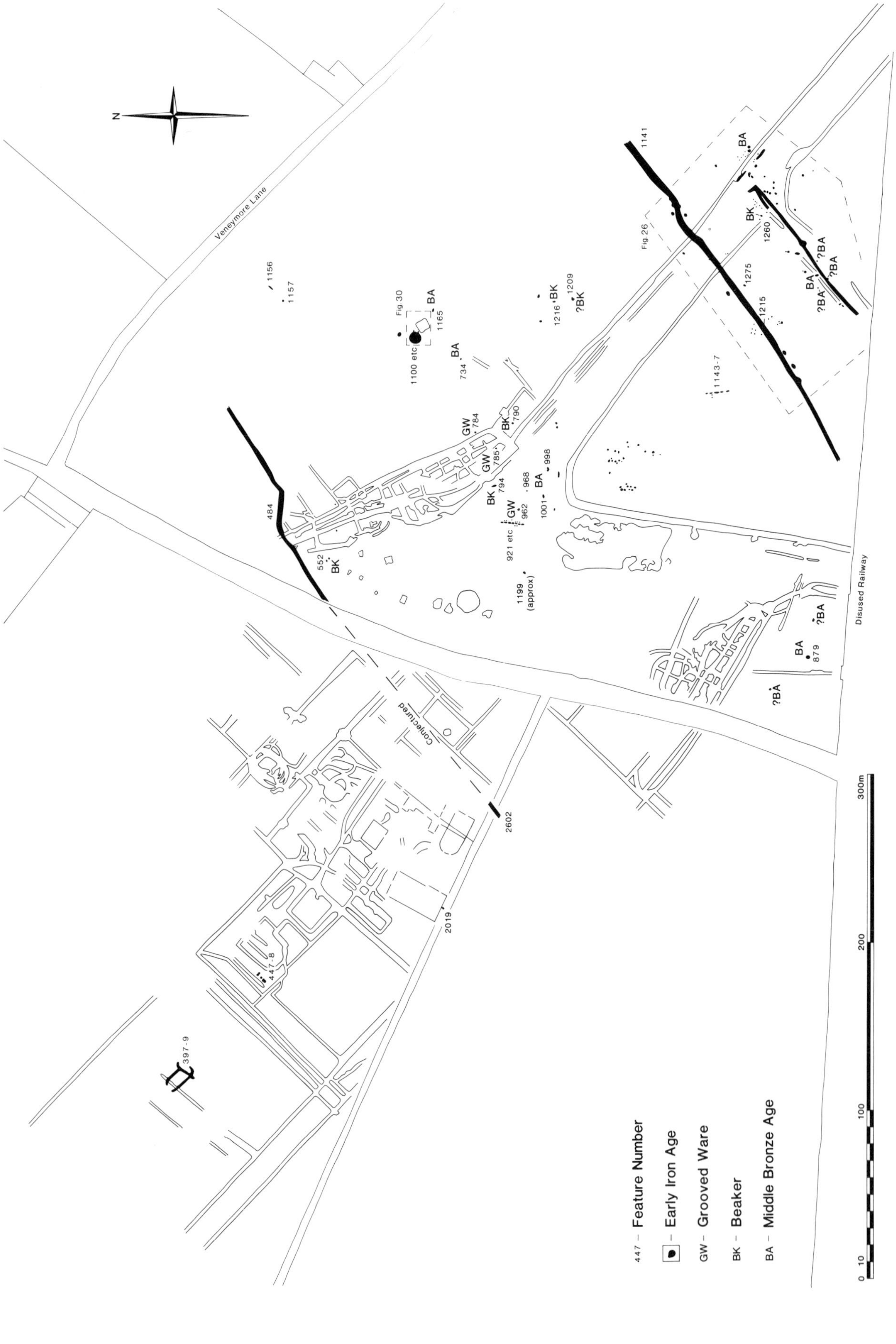

8   *Roughground Farm, Lechlade, Gloucestershire: a prehistoric and Roman landscape*

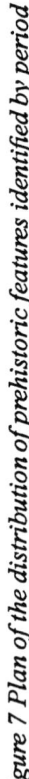

Figure 7 Plan of the distribution of prehistoric features identified by period

Chapter II

The early prehistoric period

by Timothy Darvill

Evidence for early prehistoric activity comprises features attributable to the late Neolithic and Beaker period on the basis of radiocarbon dates and distinctive ceramic assemblages, a group of undated features which contained only prehistoric flintwork, and a collection of residual and unstratified flintwork from Iron Age, Roman and later contexts. The features all occur to the east of the Lechlade-Burford road (A316), but the residual flintwork assemblage derives from the entire site (Fig. 7). All the excavated features were heavily truncated by later ploughing and by topsoil stripping.

II.A The Grooved Ware occupation

II.A.1 Description of the features

Four features, all pits or postholes, can be assigned to the Grooved Ware occupation of the site. These are 784, 785, 962 and 983. They occurred as one group within 40 m of one another (Fig. 7). For dimensions and finds see Table 1. Pit 962, which was cut by pit 983, is illustrated on Fig. 116 on Fiche 1#4.

Context	Length	Breadth/diameter	Depth	Profile	Pottery	Flint	Animal bones	Stone	Other	C14 dates
Grooved Ware										
784	—	0.90	0.18	Sloping U	P1	×46	×8	—	×2 bone	Table 4
785	—	1.00	0.12	Sloping U	P2–4	×23	×21	Hammerstone	—	—
962	—	1.37	0.20	Sloping U	P5–6	×48	×57	—	—	Table 4
983	0.83	0.73	0.25	Stepped U	—	×18	×8	—	Fired clay	—
Beaker										
552	—	0.68	0.12	Saucer	P7–14	—	—	—	—	—
790	—	0.60	0.25	U	P15	×12	—	Quartzite lump	—	—
794	2.89	0.75	0.25	Irregular	P16	×3	—	—	—	—
1216		No details			P17 18	×1				
1260	—	1.00	0.35	Bowl	P19–42	×134	×3	Cushion-stones and hammerstones	×15	Table 6

Table 1 Grooved Ware and Beaker features and their finds. Dimensions in metres. For a breakdown of the pottery assemblages see Tables 29 on Fiche 1#5 and 32, Fiche 1#12, for the flints see Tables 2 and 7, and for the animal bones see Table 3.

II.A.2 Pottery

II.A.2.a Introduction

A total of 54 sherds of Grooved Ware pottery, weighing 438 grams, was recovered. No complete or substantially reconstructable vessels were represented, but macroscopic studies of fabric, decoration, vessel size and colouration allowed portions of six different vessels to be recognized. The incidence of these by context is summarized on Table 29 on Fiche 1#5 in the microfiche report.

II.A.2.b Fabrics

Two fabrics were represented (Fabric 1: fossil shell and limestone, and Fabric 2: fine shell and quartzite). Details of these are given in the microfiche.

II.A.2.c Forms and decoration

For a full catalogue see microfiche report (Ch. 2.A.2 on Fiche 1#5).

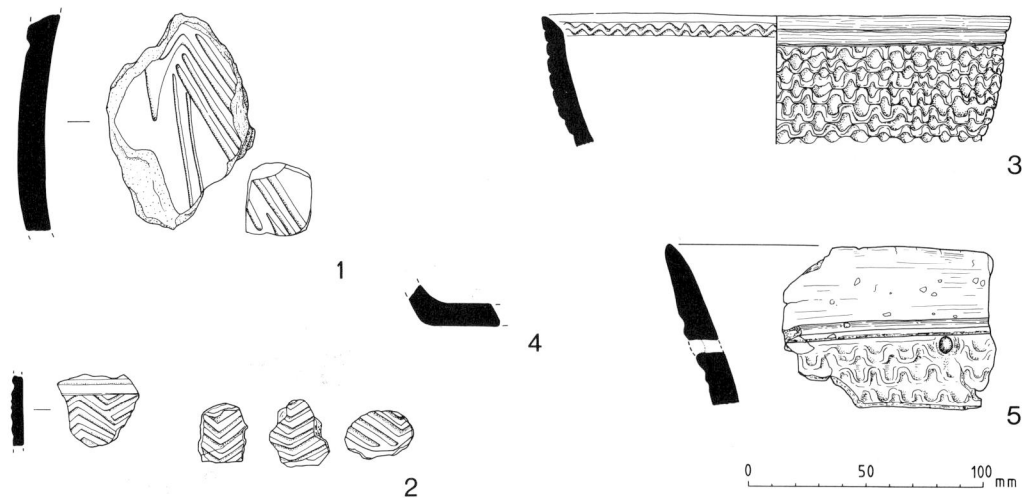

Figure 8 Grooved Ware pottery

P1 Five sherds in Fabric 1. Interior and exterior pale red-orange, core dark. Fig. 8.1.

P2 Eight sherds in Fabric 1. Exterior pinkish-red, interior and core dark brown to black. Fig. 8.2.

P3 Eighteen sherds in Fabric 1. Exterior ranges from pink through to dark brown, interior and core dark brown to black. The rim diameter is about 200 mm. The rim has a pronounced bevel on the inside (like Wainwright & Longworth 1971, type 24). Fig. 8.3.

P4 Nine sherds in Fabric 1. Possibly the base for P3. Exterior light grey, almost white in places, interior and core black. Not illustrated.

P5 Ten sherds in Fabric 1. One rim sherd has already been published (Jones 1976, Fig. 2.1). Exterior very dark brown to dark greyish-brown. Fig. 8.5.

P6 Four small sherds in Fabric 2. Exterior, interior and core dark brown to black; some sherds discoloured and vitrified by refiring. Not illustrated.

As a group, these six putative vessels from Roughground Farm are not easy to place within the scheme of four Grooved Ware sub-styles proposed by Wainwright and Longworth (1971, 236). The nearest match seems to be with the Woodlands sub-style because of such distinctive traits as the presence of thin-walled vessels and simple bevelled rims and the high incidence of incised decoration.

II.A.2.d Discussion

The pottery from Roughground Farm is different in its decoration and fabric to the Grooved Ware from The Loders on the east side of Lechlade (Darvill *et al* 1986). Indeed it stands apart from many other Grooved Ware assemblages from the Upper Thames and Cotswold region like Broadway, Hereford and Worcester (Warren *et al* 1936), Purwell Farm, Stanton Harcourt, Oxfordshire (Oxford County Museum Service SMR, PRN 3966), Sutton Courtenay, Oxfordshire, (Leeds 1934, 265) and Dorchester on Thames, Oxfordshire (Atkinson *et al* 1951, 110), in being of generally finer quality. In contrast, the assemblage from Tolley's Pit, Cassington, Oxfordshire, is very similar indeed to the Roughground Farm assemblage. The fabric is limestone shell-tempered, and there is one vessel with a simple upright rim with an internal bevel, and another with rusticated decoration of the same design as that on P3 (Case 1982a, Fig. 69.7 and 8). Whether these similarities and differences in assemblages should be seen as chronological, functional or cultural is not at present clear.

II.A.3 Flintwork

An assemblage comprising 135 pieces of flint, weighing approximately 1978 grams in total, was recovered from the features containing Grooved Ware. Table 2 summarizes the composition of the assemblage. In general, the flint is fresh with few signs of post-depositional damage or abrasion. Most pieces are lightly patinated a white or cream colour which is typical of the area. There is no evidence of settlement on the site before Late Neolithic times and it is assumed that the assemblage is a coherent group without residual material.

The raw material is exclusively good quality 'chalkland' type flint which was presumably imported to the site. Especially characteristic is material with a thin blue-grey band between the cortex and the unaltered flint. There is no evidence for the use of drift flint from the Upper Thames area, and only a few flints display the rather thick cream-coloured cortex that is common in the Beaker assemblage (see below Ch. II.B.4).

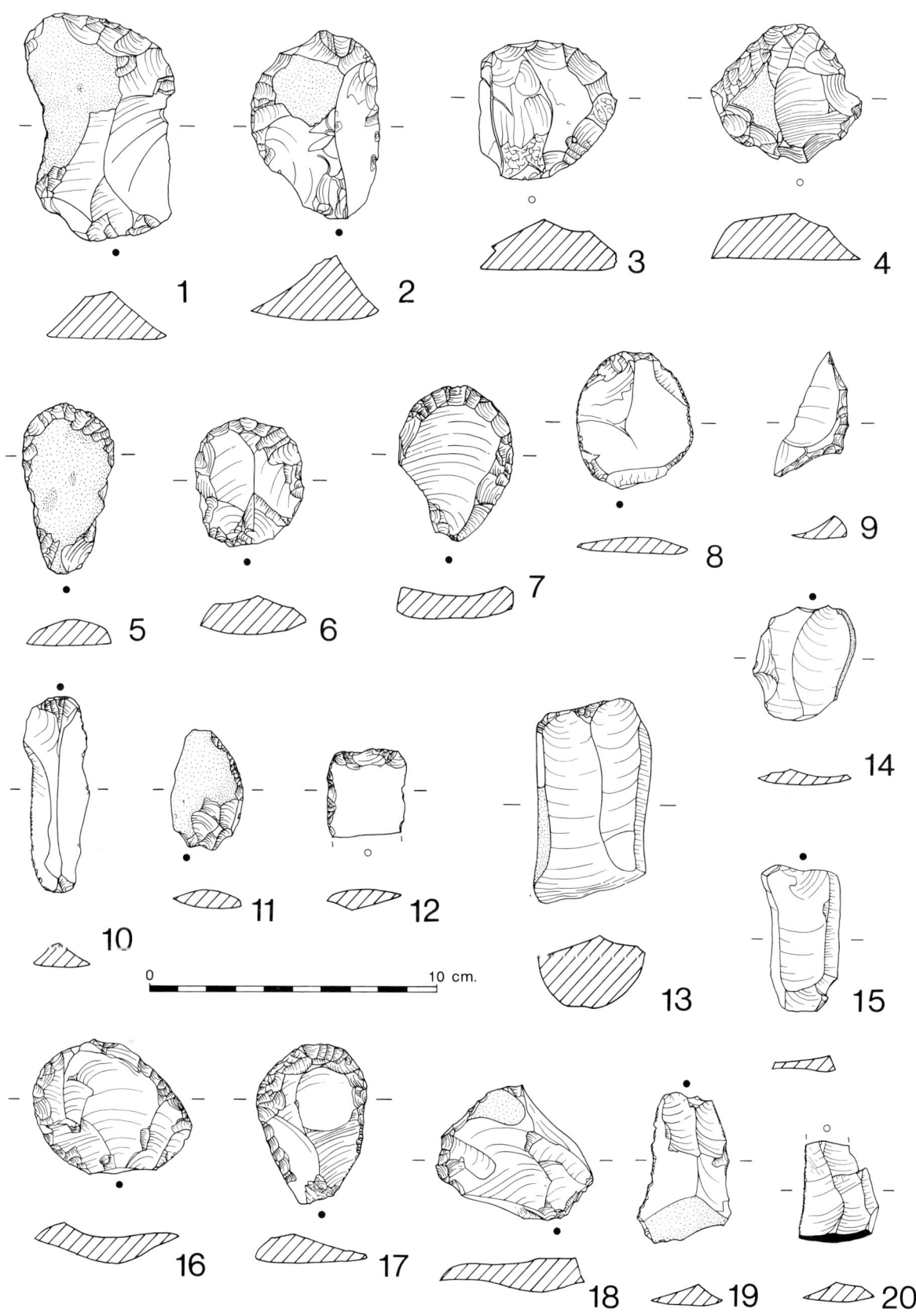

Figure 9 Flints from Grooved Ware features. Scale 1:2. Scrapers: 1-8, 16-18; Serrated flakes; 10, 19-20; Projectile point: 9; Miscellaneous retouched pieces: 11-12; Utilised flakes 14-15; Core: 13. 1-12 from context 784; 13-15 from context 785; 16-20 from context 962.

One flint nodule weighing 330 grams was recovered from 784 and may reflect the manner in which raw material was brought to the site.

Types	Features				Totals
	983	962	784	785	
Scrapers		3	8		11
Serrated flakes		2	1		3
Projectile point			1		1
Misc. retouched			2		2
Utilized flakes		2	4	2	8
Hammerstone	1			*	1
Cores		4	3	1	8
Unmodified flakes	17	36	26	15	94
Calcined lumps		1		5	6
Nodule			1		1
Totals	18	48	46	23	135

* A quartzite hammerstone was present in this feature (see Ch. II.A.4)

Table 2 Summary of flintwork from Grooved Ware features

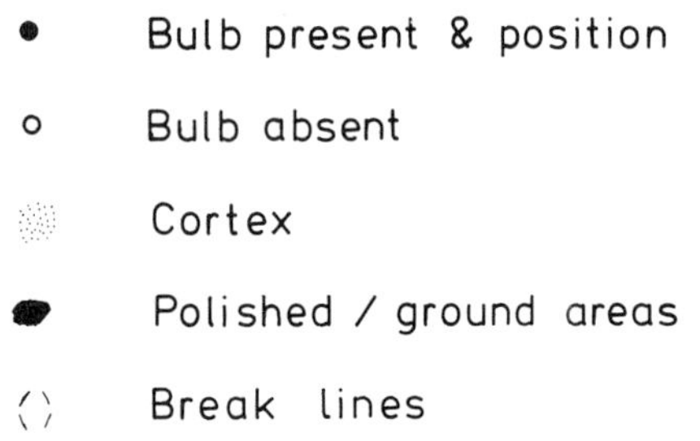

- Bulb present & position
- ○ Bulb absent
- Cortex
- Polished / ground areas
- ( ) Break lines

Figure 10 Drawing conventions used for flintwork

Fig. 9 illustrates a representative selection of the tools and worked pieces. For details of the assemblage see Ch. 2.A.3 on Fiche 1#8.

Overall, the assemblage is dominated by tools, especially scrapers and serrated blades, and by working waste. The presence of cores and hammerstones suggests that working took place nearby; and the contents of pit 785 (Fig. 11) suggest that debris from one episode of flintworking was disposed of as a single group. Implements and utilized pieces represent 20% of the assemblage, which is high even for a site away from naturally abundant supplies of raw materials, where frugal use of raw material might be expected.

Only 3 of the 19 categories of flint implements recurrently found in association with Grooved Ware were present in the Roughground Farm assemblage (cf. Wainwright & Longworth 1971, 254). Particularly notable is the absence of points/awls, knives, and axe fragments. Many of the Grooved Ware pit groups in the upper Thames Valley yield rather little flintwork, as for example at Vicarage Field, Stanton Harcourt, Oxfordshire (Case 1982c), and in this respect the Roughground Farm collection is an important assemblage. Comparable groups are known from the Thames valley, as for example at Sutton Courteney, Oxfordshire (Leeds 1934) and Cassington, Oxfordshire (Case 1982a). In both these cases scrapers and serrated blades dominated the assemblages. Little is known of contemporary assemblages from the Cotswolds, but further west at Trelystan in Powys scrapers, knives and points predominate (Healey in Britnell 1982, 175), possibly reflecting slightly different economic and subsistence practices in the uplands (Darvill 1983, 210–11).

II.A.4 Stone object

A single quartzite hammerstone was recovered from 785. This was an unmodified quartzite pebble crazed and fractured by use at both ends (Figs. 13 and 11). This stone was found associated with a worked-down flint core and at least nine unmodified flakes which probably derived from the core, suggesting than it had been used in flint knapping and discarded along with the other debris.

Hammerstones are relatively rare from sites with Grooved Ware pottery: Wainwright and Longworth list only one example, from Newport, Essex (1971, 262). In addition Pit P at Sutton Courtenay, Oxfordshire, contained a quartzite hammerstone and two flint hammerstones associated with Grooved Ware pottery (Leeds 1934, Pl. xxviii.a.)

II.A.5 Bone objects

A complete bone point/awl (Fig. 12.1) and the tip of another (Fig. 12.2) were recovered from 784. The complete point is made on a portion of long bone, probably a piece of tibia or fibia. Both were ground to shape, and are typical of the range of such artefacts known from Grooved Ware sites in Britain. At least nine awls of comparable form were found at Durrington Walls, Wiltshire, all within the size range 80–124 mm long (Wainwright & Longworth 1971, 181).

II.A.6 Animal bones

by Gillian Jones

Animal bones were recovered from all four features associated with Grooved Ware. More than half the bones were of pig, and a quarter were bovid. Of the red deer, all except three bones were antlers. Sheep or goat was represented by a single tooth, and a fragmentary atlas vertebra was from a dog or wolf. Table 3 summarises the animal bone assemblage by context.

The composition of the assemblage from the Grooved Ware pits varied, although pig was the most common species by fragment count in all the pits. 962 contained the sheep/goat tooth, the fragment of dog/wolf, and all the fairly complete antlers. It also contained relatively more cattle bones than any of the other pits.

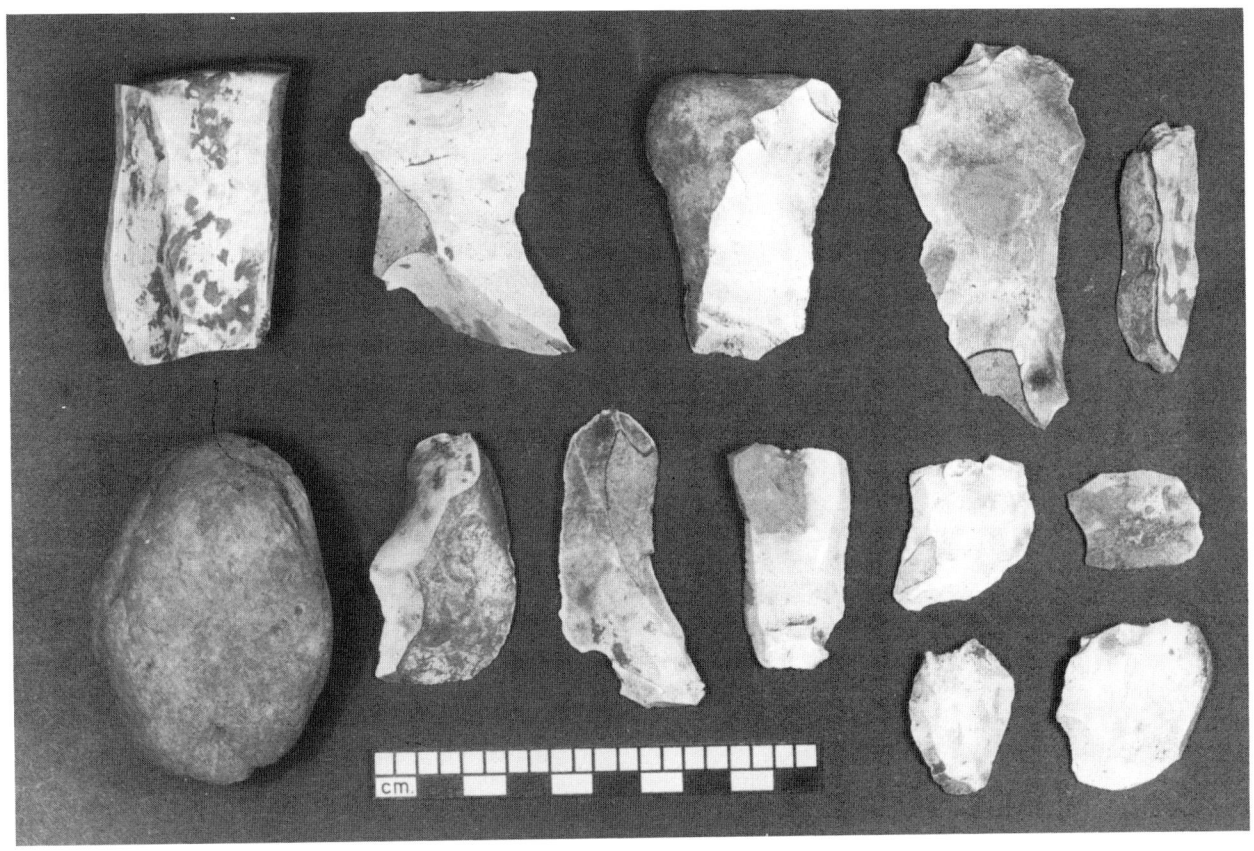

Figure 11 Flints and hammerstone from Grooved Ware pit 785 (photograph by T C Darvill)

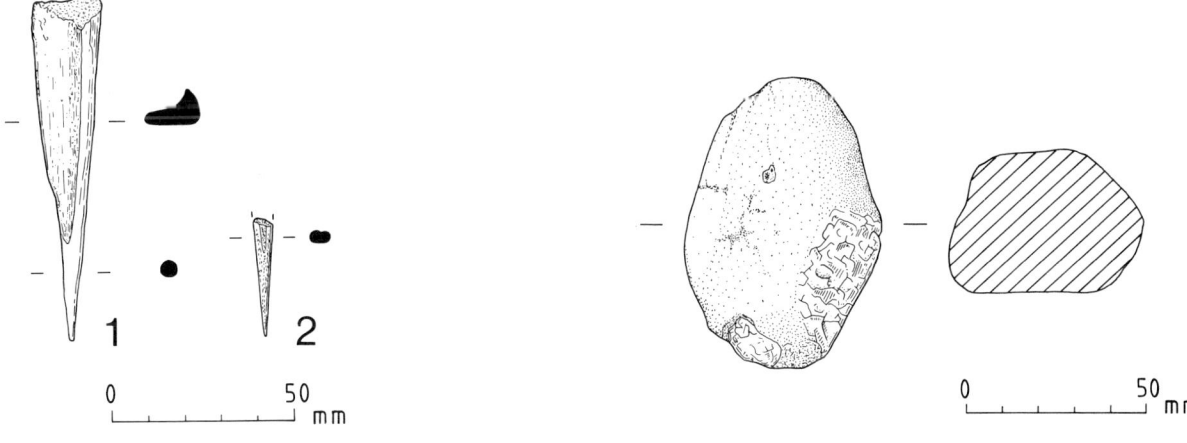

Figure 12 Bone points from pit 784

Figure 13 Hammerstone from pit 785

Species	Features				Totals
	784	785	962	983	
Pig	6	16	27	6	55
Cattle	1	1	17	2	21
Red deer	1	4	11		16
Sheep/goat			1		1
Dog			1		1
Totals	8	21	57	8	94

Table 3 Animal bones found in the Grooved Ware pits (by fragment count)

The pig bones are chiefly from domestic animals, with the exception of one male lower canine tooth, which was large and may be from a wild boar. Butchery marks were observed on one pig bone. Evidence of the age at death of the pigs suggests that few reached maturity and that they were killed at a variety of ages.

Most of the red deer remains came from 962, which contained at least four fairly complete shed antlers (Fig. 14). No signs of intentional use or wear were observed. Table 31 on Fiche 1#10 summarises the measurements taken on the antlers. In addition to the antlers in 962, three tines and two fragments were recovered from other pits.

Red deer was also hunted, to judge from the presence of three red deer metapodial bones. One of these bore many fine marks around the condyles, probably caused when skinning the animal. Animal skins would have been important, particularly bearing in mind that wool, if it was used at all, was available only in small quantities.

The cattle bones appear to be from domestic animals, none being large enough to suggest the presence of aurochs (one scapula neck — SLC 40, after Driesch 1976). A mandible and a few loose teeth indicate three individuals, all less than about five years old.

Some information on the probable season of use of two of the pits may be put forward. Most of the young of wild boar are born in late March or early April (Grigson 1982). If one assumes that Late Neolithic domestic pigs also generally produced only one litter, in the spring, then it is likely that the piglet bones in 785 were deposited some time in the summer. The find of several antlers together in 962 may be interpreted as a store. Red deer drop their antlers in February or March, and these would be collected soon after; antlers left on the ground, apart from being soon covered by plant growth, may be gnawed and damaged by the deer themselves. It is worth noting that no bones of very young pigs were found associated with the antlers. On the basis of this rather tentative argument, it can be suggested that the site was occupied or visited in both late winter and summer.

The bone sample is similar to those from the Late Neolithic sites discussed by Grigson (in Smith *et al* 1981) notably in the predominance of pig. Cattle were, as here, of secondary importance in terms of the number of fragments found, though given their greater size they may have provided the major part of the food output through milk and/or meat. Sheep were present at all sites but in very small numbers. Grigson observed that horse bones were recorded only from henge sites and not at those sites, like Roughground Farm, comprising only groups of pits.

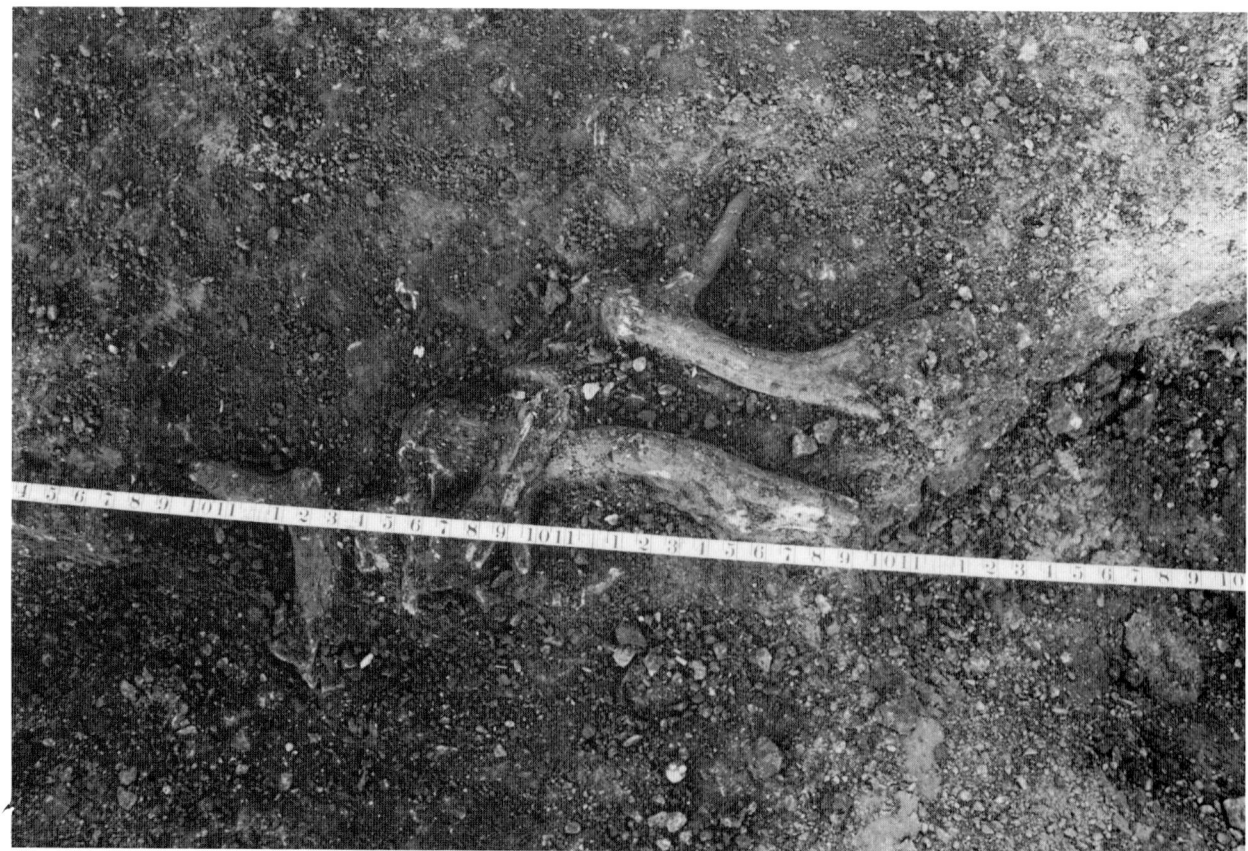

Figure 14 Deposit of antlers in Grooved Ware pit 962

II.A.7 Freshwater mollusca remains

by Mark Robinson

Fragments of the shell of a freshwater mussel belonging to the Unionidae family (*Andonta/Unio/margaritifera*) were recovered from 962. This is an extremely interesting find and may suggest that mussels were part of the Late Neolithic diet at the site. Alternatively, the shells could have been used as scoops or for the manufacture of personal ornaments.

II.A.8 Radiocarbon dates

Three radiocarbon dates were determined by the Harwell Radiocarbon laboratory on samples of bone from features containing Grooved Ware. These are shown in Table 4.

Context	Lab. No.	uncal. BP	calibrated BC		
			$+1\sigma$	(intercepts)	-1σ
784	HAR-5498	4100±100	2880	(2855, 2824, 2657, 2640, 2619)	2498
962	HAR-5500	3940±80	2573	(2466)	2343
962	HAR-5501	3820±90	2460	(2288)	2140

Table 4 Radiocarbon dates obtained from bone from features containing Grooved Ware pottery

The two dates from 962 give a weighted average of 3887±59 uncal. BP which calibrates to 2467 (2455, 2418, 2403) 2294 cal. BC at one sigma. The dates for all the features containing Grooved Ware overlap at one sigma, and probably relate to a single episode of activity. Such a proposition is enhanced by the spatial proximity of the features and the similarities in pottery styles between them. The weighted average for all three dates is 3943±51 uncal. BP, which calibrates to 2561 (2466) 2405 cal. BC at one sigma.

II.B Beaker period occupation

II.B.1 Description of excavated features

Five features contained Beaker pottery, 552, 790, 794, 1216 and 1260. All were apparently pits, and were scattered over an area more than 300 m across (Fig. 7). For dimensions and finds see Table 1. Pit 1260 is illustrated (Fig. 117 on Fiche 1#11).

II.B.2 Pottery

Fig. 15

II.B.2.a Introduction

About 200 sherds of Beaker pottery weighing a total of approximately 1297 grams were recovered from the beaker pits, the majority from 1260. Macroscopic examination of the fabrics, decoration, vessel form and colouration suggests that there are at least 36 individual vessels represented. A catalogue of these will be found in the microfiche report (Table 32 on Fiche 1#12). No complete or nearly complete vessels survive. A few scraps, representing less than 8% of the assemblage by weight, could not be assigned to particular vessel groups, but these do not include any featured sherds.

II.B.2.b Fabrics

Three main fabric groups were identified by macroscopic inspection and were subsequently verified in thin-section (see microfiche report: Fabrics 3 Grog, 4 Grog and shell, and 5 Flint). Table 32 on Fiche 1#12 summarizes the composition of the assemblage by context.

Fabric 4, the grog and shell-tempered ware, is by far the most common fabric, and was used for vessels of all types. The flint-tempered fabric (Fabric 5) tended to be used for larger and thicker-walled vessels, the grog-tempered fabric (Fabric 3) is common among the thin-walled finewares (see below). Petrological studies, however, show that these three fabrics are essentially the same clay mixed with slightly different combinations of tempering agents. This may relate to the function of different vessels, but without details of the forms it is difficult to be sure.

II.B.2.c Catalogue of illustrated sherds

For the full catalogue see microfiche.

Feature 552

P7 One sherd in Fabric 1. Decoration cf. Clarke 1970 motif 32.i. Orange-red colour throughout. Fig. 15.7

P8 Two sherds in Fabric 2. Decoration cf. Clarke 1970 motif 2 or similar. Pink-red Colour throughout. Fig. 15.8

P9 Two sherds in Fabric 1. Decoration cf. Clarke 1970 motif 1. Orange-red colour throughout. Fig. 15.9

P11 Five sherds in Fabric 2. Dark grey to black colour throughout. Fig. 15.11

Feature 1260

P19 Eleven sherds in Fabric 4. Rim and neck cf. Clarke 1970 II/IV. Decoration cf. Clarke 1970 motif 1. Pink-orange surfaces with a dark core. Fig. 15.19

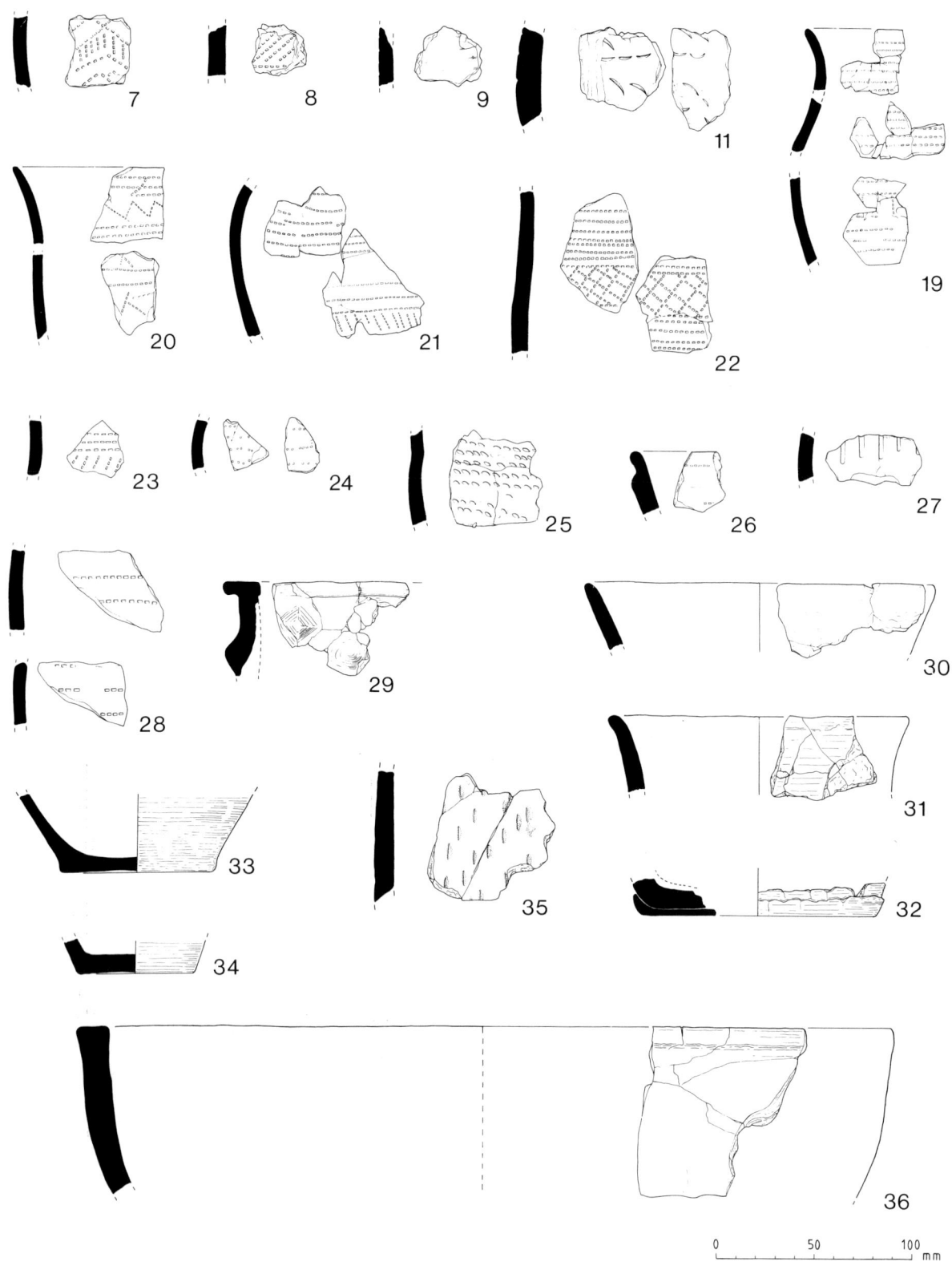

Figure 15 Beaker pottery

P20 Two sherds in Fabric 5. Decoration cf. Clarke 1970 motifs 1 and 7. Orange red surfaces with a dark core. Fig. 15.20

P21 Three sherds in Fabric 4. Decoration cf. Clarke 1970 motifs 1 and 2/12. Pink-red surfaces with dark core. Fig. 15.21

P22 Two sherds in Fabric 4. Decoration cf. Clarke 1970 motif 1 and 4. Pink-orange colour throughout. Fig. 15.22

P23 One sherd in Fabric 4. Decoration cf. Clarke 1970 motifs 1 and 2/12. Orange exterior, pink interior, dark core. Fig. 15.23

P24 Two sherds in Fabric 3. Decoration possibly barbed-wire style. Orange exterior, pink interior, dark core. Fig. 15.24

P25 Three sherds in Fabric 3. Exterior brown-red colour, interior and core dark. Fig. 15.25

P26 Rim sherd in Fabric 4. The rim is rather unusual in being cordoned. Red-orange throughout. Fig. 15.26

P27 One sherd in Fabric 4. Dark red throughout. Fig. 15.27

P28 Two sherds in Fabric 4. Decorated with widely spaced, horizontal comb-impressed lines. The knotches of the comb used were unusually large. Exterior and interior pink-red, dark core. Fig. 15.28

P29 Eighteen sherds in Fabric 4. An unusual vessel, probably some sort of bowl. The T-shaped rim was made by rolling the walls inwards and outwards. The vessel is plain, but has two projecting applied lumps of clay below the rim, and among the bodysherds there are indications of others. Exterior red-orange, core and interior dark. Fig. 15.29

P30 Two rimsherds in Fabric 3. Estimated rim diameter 175 mm. Interior and exteriors surfaces pink to red, dark core. Fig. 15.30

P31 Four sherds in Fabric 3. Estimated vessel diameter 150 mm. Exterior red, interior light-brown, dark core. Fig. 15.31

P32 Three sherds in Fabric 4. Estimated base diameter 120 mm. Coil-built. Dark red throughout. Fig. 15.32

P33 One sherd in Fabric 4. Estimated base diameter 80 mm. Pink-red exterior, brown-red interior and core. Fig. 15.33

P34 One sherd in Fabric 3. Estimated base diameter 60 mm. Red-orange exterior, interior and core dark. Fig. 15.34

P35 Ten sherds in Fabric 5. Pink-red interior and exterior, dark core. Fig. 15.35

P36 Three sherds from a potbeaker in Fabric 4. The diameter is between 300 mm and 400 mm. Red interior and exterior, dark core. Fig. 15.36

The beaker assemblage is typical of a domestic collection. There is a considerable range of vessel sizes, from small pots with rim diameters of less than 130 mm up to large vessels over 300 mm in diameter. The basic three-fold division of domestic beaker groups into fineware, everyday ware and heavy duty ware proposed by Clarke (1976) can be easily discerned in this assemblage from the size of vessel, wall thickness and coarseness of fabric. The assemblage breaks down as follows: Fineware 75% (27 vessels), everyday ware 17% (6 vessels) and heavy-duty ware 8% (3 vessels).

Typically the coarser vessels are less well decorated, often with fingernail-impressions rather than comb-impressions, and some of the heavy duty wares, such as P36, are plain. Among the fineware vessels toothed comb decoration is the most widely used, cord-impressed lines occurring only on P25. The decorative motifs and arrangements used are horizontally set parallel lines, with occasional use of zigzag and lattice work.

Very few profiles can be reconstructed, but most seem to fall into the Bell Beaker and short-necked Beaker classes. P29 is very unusual and cannot be easily paralleled among published domestic assemblages or grave deposits. Gibson (1982, 454) illustrates a lugged vessel from the mixed Beaker/Early Bronze Age collection from Mildenhall Fen, Suffolk, and there is another lugged vessel from Newgrange, Co Meath, Ireland (O'Kelly *et al* 1983, 90) but neither vessel shares the form of our example.

Chronologically, the Roughground Farm assemblage belongs to the middle Beaker phase as defined by Humphrey Case (1977, 72), and the decoration and forms fit into Steps 2–4 on the scheme of Lanting & Van der Waals 1971. The radiocarbon date of 3710±100 BP (HAR-5499) from 1260 is consistent with the typology of the Beaker assemblage (see below).

The Upper Thames Valley is fairly rich in Middle Beaker occupation, to judge from the number of burials, cemeteries and possible settlements (Case 1986, 32). A possible settlement is known from pits at Cassington, Oxfordshire (Case *et al* 1964, 59–63), and there is the well known cemetery containing at least four graves at Stanton Harcourt, Oxfordshire (Case 1963, 21–26), as well as numerous single burials and stray finds. Middle Beaker period activity is also evident on the Cotswolds from the presence of burials such as at Little Rollright, Oxfordshire (Case 1956, 2) and the radiocarbon-dated ditch deposits at Condicote Henge, Gloucestershire (Saville 1983). At this last site only fingernail-decorated coarse Beaker was recovered, but it was similar in both style and fabric to some of the Roughground Farm coarseware Beakers, suggesting a fairly widespread tradition of using limestone and grog for making coarse pots.

II.B.3 Ceramic objects and daub

Pit 1260 contained 528 grams of fired clay in Fabric 12, including two possible mould fragments. (For details see microfiche Ch. 2.A.2.b on Fiche 1#6).

II.B.4 Flintwork

Some 150 pieces of flint weighing a total of 777 grams were recovered form the Beaker pits. Over 90% of the assemblage (by fragment count) came from 1260. Table 5 summarises the composition of assemblage by context. Most of the flint was fresh and in good condition with little sign of post-depositional damage. Because the Beaker pits are spatially discrete from the pits with Grooved Ware it is assumed that the Beaker-associated assemblage is relatively uncontaminated by earlier material.

Type	Features					Totals
	552	790	794	1216	1260	
Scrapers		1			20	21
Serrated flakes		1			1	2
Knives					2	2
Polished axe*					1	1
Misc. retouched			1**	1	4	6
Utilized flakes					1	1
Cores					1	1
Unmodified flakes		9	2		36	47
Calcined lumps		1			7	8
Pieces of drift flint					61***	61
Totals	0	12	3	1	134	150

* Axe reused as a core
** Probably a broken knife
*** Including some struck and some naturally fractured flakes

Table 5 Flintwork from Beaker features

Two main types of raw material are represented. 1260 contained 62 pieces (weight 69 grams) of local drift flint, mostly small flakes and broken pebbles, but including one very small scraper (see below). This flint was presumably collected from the deposits of high-level gravels in the Thames Valley west of Lechlade, as drift flint is not recorded within the lower-level gravels of the immediate Lechlade area (Richardson 1933, 85). Only 1260 contained this type of flint; it was absent from the pits containing Grooved Ware (see above).

The remaining flint is good quality 'chalkland' type, probably imported and fairly uniformly patinated white. There are two types of cortex, a thin white-grey variety which is rare and a thicker cream-coloured variety which is softer and more porous, and which dominates the assemblage. Fig. 17 illustrates a representative selection of the tools and worked pieces.

Overall, the assemblage is dominated by utilitarian tools, particularly scrapers. In general the Beaker scrapers are smaller and lighter than those associated with Grooved Ware.

Fig. 16 shows a comparative plot of scraper dimensions for the two periods; two clusters can be clearly discerned. Excluding the broken drift flint, which contributed little to tool-making, the assemblage comprises a remarkable 40% worked and utilised pieces to only 60% debitage. This suggests that the contents of the pit derived from an area where domestic or industrial activities took place rather than an area near to the site of flintworking (see Ch. II.C). Also notable is the absence of projectile points or certain points/awls.

Compared with other flint assemblages of Beaker date from the Cotswolds and Upper Thames Valley this one from Roughground Farm is especially rich. At Tolley's Pit, Cassington, Oxfordshire, for example, Beaker pit 1 contained only seven worked flints (Case *et al* 1964, 59–63). The assemblage from the silting of the inner ditch at Condicote Henge, Gloucestershire, which on the basis of radiocarbon dates is approximately contemporary with the Beaker pits at Roughground Farm, contained only 12 worked flints (Saville 1983, 34). In comparison, pit 1260 at Roughground Farm contained 29 worked pieces.

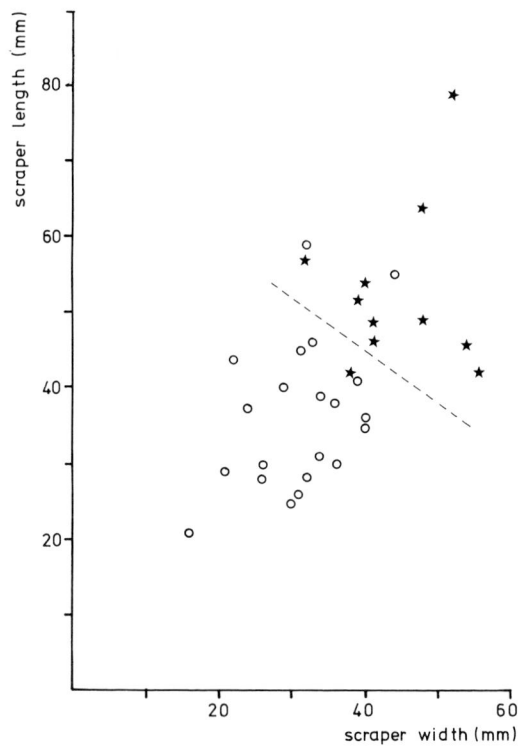

★ Grooved ware associations
○ Beaker associations

Figure 16 Graph showing the size distribution of Grooved Ware and Beaker scrapers

II.B.5 Stone objects

Parts of two sandstone cushion stones (S1 and S2) and four quartzite pebble hammerstones (S3–S6) were recovered from 1260, together with six fragments of unutilised pebbles and two roughly spherical lumps of limestone (S7–S14)(Fig. 18). One fragment of sandstone (S15) was also found in feature 790. (For catalogue see Ch. 2.B.5 on Fiche 1#15.)

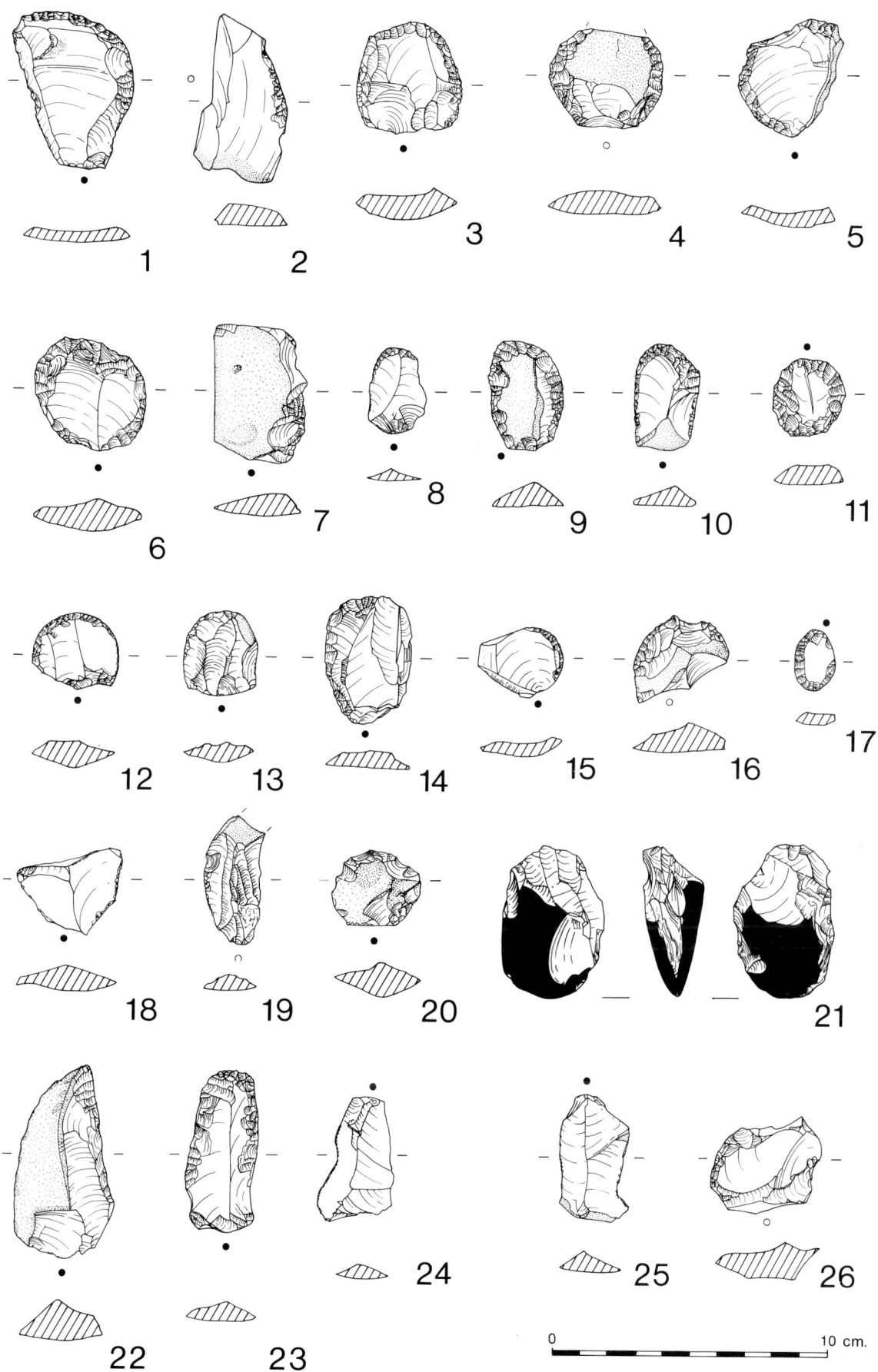

Figure 17 Flints from Beaker features. Scrapers: 1–20, 26; Serrated flakes: 24, 25; Knives: 22, 23; Polished Axe: 21. 1–24 from context 1260; 25 and 26 from context 790.

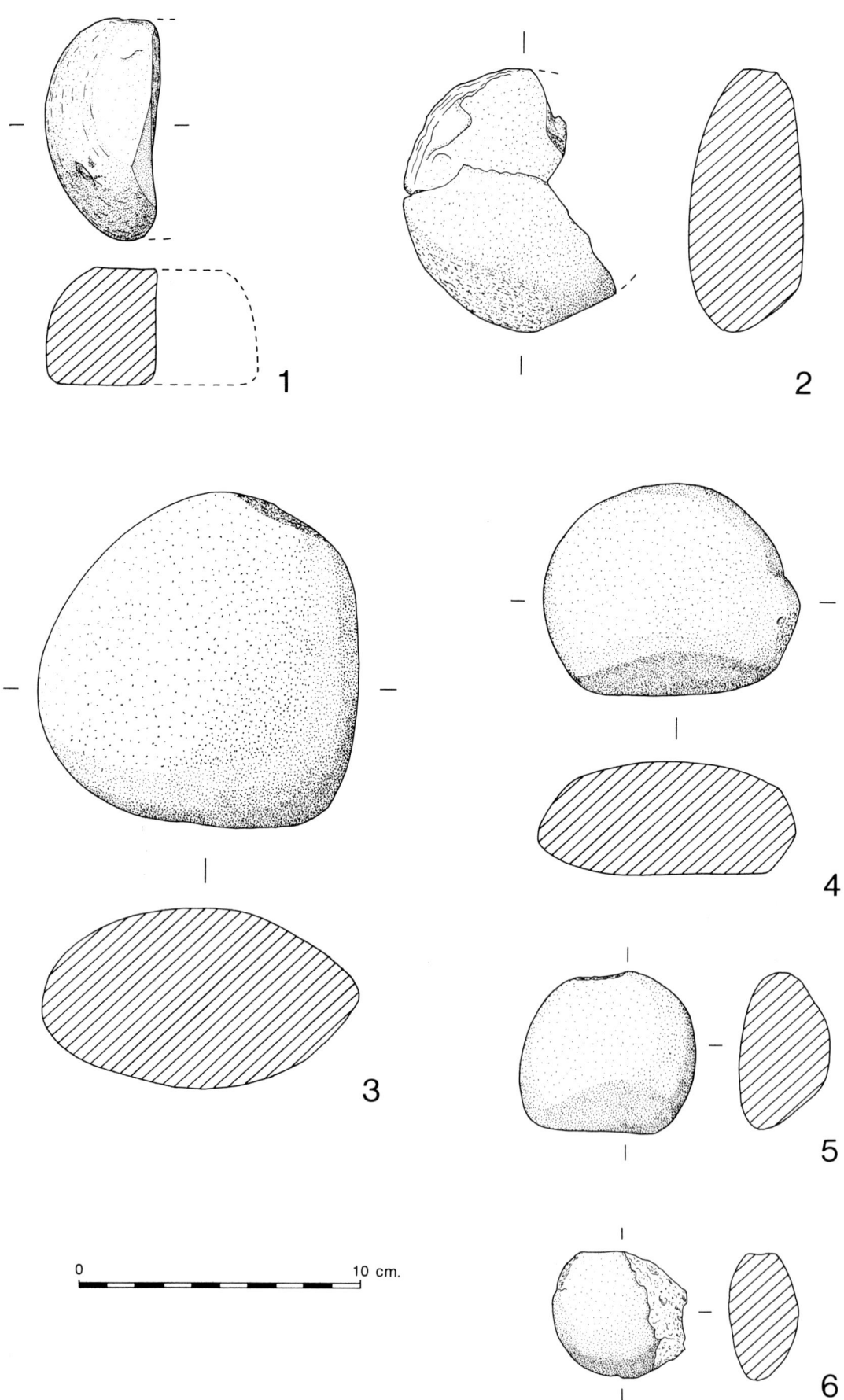

Figure 18 Cushion stones and hammerstones from Beaker pit 1260

The variety of hammerstones and stone objects from 1260 provides an interesting assemblage from a sealed Beaker context. S2 could have been used in grain processing, but it is rather small for a rubber, very fine-grained, and there are no associated fragments of quernstone. More likely is that it was used for some other task, possibly as a cushion stone like S1.

If S1 is a cushion stone then this is an important and unusual find. Both round and rectangular cushion stones have been recognised among Beaker grave goods on the Continent (Butler & Van der Waals 1966, 63), but very rarely in Britain (Clarke 1970, 573) where they seem to be more common as stray finds without any secure context. Examples from the west of England include Okus, Swindon, and Chase Hill, Hereford and Worcester (Darvill 1983, 126). Another possible example, from Whittington Wood, Gloucestershire, was exhibited at the Society of Antiquaries in 1866 (Evans 1897, 244). One interpretation of these cushion stones is that they were simple anvils used by metal workers when hammering copper, bronze and gold, but no metal ores or metal residues were found in 1260. A source to the west or south-west of Lechlade must be envisaged for the sandstones represented by S1 and S2.

The four hammerstones represent a series which although not precisely graduated increase in weight by the following factors from smallest to largest: × 2.8; × 2.0; × 3.3. In each case the working face is confined to a small area. Whether these hammers were used for flintworking or were perhaps connected with the use of the cushion stones is uncertain, but it is notable that cores are scarce among the flint assemblage from the Beaker pits, suggesting that if these hammers were for flintworking then any spent cores underwent a different deposition pattern to the hammers. All the hammerstones could have been obtained from the high-level gravels containing 'northern drift' which outcrop to the west of Lechlade. No quartzite or bunter pebbles are recorded in the low-level gravels in the immediate vicinity of Lechlade (Richardson 1933, 85).

II.B.6 Animal bones

by Gillian Jones

Three fragments of bone were recovered, all from 1260. Two were cattle, the other was pig.

II.B.7 Radiocarbon date

A single radiocarbon date was determined by the Harwell Radiocarbon Laboratory on a sample of bone from pit 1260. This is shown in Table 6.

This date is significantly younger than the dates obtained for the Late Neolithic Grooved Ware activity at the site, and suggests that the two episodes of occupation were separated by two centuries or more.

Context	Lab. No.	uncal. BP	calibrated BC $+1\sigma$	(intercepts)	-1σ
1260	HAR-5499	3710±100	2280	(2135, 2052, 2050)	1970

Table 6 Radiocarbon date obtained from bone from pit 1260.

II.C Early Bronze Age

II.C.1 Pottery

Fig. 19

A single small rimsherd of dark fired pottery was recovered from 1137 (Fig. 19.1). The fabric is grog tempered (see Ch. 2.A.2.b on Fiche 1#6, Fabric 6 for details). The inner face of the rim is bevelled and is decorated with two parallel twisted cord impressed lines. There are traces of a single line of impressed twisted cord on the outer face. Although the sherd is small, it is probably a piece of food vessel or collared urn and as such can be assigned tentatively to the Early Bronze Age. There is little else of similar date from the site, and it may be that the Roman features around 1137 disturbed or destroyed an earlier feature of some sort.

II.C.2 Discussion

Early Bronze Age activity at Roughground Farm is represented by only one sherd of pottery and perhaps a few stray implements among the residual flint assemblage. That activity of this date was present in the area can hardly be doubted to judge from the number of known ring ditches (Benson & Miles 1974; Leech 1977), but the focus of settlement must have been elsewhere.

II.D Undated prehistoric features

II.D.1 Description of the features

Twenty-six features contained flints but no chronologically diagnostic artefacts. 983 also contained only flints, but cut pit 962 and is described above (Ch. II.A.1). Some of these features may have been connected with the later Bronze Age occupation, and are discussed in Ch. III.A.1

II.D.2 Flintwork

Fig. 118 on Fiche 1#17

Fifty-nine flints weighing a total of approximately 396 grams were recovered from the undated features. The largest assemblages were from 969 and 1163, with 7 and 10 flints respectively. Ch. 2.D.2 on Fiche 1#16 in the microfiche summarises the composition of the assemblage by context; the composition of the assemblage as a whole is summarised on Table 33 on Fiche 1#16.

Most of the pieces are well preserved and fresh-looking. Chalkland type flint predominates, and most pieces have a light patina. Three pieces are of special interest, a large knife from 1209 (Fig. 118.1 on Fiche 1#17) whose retouched edge has gloss (?sickle gloss) along almost the whole length of both faces, a multi-purpose tool of unclassifiable form from 1165 (Fig. 118.2 on Fiche 1#17) and a bifacially flaked arrowhead of fine workmanship from 1288 (Fig. 118.3 on Fiche 1#17).

All the flintwork from these features could be fitted into the Late Neolithic or Beaker period of activity on the site.

II.E Flints from later features

II.E.1 General

Later prehistoric and Roman features contained residual flintwork; flints were also collected from unstratified contexts and are considered together with the residual assemblage.

The flintwork from the Later Bronze Age pits may also be residual, but is described in Ch. III.A.3 as a potentially coherent assemblage.

II.E.2 Composition

Fig. 19

The residual assemblage comprises 416 pieces of flint which weighs a total of approximately 2392 grams. Table 7 summarises the composition of this assemblage and further details of the finds from individual features/layers can be found in the microfiche. Most features contained only single flakes or worked pieces. Fig. 19 illustrates a representative selection.

In general the flints are battered, many are broken or abraded and 'rolled' in appearance. Patination was highly variable and sometimes absent. Good quality 'chalkland' type flint dominates the assemblage and no tools made from drift flint were present. One nodule of imported flint was found in 1141. Approximately 12% of the total assemblage are tools or implements.

Overall, the residual assemblage is mostly of Late Neolithic, Beaker period and Early Bronze Age character.

There is no Palaeolithic or Mesolithic flintwork and no certain examples of Early or Middle Neolithic tools. Accordingly, this collection may be viewed as an extension of material recovered from sealed contexts, and it is interesting to note that the range of arrowheads and points represent types which were virtually absent from the pit groups (see Tables 2 and 5).

Types	Iron Age	Roman	Iron Age or Roman	Unstratified	Totals
Scrapers	11	7		4	22
Serrated flakes	4				4
Arrowheads		2	1	1	4
Points		1	1		2
Knives			1		1
Strike-a-light		1			1
Misc. retouched	1	6		3	10
Utilized flakes	2	4		1	7
Cores	6	7	2	3	18
Flakes	168	80	24	69	341
Nodule	1				1
Calcined lumps	2	1			3
Drift flint nodules				2	2
Totals	195	109	29	83	416

Table 7 Summary of the residual flintwork assemblage

II.F Discussion

The earliest firm evidence of activity on the Roughground Farm site dates from the Late Neolithic period. Certainly communities were active in the area before this time, as is shown by at least three stone and flint axes from the immediate vicinity of the site (Fig. 20), but on this site no traces were left behind. The absence of earlier occupation on the First and Second Gravel Terraces is borne out at other sites in the area and in the wider region with Late Neolithic activity, notably in the Stanton Harcourt area (Barclay et al forthcoming).

The Late Neolithic expansion of settlement in the Upper Thames area has been described by Case (1986, 31). A similar pattern can be seen in the Severn Valley (Darvill 1984, 100), and there is some evidence to suggest that the changes in these two areas were related to a decrease in settlement density on the Cotswold uplands, where causewayed enclosures and chambered tombs fell out of use at the end of the Middle Neolithic (Darvill 1984, 99).

The Lechlade area emerged as in important focus of activity in the Late Neolithic. Two cursus monuments are known, one on each side of the Thames (Fig. 20). Only the Lechlade cursus, which is 500 m SW of the Grooved Ware settlement at Roughground Farm, has been explored by excavation. Three cuttings through the western ditch in 1965 revealed very little (Vatcher 1965) but more recently excavation by the Oxfordshire Archaeological Unit brought

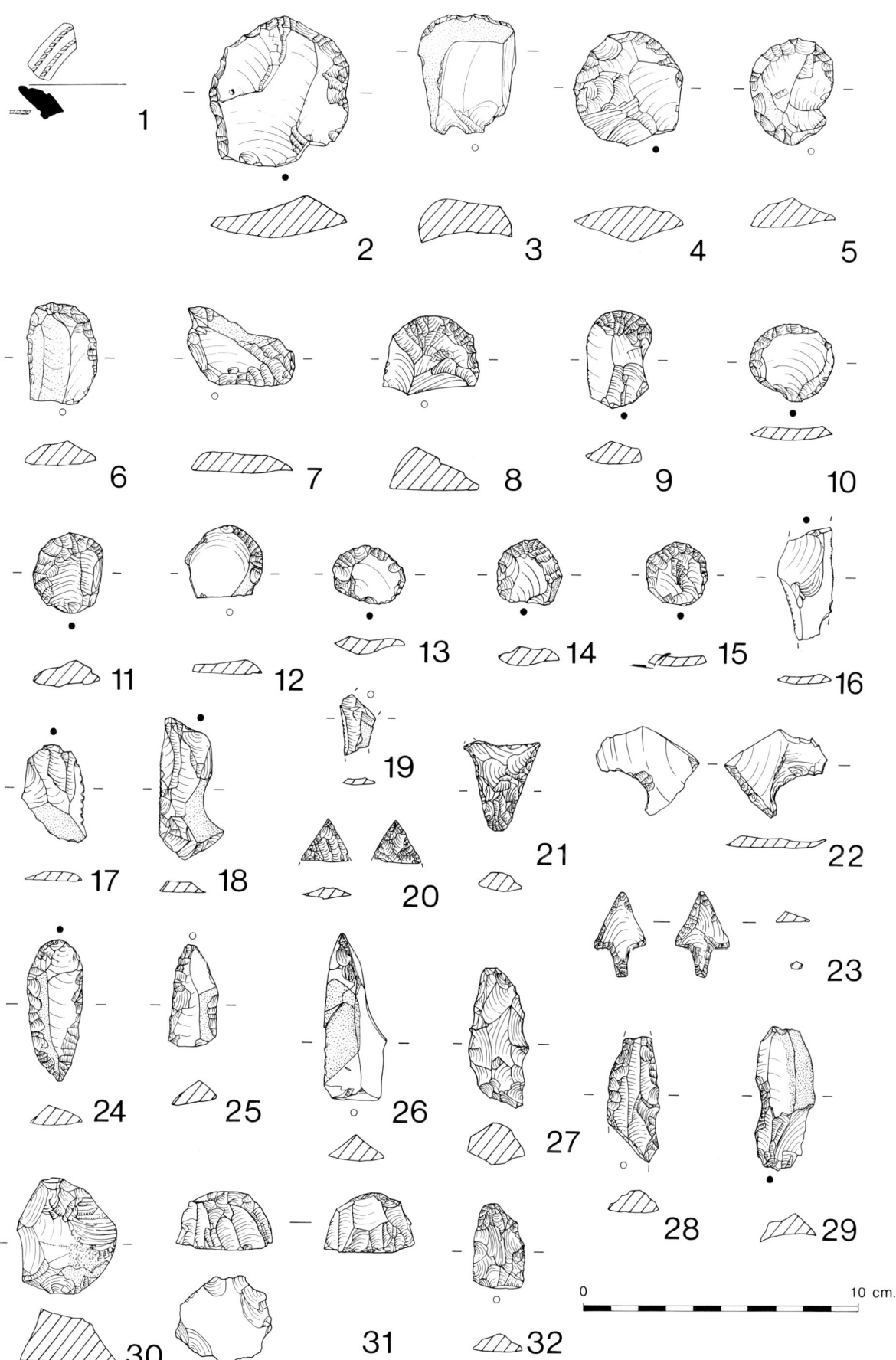

Figure 19 Pottery and flintwork from residual and unstratified contexts. Early Bronze Age sherd: 1; Scrapers: 2–15; Serrated flakes: 16–19; Arrowheads: 20–23; Points: 25 and 26; Knife: 24; Strike-a-light: 27; Miscellaneous retouched flakes: 28, 29, and 32; Cores: 30, 31.

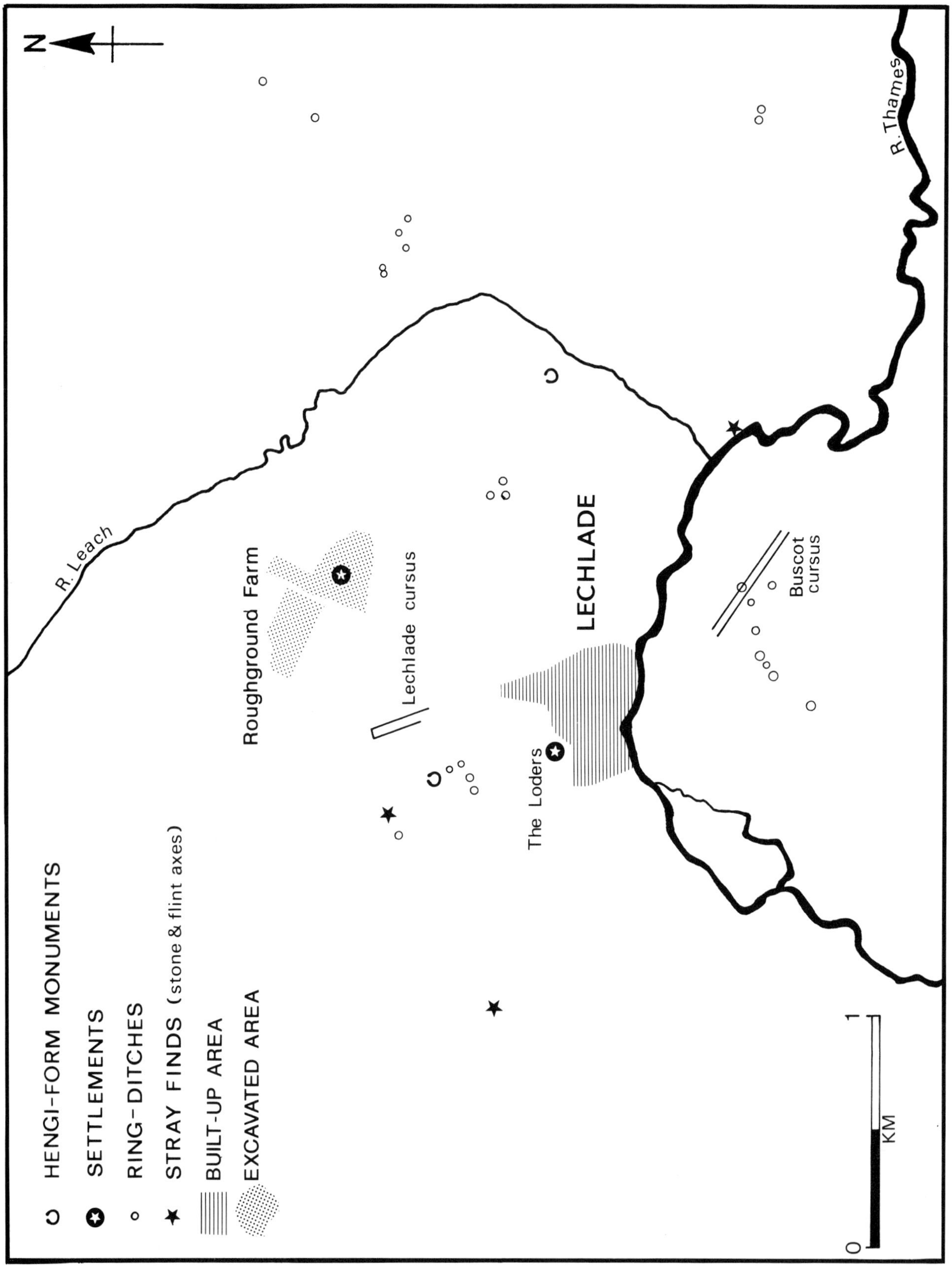

Figure 20 Late Neolithic and Early Bronze Age sites and monuments in the Lechlade area

to light an almost complete Grooved Ware vessel about one-third of the way down the fill of the eastern ditch (Moore 1985). Some of the ring ditches in the area are probably of the same date, and mention may be made of the two hengiform monuments in the area (Fig. 20; IF Smith 1971; Benson & Miles 1974; Leech 1977).

The Grooved Ware occupation at Roughground Farm is only one of a series of such sites, characterised by pits and pit groups, on both sides of the Thames in Oxfordshire, the nearest example being only 1.2 kilometres to the SW at The Loders (Darvill et al 1986). This site was discovered during the groundworks for a housing estate and could not be fully excavated to determine the extent and form of the settlement area. The pottery and the flintwork from The Loders is quite different from that at Roughground Farm, but close parallels for both pottery styles and flintwork have been noted between Roughground Farm and a site at Cassington, Oxfordshire (see above). Here a group of seven pits representing a small occupation site were excavated in the early 1950s (Case 1982a, 121).

The four Grooved Ware pits at Roughground Farm lay close to one another (Fig. 7) and may represent a single phase of occupation. Both features and finds suggest that it might have been a working area. The tools are all fairly intact, which contrasts with the flint tools from The Loders (Darvill et al 1986). The considerable number of animal bones and the group of antlers in 962, coupled with the presence of large heavy scrapers and serrated blades may point to an animal carcass processing area; some of the pit and cattle bones showed signs of butchery, and the deer bones display marks appropriate to skinning. The cache of antlers may have been stored for future use. The discarded flintworking debris, which included a core and a hammerstone, may be related to the provision of sharp fresh flakes for use as knives in carcass dismemberment and butchery.

Pig bones were abundant in all the Grooved Ware features, underlining the fact that pigs were important at many different types of site in the Late Neolithic, not just at large henges. As Jones points out above (Ch. II.A.6), however, cattle may have been just as important as pig, if not more so, in the diet of the community at Roughground Farm. No evidence of cereal production or processing was found on the site and it is doubtful whether the pits would have been suitable as grain silos; perhaps they were dug as quarries for gravel or hearth pits.

The presence of a freshwater mollusc shell is unusual; shellfish were exploited by other Late Neolithic communities, as for example at Woodlands, Durrington Walls, Ratfyn, and Woodhenge, all in Wiltshire, (Wainwright & Longworth 1971, 265), but these instances are all of marine mollusca and may simply indicate connections with coastal communities (see Darvill 1983, 92 for a review of marine exploitation in the Neolithic).

Radiocarbon dates suggest that the Beaker activity at Roughground Farm was slightly later, focused on the last quarter of the 3rd millennium BC. No features contained both Grooved Ware and Beaker pottery and the distribution of features belonging to the two traditions is quite distinct, as were the clay sources used in the manufacture of pottery by the two groups. The Beaker period occupation was spread over a wide area in contrast to the Grooved Ware activity (Fig. 7). Beaker period activity is common on sites in the Upper Thames Valley, and in view of their density further down the Thames it is perhaps surprising that no Beaker burials were located at Roughground Farm.

Beaker activity in the immediate Lechlade area is represented by a sherd of Beaker pottery from a ring ditch at Langford Downs, Little Faringdon (Williams 1947, 63) about 3 kilometres to the N, and by finds from South Lawn, Taynton, about 13 kilometres to the N (Clifford 1937, 162). The Late Neolithic was a period of renewed or continued expansion of settlement in the upper Thames Valley and Cotswolds, and it was at this time that the henge monuments at Condicote, Gloucestershire, and the Devil's Quoits, Stanton Harcourt, Oxfordshire, were in use.

Excavations at Condicote, some 29 kilometres NW of Lechlade, have demonstrated Beaker associations with the monument and radiocarbon dates of 3720 ± 80 BP (HAR-3064) and 2670 ± 100 BP (HAR-3067) were obtained from the ditch fills (Saville 1983, 46). This makes Condicote Henge contemporary with the activity related to feature 1260 at Roughground Farm, which has a radiocarbon date of 3710 ± 100 BP (HAR-5499). The Devil's Quoits, about 21 kilometres east of Lechlade, has a radiocarbon date of 4010 ± 120 BP (HAR-1887) from the primary ditch silt (Case 198632). Mention may also be made of the undated henge at Westwell only 10 km north of Lechlade (Atkinson 1949).

The nature of the Beaker period occupation at Roughground Farm is difficult to establish. Evidence for subsistence activities is very poor; there is no evidence of crop production or crop processing and animal bones are very few. This paucity of subsistence evidence possibly suggests that some sort of industrial activity rather than food processing was being undertaken, around 1260 at least. The flintwork includes a high percentage of tools, and although flintworking may have been carried out in the area, the virtual absence of spent cores would suggest otherwise. The groups of hammerstone and the cushion stones are probably the most significant clue. Metalworking is one possibility; the burnt stones and heavily burnt daub mould fragments from 1260 might support this, but there was no trace of metal ores, waste products, or partly finished implements. Other possible uses for the hammers and cushion stones include leatherworking.

Chapter III

The later prehistoric period

III.A Later Bronze Age occupation

III.A.1 Description of the features

Plan: Fig. 7

Nine features, all of them pits, were dated by pottery to this period. They were widely distributed across the site east of the Lechlade-Burford road. Other features which contained only flints may also have been contemporary but the flintworking is not sufficiently diagnostic to isolate it from Late Neolithic assemblages, which were also present on the site. Some of these features, however, clustered around known Bronze Age pits, and are mentioned below.

The pits are described from west to east.

Pit 879 was circular with sloping sides, except on the north, where it was apparently undercut more than 0.6 m (Figs. 21 and Fig. 119 on Fiche 1#19). This may have been a tree hole (see Moore & Jennings forthcoming). Alternatively the undercut may have been caused by animal burrowing, especially as an early Roman sherd was found halfway down the fill. The top fill of 879, which is described as 'old topsoil', probably indicates a slow humic build-up in the open dry conditions suggested by molluscs from the pit (see Ch. III.A.6).

Several other features in the vicinity may also have been of this period. 885 (Fiche 4#71), 897 (Fiche 4#73) and 881 (Fiche 4#72) all contained flints, bone and burnt limestones. The clay into which 897 was cut was burnt brick red, so it was presumably a hearth.

Figure 21 Bronze Age pit 879, over-excavated to show undercut

Another group of Bronze Age pits lay c 180 m north-east (Fig. 7; Fig. 119 on Fiche 1#19). 968 was cut by pit 988. A calibrated radiocarbon date of 1410–1170 cal. BC (at one sigma) was obtained from animal bone from pit 1001 (see Table 12). To the north-east were two further pits 734 (Fiche 4#41) and 1165 (Fiche 4#42). On the very north edge of the site were a crouch burial 1157 (Fig. 32) and a gully aligned upon it, 1156; the burial was radiocarbon-dated and gave a calibrated date of 1160–940 cal. BC (at one sigma) (see Table 12), and both features probably belong to the Later Bronze Age occupation. They are, however, described in the Early Iron Age section (see Ch. III.B.1 and Ch. III.B.4).

At the east edge of the site were adjacent circular pits 1296 and 1297 (Fig. 26). These pits were larger than the Iron Age ones, but were only shallow; for the section of 1297 see Fig. 119 on Fiche 1#19. Further south was an elongated pit 1290 (Fig. 26; Fig. 119 on Fiche 1#19), surrounded by small pits 1244, 1323 and 1327 which may have been of similar date (see Ch. 3.1 on Fiche 1#19). This area may therefore represent another small focus of Bronze Age occupation.

Feature 1199, salvaged by A J Baxter, produced the largest assemblage of Bronze Age pottery from Roughground Farm. Unfortunately no details other than its approximate position are available (Fig. 7).

These scattered features vary widely in shape and size, but common to all was a charcoal-laden dark fill containing occupation refuse and burnt stones. Except in the case of 897 the charcoal need not mean that the pits were the sites of fires, but does imply domestic occupation close by, in contrast to the Early Iron Age pits, many of which contained little or no rubbish (see below).

III.A.2 Bronze Age pottery

by Richard Hingley

Figs. 22, Fig. 23, Fig. 24

Nine features produced Later Bronze Age pottery, the assemblages from which varied from 1 to 134 sherds (see Table 34 on Fiche 1#21). Bone from one of these features, pit 1001, produced a calibrated radiocarbon date of 1410–1170 cal. BC (at one sigma) (see Table 12).

The pottery was classified according to fabric, form and decoration or surface treatment. Seven fabrics were identified by macroscopic examination. Fabric proportions were compared between assemblages of more than 30 sherds (following De Roche in Parrington 1978, 47). See Table 8 below.

In the Later Bronze Age the calcareous Fabrics 2, 3 and 4 account for 91.6% of all sherds, or if Fabric 6 is included, 95.2%.

Sherds of Later Bronze Age date were usually small, soft and friable, in contrast to those of Early Iron Age date. This is probably due to harder and more even firing in the Early Iron Age.

Fourteen form categories have been defined on the basis of whole profiles, rims or shoulders (Table 9).

The forms cover both the Bronze Age and Early Iron Age assemblages, as a number occur in both periods. (For definitions of the terms used see the Microfiche report).

From the assemblage of 366 sherds 34 vessels were either partly reconstructable or had distinctive traits worth illustrating (Figs. 22, Fig. 23 and Fig. 24). A classification of illustrated sherds is given below:

Form 1 Upright rims 3, 4, 14, ?22, 23, 25, 28, 32.
Form 2 Inturned rims 6, 26.
Form 4 Incurving rims 24
Form 6 Rounded and out-turned rims 5.
Form 8 Straight-sided upright vessels 7, 20.
Form 9 Concave necks of vessels (none illustrated).
Form 12 Bipartite vessels 27
Form 13 Biconical vessels 1, 2, ?11, 18
Form 14 Bucket urns 0, 13, 19, 21, 31, 33

Bucket urns (Form 14) and biconical vessels (Form 13) are predominant in these features (Table 9). Large fragments of bucket urn were recovered from 734 (No 13), 879 (No 33), 998 (No 0), 1001 (No 21) and 1296 (No 31). Small sherds, possibly from bucket urns (Form 8) came from 1199 (No 7), 1290 (Nos 19 and 20) and from 1242 (No 35). The sherds from 1242 was associated with Early Iron Age pottery and may have been residual. Four probable biconical urns (Form 13) are represented.

Six types of decoration were present (Table 36 on Fiche 1#23), the first three of which are characteristic of the Later Bronze Age. Shallow grooves, finger-tip/nail impressions and incised lines also occur, but are commoner in the Early Iron Age. The incidence of forms and types of decoration by feature is given in Table 37 on Fiche 1#23.

III.A.2.a Catalogue of the illustrated sherds

Feature 998 Fig. 22.0 Fabric 2, dense and finely sorted. Exterior red-brown, interior orange to black, break dark grey to black. Form 14.

Feature 1199 Fig. 23.1 Fabric 2 with addition of very small orange inclusions of uncertain origin. Exterior orange to grey, interior grey, break grey. Possible marks of vestigial cordon on girth of pot. Form 13.
  Fig. 23.2 Fabric 4. Exterior orange, interior and break dark grey. Possible mark of vestigial cordon on girth of pot. Form 13.
  Fig. 23.3 Fabric 4. Exterior orange to grey, interior dark grey, break grey. Form 1.
  Fig. 23.4 Fabric 2. Exterior orange, interior and break

Ch. III.A   *Later Bronze Age occupation*   29

Feature	1 Sand No.	%	2 Shell No.	%	3 Limestone No.	%	4 Shelly limestone No.	%	5 Grog No.	%	6 Shell + grog No.	%	7 Flint No.	%	Total number of sherds
1199	6	(4.5)	69	(51.5)	3	(2)	45	(33.5)	0		11	(8)	0		134
879	0		71	(80)	0		18	(20)	0		0		0		89
998	0		32	(95)	0		0		0		2	(5)	0		34
1001	0		44	(59.5)	4	(5.4)	22	(30)	1	(1)	1	(1)	2	(2.5)	74
	6	(1.8)	216	(64.7)	7	(2.1)	85	(25.7)	1	(0.9)	14	(4.3)	2	(0.6)	331

Table 8 Fabric per Feature. Fabric proportions in Later Bronze Age features (for features with over 30 sherds). Percentages in brackets.

Vessel type	Form No.	Number	Percentage
Bipartite vessels	12	2	6.9
Biconical vessels	13	4	13.8
Bucket urns	14	5	17.2
Upright rims	1	8	27.5
Straight-sided walls	8	4	13.8
Inturned rims	2	4	13.8
Incurving rims	4	1	3.5
Rounded + out-turned rims	6	1	3.5
Expanded rims	5	—	
Flared or out-turned rims	3	—	
Rounded or sharp shoulders	7	—	
Concave necks	9	—	
Tripartite bowls	10	—	
Tripartite jars	11	—	
Total		29	

Table 9 Occurrence of vessel types in Bronze Age contexts (giving absolute number and percentage as a proportion of all types

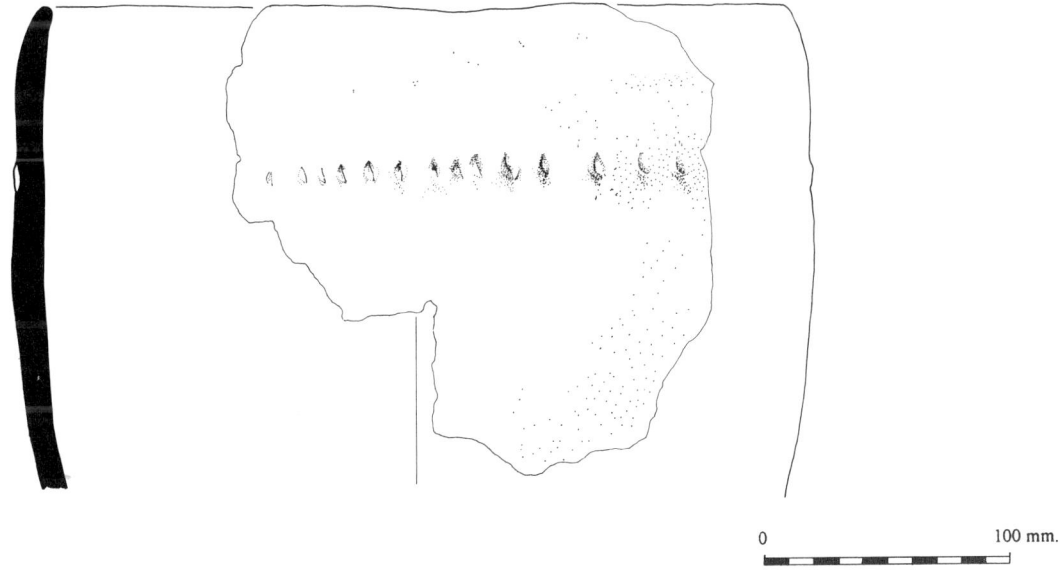

Figure 22 Later Bronze Age pottery No. 0 from context 998.

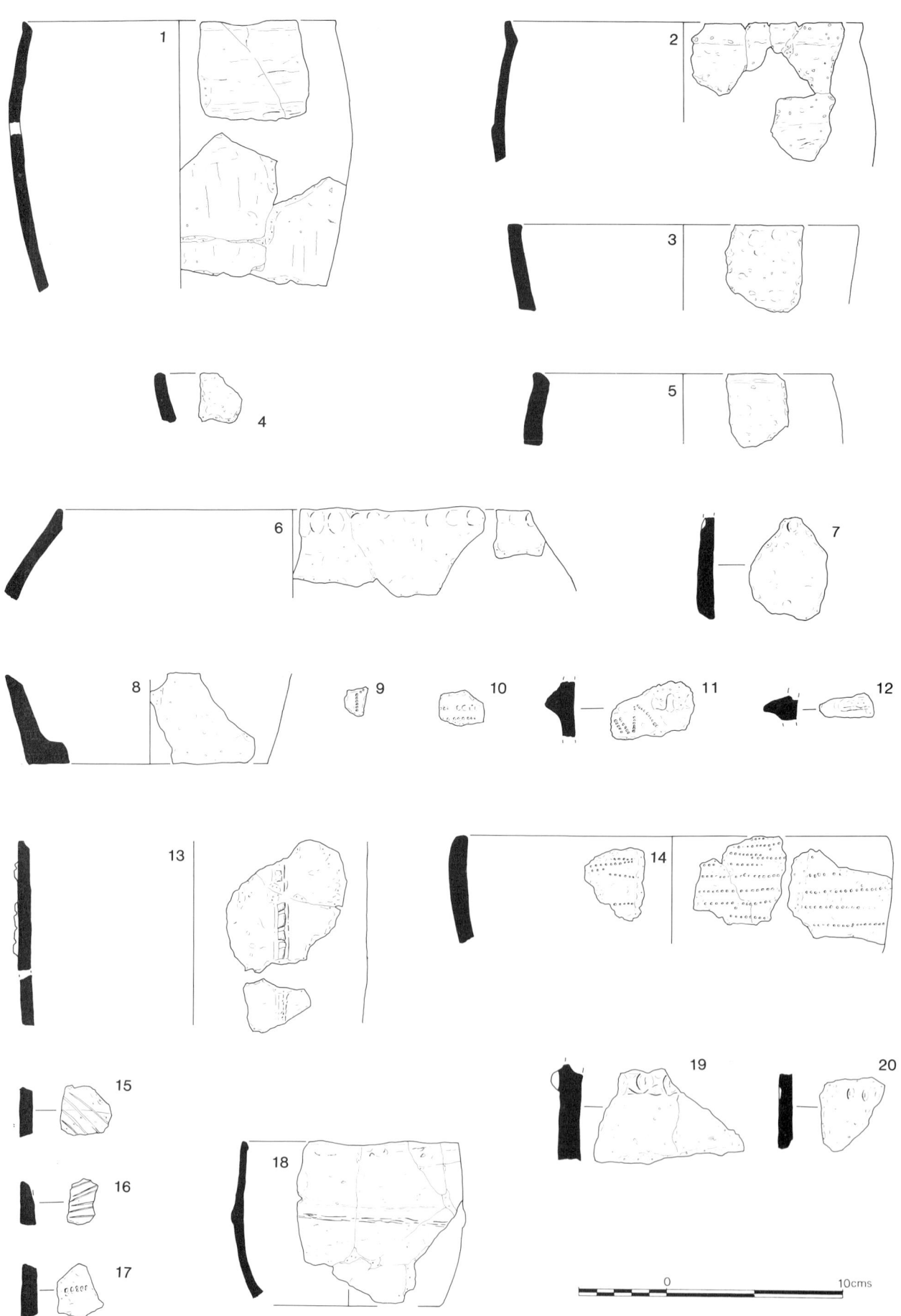

Figure 23 Later Bronze Age pottery Nos. 1–20. 1–12 from context 1199; 13–17 from 734; 18 from 1165; 19 and 20 from 1290.

grey. Angle of rim uncertain. Form ?1.

Fig. 23.5 Fabric 2. Exterior grey, interior orange to dark grey, break grey. Form 6.

Fig. 23.6 Fabric 2. Exterior and interior orange, break grey. Slight finger impressions along outside of rim. Form 12.

Fig. 23.7 Fabric 2. Exterior orange, interior and break dark grey. Possible trace of fingertip impression in outer face. Form ?8.

Fig. 23.8 Fabric 2. Exterior orange, interior very dark grey, break orange to very dark grey.

Figs. 23.9–11 Fabric 2. Exterior orange, interior and break dark grey. One sherd has a pierced lug and all three have comb tooth decoration. All three sherds may be from a Wessex biconical type urn. Form ?13.

Fig. 23.12 Fabric 2. Exterior, interior, and break orange. Applied lug.

Feature 734 Fig. 23.13 Fabric ?4. Exterior and interior orange, break dark grey. Applied vertical cordons with impressed nicks. Form ?14.

Fig. 23.14 Fabric ?5. Exterior and interior orange, break dark grey. Multiple lines of comb-tooth decoration on exterior. Form ?1.

Figs. 23.15–16 Fabric 6. Exterior, interior, and break grey. Multiple incised lines on exterior.

Fig. 23.17 Fabric ?4. Exterior orange, interior dark grey, break orange to dark grey. Line of comb-tooth decoration. Possibly from vessel 13.

Feature 1165 Fig. 23.18 Fabric 2. Exterior and interior orange to grey, break grey. Applied cordon on girth of vessel. Form 13.

Feature 1290 Fig. 23.19 Fabric 4. Exterior and interior orange, break grey. Applied horizontal cordon with fingertip impressions. Form ?8.

Fig. 23.20 Fabric 2. Exterior, interior, and break orange. Fingertip impressions. Form 8.

Feature 1001 Fig. 24.21 Fabric 2. Exterior grey, interior and break dark grey. Fingernail impressions in exterior of rim and fingertip impressions on girth. Form 14.

Fig. 24.22 Fabric 4. Exterior light grey, interior and break dark grey. Form ?1.

Fig. 24.23 Fabric 2. Exterior grey, interior and break dark grey. Form 1.

Fig. 24.24 Fabric 2. Exterior orange, interior and break dark grey. Form ?4.

Fig. 24.25 Fabric 6. Exterior and interior grey, break dark grey. Form 1.

Fig. 24.26 Fabric 7. Exterior and interior grey, break orange. Form 2.

Fig. 24.27 Fabric 2. Exterior orange to grey, interior orange, break grey. Form 12.

Fig. 24.28 Fabric 2. Exterior and interior grey, break dark grey. Form 1.

Fig. 24.29 Fabric 4. Exterior orange, interior and break grey. Applied lug.

Feature 968 Fig. 24.30 Fabric? S. Exterior orange to dark grey, interior orange, break very dark grey. Incised or impressed decoration.

Feature 1296 Fig. 24.31 Fabric 4. Exterior and interior orange, break dark grey. Fingertip impressions on girth of vessel and faint vertical striations perhaps from smoothing with finger. Form 14.

Feature 879 Fig. 24.32 Fabric 2. Exterior orange, interior grey, break dark grey. Form 1.

Fig. 24.33 Fabric 2. Exterior brown, interior grey, break dark grey. Fingernail impressions and an applied boss on girth of vessel. Height of vessel uncertain. Form 14.

III.A.2.b Discussion

It has recently been suggested that collared urns, biconical and bucket urns formed part of a 'single burial tradition' on some sites of the Bronze Age in the Upper Thames Valley (Case in Linington 1982, 87). At Roughground Farm two of these elements existed in a possible settlement context. Case has discussed the occurrence of bucket urns and biconical urns in the Upper Thames Valley (Case et al 1964). The biconical vessels discussed by Case and three of the examples from Roughground Farm are plain with only a slight trace of a cordon. By contrast a fourth decorated vessel with a pierced lug and comb-tooth decoration above is closer in type to the true Wessex biconical urn (see I Smith 1961).

No clear stratified association between bucket urns and biconical vessels occured at Roughground Farm. In pit 1199 biconical and bipartite vessels predominate and are associated with one possible sherd from a bucket urn. In contrast to this 1001, with a calibrated radiocarbon date of 1410–1170 cal. BC to one sigma (see Table 12), is dominated by bucket urns and vessels with fairly upright rims; the bipartite vessel from 1001 is not truly biconical. As a consequence the chronology of ceramic development at Roughground Farm is uncertain. Biconical urns and bucket urns may have formed distinct and successive ceramic styles. The C14 date for 1001, an assemblage dominated by bucket urns, accords well with the general cluster of dates for such assemblages (Barrett 1976, 289–307).

III.A.3 Flints from Bronze Age features

by Timothy Darvill

A collection of 72 struck flints weighing a total of 600 grams was recovered from seven of the nine features with Later Bronze Age pottery. Table 10 summarises the composition of the assemblage, and Fig. 25 illustrates a representative selection of the tools and worked pieces.

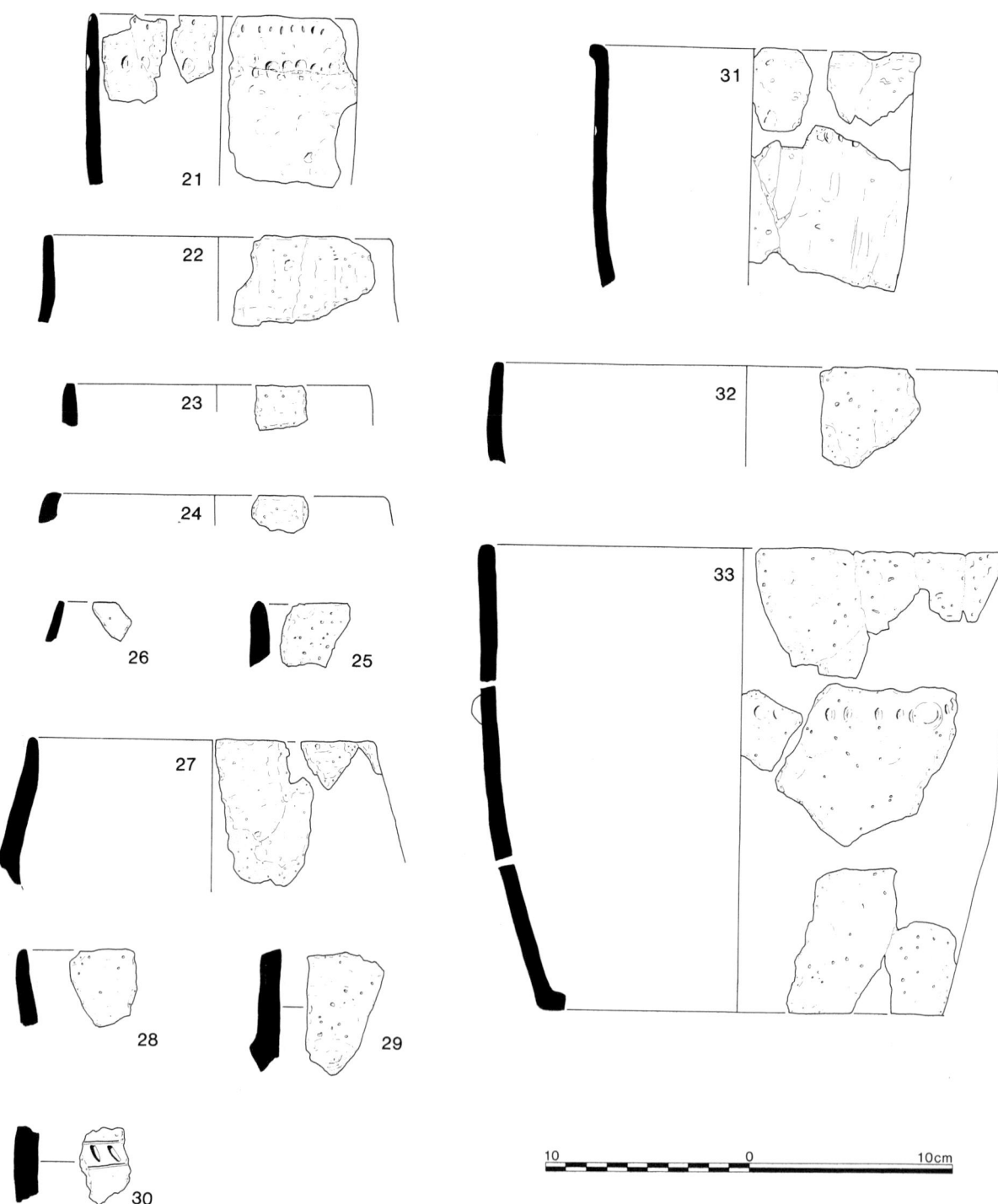

Figure 24 Later Bronze Age pottery Nos. 21–33. 21-29 from context 1001; 30 from 968; 31 from 1296; 32 and 33 from 879.

Types	Feature							Totals
	734	879	998	1001	1165	1290	1296	
Scrapers	1			1		2	1	5
Serrated flakes				2		2		4
Retouched flakes		1	1	1			2	5
Utilized flakes		1					1	2
Cores				3				3
Unutilized flakes	1	5	4*	31**	1	4	2	48
Calcined lumps				5				5
Totals	2	7	5	43	1	8	6	72

* including 2 calcined flakes
** including 1 calcined flake

Table 10 Summary of flintwork from Later Bronze Age features

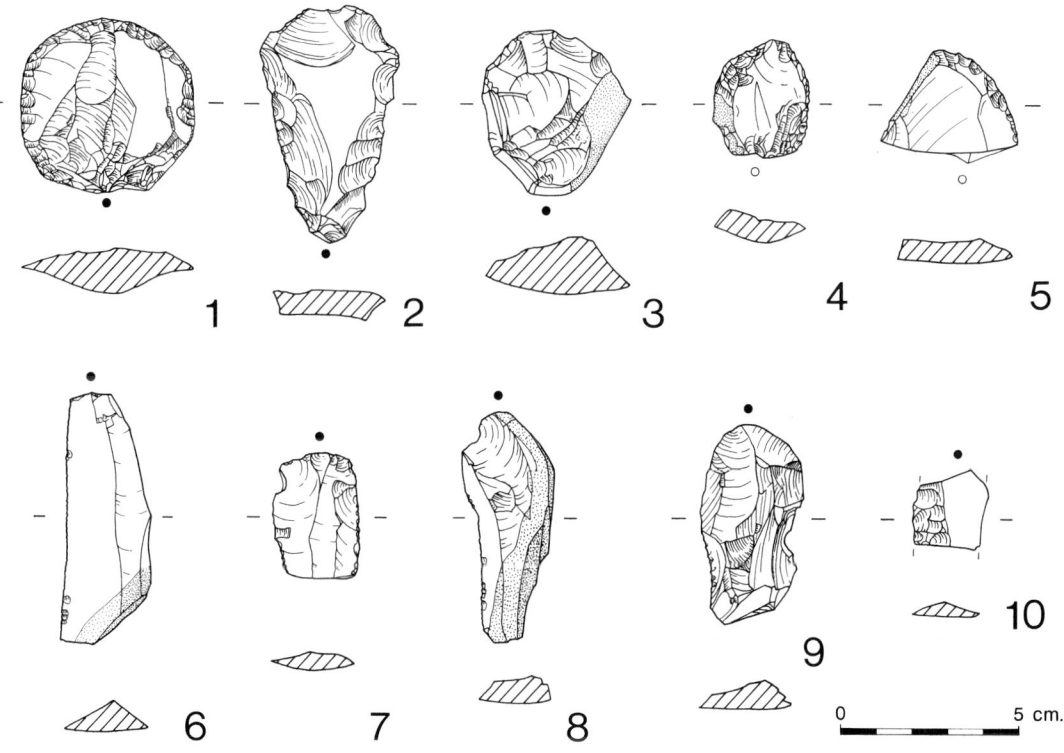

Figure 25 Flints from Later Bronze Age pits. Scrapers: 1-5; Serrated flakes: 6-9 Miscellaneous retouched flakes: 10. 1 from context 734; 2, 6 and 9 from context 1001; 3, 4, 7 and 8 from context 1290; 5 and 10 from context 1296.

With such a small assemblage it is uncertain to what extent the collection is contemporary with the pottery, rather than residual from Late Neolithic and Beaker period activity in the vicinity.

The raw material is all good quality imported flint, and is broadly similar to that used during Late Neolithic and Beaker times (see Ch. II.A.3 and Ch. II.B.4). Thin cream to light-grey coloured cortex predominates, although a few fragments display a thicker and lighter coloured cortex. Most of the flints have a light milky-white patina. No drift flint is present.

In contrast to most Neolithic/Bronze Age flint assemblages the percentage of unutilized flint flakes as a fraction of the total assemblage is rather low at about 66%; a figure of over 90% is customary (Saville 1980, 19). Several factors may account for this, among them the small size of the sample, the position of the site in an area where good flint is not available naturally and thus has to be used sparingly, and the possibility that worked pieces were preferentially collected during the excavation. The flakes represent a wide range of sizes from 18 mm in length to over 45 mm long, but no small chips or splinters from retouching and fine flaking are present. In general the flakes are squat with abundant hinge fractures and rather ragged irregular outlines. Insufficient pieces are present to allow any metrical analysis, but the general character of the cores and the flakes is similar to material from other Bronze Age sites in southern England (eg Fasham & Ross 1978).

Overall, this small assemblage is extremely difficult to evaluate. All the tool forms present could be accommodated within the typological and stylistic range represented by examples from the Late Neolithic and Beaker period features, and there are also similarities in the types of raw material represented. Given these features, together with the small size of the assemblage, it seems unlikely that flintworking was undertaken on any scale, if at all, by the Later Bronze Age inhabitants of the site.

III.A.4 Other finds

III.A.4.a Worked bone

Two bones from pit 1001 showed signs of working.

1. The point of a pin or needle, slightly curved and polished at the end, probably through wear. Length 32 mm.
2. A sheep or goat metatarsal split lengthways, much of the split edges being smoothed. There were traces of polish on the abraded exterior, and a number of short incisions or scratches down the length on one side, though these did not form any pattern. One end of the metatarsal was broken. In the Iron Age split bones such as this were often used as gouges or awls, as at Ashville (Parrington 1978, 81–82). Surviving length 94 mm, width 13 mm.

III.A.4.b Fired clay

582 grams, all in Fabric A—Mixed streaky Clays, came from four of the Bronze Age pits. (For details see Ch. 5.11.b on Fiche 2#63 and Table 53 on Fiche 2#66).

These included one possible mould fragment, part of a flat slab and daub fragments.

III.A.4.c Stone

One worn lump, probably of Sarsen sandstone, came from pit 1001. This was possibly a quern rubber.

III.A.5 Animal bones

by Gillian Jones

Under 200 animal bones were recovered from the Bronze Age pits. Table 11 lists these and gives percentages of the species.

	Cattle	Sheep	Pig	Red deer	Dog	Unidentified	
						Large	Medium
879	2	1	—	—	—	4	3
968	—	—	—	1	—	—	—
1001	7	46	—	—	—	11	107
998	2	3	—	—	—	—	1
1296	2	—	—	—	—	3	4
Total	13	50	—	1	—	18	115
Percentages of identified bones of each species							
	20	78	—	1.7	—	(32% identified)	

Large — cattle-sized fragment; medium — sheep/pig-sized fragment

Table 11 Animal bones: percentages of species from Bronze Age features

Bones from the Later Bronze Age features, all of them pits, were dominated by those of sheep or goat. The sample size is small, but comparison of the unidentified fragments gave a similar pattern, 87% being of sheep size (and few of these being at all like pig bone).

One horn core fragment was identified as sheep; no bones were positively identified as goat, and most of them are probably from sheep. Evidence of the age at death was scant. One mandible was well worn (wear stage 44E, Grant 1975), but of nine first or second molars, all probably from different individuals, only one showed sufficient wear to have come from a mature animal.

The cattle bones included two from calves (a mandible with M_1 unerupted, and a very immature femur) and only one from an adult beast. The surface of the bones was rather eroded, and no butchery marks were observed.

Deer was represented only by a single piece of large antler, presumably red deer, and no pig or horse bones were found.

Bone from these pits were collected by hand and with care, many small fragments being recovered. The sheep bones were fragmentary and the large number of sheep sized ribs and unidentified pieces were also unusually small and jagged (130 pieces, mostly 20–50 mm in length). No signs of butchering or working were observed but it seems likely that the fragmentation was intentional, perhaps indicating use of the marrow.

One of the sheep bones and 5% of the unidentified bone were burnt, whereas none of the Neolithic bone was burnt.

A bone point and a sheep metatarsal which may be worked are described above (see Ch. III.A.4.a).

Other sites of Bronze Age date have indicated a decline in the importance of the pig, with cattle and to a lesser extent sheep being more numerous (Grigson in Tinsley & Grigson 1981). The present sample is unusual in that most of the bones were from sheep. Of the sites quoted, only at the Early Bronze Age phase of Mount Pleasant were sheep more numerous than cattle. At least some reduction in woodland probably took place, since sheep require open ground, and the availability of wool points to an increased variety of clothing and coverings.

III.A.6 Mollusca and charcoal from pit 879

by Mark Robinson

The molluscan fauna from a sieved soil sample (*c* 1 kg in weight) from pit 879 suggests dry, open conditions around the pit. For details see Table 39. Wood charcoal from the pit included mature oak (*Quercus*) and alder or hazel (*Alnus/Corylus*).

III.A.7 Radiocarbon dates

Two samples for C14 dating were taken from features of possible Later Bronze Age date. The results are given in Table 12 below.

Context	Lab. No.	uncal. BP	calibrated interval ± 1 σ	calibrated interval ± 2 σ
1157	HAR-5503	2840±90	1160–940 BC	1310–820 BC
1001	HAR-5504	3040±100	1410–1170 BC	1520–1000 BC

Table 12 Radiocarbon dates obtained from bone from Bronze Age features. Calibrated using a local IML program with the data files ATM20.C14 provided by Washington University, USA (Stuiver & Reimer 1986) compiled by them from the recommended calibration data of Stuiver and Pearson (1986), Pearson and Stuiver (1986) and Pearson et al (1986).

III.A.8 Discussion

The pattern of scattered pits, occurring in several clusters but without traces of more permanent settlement, is in sharp contrast to the series of enclosures and the possible roundhouse at Corporation Farm, Abingdon (Barrett & Bradley 1980, 251 and 258). No evidence of arable agriculture of this date has been found at Roughground Farm, and the nature of the occupation evidence may reflect instead shifting settlement based upon pastoralism. Bradley (1986, 39–40) has suggested a mobile settlement pattern for the earlier Bronze Age whose domestic occupation and structures left little trace below ground. This may have persisted in parts of the Upper Thames Valley, for instance around Lechlade and Stanton Harcourt, contemporary with the establishment of organised field systems and trackways in the Abingdon-Dorchester area at Long Wittenham (Thomas 1980, 310–311), Mount Farm (Lambrick pers. comm.) and the Dorchester bypass (Chambers 1987, 64–5).

Recent work in Wessex (Bradley 1986, 42) has suggested that settlements may lie only a few hundred metres from their cemeteries, and the occupation at Roughground Farm is similarly situated in relation to the ring-ditches to its south and south-west. However, only one of these burial monuments has been excavated, that at Butler's Field (Miles & Palmer 1986, 3–4) and it is not dated.

The unaccompanied inhumation 1157, radiocarbon dated to 1160–940 cal. BC, deserves comment. Burials of this date range are more usually cremations, but there is a growing body of evidence for flat crouched inhumation burials at this period. For instance, a flat grave at Todmarton in Gloucestershire was radiocarbon dated to 1297–1001 cal. BC (Rowlands 1976, 55, 192). Two unaccompanied flat inhumations at Radley, Barrows Hills, Oxon. were radiocarbon dated to 1258–1043 cal. BC and 987–842 cal. BC respectively (A. Barclay pers. comm.). These latter burials were inserted into an earlier prehistoric monument, and flat inhumations are normally found in association with barrows or other monuments. The discovery of an apparently isolated inhumation of this date is more unusual, but burials in stratigraphic isolation are rarely subjected to radiocarbon dating, and it is likely that many more of a similar date exist amongst the those ascribed either to the Beaker period or to the Iron Age.

III.B The Early Iron Age occupation

III.B.1 Description of the features
Plans: Figs. 7, Fig. 26, Fig. 30. Sections: Fig. 27, Fig. 120 on Fiche 1#20

III.B.1.a The major land boundaries

For the overall distribution of Iron Age features see Fig. 7. The most prominent feature was 1141, a large ditch running NE–SW, whose cropmark can be traced north to Veneymore Lane and south beyond the disused railway line (see Fig. 110 and Fig. 7). Early Iron Age pottery was present throughout the fills, and 1141 was cut through by Roman ditches 959/960 and 719 (Fig. 27).

Some 300 m to the north-east another large ditch 484 ran north-east (Fig. 7; Fiche 4#3). This was cut across by Roman ditch 485 (Fig. 27), and had a deep V-profile like that of 1141, but produced no finds. It is however parallel to 1141 and both ditches kink opposite one another (Fig. 7), and it is suggested that 484 was contemporary with 1141. A probable continuation of 484, ditch 2602, was found beneath the track to Roughground Farm during the 1990 excavation (see Fig. 7 and Fig. 128 on Fiche 1#32).

A crouched burial 1215 (Figs. 26 and 32) was found in the bottom of 1141 during mechanical excavation. A calibrated radiocarbon date of 350–40 cal. BC (at one sigma) was obtained from the skeleton (see Table 16). This would suggest that the burial was most likely inserted after the ditch had partially silted up. Another crouched burial 1275 lay just south of 1141 (Figs. 26 and 32; see also below).

Both 1141 and 484 have a pronounced kink; that of 1141 lay within the excavated area. No evidence remained of any landmark the ditch might have been respecting, and alternatively there may originally have been a gap here, but this was not investigated. Alongside the kink were large pits eg 1271 and 1272 and shallower hollows eg 1311, 1312 and 1313 (Fig. 26; Fig. 27). The pits may have been for storage (see Table 76 on Fiche 3#2).

A possible four-post structure 2.25 m square (postholes 1201–1204; Fig. 26) of side 2.25 m (Fig. 28) lay just west of 1141, but the postholes may simply have been part of a scatter either side of the ditch here.

South of 1141 were three parallel slots 1150a, b and c (Fig. 26). These were undated; similar parallel marks have been found on an Early Iron Age settlement at West Heslerton, North Yorkshire (D Powlesland pers. comm.), and at Romano-British sites at Whitton and Mucking (Morris 1979, 187 Fig. 29). At the latter sites it was suggested that they represented slots for granaries on timber ground-sills.

III.B.1.b The main occupation area
Plan: Fig. 26; sections: Fig. 27

Features and occupation material were concentrated southeast of 1141 alongside a parallel ditch 1241 (Fig. 26; Fig. 120 on Fiche 1#20). Since there was no evidence of Roman occupation here, there is a potential problem in distinguishing Roman features with residual Iron Age pottery from genuinely Iron Age ones, especially ditches and postholes on alignments like those of the Roman fields, such as 1263. Most features however are considered to be Iron Age; some of the postholes were filled with dark soil and charcoal as well as Iron Age pottery, suggesting contemporary occupation, and ditch 1241 contained concentrations of Iron Age pottery remote from other Iron Age features, and was apparently cut by Iron Age pits.

No structures were found in this area. At its north end 1241 intersected with a cluster of pits. The fills of the pits and the ditch were very similar, but it was believed that the pits were later. The pits all lie east of ditch 1248-1249, which was therefore perhaps a later boundary contemporary with the pits, with an entrance between 1248 and 1249.

Parallel to 1248-9 was a line of postholes, Nos. 1251 and 1253–7 (Table 77 on Fiche 3#10). The postholes were in line with the end of Roman ditch 959/960, and both lined up with the southern part of 1241, perhaps suggesting continuity of a boundary here. East of 1241 were other phases of boundary; 1263 contained Early Iron Age pottery, but its cropmark can be traced running southeast parallel to Roman ditch 710 for several hundred metres (see Fig. 110), so was most likely also in use in the Roman period. Around these boundaries were scattered pits and postholes. Bone ostensibly from Iron Age pit 1280 gave a calibrated radiocarbon date of cal. AD 160–380 (at one sigma; see Table 16); the records suggest that this pit was cut into by a later feature, not noticed during excavation, from which the bone must have derived.

III.B.1.c Pit scatters
Plans: Fig. 78; Fiche 4#52–3, 66–8, 80, 81. sections: Fig. 27; Fig. 120 on Fiche 1#20

North-west of 1141 occupation was much more scattered. The only boundaries probably of this date were two alignments of rectangular pits, 921–935 and 1143–1147, both aligned approximately north-south (Figs. 7 and Fig. 78). Both alignments had postholes alongside; those next to 923 etc had different fill from the pits, and were probably not contemporary.

Close to and parallel to Roman ditch 959/960 were short gullies 984 and 1018 (Fiche 4#67). 984 contained Iron Age pottery; gully 1018 (possibly a continuation of 984) was undated. Between the two Iron Age pit alignments was a scatter of pits, clustered in small groups. Several pits in each group contained a little Iron Age pottery, others flints.

Ch. III.B   The Early Iron Age occupation   37

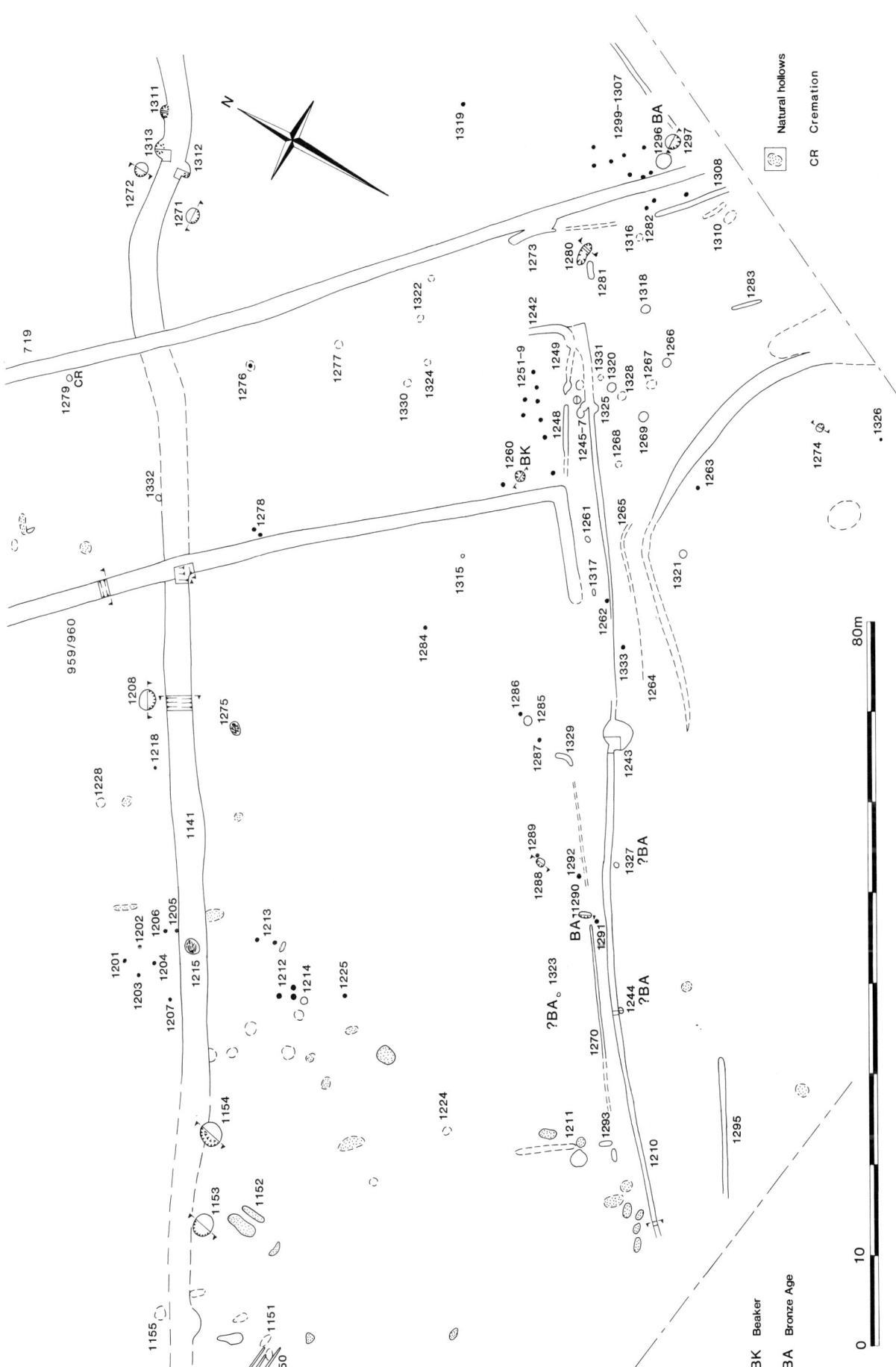

Figure 26 Plan of Early Iron Age settlement at the east of the site

BK   Beaker
BA   Bronze Age

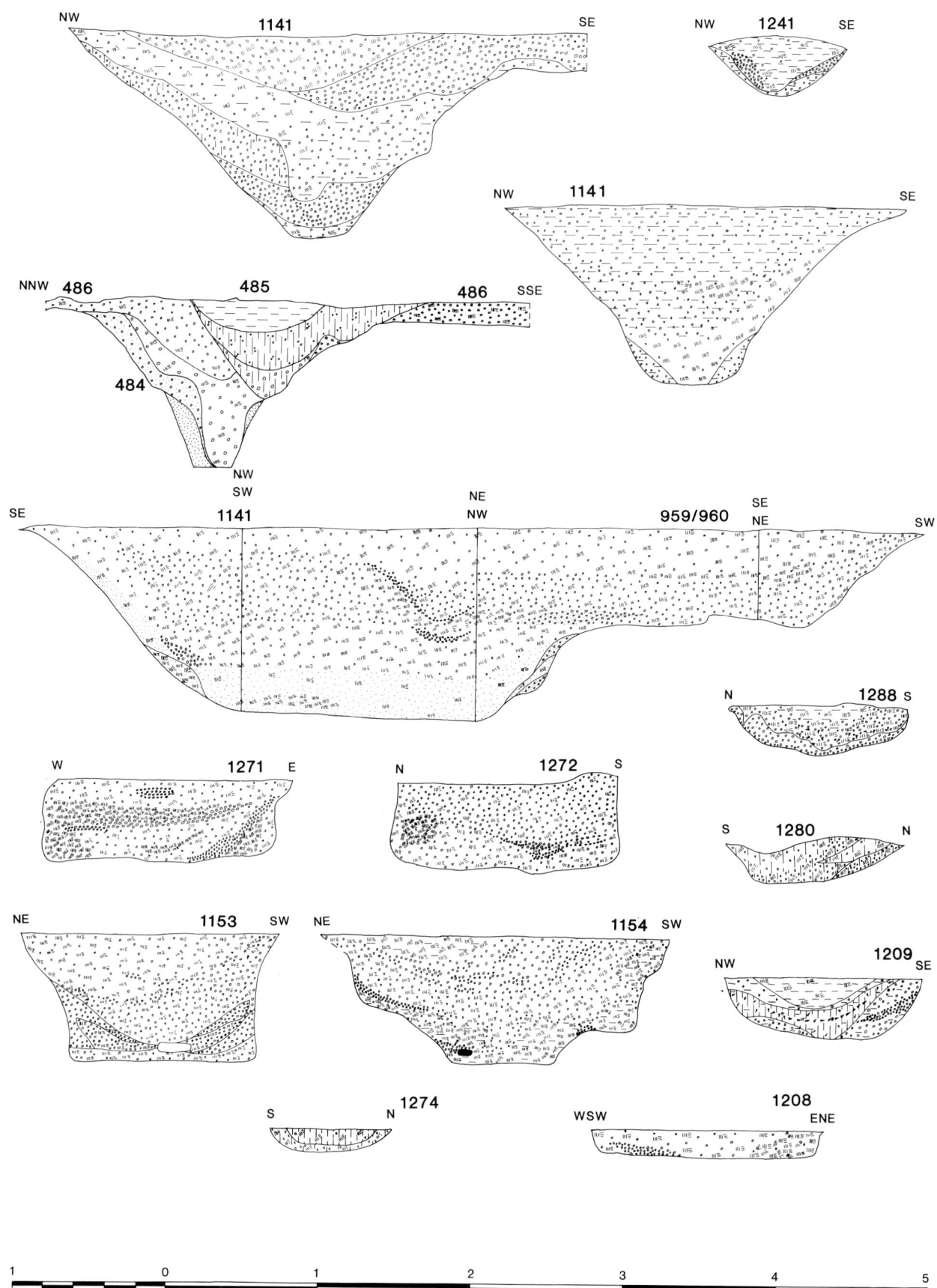

Figure 27 Early Iron Age settlement: sections

Figure 28 Early Iron Age four-post structure 1201–1204 taken from the south-east

Figure 29 Iron Age roundhouse taken from the north-east (photographed by W T Jones)

III.B.1.d The roundhouse

Plan: Fig. 30, Fiche 4#42, Fig. 29

Post-circle 1100 was found *c* 100 m north-east adjacent to a small square-ditched burial enclosure 1137. The post-circle has already been published as an Iron Age roundhouse (Harding 1972, 24–5 and Fig. 3). There were 22 postholes on the circumference, mostly grouped in twos or threes, possibly indicating that the structure had been rebuilt once or twice. The entrance to roundhouses in the Upper Thames is usually on the east or south-east, and the pair of postholes 1101 and 1132 outside on the east here may have been for a porch.

III.B.1.e Other features

Some 75 m north-east of 1100 was a crouched burial 1157 (Fiche 4#19; Fig. 32), with gully 1156 running north-east adjacent and apparently aligned upon 1157 (Fiche 4#5 and Fig. 26). The burial was radiocarbon-dated to 1160–940 cal. BC (to one sigma; Table 16). The gully contained only undiagnostic flints (see Ch. 2.E on Fiche 1#17). These features could belong either to the Later Bronze Age or to the Early Iron Age occupation. The burial is described in Ch. III.B.4.

West and north of the pit alignment 922 etc and of the roundhouse there were very few Iron Age features, though close to 484 a scatter of pits may have been prehistoric (see Ch. IV.F.5). No Early Iron Age features were found further south-east below the Roman enclosures nor any in the area of the southern Roman enclosure group (see Ch. IV.F.1 and Ch. IV.F.6).

Beneath the villa and to the north and west of it the only certainly Iron Age features were pits 447 and 448 (Fiche 4#47) and a small enclosure 397 etc (Fiche 4#16–17). See Table 76 on Fiche 3#2 for details. Iron Age pottery was also recovered from features of the Early Roman occupation area, most of it residual; pit 12 however may genuinely have been Iron Age. A few indeterminate or Middle-Late Iron Age forms occurred, for instance Fig. 31 Nos. 48 and 65, which may be Iron Age survivals in use together with Romano-British pottery in the mid-first century AD (see also Ch. V.2.c.3).

III.B.2 Early Iron Age pottery

by Richard Hingley

Fig. 31

III.B.2.a Summary

One hundred and four features produced Early Iron Age pottery. This pottery constitutes what is sometimes called a 'Decorated Ware assemblage' (Barrett 1980, 305). Features were scattered across the site, but the main concentration occurred at the south-east edge of the site (Fig. 26). The Early Iron Age assemblages are quantified in Table 35 on Fiche 1#21.

III.B.2.b Fabrics

The pottery was classified according to fabric, form and decoration or surface treatment. Of the seven fabrics identified in the Bronze Age pottery (see Ch. III.A.2) five were still present in the Early Iron Age. Fabric proportions were compared between assemblages with more than 30 sherds (following De Roche in Parrington 1978, 47). The results are shown in Table 13.

The calcareous fabrics (2–4) make up 57.6% of the whole assemblage or 58% including Fabric 6. This corresponds closely the 60.2% from the Early Iron Age features with more than 30 sherds, showing that these features are representative of the whole assemblage. This proportion matches closely the predominance of calcareous fabrics in the Early Iron Age at Ashville (Period 1: 67%) (De Roche in Parrington 1978, 70) and this has been seen as the general trend for the Upper Thames Valley (Lambrick & Robinson 1979, 38).

There is a change in the proportions of the different fabrics from the Later Bronze Age, where calcareous fabrics made up 95% of the assemblage. In the Early Iron Age calcareous Fabrics 2–4 still predominate, but their proportion has dropped considerably. In addition shell, which was the major inclusion in 60% of the Later Bronze Age sherds, represents only just over 20% of the Early Iron Age assemblage. The other calcareous groups, shelly limestone and oolitic limestone, remain at roughly the same proportion, but there is a sharp increase in sandy fabrics in the later period; at 39% sand is the largest single fabric group.

III.B.2.c Forms

Eleven forms were identified: the incidence of these is shown in Table 14.

A representative sample of the Early Iron Age forms is illustrated (Fig. 31). A classification of illustrated sherds according to form category is given below:

Form 1 Upright Rims 39, 41.
Form 2 Inturned Rims ?55, 56.
Form 3 Flared or Out-turned rims 36, 47, 50, 52.
Form 5 Expanded rims 54, 65.
Form 6 Rounded and Out-turned rims 48, ?58.
Form 7 Rounded or sharp shoulders of vessels 38, 42, ?43, 44, 57, ?63.
Form 8 Straight-sided upright vessels 35.
Form 10 Tripartite Bowls 37, ?45, 49, 51, 61.
Form 11 Tripartite Jars 34.

Ch. III.B   The Early Iron Age occupation   41

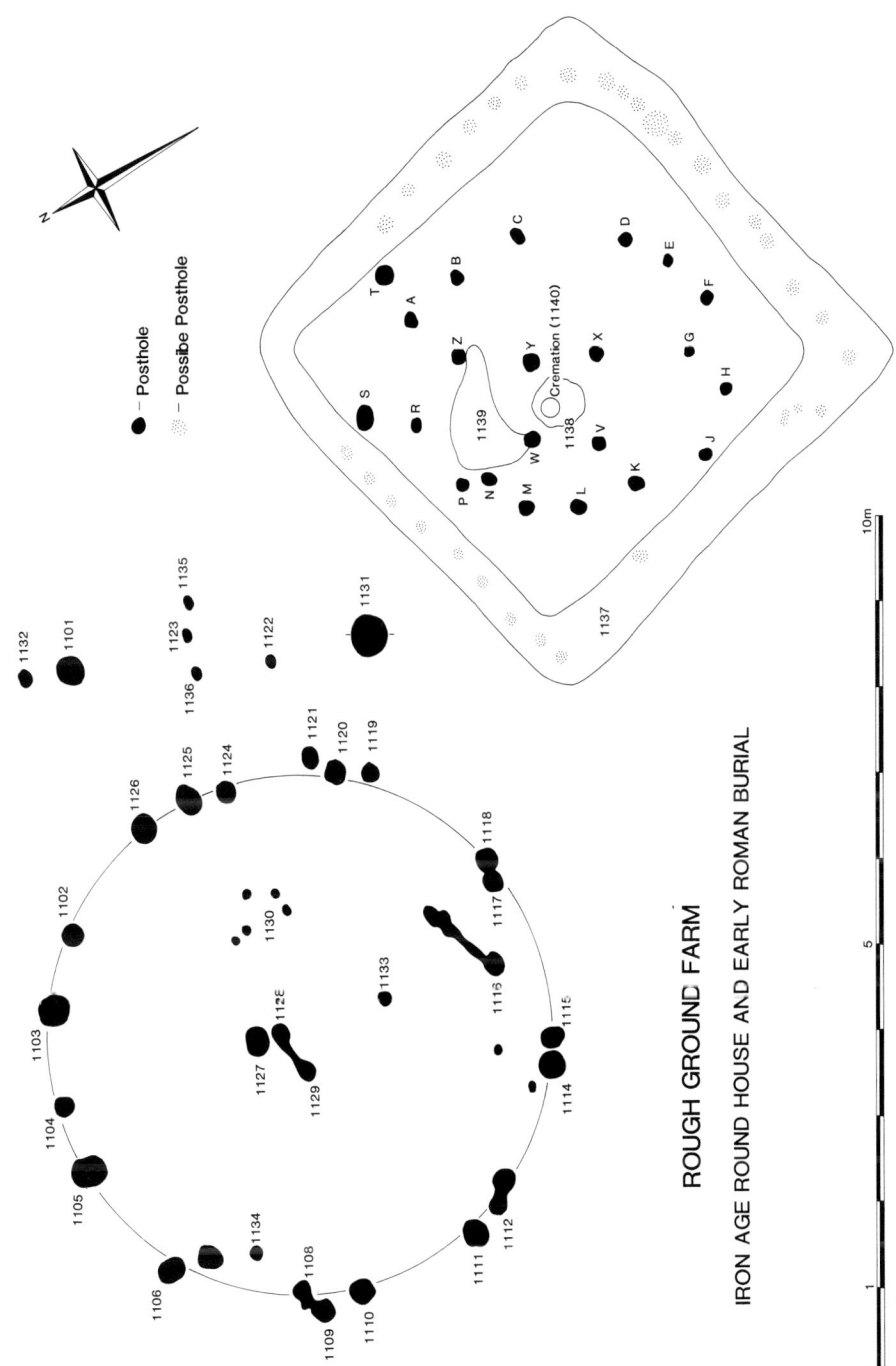

Figure 30 Iron Age roundhouse and Early Roman burial

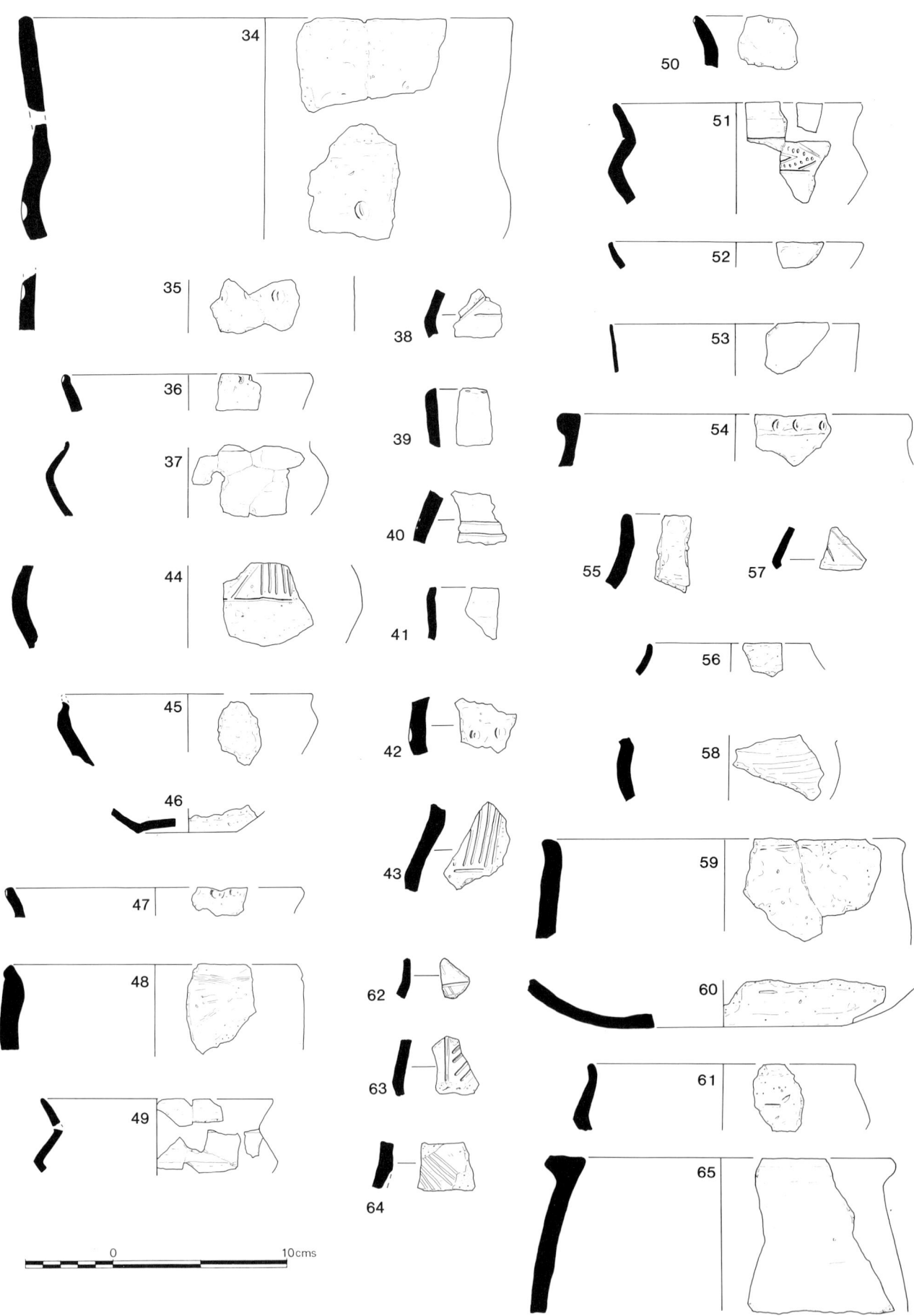

Figure 31 Early Iron Age pottery. 34–42 from context 1242; 43 and 44 from 1273; 45–47 from 1325; 48 from 332; 49 from 1137; 50 and 51 from 1274; 52 from 1280; 53 from 1241; 54–56 from 1141; 57 from 1103; 58 from 550; 59 from 413/7; 60 from 448; 61 from 1308; 62 from 481; 63 from 498; 64 and 65 unstratified.

The two most distinctive forms are tripartite jars (Type 11) and tripartite bowls (Type 10). The assemblage from feature 1242 is fairly characteristic, although it contains a couple of sherds which may have come from a bucket urn (No 35) and are probably residual. 1242 also contained a tripartite jar (No 34) and part of an angular tripartite bowl (No 37), and other sherds (Nos 37, 38, 40) are probably from tripartite bowls and have burnished outer surfaces and incised linear decoration.

Among other forms of particular note is a vessel with an expanded rim (No 65); this has parallels on other Early Iron Age sites in the Upper Thames Valley (Harding 1972, Plates 44, 45).

Some individual sherds could be of Middle Iron Age date (eg Nos 48, 55, 56), but no distinctive Middle Iron Age forms (eg globular bowls and saucepan pots; Harding 1972; De Roche in Parrington 1978) were found.

	1 Sand		2 Shell		3 Limestone		4 Shelly limestone		5 Grog		6 Shell + grog		7 Flint		Total number of sherds
Feature	No	%	No	%	No	%	No	%	No	%	No	%	No	%	
27	23	(47)	6	(12)	2	(4)	18	(37)	0		0		0		49
1141	27	(47)	15	(26)	0		13	(23)	0		2	(3.5)	0		57
1241	22	(38.5)	12	(21)	0		23	(40)	0		0		0		57
1242	31	(32)	19	(20)	8	(8)	38	(39.5)	0		0		0		96
1273	62	(38)	30	(19)	18	(11)	50	(33)	0		0		0		160
1274	12	(34)	6	(17)	0		17	(48)	0		0		0		35
1280	29	(41)	24	(34)	0		18	(25)	0		0		0		71
1325	15	(39.5)	8	(21)	2	(5)	13	(34)	0		0		0		38
Total	221	(39.3)	120	(21.3)	30	(5.3)	190	(33.6)	0	(0)	2	(0.3)	0	(0)	563
Fabric proportions of all Early Iron Age sherds															
	341	(37.4)	212	(23.3)	63	(7.0)	249	(27.3)	16	(1.7)	4	(0.4)	23	(2.5)	908

Table 13 Early Iron Age pottery: fabric proportions by context groups (for features with over 30 sherds) and for all Early Iron Age sherds. (Percentages in brackets)

	Upright Rims	Straight-Sided Walls	Inturned Rims	Incurving Rims	Rounded + Out-turned	Expanded Rims
Form No.	1	8	2	4	6	5
Number	6	2	3	1	4	2
	8%	2.7%	4%	1.3%	5%	2.7%
	Flared or Out-turned Rims	Rounded or Sharp Shoulders	Concave Necks	Tripartite Bowls	Tripartite Jars	
Form No.	3	7	9	10	11	Total
Number	12	18	6	17	5	76
	17%	25%	8%	23.5%	6.7%	

Table 14 Summary of Occurrence of Vessel Types (giving absolute number and percentage as a proportion of all types)

III.B.2.d   Catalogue of illustrated sherds

Feature 1242   Fig. 31.34 Fabric 4. Exterior and interior orange, break grey. Fingertip impressions on girth of vessel. Form 11.

Fig. 31.35 Fabric 4. Exterior dark grey, interior and break orange. Fingertip impressions. Form 8.

Fig. 31.36 Fabric 4. Exterior, interior and break orange. Fingernail impressions on rim. Form 3.

Fig. 31.37 Fabric 1. Exterior grey and burnished, interior orange, break grey. Form 10.

Fig. 31.38 Fabric 1. Exterior orange, interior and break grey. Incised lines on exterior. Form 7.

Fig. 31.39 Fabric 1. Exterior, interior, and break grey. Fingernail impressions on top of rim. Angle of rim uncertain? Form 1.

Fig. 31.40 Fabric 1. Exterior and interior grey, break dark grey. Incised lines on exterior.

Fig. 31.41 Fabric 2. Exterior and interior grey, break orange. Form 1.

Fig. 31.42 Fabric 2. Exterior orange, interior and break grey. Fingertip impressions on exterior. Form 7.

Feature 1273   Fig. 31.43 Fabric 4. Exterior orange, interior and break grey. Incised lines on exterior. Form ?7.

Fig. 31.44 Fabric 4. Exterior and interior orange, break grey. Incised lines on exterior. Form 7.

Feature 1325   Fig. 31.45 Fabric 4. Exterior orange,

interior and break dark grey. Form ?10.

Fig. 31.46 Fabric 1. Exterior and interior orange, break grey.

Fig. 31.47 Fabric 4. Exterior, interior and break orange. Fingertip impressions on exterior of rim. Form 3.

Feature 332   Fig. 31.48 Fabric ?5. Exterior and interior orange, break dark grey. Smear marks on exterior. Form 6.

Feature 1137   Fig. 31.49 Fabric ?7. Exterior and interior orange, break light grey. Form 10.

Feature 1274   Fig. 31.50 Fabric 4. Exterior, interior and break orange. Form 3.

Fig. 31.51 Fabric 1. Exterior and interior dark grey and burnished, interior grey. Incised lines and impressed dots on exterior. Form 10.

Feature 1280   Fig. 31.52 Fabric 1. Exterior, interior, and break grey. Form 3.

Feature 1241   Fig. 31.53 Fabric 1. Exterior and interior orange and burnished, break grey. Form 1 or 3.

Feature 1141   Fig. 31.54 Fabric 4. Exterior and interior orange, break grey. Expanded rim with fingertip impressions in exterior. Form 5.

Fig. 31.55 Fabric 7. Exterior grey, interior and break dark grey. Form ?2.

Fig. 31.56 Fabric 1. Exterior grey, interior orange, break grey. Form 2.

Feature 1103   Fig. 31.57 Fabric 1. Exterior and interior grey, break light grey. Incised lines on exterior. Form 7.

Feature 550   Fig. 31.58 Fabric 1. Exterior orange and burnished, interior and break orange.

Feature 413/7   Fig. 31.59 Fabric 4. Exterior grey, interior orange, break grey. Form 6.

Feature 448   Fig. 31.60 Fabric 7. Exterior, interior, and break grey.

Feature 1308   Fig. 31.61 Fabric 4. Exterior dark grey to grey, interior and break dark grey. Form 10.

Feature 481   Fig. 31.62 Fabric ?1. Exterior, interior, and break grey. Incised lines on exterior. Form ?10.

Feature 498   Fig. 31.63 Fabric 1. Exterior dark grey, interior and break light grey. Incised lines on exterior. Form ?7.

U/S (1240)   Fig. 31.64 Fabric 4. Exterior dark grey and burnished, interior grey, break orange. Incised lines on exterior with white paste infill.

U/S (70)   Fig. 31.65 Fabric 1. Exterior, interior, and break dark grey. Expanded rim. Form 5.

III.B.2.e   Decoration

Of the 916 sherds 43 (4.7%) were decorated either with fingertip or nail impressions (23) or with incised lines (20) (see also Table 36 on Fiche 1#23).

III.B.2.f   Discussion

The Early Iron Age pottery at Roughground Farm represents a 'decorated ware' assemblage (see Barrett 1980). Sites with decorated ware assemblages are common on the Upper Thames gravels (Harding 1972; De Roche 1978; Lambrick 1984,).

Another Early Iron Age assemblage was recovered from only 1 kilometre away at The Loders, Lechlade (Darvill *et al* 1986). This shared the tripartite jar and bowl form (Forms 10 and 11) at Roughground Farm; calcareous and sandy fabrics were equally represented at *c* 48% each. It is suggested that the high representation of sandy fabrics at The Loders resulted from the high proportion of fineware angular vessels, which are almost always made in sandy fabrics. The representation of sandy fabrics at Roughground Farm, however, and in a small assemblage from Hambridge Lane nearby (J Moore in prep), suggests that in general sites in this area conform to the trends evident further down the valley (Lambrick 1984).

In spite of the differences between the Later Bronze Age and Early Iron Age assemblages there is also considerable overlap in form, decoration and fabric. Gingell has recently argued a late date for the occurrence of Deverel Rimbury ceramics at Burderop Down, 20 km south of Lechlade (Gingell 1980, 218), while on Cranborne Chase it is evident that Deverel Rimbury ceramics were replaced directly by a decorated ware assemblage (Barrett *et al* 1981, 232–4). A similar succession, with bucket urns giving way to a decorated ware assemblage could be indicated by the Roughground Farm material. If this is so the sequence at Lechlade differed from that in the Thames Valley downstream of Abingdon, where Deverel Rimbury ceramics appear to have been replaced by 'plain ware ceramics' and then in turn plain ware by decorated ware assemblages (Barrett 1980; Bradley *et al* 1980).

III.B.3   Other finds

III.B.3.a   Stone

Thin-sections by Timothy Darvill

Fig. 122 on Fiche 1#26

One fragment of Sarsen quernstone came from pit 1257, a thin flat slab tapering to a point at one end, the other broken off. Both flat faces and one side were worn smooth. The point appears to have been battered, suggesting that this stone was used as a hammer. 102 mm × 88 mm × 23 mm.

Two fragments of sandstone also come from pit 934 in the rectangular pit alignment.

III.B.3.b   Fired clay

Only 33 grams were recovered from the early Iron Age features, of fabrics A—Mixed streaky Clays, F—Quartz and C—Organic. (For details see Ch. 5.11 on Fiche 2#62). These included one possible mould fragment and one highly fired piece that may have come from a crucible, though there were no metal residues upon it.

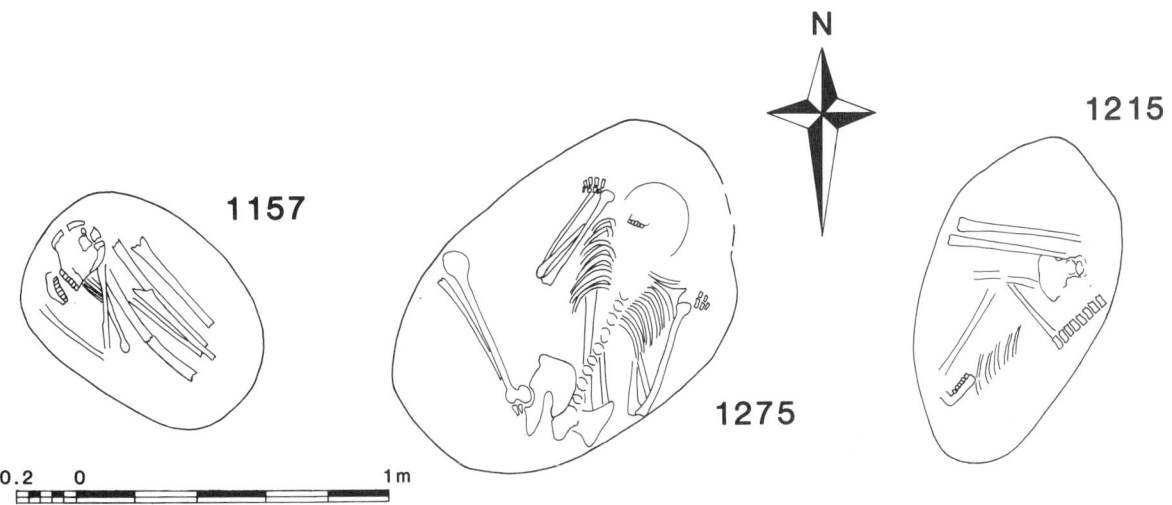

Figure 32 Later prehistoric burials: 1157 Bronze Age; 1275 & 1215 Iron Age

III.B.4 Contracted or crouched burials

Fig. 32

Three such burials were excavated at Roughground Farm. For details of the skeletal analysis see Table 64 and Table 65. 1157 (Fiche 4#19) was an isolated oval pit containing a contracted burial lying on its left side. The head lay to the south-east and was bent forwards with the arms and legs tightly folded up so that its knees rested against its forehead. The body was that of an adult male aged 30–35 years, and there were no grave goods. Bone from this burial has been radiocarbon dated to 1160–940 cal. BC (to one sigma).

1215 was a crouched burial at the bottom of the Early Iron Age ditch 1141 in an oval pit cut 0.15 m below the bottom of the ditch. Their relationship was not established as the ditch was emptied by machine along this length, but the pit is unlikely to have cut prior to the ditch 1.2 m into the gravel. The head was at the south and was bent forwards. The arms were bent up to the head, and the legs drawn up almost touching the elbows. The body was that of a young adult aged 18–23 years. There were no grave goods, but bone from the skeleton was radiocarbon dated to 350–40 cal. BC (to one sigma).

1275 was another crouched burial in an oval pit south-east of 1141. The body was prone with the head to the north-east turned to the left side. The arms were raised against the shoulders with the elbows at the sides, and the legs were bent up, the right one underneath the body, the left knee out to the left side. The body was that of an adult male aged 30–35 years. There was no dating evidence for this burial, but it was probably associated with the adjacent Early Iron Age settlement.

Crouched burials are quite numerous from Iron Age sites, though few are known from the Upper Thames Valley. Moderate contraction, in other words in a grave about 1 m in length, is more common than extreme contraction (Wilson 1981), and at Roughground Farm burials 1215 and 1275 are of this order of size. With moderately contracted burials the hands and feet are often tied, but at this site neither burial was; unusually 1275 was prone rather than lying on one side. 1157 had a smaller grave-pit, but did not even occupy all of this, and the body was probably tightly bound, as is common in more extreme cases of contraction (Wilson 1981).

Burials within settlements become more common as the Iron Age progresses, Early Iron Age adults tending to occur in perimeter ditches or outside settlement boundaries (Wilson 1981). The three burials at Roughground Farm fit this suggested pattern, 1157 being isolated (and clearly Late Bronze Age), the other two lying in or close to a boundary ditch at some distance from the main focus of Iron Age settlement.

III.B.5 Animal bones

by Gillian Jones

Only c 170 animal bones were recovered, and the density of bones was low, 24 features producing only 42 identifiable pieces. The percentages of species identified are given in Table 15.

Number	Cattle	Sheep	Pig	Horse	Deer	Others
42	31%	52%	12%	*	*	—

* indicates a species represented by a single bone

Table 15 Animal Bones: Percentages of species in Early Iron Age contexts

Despite its small size, this sample contrasts with the earlier groups in suggesting that by the early Iron Age, sheep and cattle were the two major species, with pig also of some importance. One sheep bone and 12% of the sheep-sized unidentified fragments were burnt. The one deer fragment had been worked and may be a gaming piece. The presence of horse (one bone) is of note, horse being absent from the earlier samples.

Context	Lab. No.	uncal. BP	calibrated interval ±1 σ	calibrated interval ±2 σ
1215	HAR-5502	2130±120	350–40BC	400BC–120AD
1280	HAR-5505	1760±100	160–380AD	20–530AD

Table 16 Radiocarbon dates obtained from bone from Iron Age features. Calibrated using a local IML program with the data files ATM20.C14 provided by Washington University, USA (Stuiver & Reimer 1986) compiled by them from the recommended calibration data of Stuiver and Pearson (1986), Pearson and Stuiver (1986) and Pearson et al (1986).

III.B.6 Charcoal from Iron Age features

by Mark Robinson

Hand-picked samples of charcoal from 5 Iron Age features included both *Quercus* (oak) and cf. *Crataegus* (Hawthorn). For details see Table 40.

III.B.7 Radiocarbon dates

Two radiocarbon dates were determined by the Harwell Radiocarbon laboratory on samples of bone from the crouched burial 1215 and from pit 1280.

A radiocarbon date calibrated to cal. AD 160–380 (at one sigma) was obtained from bone in pit 1280. This pit contained a large assemblage of Early Iron Age pottery, which is unlikely to be residual, and the date must therefore be regarded with suspicion. The records suggest that possibly there was a later feature cutting into the Early Iron Age pit, from which the dated bone may have come.

A date of 350–40 cal. BC (to one sigma) was obtained from a crouched burial 1215 within ditch 1141. Sherds from the ditch are of Early Iron Age date and the burial therefore appears to be a later Middle Iron Age insertion.

III.B.8 Discussion

III.B.8.a The major land boundaries

Ditches 1141 and 484 are interpreted as contemporary linear boundaries dividing up the gravel terrace at right angles to the river Leach. 1141 is visible as a cropmark both north and south of the excavated area (Fig. 110), and a probable continuation of 484 was excavated some 600 m to the south in Butler's Field, Lechlade (Miles & Palmer 1986, 4). At right angles to this continuation were smaller contemporary ditches, and this subdivision was also evident at Roughground Farm (Fig. 26) in ditch 1241 and cropmarks further north.

It is tentatively suggested that kinks in both 1141 and 484, which occurred roughly opposite one another, may originally have been gaps c 30 m wide for a trackway parallel to the river Leach and on the line of the later Romano-British droveway. Short lengths of Early Iron Age ditch lay alongside the Romano-British ditches of the droveway (see Ch. III.B.1.c above), and ditch 1241 also turned a corner into 1242 in line with this (Fig. 26). This trackway was apparently temporarily blocked and the gaps in 1141 and 484 dug through. Alternatively there may have been landmarks where the kinks occurred which were respected by the Early Iron Age boundaries, and which survived to be used again by the Romano-British boundary. However no trace was found of any such features, and the obvious importance of a route alongside the winding course of the river Leach makes it likely that there would have been gaps left for this in digging the major Early Iron Age ditches.

Evidence of land-division as early as this is uncommon on the Upper Thames gravels. Double-ditched trackways or boundaries probably of the Bronze Age have been found at Dorchester crossing the cursus (Atkinson *et al* 1951; Chambers 1987, 64–65) and at Mount Farm (Lambrick 1979, 113–4), and a Bronze Age field system has been proposed from cropmark evidence at Long Wittenham (Thomas 1980, 310–311). Ditched field boundaries of Middle and Late Iron Age date have been excavated at Gravelly Guy and Blackditch, Stanton Harcourt (Lambrick 1985, 108; Lambrick 1983, 144–5), and at Gravelly Guy the settlement layout suggests that the boundaries, though not the ditches, were present in the Early Iron Age. The gravels north of Lechlade however provide the only evidence so far for the large-scale division of the valley bottom at this date.

On higher ground the parcelling-out of the landscape in the Early Iron Age is attested at Rollright on the Cotswolds (Lambrick 1988, 80–82), and probably in the Later Bronze Age at Grimsbury near Banbury (Allen 1989, 41–2).

III.B.8.b Pits and pit-alignments

The main settlement consisted of a cluster of storage pits alongside ditches 1241 and 1247. Clusters of storage pits are often the only element of Early Iron Age settlement found on the Upper Thames gravels, and at sites such as Farmoor (Lambrick & Robinson 1979, 19 and 37–8) may genuinely reflect agricultural activity separate from permanent settlement, cultivation of the narrow gravel terrace by settlements on higher ground. At Roughground Farm however the concentrations of pottery in both the ditches and the pits suggests that there were houses close by.

A number of pits also occurred alongside 1141 and possibly 484 (Figs. 26 and Fig. 27). These were not closely spaced like the pit alignments alongside the ditch at Butler's Field (Miles 1986, 4), but may have been storage pits; it has been suggested on the evidence of linear alignments of pit groups at Stanton Harcourt (Case 1982c, 107ff) that pits were sometimes dug alongside the edge of arable fields at some distance from settlements, and excavation at Gravelly Guy there (Lambrick 1986, 112–113) has recovered small groups of such pits. Pit 1313 was, however, respected by ditch 1141, showing that, as at Butler's Field (Boyle *et al* forthcoming), the large linear ditches were secondary developments.

Two short alignments of linear pits (Fig. 78) may also have been contemporary, as similar pit alignments of this date were found alongside the linear boundary at Butler's Field (Miles & Palmer 1986, 4). Neither alignment at Roughground Farm, however, contained more than scraps of Iron Age pottery, and the longer one was adjacent to Roman (or later) posthole-lines (Ch. IV.F.9). Similar alignments are known from Middle Iron Age and Roman contexts at Mingies Ditch, Hardwick, Oxon (Allen & Robinson forthcoming) and Watkins Farm, Northmoor, Oxon (Allen 1990, 27–30) respectively, and those at Roughground Farm may also be later.

III.B.8.c Structures

No buildings were identified in the main settlement area, with the exception of a possible four-post structure adjacent to 1141. Scatters of postholes may represent the position of former buildings but the only recognisable patterns appear to be fence-lines. The absence of recognisable structures is likely to be the result of truncation by medieval agriculture. Few houses of this period have been found in the region (see Allen *et al* 1984, 89-100), and identification is made more difficult by the apparent absence of drainage ditches around them at this date; the largest early group of houses, recently excavated at Gravelly Guy, Stanton Harcourt, Oxon, are all without surrounding gullies (Lambrick 1985, 111 Fig. 27).

One post-circle, feature 1100 etc, was found in apparent isolation midway between the large boundary ditches (Fig. 30). The lack of associated features or occupation material makes interpretation as a house less secure. 1100 etc was found immediately adjacent to an Early Roman ditched cremation burial, and the Iron Age dating evidence consisted only of a few small abraded sherds from two postholes. Other possibilities are that it was either not Iron Age, or that the post-circle revetted a mound, hence the survival of its position into the Roman period and the positioning of the cremation burial adjacent.

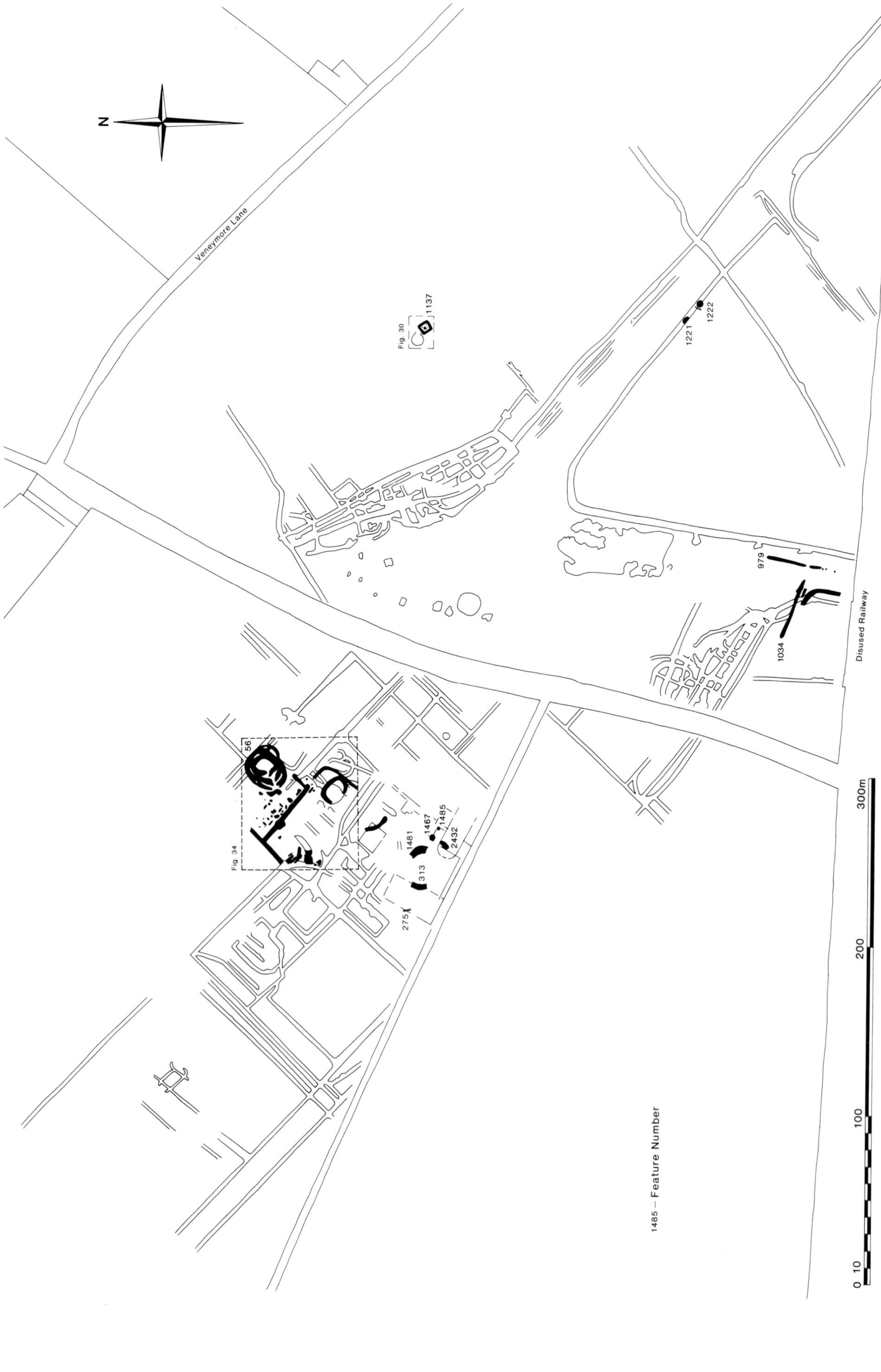

Figure 33 Early Roman settlement plan: overall distribution of features

Chapter IV

The Roman occupation

IV.A Introduction

IV.A.1 Excavation and post-excavation methodology

The manner of excavation and the techniques of site-recording employed largely dictate the level at which analysis is possible and influence the conclusions drawn from it. A brief resume of the site-recording adopted in each area, and of the consequent post-excavation strategy, is therefore given below.

The basis of the recording was the finds notebook, a day-by-day listing of the principal finds bagged from each excavated trench, box, cutting or individual feature. Due to the use of untrained labourers for most of the excavation work, who could not distinguish between features, there was however no unique context numbering system, and description of the provenance of the finds varied considerably.

In the Early Roman area (see Fig. 34) and the western enclosures (see Fig. 59, Fig. 131 on Fiche 1#35) features were numbered individually and separate cuttings distinguished by letter. Within features layers were sometimes distinguished, or the depth given below surface.

In the 1957–59 villa excavations finds were attributed to trench or box on the grid, and were given a depth below surface, usually accompanied by a brief description of the soil, *eg* Trench S, brown soil below black, 2'6" down. The position within the trench was sometimes indicated, *eg* W side. One or more plans of each trench was drawn, usually either at the level of undisturbed gravel or, within a building, at floor level, and at least one section of each trench was usually drawn. It was thus often possible to attribute finds to a particular context. Some trenches, particularly in the villa courtyard, were not however drawn, and others were only sketched.

Only very limited areas were opened up due to the shortage of resources (see Fig. 37 and Fig. 42, Building III); no overall phasing linking the various deposits between separate trenches was undertaken on site, and no levels were taken. Where the sections on opposite sides of a trench differed, the relationship between them was often not stated. Understanding of the complex stratigraphy was thus limited.

Both sets of enclosures east of the villa were stripped to gravel prior to excavation (Fig. 1; 138 on Fiche 1#44; 142 on Fiche 1#48) and the excavation strategy was aimed at obtaining an overall plan and on excavating the intersections between features to clarify the chronology. The site was gridded in 10' squares on an alpha-numeric grid, and the excavated intersections were labelled by grid square, not according to the features involved, which were not distinguished. Finds were not separated between the intersecting features; the intersections were excavated and the most significant finds recorded and planned in spits. Sections of the relationships were drawn after excavation.

Using the sections and the plans of the spits it was possible to number features individually and separate some of the finds between them, and this was carried out in order to date the broad sequence of development. Many of the enclosure ditches were frequently recut, but in most cases no attempt was made to distinguish the individual recuts.

Ernest Greenfield, who excavated the SE half of the northern enclosure group, adopted a different strategy. Having recorded an overall plan he excavated only the discrete features, which he numbered individually, but drew very few sections. The sequence of enclosures in this part of the site is thus not as clear.

The areas east of these enclosure groups were stripped and salvaged. Features were given grid references and were distinguished individually. Only very limited excavation was possible with the resources available.

In ordering the site information for publication a choice had to be made between full description, often involving lengthy discussion of the doubtful validity of particular pieces of evidence, or more summary description, based around whichever interpretative framework best fitted the available data. The second approach has been adopted here; the description of the Roman stratigraphy is thus only a summary of the evidence, and for reasons both of brevity and clarity much of it is presented through an interpretative rather than a purely descriptive framework. This is drawn from a fuller description of the stratigraphy, which can be found in the Archive.

Where stratigraphic evidence is lacking, the dating of the sequence of Roman occupation is based upon the finds. Where coins occur they are mentioned in the description, but these were few (see Ch. V.3), and dating relies largely upon the pottery. Because of the problems of attributing pottery described above, and because some of the pottery was discarded (see Ch. I.4), the pottery is not presented in phased sequence or by context groups (see Ch. V.2),

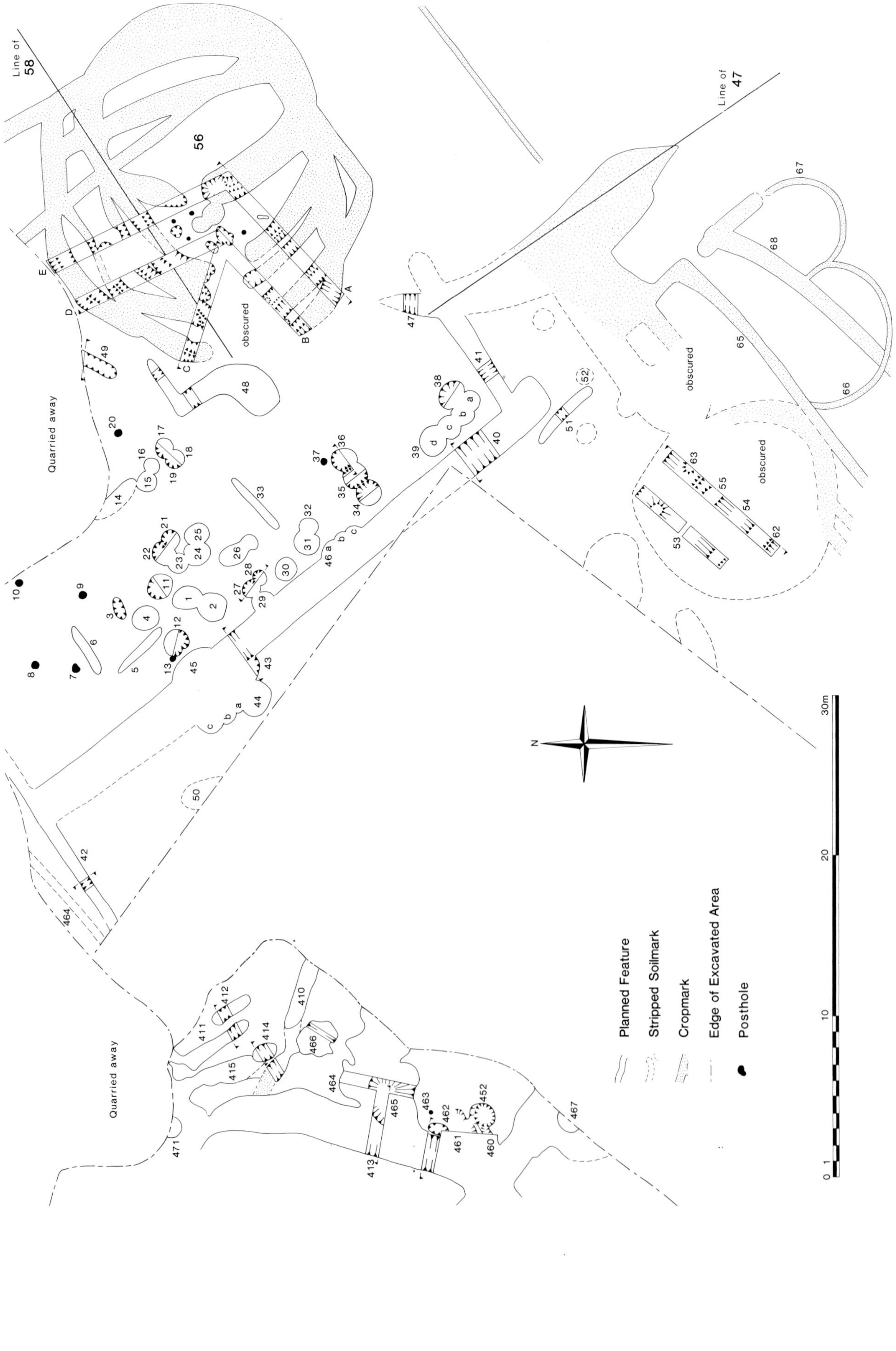

Figure 34 Early Roman occupation: plan of House-enclosure 56, pits and ditches

and only brief information as to the pottery from crucial contexts is given in the site description. A full breakdown of the pottery from individual contexts will however be found in Table 79 on Fiche 3#16.

IV.B The Early Roman occupation

Plans: Figs. 33, 34. Sections: Figs. 122 on Fiche 1#26, 123 on Fiche 1#28, 124 on Fiche 1#29, and 125 on Fiche 1#29

IV.B.1 Introduction

The overall distribution of Early Roman features is shown on Fig. 33. A large area photographed after topsoil stripping shortly before excavation began (Fig. 3) shows the circular or oval enclosures, pits and ditches characteristic of Iron Age or early Roman settlement. Part of this area was excavated (Fig. 34); the rest was extracted before excavation began. North of enclosure 56 virtually nothing is known, although local reports hint that occupation was thinning out, and that only the linear ditches of a later Roman field system were present. Another cluster of pits and gullies was found further west (Fig. 34 features 410 etc), and these represent the limits of early occupation in this direction. Further south early Roman pits and ditches also occurred below the Roman villa buildings (Figs. 129 on Fiche 1#33, 127 on Fiche 1#31, and 130 on Fiche 1#34), and continued south beyond the excavation area. The eastern limits of this occupation lay in the extracted area west of the Lechlade-Burford road; no early settlement was encountered in the excavations east of this (Fig. 33).

The middle of this settlement was extracted without record (Fig. 1 and Ch. I), and only small trenches were dug into features below the villa, so these do not form a coherent whole. Characterisation of the settlement is therefore based upon only a small sample.

IV.B.2 A ditched compound containing House-enclosure 56, pits and pen

An oval enclosure, 56, whose ditches were recut many times, was occupied from the mid-1st to the mid-2nd century AD. The ditches contained domestic refuse and the enclosure probably surrounded a house; a short arc of postholes on the inner lip of one ditch circuit may have been part of this. The size of the enclosure varied from 9 m to over 20 m from front to back, but it was not possible to establish the sequence of the ditches. One or two of the ditches could have held a wall or fence slot (Fig. 123 on Fiche 1#28). Outside the entrance was a group of pits contemporary with it, mostly filled with dark occupation soil including charcoal and domestic refuse (Fig. 124 on Fiche 1#29). The pits could have been used for storage, and one or two may have been lined with stones. One or two pits contained only Iron Age pottery, and may have been prehistoric.

Most of the pits were contained within a rectangular enclosure formed by ditches 40, 41 and 42. Ditch 40 cut some of the pits, but contained no finds later than the mid-2nd century, and was probably contemporary with 56 and the later pits. Ditch 41 was in line with the south-east side of 56, which was thus probably incorporated within the rectangular enclosure. A dump of raw clay was found in 40, and smaller lumps of the same in the pits; this may have been intended for constructing ovens, of which numerous fragments were found in this area. What was probably the stoking end of an oven, feature 49, was found on the quarry edge just north of 56. Alongside ditch 40 a group of short shallow slots, 5, 6, 33 and 48, defined a rectangular pen adjacent to 56.

This area formed a coherent domestic compound with house, pits, a pen and ovens. It went out of use by the mid-2nd century AD, and was cut across by the ditches of a regular enclosure system 58 and 47 (Fig. 34).

IV.B.3 'Well' 54 and adjacent features

South of this compound was a large deep pit 54, which may have been a contemporary unlined well (Fig. 124 on Fiche 1#29). Around 54 were a series of gullies, some cut by it, others possibly surrounding it. These appear to have formed a small enclosure, possibly sitting inside the corner of another compound bounded by ditch 40 and its return, ditch 65 (Fig. 34). Just south-east of this corner was another circular enclosure 66, 6 or 7 m across, with an annex 67 on the east, but this was not investigated.

IV.B.4 Pits, postholes and gullies to the west

West of this area shallow gullies, postholes and deep pits were found. These included 465 and 471, two pits much deeper and larger than the majority of those close to 56 (Fig. 125 on Fiche 1#29). Another pit had a primary charcoal fill overlaid by a layer of stones, possibly indicating firing to sterilise the pit after storage and then laying a secondary floor of stones. However, this group of pits and gullies did not have the dark fill of features adjacent to 56, and may have belonged to a more peripheral area of settlement. 465 had fragments of several rotary querns and complete gate-pivot stones in its backfill, implying a major reorganisation when it was backfilled in the early to mid-2nd century.

Yet further west well 470 was excavated to the level of the water table 2.4 m down. (Fiche 4#62; Fig. 128 on Fiche 1#32; Fig. 133 on Fiche 1#37). The well was silting up by the end of the 2nd century, so may have been dug during the pre-villa phase of occupation.

IV.B.5 Features below the villa buildings and courtyard

South of this early features were seen only beneath later buildings and in narrow trenches. The terminals of another 1st and 2nd century enclosure ditch lay below Building I south of 54 (Fig. 127 on Fiche 1#31). Other deep curving ditches south-west of these (Fig. 43, 48, 130 on Fiche 1#34) may have belonged to one sub-rectangular enclosure up to 22 m across; these had many recuts with gravelly fills and few finds, and dated to the 1st century AD. Similar enclosures of the same date excavated at Claydon Pike and Thornhill Farm, Fairford, nearby (Miles and Palmer in prep.) have been interpreted as stock enclosures.

West and east of this enclosure were further pits, postholes and gullies, most of which had clean gravelly fills with few finds. One deep pit 320 (Fig. 53) had a black charcoal-impregnated fill and much early 2nd century pottery, but this dark fill generally only appeared in later features in this area. Further north-west however a couple of hearths or ovens 365 and 372 (Fig. 58) lay on the edge of the unexcavated area within what may have been the corner of another larger enclosure. These features went out of use soon after the mid-2nd century AD.

IV.B.6 Features east of the main settlement
Fig. 33

There were a few features adjacent to or beneath the linear boundary ditch 959/960 (Fig. 126 on Fiche 1#30). Two lengths of gully and a few pits or postholes ran parallel to it (Fig. 74 Stage 1; Fiche 4#74 and 88) and both at its north-west corner and down its eastern arm pits were cut through by the ditch (Fiche 4#66–7 and 98). These features contained early-mid 2nd century pottery, and their coincidence with the ditched boundary probably implies that the boundary, if not the ditch, was in existence when they were dug.

Figure 35 Early Roman square-ditched cremation burial 1137, from the east (photographed by W T Jones)

IV.B.7 Early Roman cremation within square ditched enclosure

Plans: Fig. 30, Fig. 33, Fig. 69, Fiche 4#42

A square enclosure 1137 *c* 6 m across was found some 250 m east of the Early Roman settlement, with the cremation of an adult (1140) buried in an upright grey-ware jar in a pit at its centre (Fig. 30; Fig. 35). The ditch was continuous, shallow and flat-bottomed; a slightly deeper channel at the north-east corner may indicate a recut. There were slight circular depressions along the bottom on the south, north and the southern part of the east side. It is not stated whether these were visible in the fill, but were probably sealed by it; they were very faint, and may simply have been undulations in the gravel.

Within the square was an oval of postholes whose long axis was aligned between the south-west and north-east corners of the square, and which surrounded the burial pit 1138 and one other feature 1139. Outside the oval on either side of the north-east corner were two slightly larger postholes on the inner edge of the ditch. Inside the oval was a line of four postholes along its long axis, with between two and four more parallel to them on the north-west side. The burial pit 1138 lay slightly north-west of the long axis within the central four postholes, 1139 at right angles to it and overlying the two most north-easterly postholes. 1138 had a dark soil fill with charcoal and burnt clay in it, 1139 brown loam. Dark soil spread out from the top of both features, surrounding posthole X and apparently Z adjacent to the end of 1139.

Probably these soil spreads lay within shallow features around the pits, but just possibly they may indicate that the interior of the enclosure was cleared down to gravel when the features were first dug. The dark soil could then represent burning of the posthole structure around the burial. It is not certain that the dark soil was fill of 1139, which may have been an earlier feature cut by the postholes.

For details of the cremation see Ch. V.16. The cremation urn is of early 2nd century date, and pottery of similar date came from the surrounding ditch. This appears to be an isolated burial, not part of a cemetery. The burial belongs to a tradition originating in the Marnian region of France (see for instance Brisson & Hatt 1955 and Stead 1979) and present in Eastern Britain in the 1st centuries BC and AD (see also Discussion, Ch. VI.1).

IV.C The villa buildings and courtyard

IV.C.1 Introduction

Parts of four stone buildings were excavated (see Fig. 36). For none of these however was a complete plan recovered. Most of the buildings were very thoroughly robbed.

IV.C.2 Building I

Plans: Fig. 37, 127 on Fiche 1#31; Sections: Fig. 38

Parts of three rooms at the east end of Building I were stripped (see Fig. 36). Room 1 was L-shaped and only 2.1 m wide, running the whole length of the east side and continuing along the S, Room 2 was c 2.4 m wide and Room 3 some 3.0 m wide. Room 1 was possibly a corridor. Foundations of pitched stones survived in places, and although floors had been ploughed out there were make-up layers of pitched stones with a layer of mortar in between in Room 1 (Fig. 38 layers 87–85), and loose grey and white tesserae overlying them from a tessellated floor. Rooms 3 and 2 also had traces of mortar make-up or flooring (Fig. 38 layers 76 and 75). Painted plaster, plaster pilaster fragments and a quarter-round moulding came from the debris, as well as *opus signinum* flooring (see Ch. V.12 and Ch. V.13). The roof was probably of tiles, though stone slates were also recorded.

One wall of this building was traced westwards (Fig. 37 features 112, 116 and 115). Building I was thus 11.1 m wide and at least 14.4 m long, but this may not have been its full extent. A dark rectangle shows up on the cropmark photographs just west of this, which may indicate a hypocausted room (Fig. 3; Fig. 1); flue tiles found amongst the debris may have derived from here.

Alongside the south wall and the wall between Rooms 1 and 3 were postholes (Fig. 37), one of them (96) sealed by the make-up in Room 1; there were no associated floors to suggest an earlier phase of building, and they were probably scaffolding-holes. Two larger postholes outside the south wall (102 and 103) may have been separate, perhaps for a porch.

Building I overlay ditches and gullies dating up to the mid-2nd century (Fig. 127 on Fiche 1#31), and since the upper parts of these ditches were backfilled the building was probably constructed soon after this. East of Building I was a deep ditch 132 whose lower fills contained high-quality pottery and glassware of the mid 2nd century (see Microfiche Pottery Catalogue, Fig. 101, Samian report Ch. V.2 and Glass Ch. V.7). This probably came from the villa, and the ditch was probably an enclosure ditch around Building I. (Fig. 41; Fig. 59).

IV.C.3 Building II

Plans: Fig. 37; Section: Fig. 41

Building II lay east of Building I, and consisted of several rooms alongside a boundary wall traced for 22 m (Fig. 36). Most of the trenches were only taken down to the destruction levels and the robber trenches then excavated. The excavated plan thus probably reflects only the latest phase of this building. Room 1 appears to have been long and thin, c 6 m by 2 m, Rooms 2 and 3 wider but of unknown length. A short length of wall 153 survived, faced with small roughly-squared blocks infilled with smaller rubble; in other trenches pitched foundations survived. Mortar flooring or make-up covered Rooms 1 and 3, and *opus signinum* flooring, painted wall-plaster and tesserae were found in the debris (see Ch. V.12 and Ch. V.13). The last two were concentrated in Room 3. The roof was

54 *Roughground Farm, Lechlade, Gloucestershire: a prehistoric and Roman landscape*

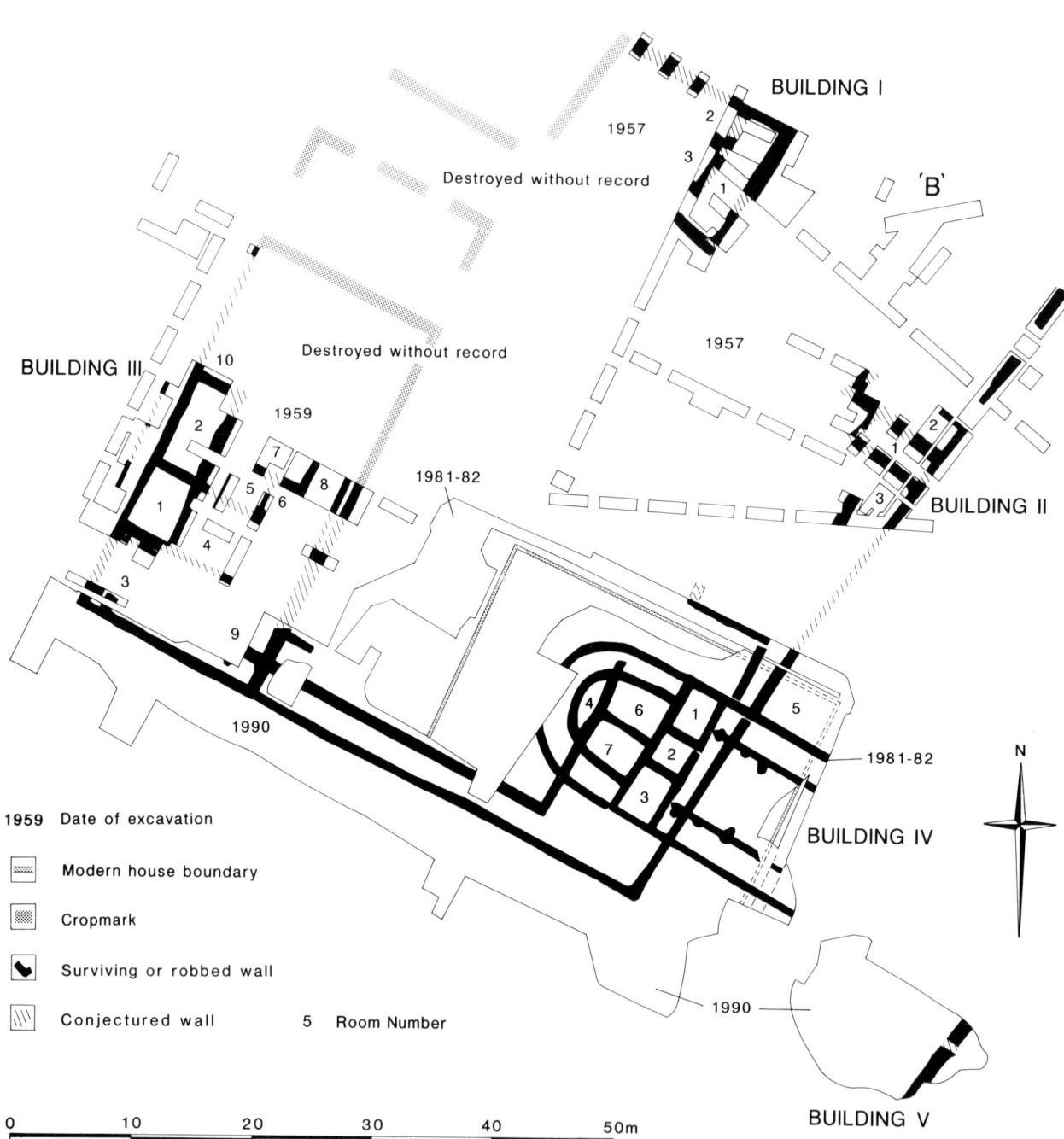

Figure 36 Plan of layout of trenches and villa buildings

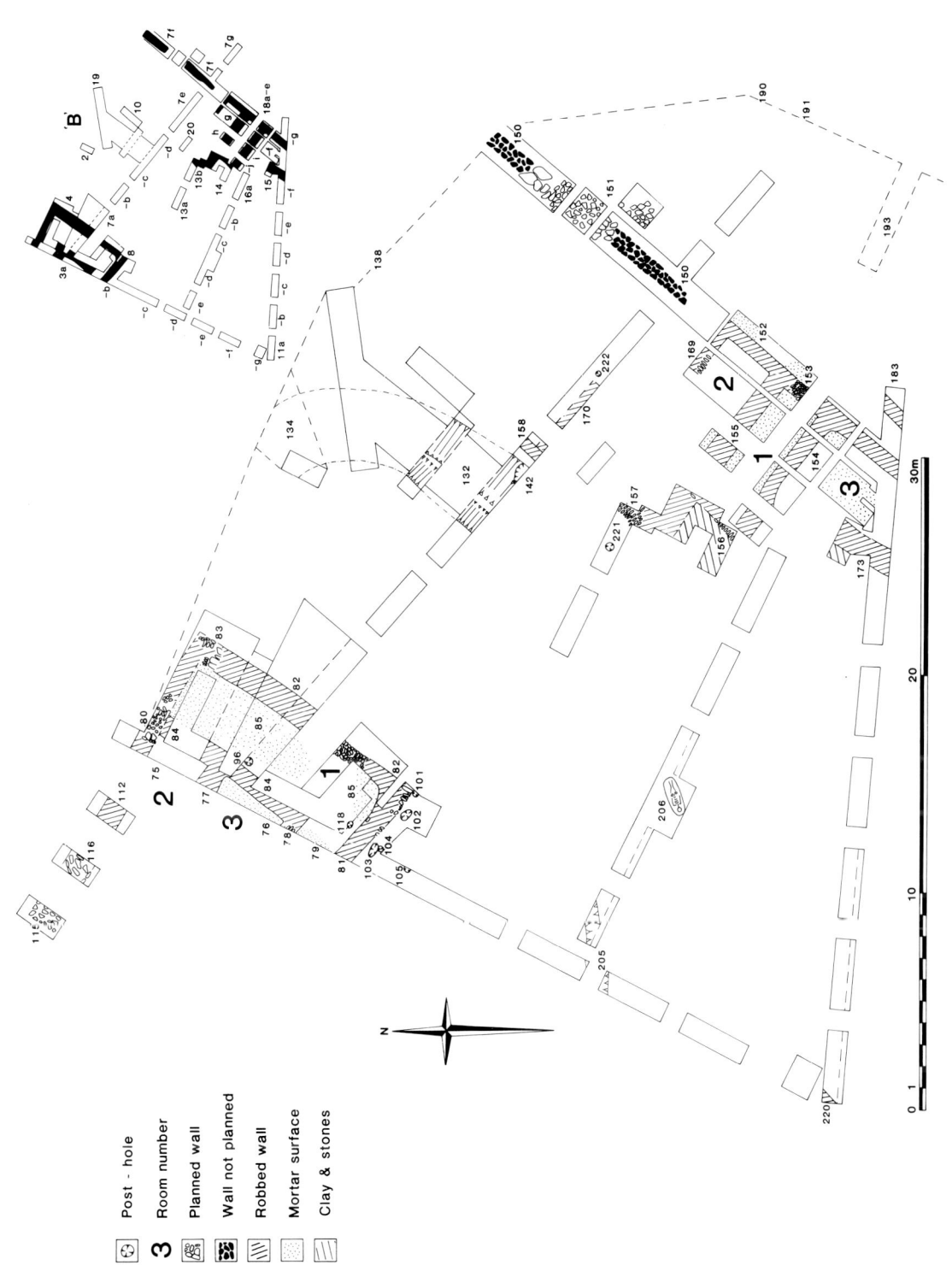

Figure 37 Plan of Buildings I and II

56 *Roughground Farm, Lechlade, Gloucestershire: a prehistoric and Roman landscape*

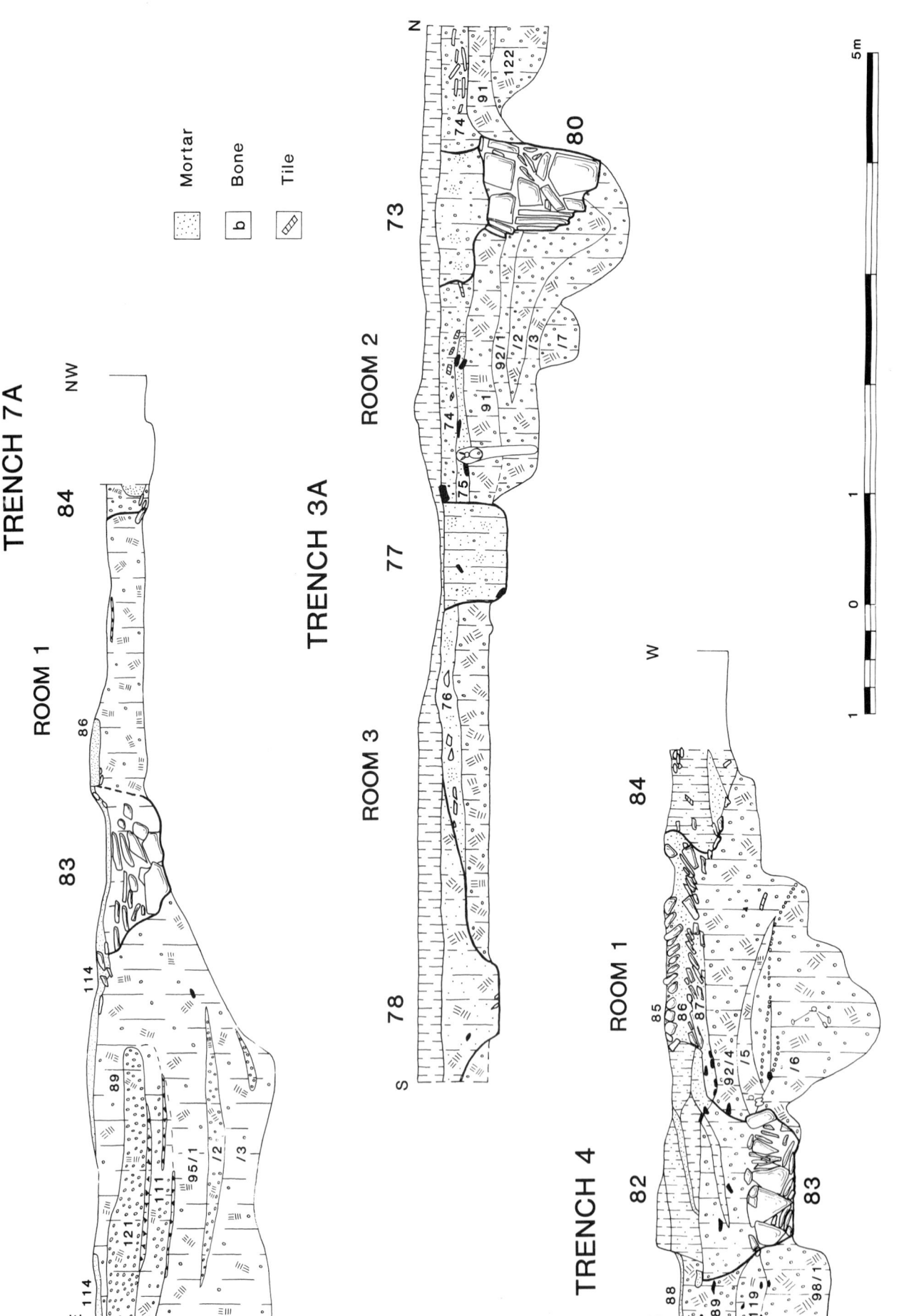

Figure 38 Building I: sections

Figure 40 Building II: Wall 153 and trenches from the east

Figure 39 Building I: Trench 7a from the south-east, showing the floor make-up layers 85–87 overlying posthole 98 and pit 94, with wall 83 in the foreground

probably of tile. East of Building II there may have been a corridor or an earlier wall, as a possible robber trench (183) was recorded 2 m east of the boundary wall (Fig. 37).

No pre-building features were found in the limited excavation to date the construction of this building. The plan as recovered probably dates to the 4th century AD, as 2496, the southern continuation of boundary wall 153, cut through Building IV and abutted Building III (Fig. 49 and below). The pre-villa subsoil alongside the robber trenches contained mid-2nd century pottery, and mixed with the 4th century sherds in the debris were many later 2nd century ones. It is possible that the building was first constructed in the late 2nd century.

To the north there was possibly an entrance between the building and the boundary wall 150, which continued north into the quarry face. Halfway along this was another entrance paved with flat stones 151, which led into a stone-floored yard between it and the ditch. The northern limits of Building II are uncertain; possible robber trenches 158 and 170 were seen along the east side of the ditch parallel to the boundary wall and at right-angles to it in Trench 7e (Fig. 37). These may have bounded the yard on the west and south sides.

IV.C.4 Building 'B'

Fig. 37

In the 4th century the upper part of 132, the large ditch just west of this yard was filled with charcoal and black soil, probably from a hypocaust (Fig. 41). Pilae tiles found on the very north edge of the area, some apparently *in situ*, together with painted plaster and *opus signinum* flooring, suggest that another Roman building lay just outside the excavated area. This is labelled B (Fig. 37). Demolition material from the yard's west wall, layer 131, overlay this charcoal.

IV.C.5 Quarry hollows 190–193 east of the villa buildings

Plan: Fig. 37; Section: Fig. 41

East of the boundary wall several very large hollows were salvaged. These are similar in character to the extensive area of gravel quarries further east (see Ch. IV.F.8), and were probably dug for the same purpose. One was backfilled with dirty sand and stones, another had a primary fill of charcoal containing much smithing slag: both were probably connected with metalworking (see microfiche report Ch. 5.15 on Fiche 2#82). They appear to range in date from the later 2nd century to the late 3rd or early 4th century.

IV.C.6 Building IV

Plans: Figs. 42, 43, 47 and 49; Sections: Fig. 44, 46 and 48

Building IV was discovered in 1981 when a narrow archaeological trench was dug around the perimeter of a modern house south of Buildings I and II (see Figs. 36, 46, and 48). When the house was demolished and the site redeveloped for housing in 1990, area excavation became possible, resulting in a fairly full plan of the west part of this building. Due to the omission of any archaeological condition in the planning consent however the excavation was carried out in salvage conditions, and it was not possible to link the 1981–2 trenches fully to the new area, nor to integrate the development of Buildings III and IV. In addition, there was not time to investigate the pre-building deposits thoroughly.

IV.C.6.a Pre-building deposits

Throughout the area of Building IV Pleistocene gravel was overlaid by an orange-brown silty clay subsoil, 2488. One early Iron Age pit 2019 underlying Building III appeared to have been truncated at the surface of the gravel and was overlaid by 2488 (Fig. 55), implying that this was a ploughsoil of Iron Age or Early Roman date, but 2488 contained very little gravel, and the absence of a clear worm-sorted gravel horizon on the interface between the pit and the layer above suggests that ploughing was only of short duration.

The top of 2488 was mixed, containing finds dated to the late 1st or early 2nd century AD. Pre-villa features cut this subsoil: pits 1467, 1492 and 2432 and ditches 1481 and 2503. 1467 cut 1492, and 2503 also cut an Early Iron Age feature 2504. Few finds came from these features, but 1481 contained 1st century AD pottery, and the finds from 2488 clearly represent contemporary occupation around them.

Overlying 2488 was an occupation layer containing charcoal, numbered variously 2480, 2491, 1465, 2502 and 1559. 2502 was dated to the 2nd century. Pit 1485, pit 2463 and feature 2432 were cut into 2480. 1485 was circular and was backfilled with large limestone slabs set on edge, 2463 was small, dated to the early-mid 2nd century and was overlaid by the north-west corner of Building IV phase 2. 2432 was large and irregular, underlying the west end of Building IV. Its north limit was not established, but it appears to have extended at least as far as wall 2452, since no subsoil was encountered in the slot dug between walls 2420 and 2452 (Fig. 129 on Fiche 1#33). Feature 2432 silted up until the top was backfilled with clean gravel (2507).

Pottery from 2432 dates to the first half of the 2nd century AD. None of the finds from any of the pre-building contexts need be any later, with the exception of three small joining sherds from layer 2491, which are late 3rd or 4th century. These are however thought to be intrusive, derived from a

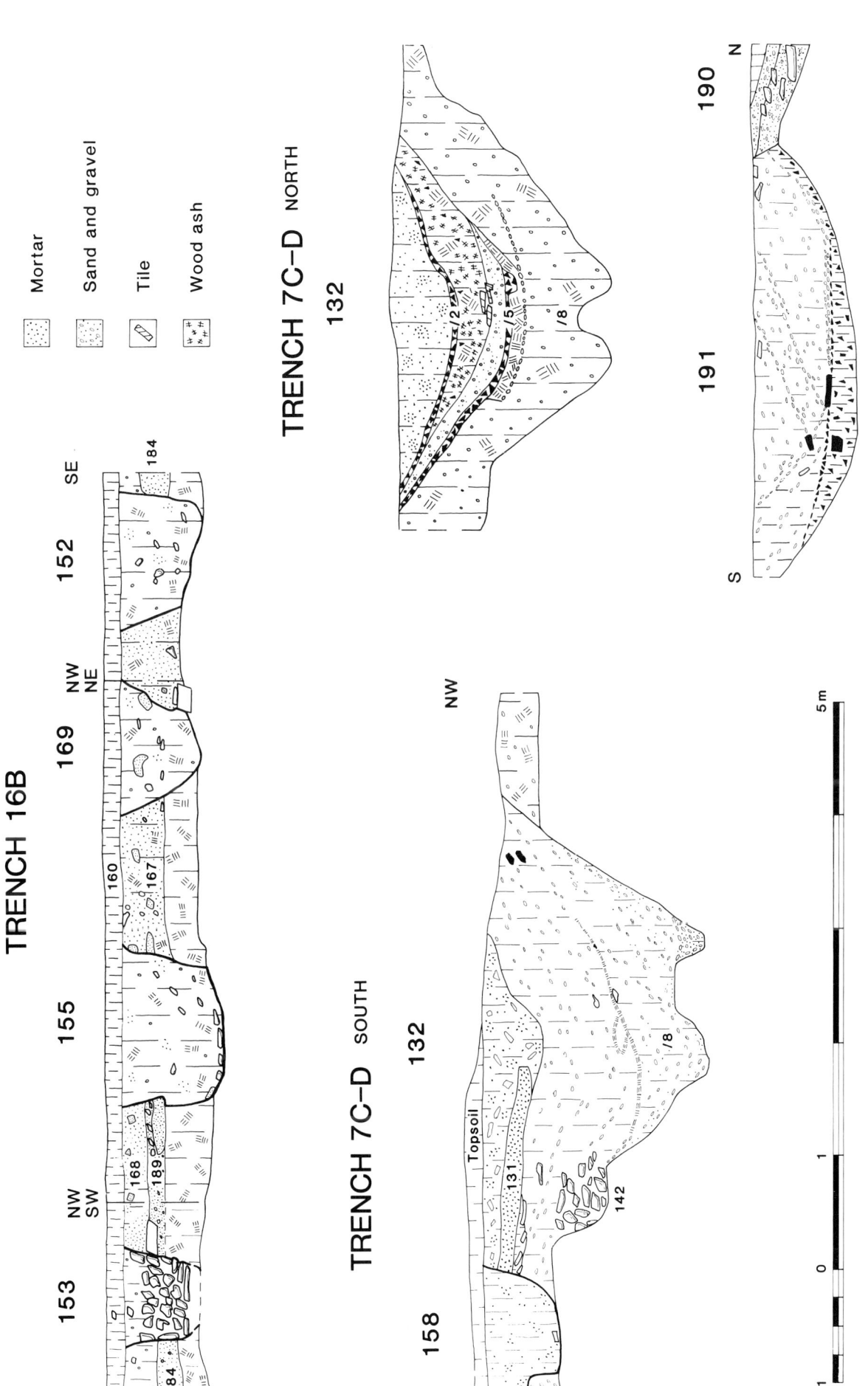

Figure 41 Building II and courtyard: sections

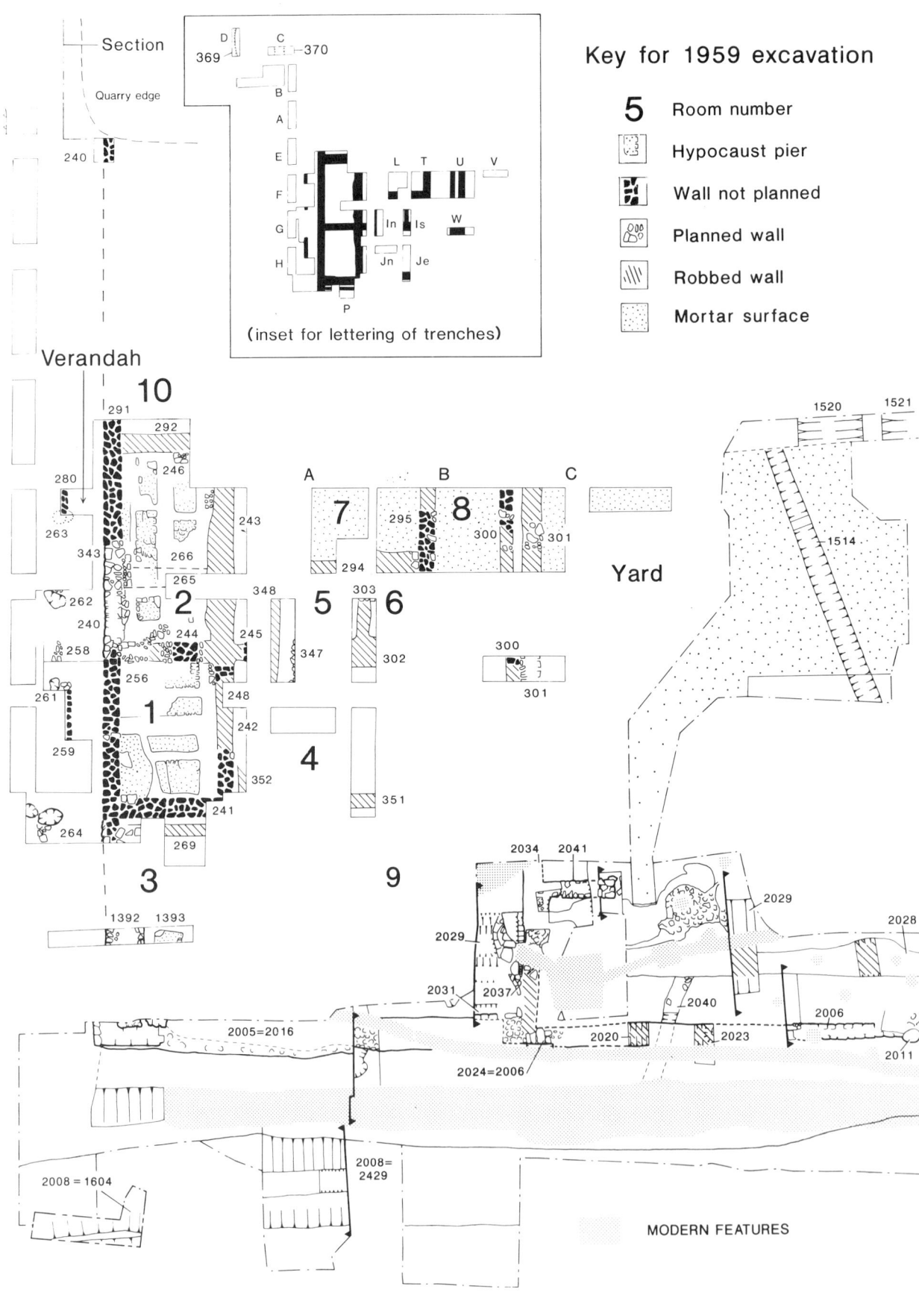

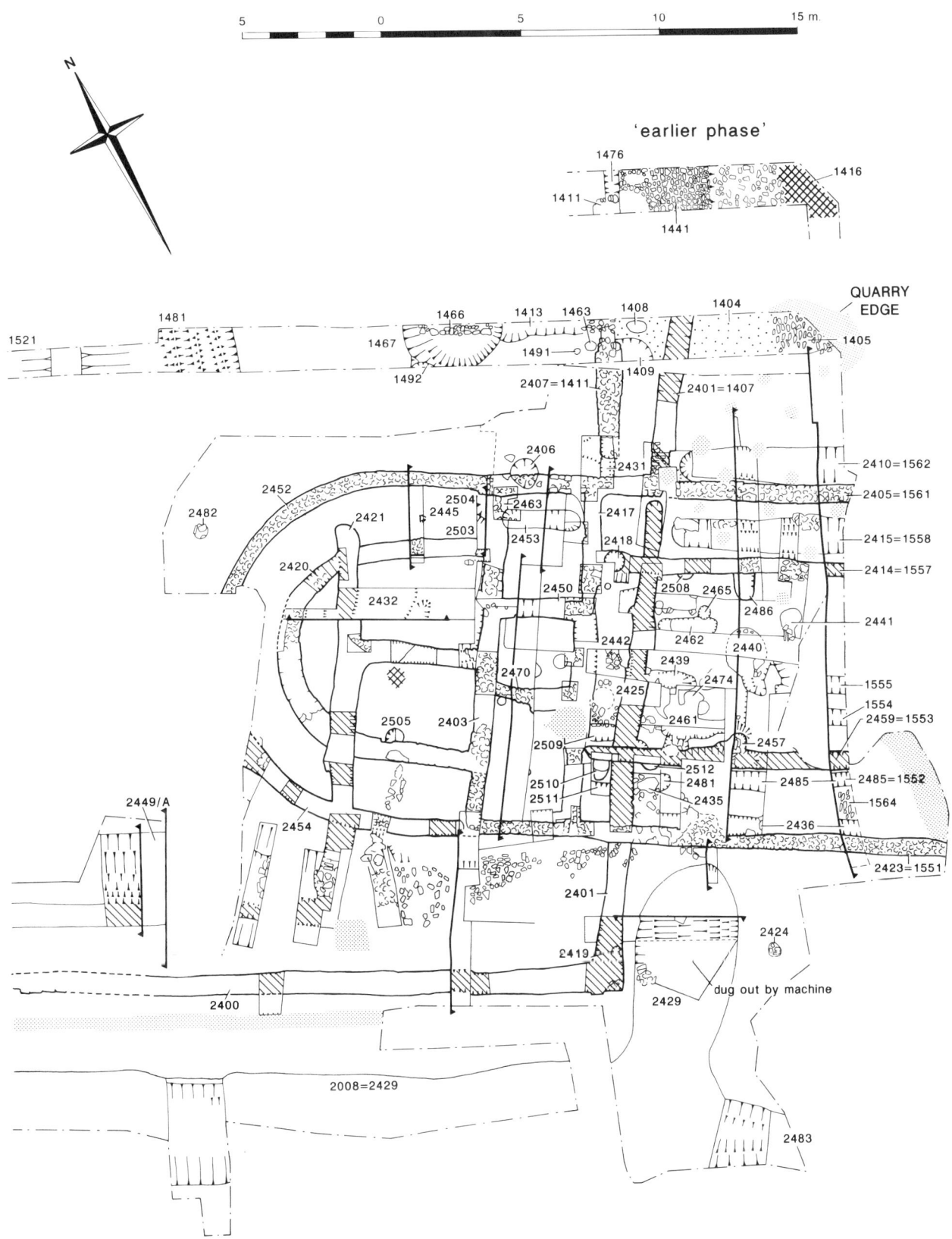

Figure 42 Plan of Building III and Building IV

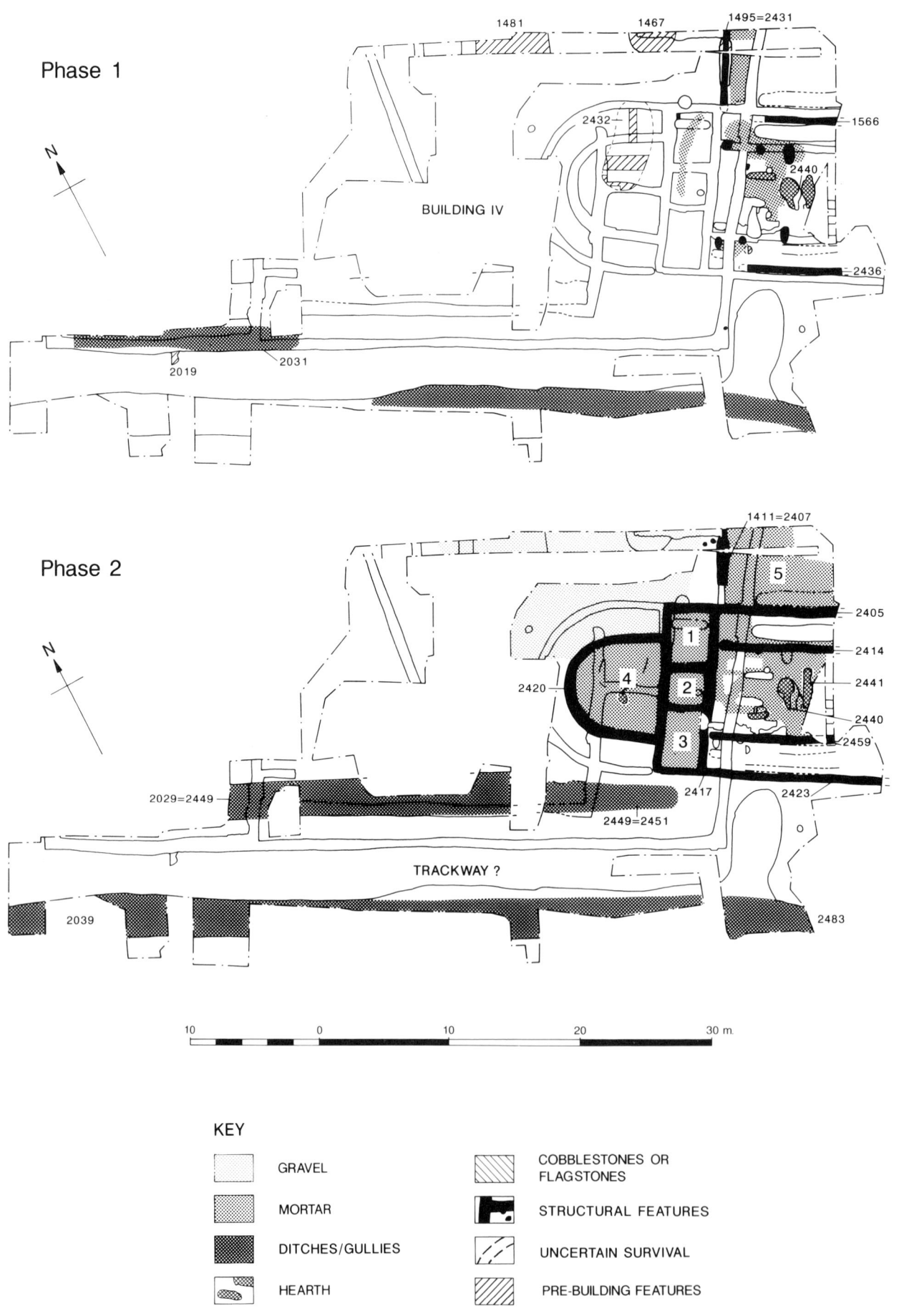

Figure 43 Building IV: phases 1 and 2

posthole 2516 which cut through the floors of Building IV from higher up (see also phase 6 below).

IV.C.6.b Phase 1

This consisted of an aisled rectangular structure aligned east-west. The east end of the building was destroyed without record by gravel extraction in the 1950s (see Fig. 42).

The aisles were supported on posts in oval postholes 0.75 m deep and with post-pipes c 0.6 m across. Only the three westernmost pairs of postholes were uncovered; these were not exactly opposed, the posthole centres in each row being spaced between 1.75 and 3.0 m apart. The posts were surrounded by a thin mortar floor 2464=1563 in both the aisles and the main hall of the building.

The form that the outer walls took in this phase is uncertain. The excavated external walls were of masonry, but no direct relationship was obtainable between the aisle postholes and these outer walls, since the mortar floor did not survive up against them (Figs. 44 and 46). The aisle posts may have been surrounded by these walls (see below Phase 2), but the westernmost pair of aisle posts lay immediately adjacent to the west wall of the aisled part of the stone building, which is structurally unlikely. In other aisled buildings the first aisle posts occur either within the end wall or at the end of the first bay. The posts are thus thought to predate the stone walls.

Just inside the north wall 2405 the subsoil was directly overlaid by 1566=2521, a band of large flat limestones up to 0.8 m wide and in places two courses deep (see Figs. 44 and 46). These extended for several metres east-west, and no mortar floor existed over these stones. In the 1990 excavation the cut for these stones was obscured by later ditch 2415, but 1566 is shown on Fig. 46 drawn in 1982.

A similar feature 2436 ran east-west parallel to it just inside the south wall 2423 for over 6 m. 1566 and 2436 may have contained the sleeper walls of the first phase aisled building. The overall width in this phase would then have been 10.5 m internally, and the aisles c 1.5 m wide (Fig. 43 phase 1). Both 1566 and 2436 however end 1.5 m short of the westernmost pair of aisle posts, and it is unlikely that this represents an entrance, since the posts closest to their ends are not opposite one another. This may suggest that 1566 and 2436 in fact belong with phase 2 (see below), and that no trace of the phase 1 outer wall survived.

The western end of the building in this phase was not recovered; this presumably lay below the phase 2 masonry building, Rooms 1–4. Feature 2463 lay in line with 2521 and was sealed beneath the phase 2 building, so may have been connected with the west end (see Fig. 43). Below Room 3 pre-villa occupation 2480 was overlaid by dark soil and charcoal, possibly equivalent to 1461 (see Fig. 48), below Rooms 1 and 2 pre-villa occupation soil 2491 was overlaid by an intermittent thin floor of yellow sand surfaced with white mortar (Fig. 44). This was covered by dark ashy soil 2492, and was overlaid by a further thin floor of clean compact clay 2493, laid on a sand bed and surfaced with white mortar and small stones. This layer was cut by the foundation trenches of the phase 2 walls 2450 and 2405, and these floors are believed to belong to the first phase aisled building.

Beneath the apsidal Room 4 the top of 2432 was filled with gravel 2507. This was overlaid by soil 2444 containing lenses of charcoal and fired clay and fragments of burnt limestone. This may be equivalent to layer 1461 further north, charcoal overlying pre-villa occupation 1480 etc, and probably created during phase 1 of Building IV. 2444 was followed by 2443, a thin spread of mortar, plaster lumps and gravel (Fig. 129 on Fiche 1#33), which is interpreted as debris from the phase 1 demolition prior to Phase 2 (see below). Layer 2443 was dated to the early to middle 2nd century, as were finds from the aisled building floor 2464.

Within the aisled hall were several ovens. Both of those dated to the 2nd century, 2440 and 2441, were oriented north-south; all those backfilled in the 3rd or 4th centuries lay east-west, and so all the north-south ovens are attributed to the early phases (see Fig. 43). The floor was also cut by posthole 2468, dated tentatively to the first half of the 2nd century.

North of the building finds from 1461 date to the early to middle 2nd century, and this is interpreted as occupation contemporary with phase 1 (see Fig. 48). Cutting 1461 and running at right angles to Building IV was slot 1495=2431. This continued north into the quarry and south up to the phase 2 wall 2405, which cut it. This slot and wall 1411 which overlay it followed exactly the same alignment, and it is possible that 1495 represents the west side of a phase 1 timber building attached to the north side of Building IV (see also below Phase 2). 1461 was directly overlaid by the first gravel mortar layers adjacent to wall 1411, the earliest of which may in fact have been contemporary with 1495 (see also Phase 2).

South of Building IV was a large boundary ditch 2008, which cut a smaller ditch on its north side. This earlier ditch was only seen in a single section, but the soilmark suggests that it ended just south-west of the building (see Fig. 42).

Another ditch lay north-west of this below the south wall of Building III, and it is tentatively suggested that these may have been contemporary (see Fig. 43, phase 1). Neither ditch was dated.

IV.C.6.c Phase 2

The external walls of the aisled building were rebuilt in masonry, set on foundations of unmortared limestones laid in rough courses between vertical edging stones; the foundation trenches were 0.5 to 0.6 m wide and bottomed on gravel. One course of wall proper survived in places,

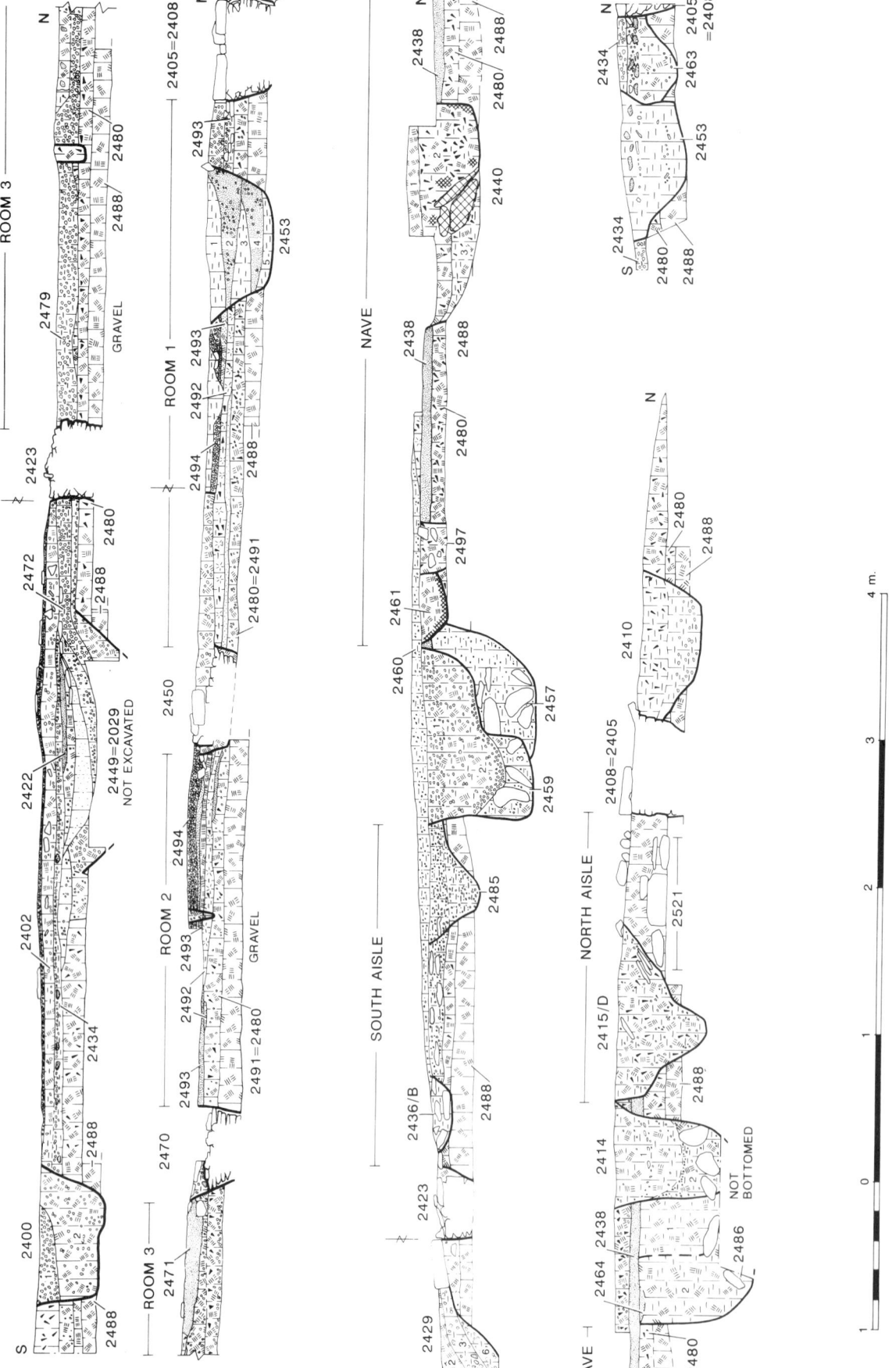

Figure 44 Building IV: N–S sections

Figure 45 Building IV from the north-west showing the apsidal west end

and consisted of roughly-squared limestone blocks bonded with cream gravel mortar. The north, south and west walls of the rectangular aisled block, 2405, 2423 and 2403, were between 0.6 and 0.7 m wide, the curving apsidal wall 2420 was wider, 0.85 m across. The aisles were 2.25 m wide, the central hall 7.0 m wide. A little pottery, dated early to middle 2nd century, was recovered from the foundation trenches of 2403.

It was probably at this stage that the aisle postholes were replaced by aisle slots, 2459 on the south, 2414 on the north. Both were completely robbed, but both had been dug up to 0.2 m into gravel, showing that they had been intended to take a great weight (Fig. 44 and 46). These slots cut through the former aisle postholes, so that the width of the central hall and aisles remained much the same. Both slots ended on the west just short of wall 2417.

The central hall was refloored with cream mortar 2438; this either overlay 2464 directly or sealed charcoal from the phase 1 ovens. In places it had a clay make-up layer 2466, pottery from which was entirely 2nd century. Some of the phase 1 ovens were not overlaid by floor 2438, continuing in use in phase 2. 2438 extended across the north aisle but not the south aisle.

The west end of the main rectangular block was divided off by wall 2417 parallel to 2403, and the 3 m wide strip between them was subdivided by cross-walls 2450 and 2470. The cross-walls were symmetrical, creating rooms 4 m long on the north and south (numbered 1 and 3 respectively) and a central area 2.5 m across between them (Room 2). Room 2 was probably an ante-room or passageway into an apsidal room to the west, Room 4.

Within Room 3 phase 1 charcoal and ash was covered by a mortar floor 2479, which gave way to a white mortar 2471 on the north. In Rooms 2 and 1 a gravel floor 2494 was laid overlying both 2493 and the wall foundation trench of 2450.

Unlike 2470 and the other walls of Building IV 2450 had shallow foundations, bottoming upon the subsoil 2488 rather than on gravel (Fig. 44). Its method of construction was however the same, and it was bonded into 2403 and 2417 at the west and east ends.

In the apsidal Room 4 a spread of gravel and plaster specks 2443 from the phase 1 structure was covered by levelling-up layer 2499 overlain by a gravel and mortar floor 2506. Similar mortar also continued north of 2420; this too was mixed with plaster specks and was cut by Phase 3 wall 2452 (see Fig. 129 on Fiche 1#33). Near to the centre of Room 4 a circular area of 2506 was reddened and blackened by burning; this was perhaps where a brazier had stood.

The date of the rebuilding is uncertain, as few finds came from the floors and most of the walls were robbed out. Early to middle 2nd century pottery came from the phase 1 debris 2443, from the construction trench 2403 and from beneath floor 2438 overlying one of the aisled postholes. The pottery from the trackway ditches to the south (see below) suggests that activity began c 130–140 AD; it is not however possible to establish whether this material is derived from Building IV phase 1, phase 2 or from both. There is however no appreciable difference between the dating offered by the finds for the start of phase 1 and for phase 2, and the occupation spreads relating to the first phase of Building IV are thin, perhaps implying that the duration of the timber phase 1 was relatively short.

About 1.4 m north of the main building and at right angles was wall 2407=1411. This had similar foundations in a trench 0.3 m deep and 0.7 m wide. 1411 ended only 4.6 m from 2405 over pit 1485, which had been backfilled with large limestone slabs set on edge when the wall was built. The wall also overlay slot 1495=2431, exactly following its alignment. At the south end the construction trench of 2407 ran on 0.75 m further than the wall; this was perhaps a mistake in construction.

East of 1411 was a series of thin mortar layers interspersed with sandy clay loams, the latest of which was 1410 (see Fig. 48). These layers continued north of 1411, stopping against a slot 1476, which continued north along the projected east edge of the wall. This slot may have been for the threshold of a doorway into the yard to the west, perhaps associated with postholes 1463 and 1491 (see Fig. 42). Away from wall 1411 there was only one layer of mortar, 1418. This floor continued east and north into the quarry. The area between 1411 and 2405 may have been an open yard, but the mortar flooring, which was replaced by further floor surfaces in later phases, suggests that part if not all was covered.

This may therefore have been a 'fore-building' with a room at least 8.5 m east-west and 5.5 m north-south abutting the aisled building on the north side.

Overlying 1410 was a limestone cobbled floor 1441 (see phase 3). This was cut on the east by 1416, a shallow hollow filled with burnt clay, charcoal and sandy loam, probably a hearth of sorts. In the south part of the room there were few stones over 1418, so possibly this area was not cobbled.

Pottery from the cobbling 1441 suggests a date no later than the late 2nd century, so the 'room' may have been built contemporarily with the phase 2 reconstruction.

West of Building IV was an extensive gravelled surface 1473. This overlay features 1467 and 1481. As their fills settled the floor subsided into them, and in the shelter of the resulting hollows fires were lit. The hollows were overlaid by a second gravel surface 1497. Like 1473 this began several metres west of 1411 and ran up to and over 1481, but was patchy and eroded in places. Finds from 1473 and the soils overlying it below 1497 were all 2nd century.

South of the building was ditch 2449=2451. This cut pre-villa occupation 2480 etc, and silted up, containing pottery dating to the early to middle 2nd century. The east terminal was not excavated, but was evident from the slumping of later gravel and cobbled surface 2472. This ditch was traced west in a straight line for 34.5 m, and was overlaid by Building III (see Fig. 52 below).

Parallel to 2449 and 6 m to the south was ditch 2039=2483. This was traced for 62 m, and continued beyond the excavated area both east and west. It deepened from 0.8 m on the east to nearly 2 m on the west. This ditch also cut the pre-villa occupation layer and contained early to middle 2nd century pottery.

2449 and 2483 probably formed a trackway leading to Building IV, alongside which 2449 ended. The continuation of 2483 however suggests that the track continued. 2483 was not visible in the trench which revealed Building V further east (see Fig. 36); it may have curved slightly southwards and missed this, or may have ended (see Fig. 128 on Fiche 1#32).

IV.C.6.d Phase 3

The apsidal room was surrounded by a parallel wall 2452=2454, abutting wall 2403 and creating an ambulatory the full width of the aisled building (see Fig. 45). This wall had similar foundations to those of phase 2; the foundation trench was 0.6 m wide and bottomed on gravel. The wall proper had been completely robbed out.

There was no direct relationship between 2420 and 2452=2454; for most of the apse area nothing survived above layer 2506. A possible floor 2501 in the north-east corner overlay 2420 but appeared to respect 2452 (Fig. 129 on Fiche 1#33), and a patch of mortar flooring 2477 on the south overlay 2506 and 2420 (Fig. 47); neither however produced any dating material, and both may have belonged instead to phase 4 (see below). The first course of wall 2420 was found still standing on the west side; if 2452=2454 replaced 2420 the floor must have been raised to cover this, and it is more likely that 2420 remained in use (see also phase 4 below). The gap between 2420 and 2452=2454 was 1.6 to 1.9 m wide, and may have been an ambulatory. While it is possible that 2420 was replaced by 2452=2454, this would have created a room 11.5 m wide north-south and over 8.5 m east-west, which would have been difficult to roof.

The floor of the original apse was cut into by a small pit 2505 against the south wall containing fragments of burnt and unburnt animal bone. This was dated late 2nd century or later.

Ovens were now constructed on an east-west alignment. Most of those that were investigated were fire-reddened to a considerable depth around the sides, showing that they were used for some time. Some, such as 2461, were secondarily lined with slates set vertically on edge along the sides of the chamber, others such as 2462 were recut and extended at one end. No detailed sequence of the ovens was established.

Within both aisles stone-filled gullies or trenches were

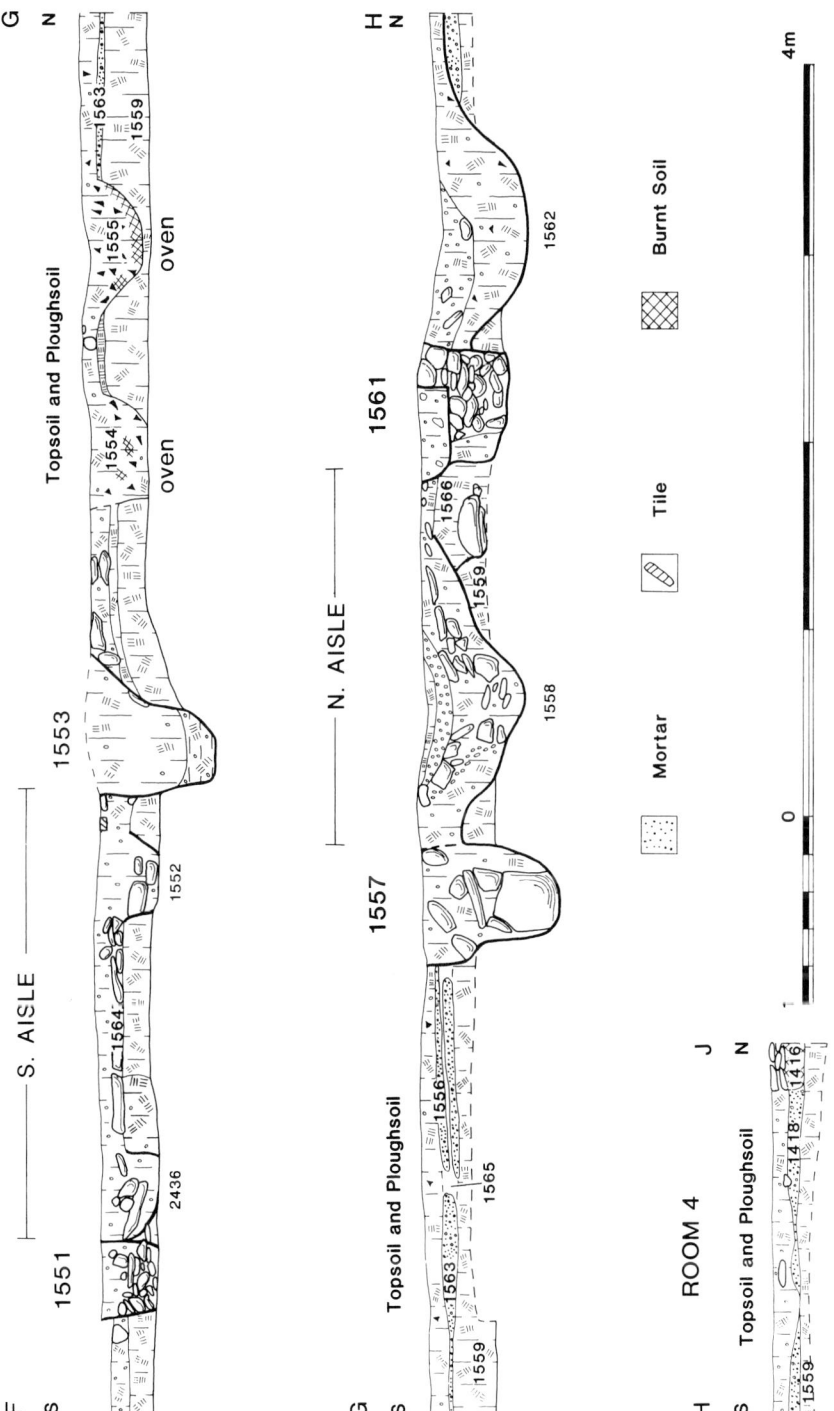

Figure 46 Building IV machine-cut trench: N–S section drawn in 1982.

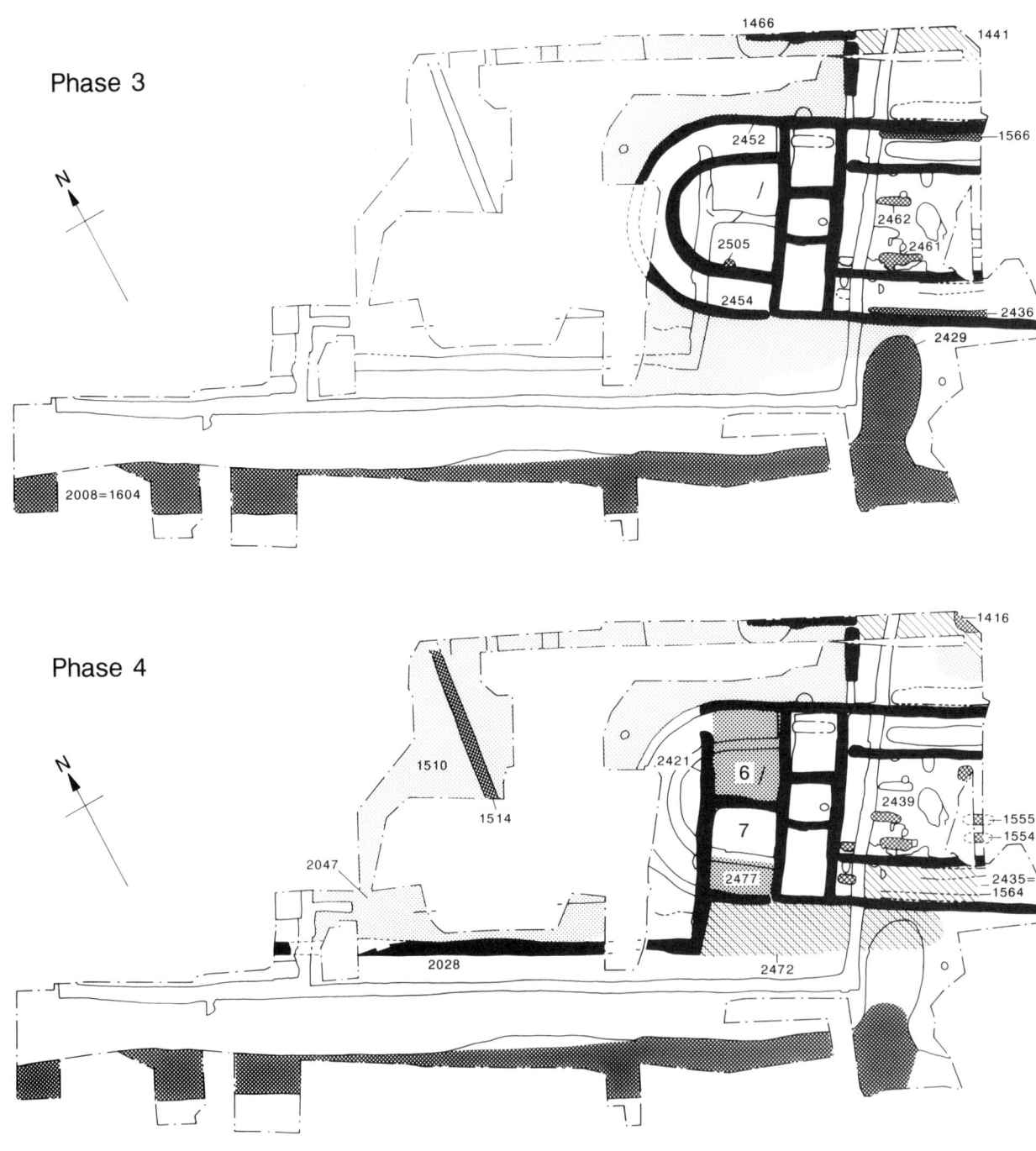

Figure 47 Building IV: phases 3 and 4. For key see Fig. 43.

found alongside the walls, 1566 on the north, 2436 on the south. These features lay right up against the foundations of the outer walls, but were not of the same construction, so were not contemporary with the phase 2 rebuilding. It is suggested (see above) that they were the sleeper walls of the phase 1 building. Alternatively however they may have been dug within the masonry building, although exposing the foundations of both north and south outer walls would have endangered the stability of the building. 2436 was overlaid by stone paving 2435 (see phase 4), but may either have cut through or have been abutted by soil overlying the first mortar floor 2464, and there was no relationship with either mortar floor 2464 or 2438. They might have functioned as drainage gullies, the stones belonging to the backfilling. These two features ended on the west opposite one another just over 2 m short of wall 2417, possibly to allow access to the building at this end; it is noticeable that the terminal of ditch 2429 just outside (see below) is in line with the ends of 2436 and 1566.

South of the building ditch 2039=2483 was recut as 2008=2429, which turned north opposite Building IV and terminated close to it, blocking the former trackway alongside. The northern trackway ditch 2449 was backfilled and overlaid by a layer of gravel (Fig. 44), probably when the ambulatory was added around the apsidal room. This gravel respected the south wall of Building IV, 2423, and skirted the end of 2429. As the backfill of 2449 settled, this surface slumped into its top. Finds from the lower silting of the terminal of 2429 were Antonine. Late Antonine pottery was recovered from the upper fills of 2483 east of the new ditch terminal, suggesting that where not recut the earlier ditch continued in use.

No direct dating evidence is available for the addition of the peristyle or ambulatory; there are no occupation deposits surviving on the floor of the original apse and no finds from the construction trenches. The infilling of ditch 2449, which may have been connected, and the recutting of 2483, can be dated to the late 2nd century. The peristyle may however have been added as late as the early third century (see also Ch. VI.2).

North of the aisled building a western extension was added to the 'fore-building'. Wall 1466 was built, without foundations, upon the courtyard gravel surface 1497, running west for 7 m. Two courses of limestones bonded with yellow mortar survived in places, elsewhere the wall had been robbed by feature 1413. The north face of 1466 had been removed by the quarry, but a bedding layer of sand survived to indicate its former width. At the east end 1466 ran over the possible threshold-slot 1476 as far as the inside edge of 1411, and may have continued onto 1441 inside the building. This area was much disturbed by a later pit 1409 and by posthole 1408, but a ridge of mortar continued for 1 m eastwards across the floor in line with the south edge of 1466, and could represent its continuation. Wall 2466 was built directly onto gravel surface 1497,

which may have been laid in preparation for this extension. Finds from below 1497 are exclusively 2nd century, and a date at the very end of the 2nd or early in the 3rd century seems likely for 1466.

IV.C.6.e Phase 4

The apse was converted into two rectangular rooms of equal size (Rooms 6 and 7) by building wall 2421 parallel to 2403 across the end of the apse 2452=2454, and an east-west wall joining 2421 to 2403 along the central axis of the building. At the north end there was an entrance just over 1 m wide between 2452 and 2421, which ran south through 2420, 2432 and 2454 and over ditch 2449 before turning at right angles to continue west. The construction of the east-west wall right down the middle of the former access from Room 2 suggests that access from the aisled building was no longer possible, and Room 7 must presumably have been entered either from Room 6 or from the south-west.

Where the wall passed over 2449 the ditch was dug out and infilled with pitched limestone slabs. 2421 was robbed out throughout its length, but bottomed on gravel, and the robber-trench was 0.7 to 0.95 m wide; the robbing of the western arm of 2421 was numbered 2028.

The first course of the original apse wall 2420 survived west of (and outside) 2421, but the wall was robbed to foundation level east of 2421, suggesting that 2420 was only robbed out when 2421 was built. The robbing of 2420 contained a few sherds dated late 2nd century or later.

There were no floors that must stratigraphically belong to this phase, but it is likely that both 2501 adjacent to 2403 and 2477 which overlay 2420 belong here (see Figs. 47 and 129 on Fiche 1#33). Both floors survived only in small areas (see also phase 3). South of 2452 the hollow overlying infilled ditch 2449, into which the gravel yard surface had slumped, was filled in, and a new gravel make-up surfaced with cobbling 2472 was laid over it (Fig. 44).

This cobbling ended against wall 2421, and the gravel make-up extended east over the end of ditch 2429 and slumped into the ditch (see Fig. 55 layer 2429/A/3). This perhaps implies that the ditch was backfilled immediately before laying the cobbling, and the fills then settled. The backfilling, which included building debris that could have resulted from the phase 4 alterations, was dated to the later 3rd century AD, and finds from upon the cobbling to the late 3rd and early 4th centuries.

The Building IV phase 4 alterations are only dateable in relation to earlier and later stratigraphic events. The phase 3 alterations are tentatively assigned to the very late 2nd century AD (see above), and the phase 4 villa boundary wall 2028 was abutted by mortar 2029/B/7 laid after 250 AD, and overlain by the extension of Building III (see Figs. 49 and 52), which was built by the last quarter of the 3rd century. Cobbling 2422, laid in the later 3rd century, certainly respects 2421, but need not have been

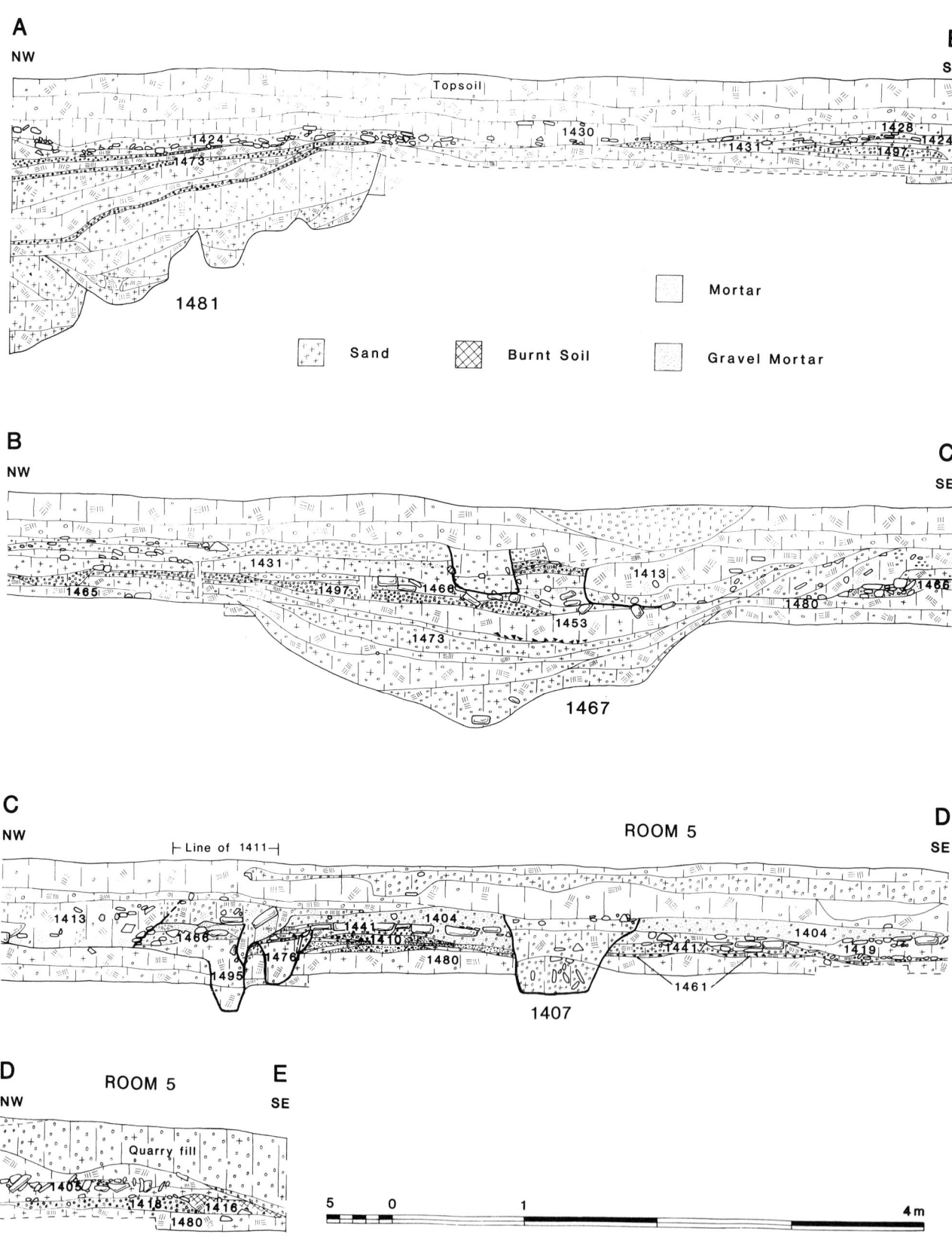

Figure 48 Building IV: NW–SE section

laid until some time after the wall had been built. Allowing for use of the phase 3 apse, phase 4 most likely dates to the middle of the 3rd century.

Within the aisled building stone paving 2435=1564 was laid in the south aisle over a build-up of loam dating to the late 2nd and early 3rd centuries. This abutted aisle-slot 2459 and overlay linear feature 2436 alongside wall 2423.

IV.C.6.f Phase 5

The structural alterations of this phase refer to Building III to the west (see Ch. IV.C.8.d). Building IV continued in use; within the aisled block ovens 2439 and 2425 were not backfilled until the 4th century. In the south aisle gully 2485=1552 was dug through paved floor 2435 roughly parallel to the walls of the building (Fig. 44). An east-west trench 2453 was dug right across the north side of Room 1, ending just short of 2403 and 2417 (Figs. 49 and 44). Finds from both 2485 and 2453 date to the late 3rd or 4th century AD.

In Room 5 north of the aisled building hearth 1416 contained a 4th century colour-coated sherd. This was overlaid by a sandy make-up layer 1419 in preparation for a tightly-packed floor of pitched stones 1405 (Fig. 48). At the west end of the room cobbling 1441 had been resurfaced, and was probably in use together with 1405. Both this resurfacing and 1405 were in turn overlain by a gravel mortar floor 1404, which was limited to a band 4.5 m wide running down the west side of the room. The absence of much soil or debris upon 1405 below 1404 suggests that there was not a long interval of use between them.

South of Building IV soil accumulated upon cobbling 2472, which was eventually replaced by another cobbled surface 2422. This too was confined east of wall 2421.

IV.C.6.g Phase 6

Room 5 and the aisled building were cut across by wall 2517=2496 on a north-north-east alignment. This was almost entirely robbed out by trench 2401, but unmortared pitched limestone foundations survived just north of the aisled building. South of Building IV and just north of ditch 2008=2429 the wall turned west, running up to about the south-east corner of Building III. This wall too was mostly robbed by trenches 2400 and 2020, but short lengths 2024 and 2006 survived, constructed of squared limestone blocks bonded with cream gravel mortar on a foundation of unmortared limestones. The surviving wall was 0.55 m wide. The foundation trench bottomed on gravel, except at the west end, where the bottom course of wall 2024 was laid directly onto the bottom of the construction trench.

The construction trench of wall 2517 butted up to the foundations of the north wall of the aisled building 2405, implying that 2405 was still visible at this date, and 2517 presumably overlay the foundations of the earlier wall. The robbing of wall 2517 cut all other features except the north aisle slot 2414, whose robbing cut through 2400. 2414 was completely robbed for most of its length, but at the east end vertical slabs were set across the trench bottom (see Fig. 46), and two courses of unmortared limestone slabs ran along the top of the trench. These are not likely to belong to the original walls, which were probably robbed when the building went out of use, but may represent a wall built out of the rubble which was later robbed in its turn.

Wall 2517 runs obliquely across Building IV, which must have gone out of use; ditches 2415=1558 and 2410=1562, both starting just east of the wall, were dug alongside the former walls 2405 and 2414. 2415 cut the mortar floors in the north aisle, 2410 exposed the foundations of 2405 in its south side. Both ditches had dark occupation-rich fills, 2410 dating to the late 3rd or 4th century, 2415 to the first half of the 4th century. 2410 also contained a radiate coin of Tetricus II minted 270–274 (see Table 21 No. 1411). It is unlikely that both ditches were open contemporarily, so 2415 probably succeeded 2410. 2415 deepened as it ran east, and the upper part was filled with limestones which appeared to have tumbled in from the north side. The absence of mortar however seems to indicate that this stonework was not derived from the walls of Building IV.

Dug into the floors of Building IV were postholes 2437, 2465, 2467, 2473, 2516, 2518 and 2519. These do not form any recognisable structure. 2437 was cut by 2400, the robbing of 2517, and 2516 may have contained late 3rd or 4th century sherds (see pre-building contexts above), the other postholes were undated. A shallow pit 1409 and a large oval posthole 1408, which was packed with limestones around a square post-pipe, cut the latest mortar floor 1404 in Room 5. 1409 was undated, but the fill of the post-pipe of 1408 contained a coin dated 350–360 AD (Table 21 No. 23). This feature also contained fragments of human skull (see Ch. 5.16 on Fiche 2#84).

West of Room 5 wall 1466 was robbed by 1413 and overlain elsewhere by a thick sandy loam 1431. This in turn was overlaid by a layer of shattered slates 1424, with patches of mortar from the destruction of the building (Fig. 48).

1424 is probably equivalent to layer 2042=2048 west of Building IV, representing the latest courtyard surface, the slates possibly derived from the roof of the demolished building (see Fig. 52). These stone spreads were however part of an extensive yard surfacing, as similar layers were recorded in various trenches across the courtyard south of Building I and west of Buildings II and IV. Overlying 1424 was a thick build-up of dark loam containing much occupation debris and charcoal (layers 1428, 1430 and 1503) and a coin of 348–360 (Table 21 No. 28), demonstrating that occupation was still continuing in the latter half of the 4th century.

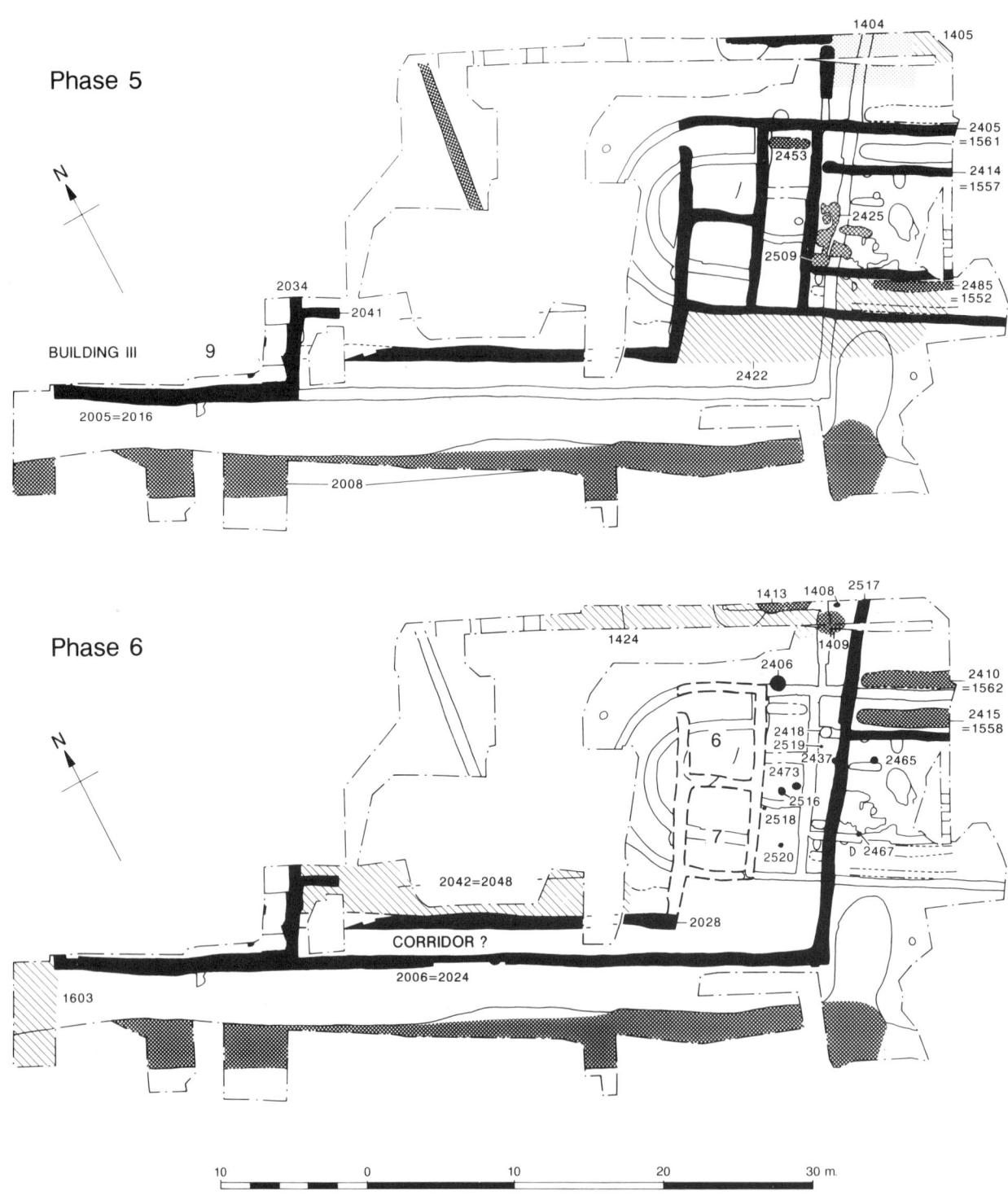

Figure 49 Building IV: phases 5 and 6. For key see Fig. 43.

IV.C.7 Building V

Fig. 128 on Fiche 1#32

South-east of Building IV was a north-south wall, 2610 (see Fig. 36). This wall was very substantial, 1.0–1.1 m wide with a foundation-trench dug 0.35 m into gravel. No trace of any associated floor survived. Pottery from the robbing of the wall dates to the late 2nd century. This wall is likely to have belonged to a building rather than simply to a boundary wall; none of the other three villa enclosure walls were similarly massive. Whether a building or a boundary wall, this may indicate that trackway ditch 2483 ended before reaching this trench; the trackway was possibly heading for this structure.

IV.C.8 Building III

Plan: Fig. 36, 42; Sections: Fig. 55, 50, 53, 52, 58

IV.C.8.a Introduction

From separate seasons of excavation in 1959, 1981–2 and 1990 an outline plan of the southern half of this building has been recovered. The building was not well-preserved however, as both floor and wall-robbing had been extensive. It consisted of a rectangular block oriented north-north-east, 16.5 m wide and at least 33 m long, with a verandah on the west and what seemed to be a paved yard on the east (see also Fig. 115). Parts of ten rooms were uncovered, two along the west side being excavated completely. The northern limits are unknown, as the building was first picked up on the quarry face of the area west of Building I.

The topsoil was removed by machine, but below this all trenches were dug by hand. In 1982 and 1990 areas were opened up by machine east of the building, but in neither case was there time to excavate these to natural.

IV.C.8.b The hypocausted rooms on the west: Rooms 1, 2, 3, 9 and 10

Fig. 51

The foundations of the west outside wall 240 consisted mostly of small pitched stones (Fig. 50), with up to four courses of roughly dressed blocks bonded with yellow mortar surviving above. The wall proper was 0.67 m wide. Inside along the west was a series of hypocausted rooms. Rooms 1 and 2 had mortar sub-floor and masonry piers. These were probably stoked from Room 10, which had thick layers of ash on its earth floor, but the wall containing the flue arch (292) was robbed out. Charcoal and ash among the flues in Rooms 1 and 2 was directly overlaid by destruction debris, and from the fact that some piers were robbed the raised floors had clearly been deliberately removed. Mosaic fragments were recovered from the flues of Room 2, which had apparently been floored with a geometric mosaic in three colours (Ch. V.12 and Fig. 151 on Fiche 2#71). No sections of Room 1 or Room 2 were drawn.

Below the sub-floor in Room 2 was an earlier wall 265, at right angles to 240 and in line with wall 294 (Fig. 42): this was not planned by the excavator. It was bonded into 240 at the north-west end, demonstrating that the channeled hypocaust in Room 2 was secondary; there was possibly also masonry below the floor in the north-west corner of Room 1, whose hypocaust may thus not have been original. Walls 241 and 242 however appeared to be contemporary with 240, so that much of the original building was retained in the later phase. No trace of floors associated with the earlier phase of this building survived; these had presumably been removed by excavation for the hypocausts, but an infant burial 343 lay beneath the sub-floor adjacent to 265.

South of Room 1 in the south-west corner of the building was Room 3, another hypocausted room. At the north end this contained a narrow sleeper-wall 269 and a layer of ash at the level of the sub-floor in Room 1 adjacent. The sub-floor appears to have been of earth. Further south a narrow trench into the west side of the room revealed a mortar sub-floor upon which was a masonry pier 1393 (see Fig. 50). At both ends the main west wall of the building surrounding this room was 1.3 m wide, incorporating a sleeper wall for the raised floor. The sleeper walls were bonded into the main wall, showing that these rooms were hypocausted from the start, unlike Rooms 1 and 2. Along the west side of Room 4 there was apparently another sleeper wall, and elsewhere within it mortar and stone spreads at the level of the sub-floors, so this room may also have had an hypocaust. This was presumably fed from the east side of the building like Room 9 (see below).

The full length of the south wall, numbered 2005 on the west and 2016 on the east, lay within the excavation. Most of this wall had been robbed down to foundation level or below (see Fig. 55), but at the west end 4 courses of the wall proper survived. 2005 was 0.6 m wide, built of roughly squared limestone blocks bonded with cream mortar, and survived 0.4 m high; the foundations were of unmortared small flat limestones laid in rough courses, and the foundation trench generally bottomed on gravel. At the east end the wall overlay an earlier east-west ditch or large pit 2031 (Fig. 52), and at the south-east corner of the building the foundations were 0.3 m deeper. 2031 contained sherds of black-burnished pottery, and so dates to the 2nd century or later. The east wall 2034 was again badly robbed, but was traced northwards for 5.3 m before it was destroyed by the quarry. Its alignment corresponds to that of wall 301 further north. This wall was 0.65–0.7 m wide and ran over both ditch 2449=2029 and wall 2028. Where it crossed 2029 the upper part of the ditch had been dug out and refilled with large limestone slabs 2036 to provide a firm foundation.

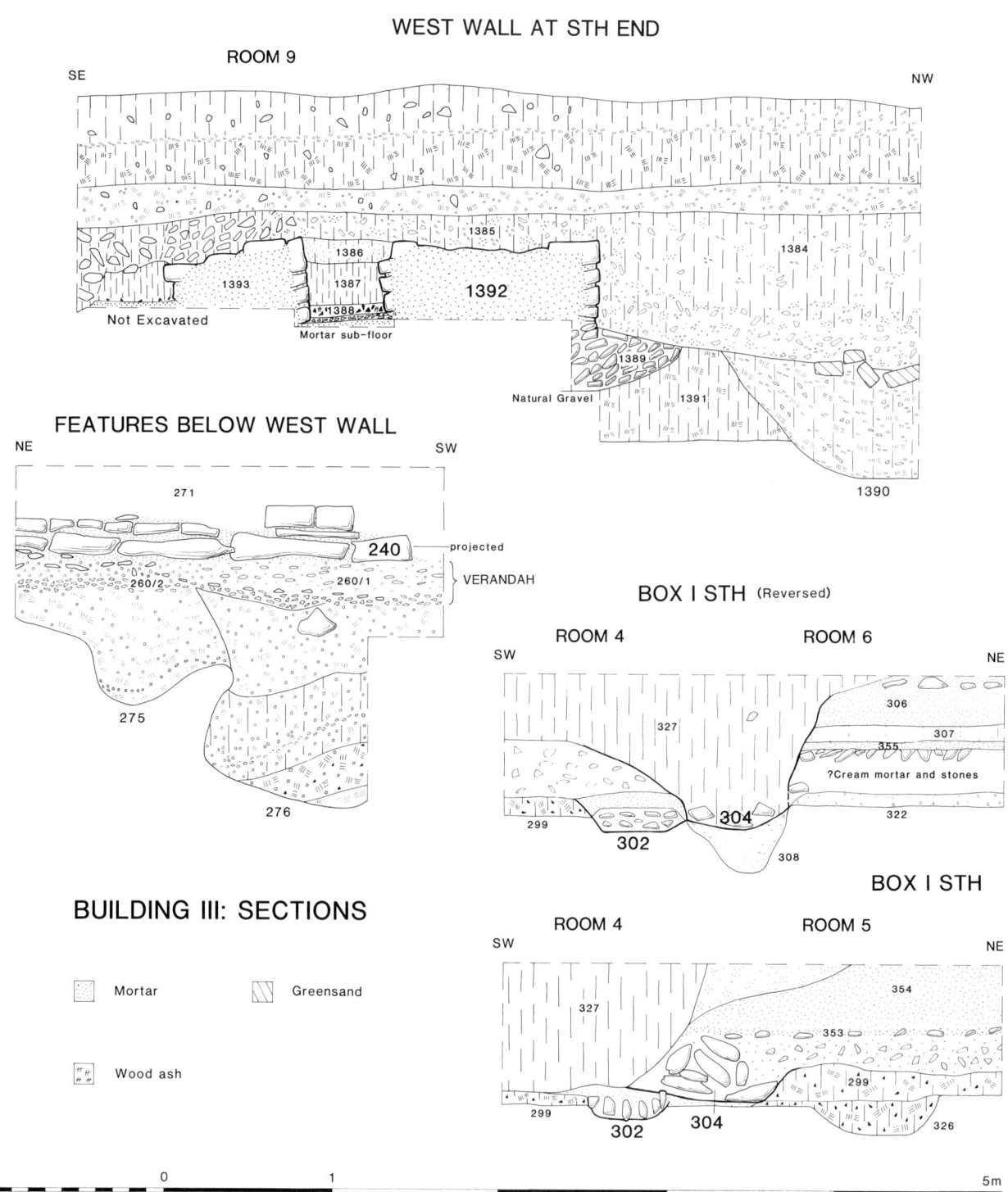

Figure 50 Building III: sections of west wall at the south end, of Box I, and of features below the west wall

Figure 51 Building III: Rooms 1 and 2 showing the channeled hypocaust from the south-west

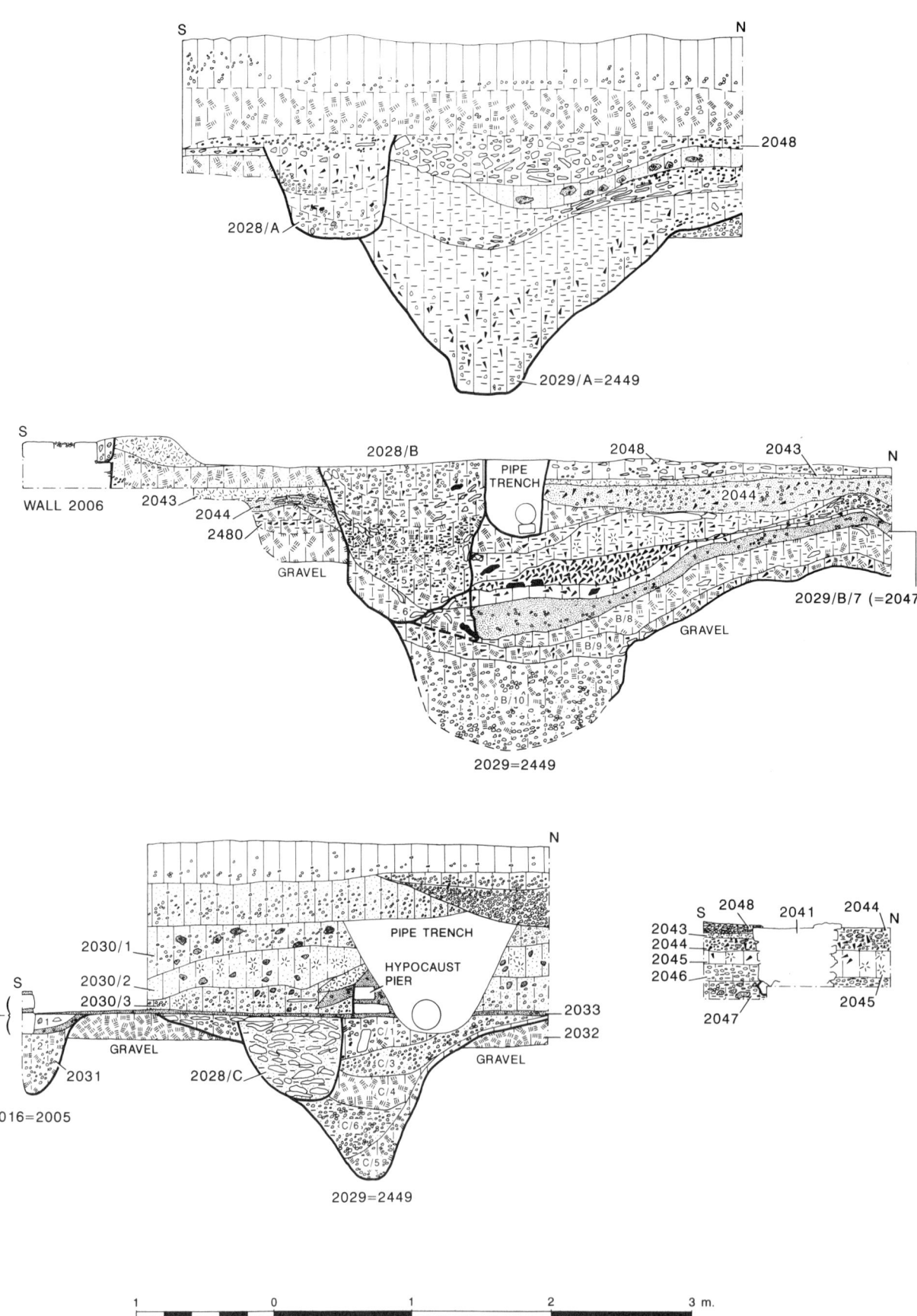

Figure 52 Building III: sections across ditch 2029 and wall 2028

Projecting from the east wall 2034 was a short length of wall 2041. This was 2.4 m long and 0.65 m wide, was built of squared limestones and survived 5 courses and 0.42 m high. The wall had pitched limestone foundations set into a gravel mortar surface 2047 (Fig. 52); the lower courses were bonded with yellow gravel mortar, the upper ones with a cream mortar. The deposits of soot and ash adjacent to 2041 perhaps suggest that it was connected with a stokehole for the hypocaust in Room 9 (see below). 2047 probably corresponds to 2029/B/7 further east (see Ch. IV.C.8.d below), which is equivalent to the make-up for the rebuilding of Building III further north. It therefore appears that 2034 must correspond to the later east wall 301 further north.

Inside Building III the room at the south-east corner (Room 9) was hypocausted. A thin mortar sub-floor 2035 overlay subsoil 2032 and ditch 2029, wall 2028 and ditch 2031. Upon the sub-floor triangular mortared limestone piers were built, 2037 surviving up to 0.37 m and 4 courses high; alongside the east wall was a narrow sleeper-wall, courses of limestones overlying pitched mortared masonry (Fig. 54). As in Rooms 1 and 2 the piers and sleeper wall were part of a channeled hypocaust supporting the floor, nothing of which survived; overlying the sub-floor was a layer of grey ash and charcoal, and this in turn was covered by mixed destruction layers. This hypocausted room extended for at least 5.5 m east-west and 4 m north-south. A modern pipe-trench which destroyed the north edge of 2005 made it impossible to find the western limits of this room, but it presumably adjoined Room 3, also hypocausted, which lay in the south-west corner of the building.

IV.C.8.c The rooms on the east side: Rooms 5, 6, 7 & 8

These had solid mortar floors. In Rooms 5 and 6 stone and mortar make-up was overlaid by pitched stones surfaced with mortar, layers 353 and 355. In Rooms 7 and 8 clean mortar floors 309 and 312 were bedded only on a thin layer of gravel or soil and pebbles. Beneath the make-up in all these rooms was a layer of black soil 299, which infilled earlier pits and postholes and overlay subsoil and gravel between them. It also seems to have lain beneath the mortar sub-floor in Room 1. This may have been an extensive clearance layer before building, like that in Building IV, but its depth and extent suggests it was dumped, possibly from a hypocaust.

There were two phases of the east wall of Building III, the later 301 being the outer and more substantial wall (Fig. 53). 302, the south wall of rooms 5 and 6, and 303, the wall between them, were also replaced by wider walls 304 and 305, and a second phase of mortar floor (306, 310 and 354) was laid in all four rooms. The surface of this did not survive, but the mortar make-up was over 0.3 m thick. In this phase the stratigraphic sequence in Rooms 6 and 8 was identical, and these may have been parts of one L-shaped room. Similarly Room 7 appears to have extended right from Room 2 to Room 8. The sections on the east side of Room 5 and just east of Room 2 are however dissimilar, and a shallow trench 348 parallel to the east wall of Rooms 1 and 2 suggests that there was later a narrow corridor dividing Rooms 5 and 4 from Rooms 2 and 1 (Fig. 42). It is not known how this might have related to the supposed hypocaust in Room 4.

The debris from Building III included both *opus signinum* flooring and yellow mortar surfaced with crushed tile in imitation of it. The painted wall plaster of the later phase showed a wide range of colours and of designs, and its distribution suggests that Building III was brightly painted throughout (Ch. V.13). Shattered limestone slates from the roof were common all along the west side of the building; ceramic roof tiles in the debris may have been reused (see also Ch. V.14).

IV.C.8.d The yard east of the building and the boundary ditches to the south

The yard was examined in two areas, east of Rooms 6 and 8 and alongside Room 9. East of Room 8 the mortar make-up for the later floors (here numbered 1510) had a flat level surface; one or two slabs found upon it suggest that it was originally paved. Cutting across it was a gully 1514 filled with fine silt, probably a drain (Fig. 42). Sealing both the gully and the mortar layer was a deposit of painted plaster with some *opus signinum* and tiles; this was not in situ collapse, but material dumped from the adjacent building, perhaps in robbing the floors. Overlying this debris was a dark loamy soil containing coins (Table 21 Nos. 24, 27 and 28) and pottery dating to the mid-4th century. This soil was probably equivalent to layers 1428–1430 overlying the destruction of Building IV (Fig. 48, Ch. IV.C.6 above).

The mortar make-up 1510 contained a little painted plaster in simple colours, indicating that the earlier phase of Building III had had some painted walls. Below this were successive gravel and mortar layers of the construction and the earlier floors. The latter probably corresponds to the second courtyard floor 1497 further east towards Building IV.

East of Room 9 below wall 2041 and cut by its foundations was a layer of gravel mortar 2047, which may correspond to layer 2029/B/7, a mortar surface in the top of ditch 2029 (see Fig. 52). This appears to be a continuation of mortar surface 1510, which here had slumped into the ditch top and which abutted the bottom of wall 2028 on its north side. It was separated from the uppermost ditch fills by a substantial depth of clay loam, implying a considerable time gap between the infilling of 2029 and the construction of wall 2028 and the laying of the adjacent mortar floor. Finds from this mortar further north date to the later 3rd century. Wall 2041 was built from the surface of this layer,

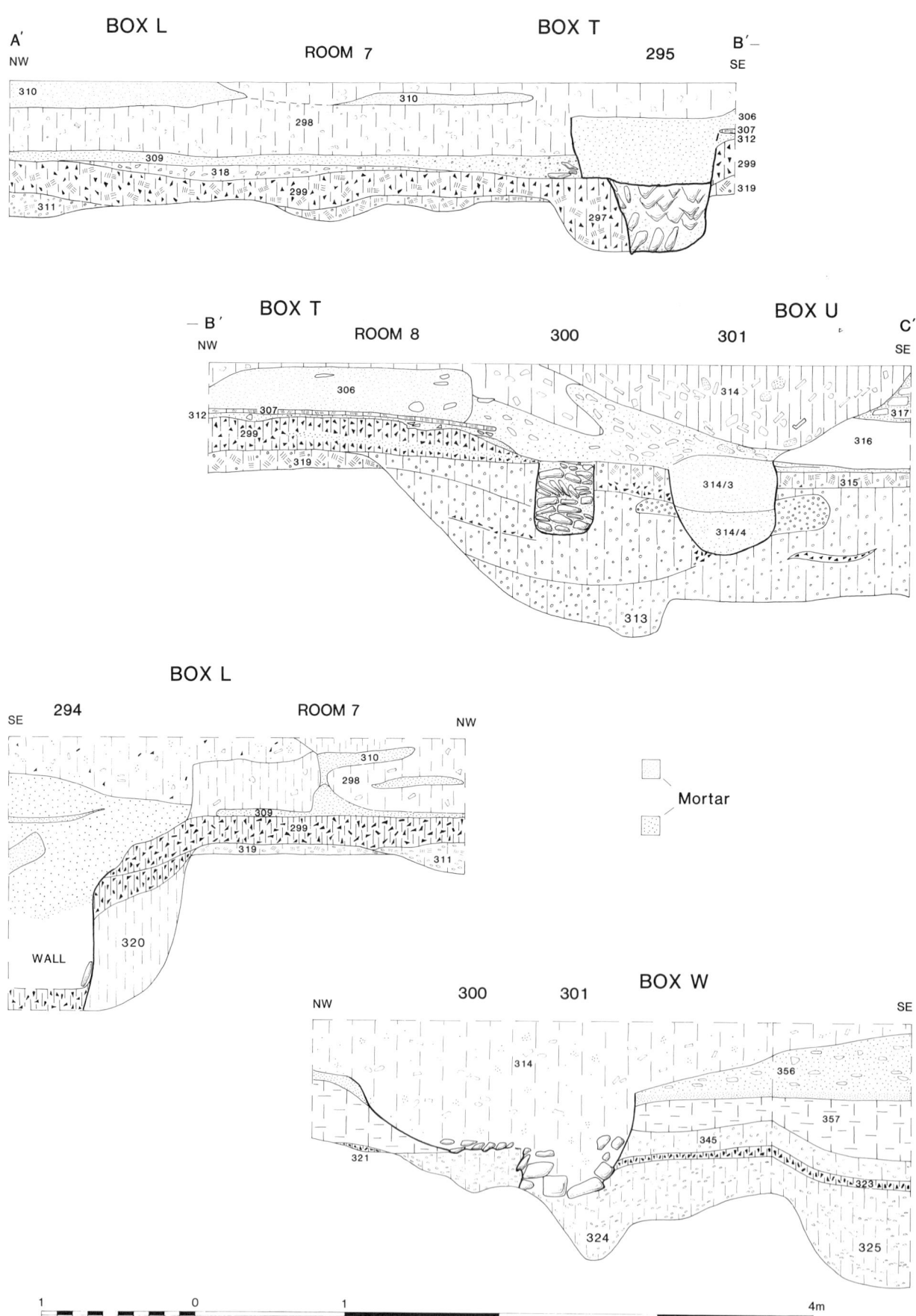

Figure 53 Building III: sections of Boxes L, T, U and W

Figure 54 Building III: Room 9 showing sub-floor and hypocaust piers

showing either that the rebuilding of Building III followed close upon construction of 2028, or that the mortar floor surface was kept clean.

Surrounding the wall was a substantial build-up of successive layers of loam mixed with limestone rubble, ash lenses and mortar, 2044–2046. 2046 may correspond to 2029/B/5 and 2045 to 2029/B/3. The last of these 2044 had a level surface, and may well have been a courtyard floor; it was overlaid by an extensive ash and charcoal layer 2043. The soils infilling the top of 2029 at this point, and even more so those overlying floor 2029/7, were full of ash, coal or charcoal deposits, and suggest raked-out material from an hypocaust flue nearby.

2043 was in turn overlain by limestone and Stonesfield slate rubble, 2042=2048, which overlay wall 2041 of Building III. This was levelled off to an even surface and was probably another courtyard hard-standing, corresponding to the upper courtyard surface further east, which occurs at a similar level overlying 2029 and is cut by the robbing of wall 2028. Since both wall 2041, which appeared to be contemporary with Building III, and wall 2028 further east, are abutted by 2048, it is clear that the Building IV phase 4 boundary wall 2028 had remained in use outside Building III, although the western part of the wall was overlain by the building. Robber-trench 2028 was visible through all the Roman deposits, and its wall may still have been in use alongside the phase 6 wall 2006=2024, forming a portico along the south side of the villa enclosure. 2006 ran up to the south-east corner of Building III, which it abutted. It cut ash layer 2043 on the north side (see Fig. 52), but no stratigraphic relationships survived above this.

Building III lay just 7.5 m north of boundary ditch 2008=2429. Both were cut through 2018, a probable ploughsoil overlying both gravel and Iron Age feature 2019, and through 2015 which overlay it (Fig. 55). 2018 may belong to the same episode of ploughing observed west of Building III (see Ch. IV.C.9 and Fig. 58), but may be earlier. 2015 was a similar soil but contained Early Roman occupation debris. The level from which the earliest phase of the boundary, 2039=2483, was cut was not ascertained, as its recut 2008=2429 removed this. The later ditch cut was nearly 4 m across. This contained two horizons of building debris, one on the interface of layers /9 and /6, the other in layers /4 and /3. The earlier may relate to the construction of Building III, the later to its destruction.

A small trench dug into the boundary ditch at the west end of the excavated area and just opposite the southwest corner of Building III in 1982 showed that it was overlaid by a deposit of limestones laid horizontally, probably to form a yard surface. The ditch here was numbered 1604, the limestones 1603. 1603 incorporated a little-worn coin of 310–312 (Table 21 No. 25), implying that the ditch went out of use during the first quarter of the 4th century. Further east however there was no sign of the limestone layer, and

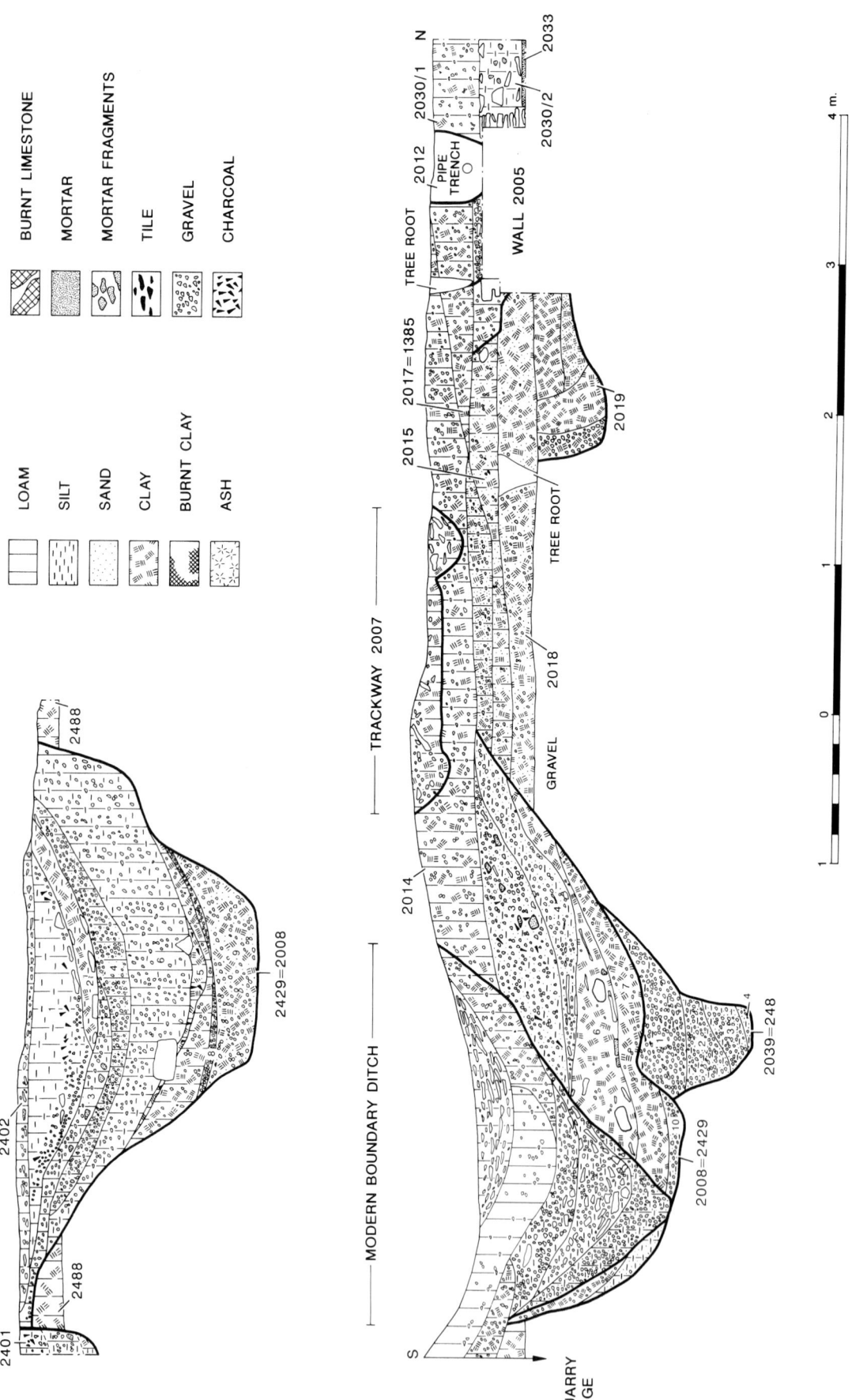

Figure 55 Building III: section to south across boundary ditches

pottery from the upper fills of 2008 continued to accumulate until the mid-4th century. Possibly the limestone was a localised infilling for access down the west side of Building III (see Fig. 49).

Destruction debris adjacent to the building is represented by 2017, after which the building and the ditches were overlaid by a gradual soil accumulation 2014. The robber trench of 2005 is cut from some way up, demonstrating that parts of the walls remained standing for some time after the building was disused, and were only robbed thereafter. On the east wall 2041 was overlaid by the slate rubble surface 2042. Further north this was overlaid by dark occupation soils 1428, 1430 and 1503, which also sealed layers of painted wall-plaster from Building III.

The post-Roman build-up was overlaid in the post-medieval period by a narrow trackway 2007 leading to Roughground Farm. South of this the Roman boundary ditches were cut by a field-boundary dug alongside this track (see Fig. 55).

IV.C.8.e The verandah on the west

Figs. 42, 56 and 57

West of the building was a verandah or passage. The floor consisted of a layer of greenish sandstone chippings 260, probably from final wall-dressing, overlaid by a layer of gravel, and this was bounded by a line of postholes 261–264. In between the postholes were traces of a dry-stone wall 258. Later the verandah was narrowed slightly, and a continuous dry-stone wall 259 built on top of the gravel floor (Fig. 57) leaving a walkway 1.2 m wide. The verandah did not apparently continue south alongside Room 9. The excavation-boxes west of this were only cleared down to destruction level, so it is not known what happened beyond it.

Ten metres further north the west wall (240) was picked up again, and outside it an extensive spread of painted plaster 0.3 m thick, apparently derived from a different set of rooms to the fragments found further south. Like the plaster east of Building III, this was probably dumped, but most likely indicates that there were further rooms and not simply a boundary wall here. The verandah floors did not appear here, but a horizon composed variously of stones (376) and *opus signinum* (362) may have been an alternative flooring at some stage (Fig. 58). This was apparently bounded by a narrow dry-stone wall (375).

IV.C.8.f Pre-building features

Plan: Fig. 127 on Fiche 1#31; Sections: Figs. 50 and 53

The west wall and the verandah overlay deep pits 276 and 279 of the later 2nd century AD, and 276 cut a gully of the 1st century AD, 275 (Fig. 50). Other pits were found in Boxes L and T, 296 being a series of intercutting features all filled with black soil 299, whereas 320 contained a dump of early 2nd century pottery in its top sealed by 299. Smaller pits and postholes, mostly filled with more of 299, occurred beneath the mortar sub-floor in Rooms 1 and 2 and in Boxes I north and I south. A large 1st century ditch, frequently recut, was found beneath the east walls of the building (Fig. 53). This is numbered 313 and 324 in separate boxes, but was probably one feature, possibly part of the same enclosure as 1481 further east (Figs. 42 and 48). Other large ditches 293 and 1390 were clipped further south, but their full dimensions were not established nor were they dated.

IV.C.8.g Dating

The extensive black layer 299 just beneath the building contained only 2nd century finds with the exception of one Oxford colour-coated sherd. Pits 276 and 279 beneath the verandah may have been as late as the early 3rd century, and the verandah floors (260) included definite early 3rd century sherds. This suggests a date after 225 AD for construction; the Oxford colour-coated sherd would imply a date after 250, but may be intrusive.

More than one phase of construction has been recognised in various trenches. On the west rooms 2 (and probably 1) overlay original cross-walls, on the east the outer wall was replaced by another alongside, and in between several other walls were rebuilt either on the same line or immediately adjacent. It is not possible to link up these alterations stratigraphically nor, from the limited dating evidence, to show whether they were contemporary or piecemeal, but the close correspondence between the earlier and later walls in most cases argues that they all represent modifications to a single building rather than successive independent structures.

At the south end the east wall 2034 had been robbed out, and there was no evidence for the two phases of east wall, 300 and 301, seen further north. Based upon the evidence of the 1959 excavation plan the main west and south walls appear to be original, so that Building III was built over boundary wall 2028 from the first, but the alignment of 2034 and the fact that 2041 overlay 2047, which almost certainly equals 1510, strongly suggests that this is the second phase east wall. Possibly the earlier east wall 300 stopped at the north side of Room 9. Alternatively, since 300 and 301 would have coincided by this point, 301 may have overlain 300. It is possible that 300 returned not as 2005 but as 2028; the width of their construction trenches was similar. The first phase of Building III may thus coincide with Building IV phase 4, or may belong a little earlier.

The make-up of the later mortar floors on the east side included Oxford colour-coated sherds, but gully 1514 in the yard to the east, which was cut through this make-up, contained large unabraded sherds of the early 3rd century. The building was thus probably re-floored and enlarged during the third quarter of the century, AD 250–275.

Figure 56 Building III: verandah from the east-south-east with ranging rods in the first phase postholes

Figure 57 Building III: verandah from the north-east alongside the west wall 240, showing the second phase dry-stone wall sitting upon the first phase floor

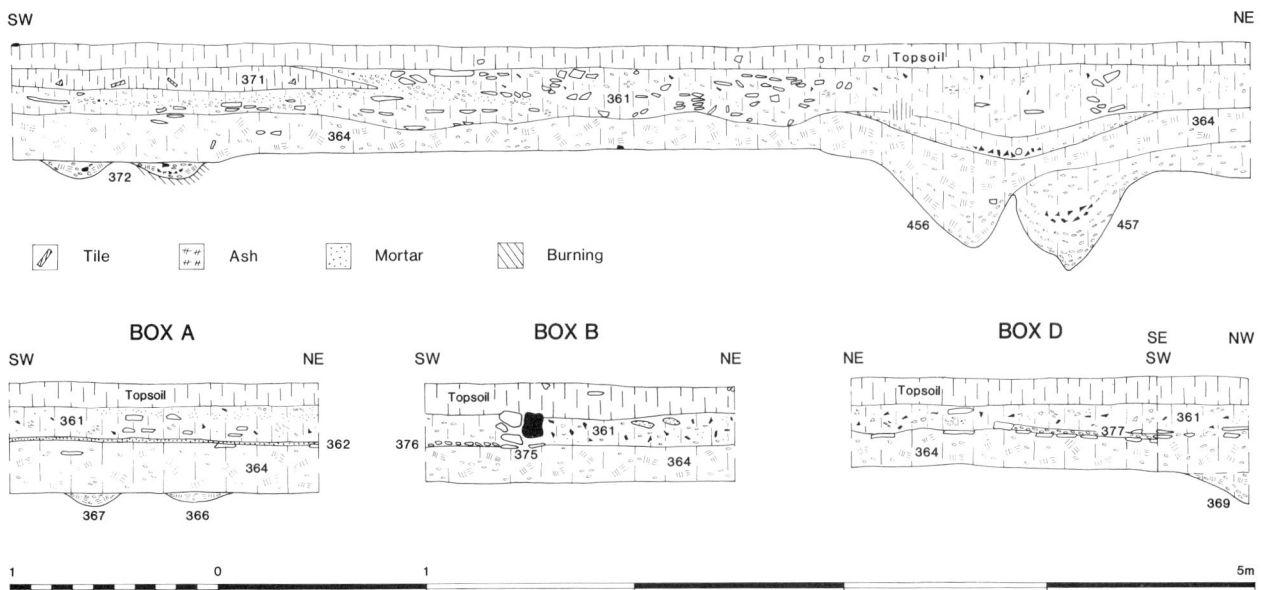

Figure 58 Trenches north-west of Building III: sections

A coin of 355–360 came from the debris among the flues in Room 3 ((Table 21 No. 21), another from an occupation soil overlying destruction debris in the yard to the east (Table 21 No. 28), and later 4th century pottery from debris over the verandah. There was also a clipped siliqua of Honorius in the upper debris (Table 21 No. 16), but it is not certain that this was deposited when the building was first destroyed. More than one phase of robbing may be represented within the debris.

IV.C.9 The villa courtyard

Plans: Figs. 36, 37; Sections: Figs. 44 and 58

The courtyard surrounded by the buildings was only investigated by narrow trenches, and except in the trench west of Building IV only sketch sections were drawn. Two layers of gravel mortar and stone were recorded south of Building I, the lower probably construction spread from it, and gravel or stone spreads occurred in most other trenches. Possibly these layers linked up with those west of Building IV, but were not traceable far as continuous horizons, and there were no spot-heights to help compare levels.

Cut through both surfaces in the middle of the courtyard was an east-west grave 206 containing the body of an adult female, with a piece of gravel conglomerate by her feet (see Table 26). A horse astralagus also came from the fill, but there was no dating evidence. An infant burial was also found in the courtyard beneath a stone (Table 64 on Fiche 2#84), but its precise location is not known.

North-west of the recorded limits of Building III further spreads of gravel or flat stones were recorded (Fig. 58). Beneath these and extending southwards just west of the building was a plough or garden soil (364) truncating the early Roman features. This probably dates between the mid-2nd century and the 4th century, since the overlying surface (362) and dry-stone wall (375) were apparently contemporary with Building III.

IV.D The enclosures west of the villa

Plans: Fig. 59; Fiche 4#16, 17, 29–33, 43–8, 58–9 and 61–2; 131 on Fiche 1#35; 135 on Fiche 1#39. Sections: Figs. 132 on Fiche 1#36, 133 on Fiche 1#37, and 134 on Fiche 1#38

IV.D.1 Introduction

This area showed on air photographs as a trackway with a parallel field boundary 110 m to the north, subdivided into fields and with a group of smaller enclosures along the north edge close to the villa buildings. This was stripped to gravel using John Deere scrapers, removing between 0.2 and 0.35 m of stratigraphy below ploughsoil, which was not recorded.

Only a small sample of the ditches was excavated; many intersections were not investigated and finds were few. Fig. 131 on Fiche 1#35 shows the excavated trenches and the position of the illustrated sections.

IV.D.2 Development

Fig. 59 illustrates a likely sequence:

1. A trackway 433–434 with parallel boundary 387 was laid out on a northwest alignment. Cross-ditches were then dug between 433 and 387 at right angles, creating large rectangular fields. The north ends of the cross-ditches 426 etc lay outside the excavated area, but cropmarks do not continue as far as 387, so access between fields was probably on this side. There are no gaps along 433, although changes in fill hint that these may have been dug through.
Within the easternmost field was a well 470 and an enclosure, 422–430, with one entrance from the track alongside 387 and another at the rounded end.
Ditch 413–417 cut across pits of the mid-2nd century (Fig. 125 on Fiche 1#29), and its continuation 439 across ditches slightly later. The field-system thus probably post-dates AD 160, but since the pottery from it was also 2nd century it was probably laid out soon after this. The relationship of this system to the ditches surrounding the villa buildings, 2449, 2429 and 132, which are on a different alignment, is not clear (see Ch. IV.C.2 and Ch. IV.C.6).

2. A square field made up of ditches 440, 421 and 436 was created south of enclosure 422 and 430, defining the other sides of trackways alongside 413 and 426. Access to this from enclosure 422–430 was facilitated by an entrance created across the south side of 422. The track alongside 387 may have been blocked by 423 and alternative access provided across 433.

3. The entrance between 422 and the field south of it was modified by the addition of ditch 435 to create a three-way junction with gateways of equal size. Further north-west it was possibly at this stage that cross-ditch 391 was replaced by a parallel ditch 392. Neither ditch was however dated.

4. Ditch 421 was extended, blocking access from the small enclosure to the square field. A new ditch 424 was dug alongside 423 curving to meet 387. This prevented direct access between fields alongside 387. A small blocking ditch 479 across the line of trackway 433–434 may have been dug at this stage, and a curving ditch 386 dug to replace 434 was probably added soon after (see Stage 5). Entry to the fields further north was now via the gap between 433 and 479 or following 426 and 424.

5. A new rectangular enclosure 403 etc was tacked onto the north of the field 421, and cut across 430, the east side of the round-ended enclosure (Fig. 133 on Fiche 1#37). 421 was perhaps shortened to allow access from the field both to this new enclosure and to 422, which continued in use. The north side of 430 presumably continued in use, as without it 422 would not make an effective enclosure. Probably at this stage 416 was dug, using the disused well 470 as a sump at the west end. This cut across the former track alongside 413. Cropmarks suggest (Frontispiece and Fig. 3) that 416 may have joined 132 at its east end, modifying the villa enclosure on the north side.

6. At the northern end of the field closest to the villa ditch 426 was replaced by a pair of parallel ditches 425 and 427 forming a trackway. These cut across trackway 433–434 and access between the small enclosures and the fields further north-west. The former entrance between 424 and 426 was blocked off by ditch 432; unlike 405 ditch 424 was not recut.
A new enclosure 402 was dug respecting ditches 421 and 401, and joined onto a new south-eastern boundary to the fields, ditch 419. Access to 402 was probably at the east corner, where the line of 402 was offset from that of 416. There was no direct access from the villa buildings; and the recutting of 416 and digging of 419, both as deep V-profiled ditches, probably represented the creation of a more substantial enclosure ditch around the villa (Fig. 134 on Fiche 1#38). This would presumably have joined ditch 1604=2008 on the south side of Building III.
Later ditch 418 was added continuing the line of 419 across the end of enclosure 402, and 416 and 419 were recut.

7. A stone culvert was built within 418, probably to support a bridge to maintain access to enclosure 402. The sides of 402 and 418 at their junction were revetted with rough stone walling (Figs. 62 and 63; Fig. 135 on Fiche 1#39). Ditch 420 and a large shallow hollow 409, measuring 16.75 m × 3.95 m × 0.60 m deep, were dug along the north-east side of 402 (Fig. 60), 420 running into 418.
409 was filled with black soil and charcoal, which also occurred in the lowest fills of 420 and the north corner of 402 adjacent (Fig. 134 on Fiche 1#38). There was no sign of in situ burning in the cuts across 409, but these were too few to be certain that burning did not occur within it. There was similarly no sign of any postholes or other structural traces. Sunken features like 409 have been interpreted as structures with turf walls, particularly animal pens (Neal 1978, 48–9 and Fig. 15) but there was no indication that the floor had been trampled, or was covered in manure. Possibly 409 was a repository for hypocaust-ash, which was later mucked out onto the fields.
At some stage a dry-stone wall was built at the junction of ditches 422, 408 and 405, and 405, 408 and 432 were backfilled behind it with gravel and grey silt while 422 was deepened (Fig. 133 on Fiche 1#37). It is possible that the enclosure consisting of 403, 401 and 406 was backfilled at the same time, as this also contained grey silt, but there was a large quantity of building debris

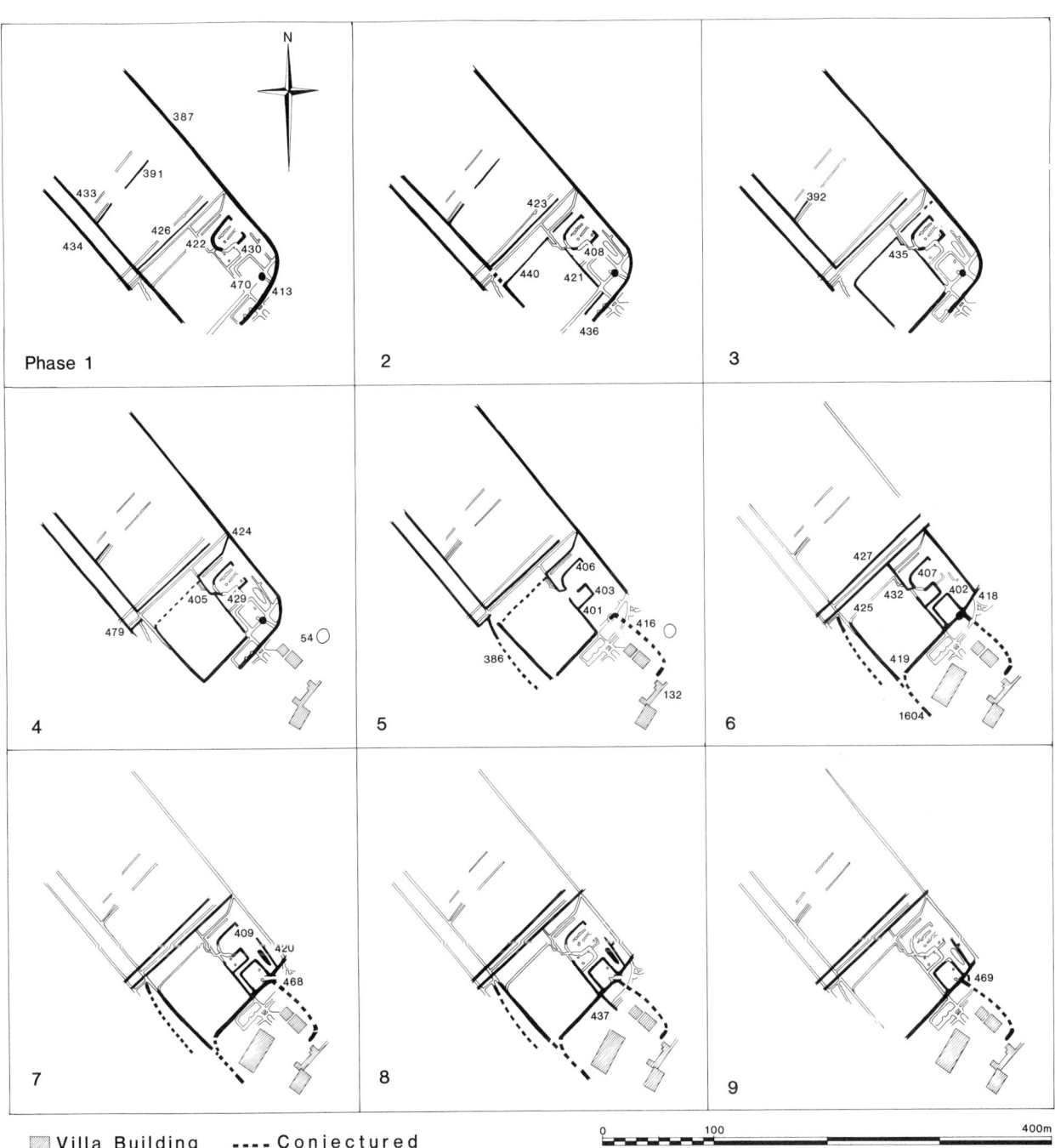

Figure 59 Phased plan of the development of the western enclosures (2nd–4th centuries)

Figure 60 Enclosures west of the villa: Pit 409 from the north-west

Figure 61 Enclosures west of the villa: 'Corndrier' 469 from the north-east

Figure 62 Enclosures west of the villa: Culvert 468 and 'Corndrier' 469 from the west, showing how 468 was cut away by recutting ditches 402 and 416

in this, and this enclosure was probably backfilled later on.

8. Enclosure 401, 403 and 406 was filled in, together with adjacent pits 451 and a slot 431 to the north. It may have been at this time that ditch 437 was dug running southeast from 419 parallel to 416. If this ditch continued it would have divided Building I from Building III.

9. Ditches 418, 416, 419 and 402 were recut, cutting through the west wall of the culvert, now silted up (Fig. 62 and 63). All these ditches and 420 silted up with a distinctive grey silt. The north corner of 402 contained building rubble, and may have been backfilled to provide access into this enclosure; this may alternatively have occurred earlier when enclosure ditches 401, 403 and 406 were backfilled. At the corner of 416 and 418 two parallel narrow stone walls were built, feature 469, with a channel cut into the gravel leading from one end down into 418. This was presumably for drainage (Fig. 135 on Fiche 1#39 and 61).

This channel cut the gravel infill behind the culvert walls, but it is not known whether it was contemporary with the culvert or the later recut. However since 469 lay across the line of access it is considered to be later. 469 was interpreted by Margaret Jones as a corndrier, but there was no evidence of burning inside the walls or at either end. Possibly the walls supported a water-trough or similar container.

IV.E The enclosures north and immediately east of the villa

Figs. 34 and 112

A regular grid of small rectangular enclosures was visible as cropmarks in this area (Fig. 2), and the cropmark evidence was partly confirmed by soilmarks seen from the air after stripping (Fig. 3). Only two of the ditches lay within the excavated area, 47 and 58, and these cut early Roman enclosures 56 and 40–41, so date after the mid-second century (Fig. 34). At the south end cropmarks suggest that the system was tied into the boundaries of the southern enclosure group (Frontispiece and Fig. 112), which were in use from the late 2nd century until the 4th century AD.

Two phases of the ditches around the villa are visible both on the cropmarks and in the stripped areas photographed from the air in 1957. These are on different alignments some 5–10 degrees apart, but the relationship of these two ditch systems was not tested by excavation. One of these alignments, to which 47 and 58 belong, clearly matches that of the trackway and fields west of the villa, and these probably originated in the later 2nd century (Ch. IV.B.2 and Ch. IV.D.2). This enclosure system does not however match the orientation of the early villa buildings I and IV. The other alignment corresponds closely to that of these buildings and of the mid-2nd century villa enclosure ditches (see Ch. IV.C.6 etc), and this may be the original alignment.

The basic unit of the layout was approximately 27 m (90′) long and 16.3m (54′) wide, and multiples of this also occurred in the ditch system west of the villa. The cropmarks did not extend east of the road, and stripping confirmed that the enclosures did not extend this far. Attached to later Roman enclosures north-east of the villa however (Fig. 73 Phase 11) were 3 parallel ditches forming two more of these strips of standard width. Further strips may have existed south of the later Roman enclosures south-east of the villa (see Figs. 112 and 115 and Ch. VI.3). These ditches were later 3rd or 4th century AD.

The northern limit of the regular enclosures is not known; recollections by local amateurs of stripping prior to 1957 indicate parallel ditches running from north-east to south-west. Some radical change must have occurred where the regular grid met the boundary ditches 532, 719 etc running north-west (see Ch. IV.F.5).

IV.F The Later Roman enclosures and droveways east of the villa

IV.F.1 Introduction

(see Figs. 1 and 66)

East of the small rectangular enclosures around the villa buildings was an open area at the junction of two ditched droveways approaching from the south and south-east. The northern boundary ditch of the south-eastern trackway and the western boundary ditch of the south one, which turned north-west, formed the north and south limits of the open area. These ditches were overlaid by a succession of small ditched enclosures, forming two groups facing one another across the open area. Alongside the eastern boundary of the open area a gravel-pit developed, and north of this at the junction of the droveways were pens or timber buildings. In the middle of the open area a small circular enclosure was dug.

When excavation resumed in 1961 two areas had already been extracted, one next to the modern road north of the enclosures and another between the two enclosure groups. The air photographs, which show the enclosure groups very clearly, do not indicate anything substantial in these areas. In contrast to the field in which the villa buildings lay this field had been disturbed by medieval ridge-and-furrow, and preservation above gravel was poor. By the

Figure 63 Enclosures west of the villa: Culvert 468 and 'Corndrier' 469 from the north-east, showing the channel running from 469 into 468 and the south wall of 468 cut away by the recut of ditch 418

time excavation began the western part of the northern enclosures had already been stripped. Sections on the edge of the stripped area show that 0.15 m of subsoil at most had survived beneath the ridges, and that the furrows came right down onto gravel. The remaining part of these enclosures was stripped down to gravel and excavated as before.

The southern group of enclosures was trial-trenched before stripping. The trenches were only 3 m × 0.9 m, but it appeared that ridge-and-furrow had again left only 0.15 m of subsoil surviving beneath the ridges. The trial trenches showed that the cropmarks were of ditched enclosures similar to the northern group, and that there were no substantial Romanised stone buildings, so the southern enclosures were also stripped to gravel before excavation.

In 1963 during Margaret Jones' absence the eastern end of the northern enclosure group was excavated by Ernest Greenfield. The surviving evidence from both enclosure groups suggests a similar range of features and functions, and both seem to have been active in the later 3rd and 4th centuries. The ditches themselves are numerous, usually recut, and their interrelationships complicated and often unclear. It has therefore been decided to treat certain classes of feature common to both enclosure groups together, and then to discuss the development of the ditched enclosures separately. Discrete features such as the circular enclosure 481 and the gravel-pit area (660 and following) will be described last.

IV.F.2 'Corndrier' and ovens

Distribution: Fig. 64.
Plans: Fiche 4#10, 24, 38–9, 53–4, 77, 91; Fig. 133 on Fiche 1#37 and 134 on Fiche 1#38.
Sections: Figs. 136 on Fiche 1#40, 137 on Fiche 1#41, 139 on Fiche 1#45, and 144 on Fiche 1#50

One T-shaped 'corndrier' 590 was found in the northern enclosure group, oriented with the bar of the T to the north-west and parallel to the linear droveway ditch. The raised floor did not survive; the unmortared walls of limestone survived two courses deep (Fig. 136 on Fiche 1#40). A sample was taken from the burnt soil in between the walls (see Ch. 5.16 on Fiche 2#84).

Within the enclosures there were 33 features with reddened gravel sides (Table 41 on Fiche 1#42). These were of two types, 7 circular or oval pits and 26 linear features. At the simplest the linear type consisted of a trench, one half of which was burnt, eg 822 and possibly 781 (Fig. 137 on Fiche 1#41), but most were 'tadpole-shaped', with a bulbous and usually deeper 'head' and a narrower and generally longer 'tail'. Burning almost always occurred around the bulbous end, especially at its junction with the narrower channel; the head was the chamber, the tail the flue and the stokehole. The high degree of burning suggests frequent use.

Figure 64 Late Roman enclosures: distribution plan of ovens and 'corndrier' east of the villa

The largest group surrounded the 'corndrier'. The 'tadpoles' in this group were all from 1.2–2.00 m long with the chamber about 0.6 m wide and 0.20–0.35 m deep. Some had wide flues with stone slabs at the junction of the flue and chamber (Fig. 137 on Fiche 1#41 Nos. 778 and 780), presumably to increase draw as at Winterton (Stead 1976, 32–5 and Fig. 18). This probably reflects a different method of stoking. The narrow tadpole flues were too small to stand in and were presumably worked from the ground surface, the wider-flues by standing in the stokehole. Some chambers were rectangular, and that of 601 was larger than its short flue. 593 (Fig. 137 on Fiche 1#41) apparently consisted of three chambers in series, and may have been stoked from two ends at once.

The absence of pottery wasters or of ironworking debris makes it unlikely that these features were kilns or furnaces, and their concentration around 590 probably indicates a connection between it and them. Soil samples from them contained hardly any grain or chaff (Ch. V.18); possibly they were bread ovens.

Other features without reddened sides but with burnt fills and the characteristic 'tadpole' shape are also listed in Table 41 on Fiche 1#42. Given the low temperature at which reddening occurs (Stead 1976, 30–35) however, they were probably not ovens.

There was a stone lining around the chamber in, for example, 521 and 598, and one oven was possibly clay-lined. Layers of burnt stones might have been from collapsed floors, but no supports for such floors were found in situ. One possible clay pedestal fragment was recovered (Ch. 5.11.j on Fiche 2#68), and temporary floors using clay plates like the fragments from the early Roman occupation (Ch. V.11) may have been employed. However, most of these ovens did not appear to have raised floors; in 598, 781, 530 and 594 charcoal and ash on the oven bottom was directly overlaid by collapsed oven superstructure.

Fired clay was found in most 'tadpole' ovens, though samples were only kept from 781. The superstructure seems to have consisted of a criss-cross vertical framework of wattles plastered thickly with clay (see also Ch. 5.11.j on Fiche 2#68). Oven walls were at least 90mm thick. Layers of burnt clayey soil could indicate superstructures made of turves, as in surface-built pottery kilns of the early Roman period in the Nene Valley (Woods 1974, 262–281). Burnt stones in the top of one oven may have come from a stone superstructure. These materials are suitable for temporary rather than permanent structures.

The circular pits also contained fired clay and were possibly roofed with clay domes. 647 was lined with flat stones and fired clay surrounding a circular Stonesfield slate (Fig. 65; Fig. 106 No.131). Pit 494 was oval and burning was concentrated at the deeper end. It had a secondary lining of stones, which may have divided the pit into a small circular chamber with a stokehole to the south-west. Elsewhere however vertical stones were probably simply to stabilise the side where ovens were cut into earlier features.

The ovens in the south-eastern enclosures of the group were more varied. Two were simply lengths of trench burnt at one end, such as are known at Winterton (Stead 1976, 30–35 and Fig. 18). 782, 783 and 787 were extremely small with very short flues, sometimes wider than the chambers (Fig. 137 on Fiche 1#41). 697 apparently had a narrow small chamber and a very broad stokehole, which is unusual for this site, although the type is common enough at Winterton.

The majority of the ovens were orientated with the head to the north-west (Table 41 on Fiche 1#42), probably in response to the prevailing wind direction. The gullies forming a circular enclosure 12–13 m across around corndrier 590 (Fig. 73 Phases 6–9) may however have held windbreak fences; at the Churchill pottery kilns a circular stone building was built around a pottery drier (Young 1977, 24–6). The ovens further east had a much greater range of size, shape and orientation. One closely-spaced group (697–699 and 772) were all oriented in different directions, and may have been roofed over.

The ovens around 590 included several intercutting groups, and were thus in use for a long time. 609 contained only 1st/2nd century finds, which would accord with the first phase of enclosure, while the corndrier was not abandoned until the later 3rd or 4th century. These ovens too could well have continued into the 4th century.

The southern enclosures contained only four ovens, two 'tadpoles' and two simple circular pits (Table 41 on Fiche 1#42). Unusually one 'tadpole' had a stone lining, as did oval pit 860. 860 cut ditch 836 and was probably late 3rd or 4th century, and 884 was also probably late. There were no large groups of ovens, suggesting that activities connected with ovens were concentrated in the northern enclosures (Fig. 64).

IV.F.3 Pits and hollows

All pits and hollows are listed in Table 76 on Fiche 3#2. Those in the northern and southern enclosure groups can be divided into three groups, large shallow hollows with a characteristic grey silt filling (3a), deep pits (3b) and an assortment of smaller pits and scoops. The last category is dealt with in describing the development of the two enclosure groups, Ch. IV.F.5 and Ch. IV.F.6.

IV.F.3.a *The silt-filled pits*

Distribution: Fig. 66.
Plate: Fig. 67.
Plans/Sections: Figs. 68, 141 on Fiche 1#47 and 143 on Fiche 1#49

This was a distinctive group of large shallow hollows with one homogeneous clayey silt fill. Five lay roughly in line north of circular feature 481, and several others close

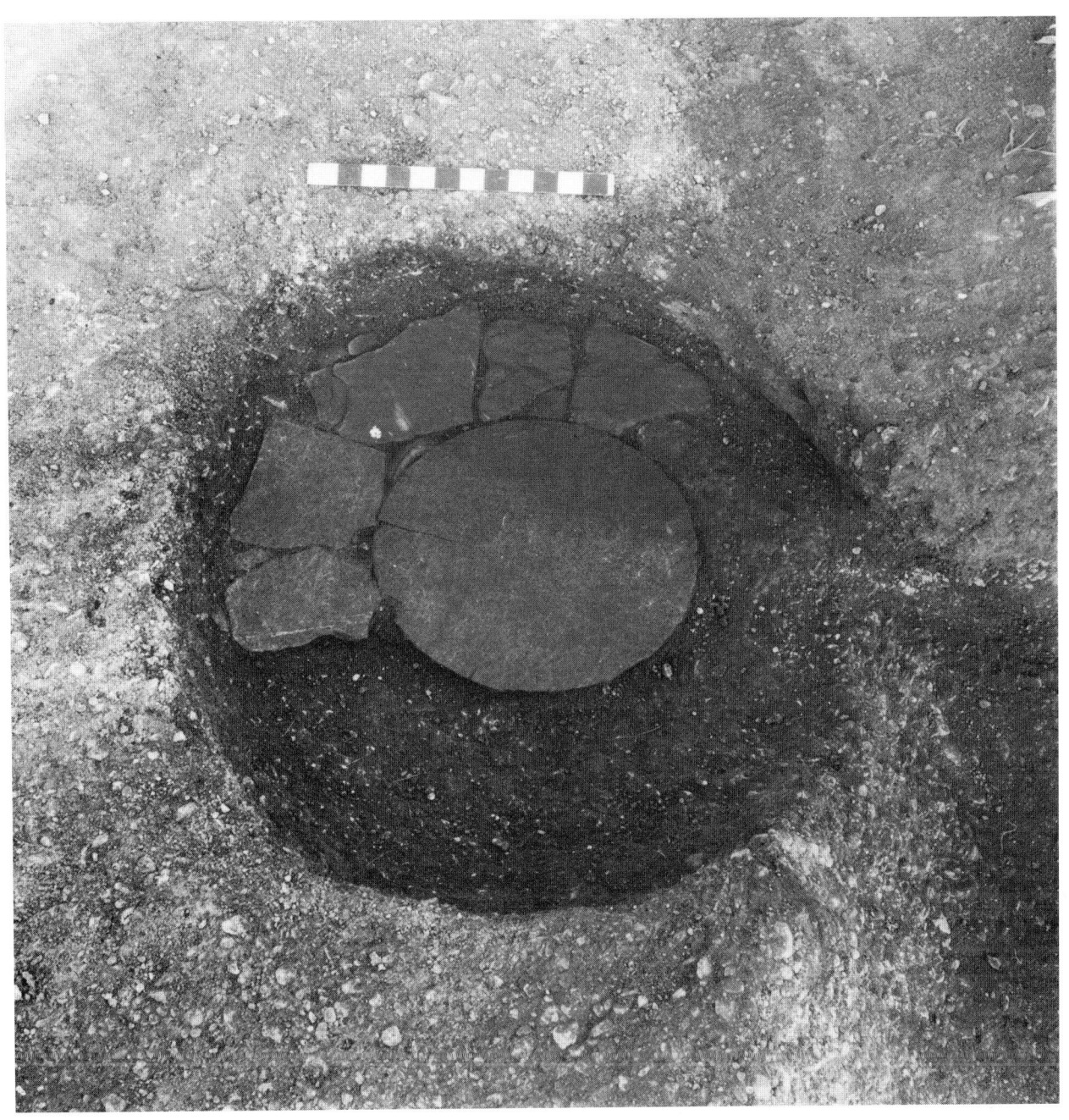

Figure 65 Enclosures east of the villa: oven-base of Stonesfield slate in 647 from the south

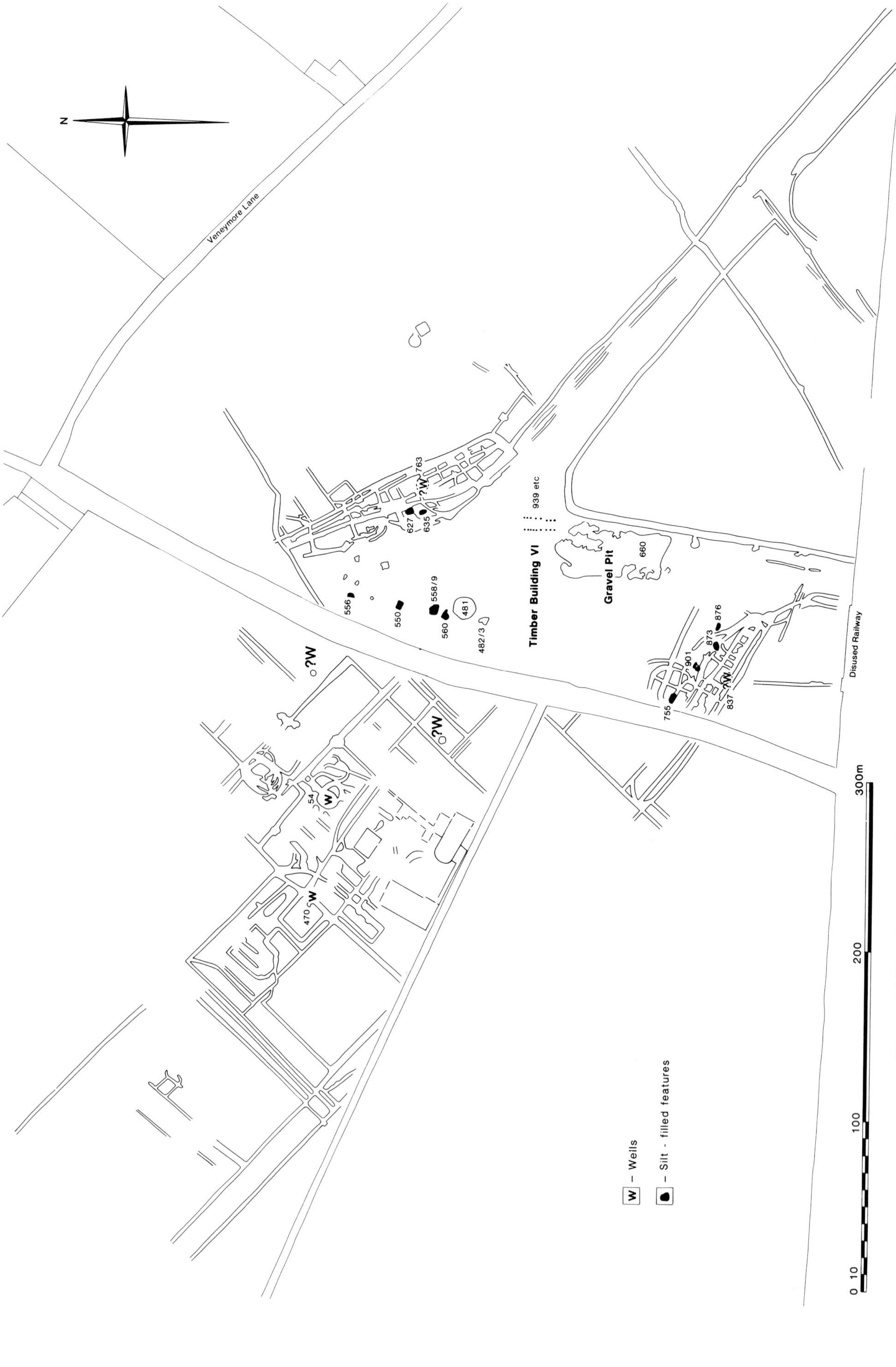

Figure 66 Distribution of wells and Late Roman silt-filled features

to or overlying the ditches of the northern and southern enclosure groups (Fig. 66). They were approximately sub-rectangular, and most had steep sides and flat bottoms, but some had deeper areas or scoops in the bottom or cut-outs in the sides (Fig. 68; Fig. 67). 550 and 558 had a small circular pit in the middle, containing the same fill as the rest of the feature, and there were single postholes at one corner or side in others. Layers of flat stones commonly occurred towards the top of the fill, and in the southern enclosures pitched stones (876) had been laid over pit 873 and were covered by an occupation layer (875).

Almost all these hollows contained 4th century finds, often in very large quantities, and 560 and 855 were dated by Constantinian coins to after 337AD and 350AD respectively (Table 21). None were cut by Roman features, but the pitched stones and subsequent occupation over 873 shows that they were part of the late Roman settlement.

The homogeneity of their fills and the absence of gravel spills suggests that these features were backfilled. This is supported by the character of the finds, which included small quantities of building debris, painted plaster and tesserae in particular, and bits of worked stone. The worked stone and occasional tesserae perhaps suggest that this is the residue sorted out from robbing but later discarded. Alternatively, in view of the large quantities of pottery, it may have come from middens.

The function of these features is difficult to determine. None of them contained the two opposing postholes characteristic of Anglo-Saxon sunken huts, and the majority are rather irregular for buildings. Postholes in the corner of 877, 560 and 873 may however indicate a structure over these pits, and the central deeper hollows in 550 and 558 could have been for a central post. Alternatively these might have been sumps for drainage. The deliberate recesses in the sides of some of these pits suggest steps down into them. Sunken-floored structures are attested on other Roman sites, and have already been discussed in relation to feature 409 (Fig. 131 on Fiche 1#35; Fig. 134 on Fiche 1#38; Fig. 60); they may have been underground stores, perhaps connected with dairying, for which sunken structures were in use until quite recently in France (Chapelot & Fossier 1985, 120–121). Other interpretations such as gravel pits are possible in some cases, but others of these pits were only cut a little way into gravel.

IV.F.3.b Deep pits

Plans: Figs. 73, 74, Fiche 4#24–5, 39–40, 54, 90–92; Sections: Fig. 139 on Fiche 1#45; Fig. 144 on Fiche 1#50

Five deep pits (579, 582, 611, 763 and 764) were excavated in the northern enclosure group and two (837 and 868) in the southern group, some of which were not bottomed. An equal number of large soilmarks were not investigated.

Those that were fully excavated were not above 2 m deep (Fig. 139 on Fiche 1#45), and since they were largely backfilled with occupation debris were probably rubbish pits. 837 contained six unused joiner's dogs and usable rotary querns, perhaps thrown out during a major reorganisation (see Ch. V.6 and Table 51 on Fiche 2#58). One or two had little debris in their lower fills, and their use for rubbish may have been secondary. A cluster (579, 582 and 611) in the same enclosure as the 'corndrier' and ovens may possibly have been storage pits of Iron Age type, as this area seems to have been connected with grain processing. One of the partly excavated pits in each enclosure group (763 and 837) had vertical and undercut sides and may have been a well. There is no other evidence for a water supply in these enclosures.

Most of the pits were dated by coins or pottery to the 4th century (see Table 21 and Table 79 on Fiche 3#16). This late date is also emphasised by their stratigraphic positions, almost all of them overlying intermediate or late phases of the enclosure ditches, viz. 579, 582, 763, 764, 837 and 868. One or two however were overlaid by ditches (eg 611 by 612).

IV.F.4 Later Roman burials

IV.F.4.a Distribution

Figs. 69–72 and 30

Seventeen extended inhumation burials were found during the 1957–1965 excavations, all but one in and around the enclosures east of the villa. Six others had previously been hastily recorded south-west of the southern enclosures in 1928, and a seventh was found further south in 1984. There were also three neonatal infant burials, two in the villa and one in the northern enclosures. A more detailed description of the burials by Mary Harman will be found in Ch. V.16 and a summary of the age, sex, orientation and other information is given in Table 26. The full tables of the skeletal information (Table 64 on Fiche 2#84 and Table 65 on Fiche 2#87) are included in the microfiche report.

IV.F.4.b Burials in the villa

Grave 206 lay in the middle of the villa courtyard (Fig. 37). It was cut through the latest laid gravel surface, and its position suggests a very late date in the occupation. Fragments of skull probably belonging to another such burial were recovered from pit 1408 cut into the corridor of Building IV. This feature is dated by a coin to after AD 350 (Table 21).

IV.F.4.c Burials in the northern enclosure group

Ten burials were found in two groups, four in one enclosure towards the west end and five within the southernmost enclosure 825, with one more just outside it. 584 was a double burial. 584 and 585 were adjacent and in line, lying in a shallow ditch 586 parallel to the enclosure boundary

Figure 67 Enclosures east of the villa: Silt-filled pit 550 from the south-east

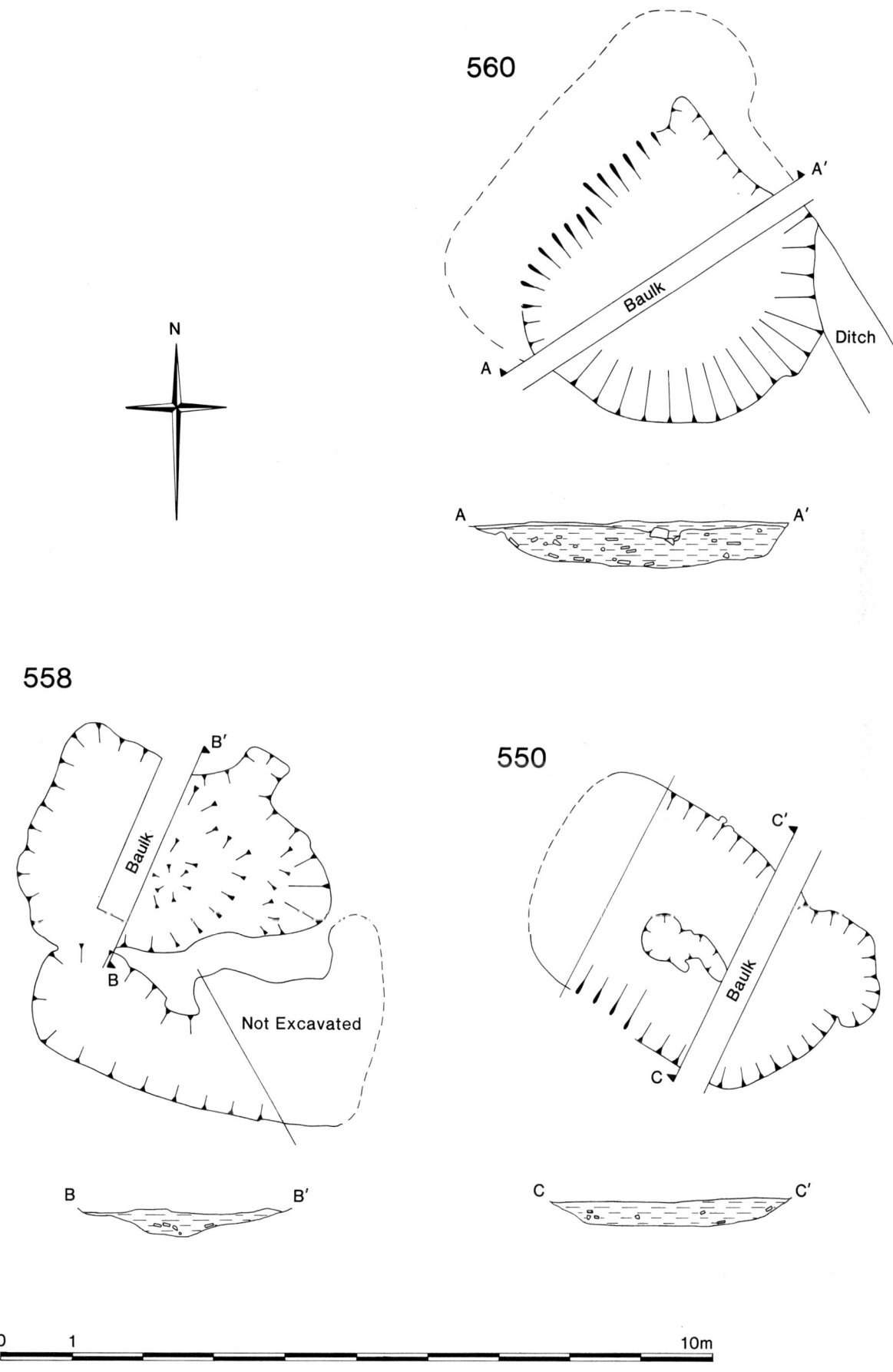

Figure 68 Late Roman silt-filled pits: plans and sections

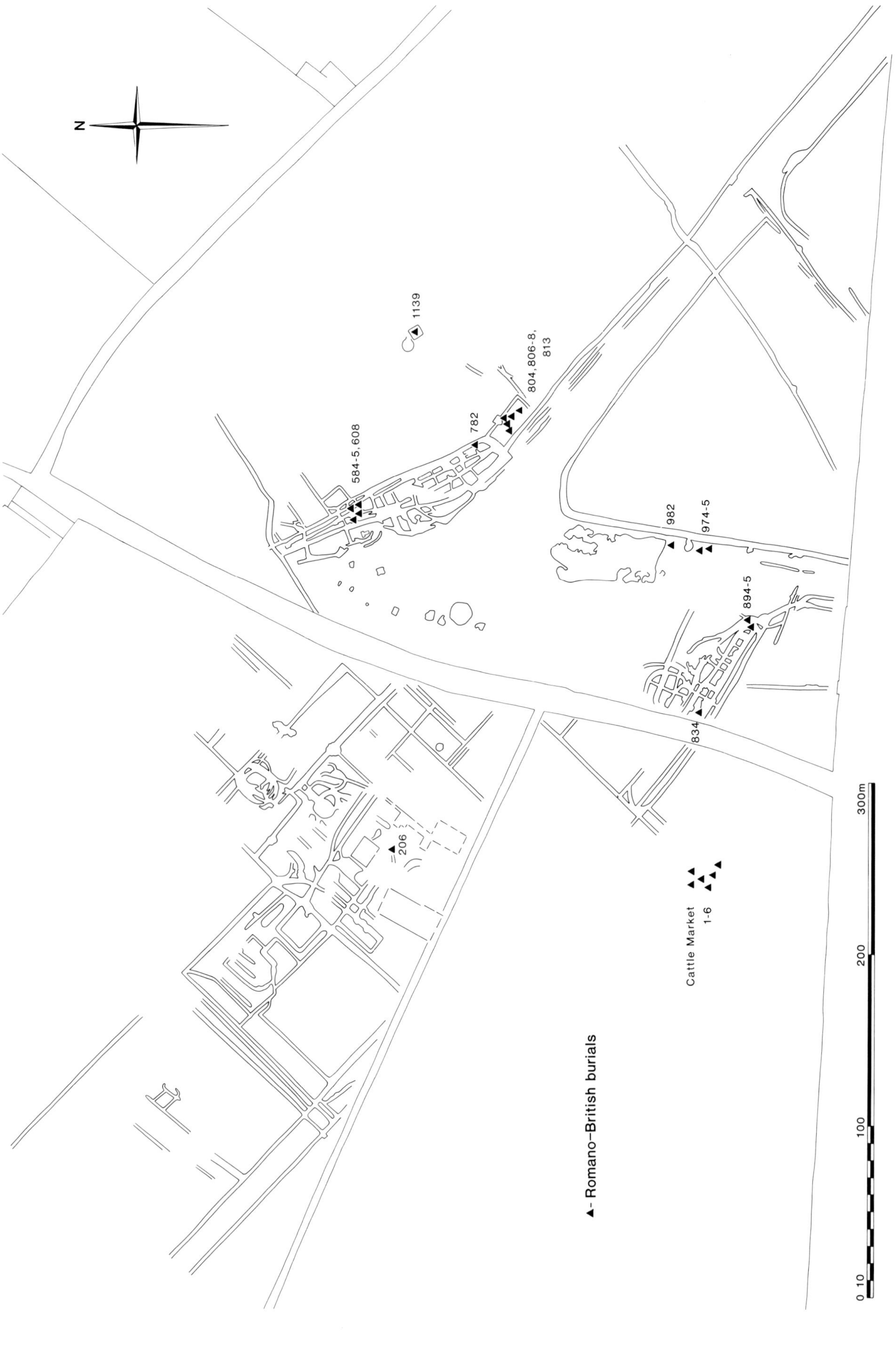

98 *Roughground Farm, Lechlade, Gloucestershire: a prehistoric and Roman landscape*

Figure 69 Distribution plan of Romano-British burials

Figure 70 Late Roman burial 206 found in the middle of the villa courtyard, taken from the east

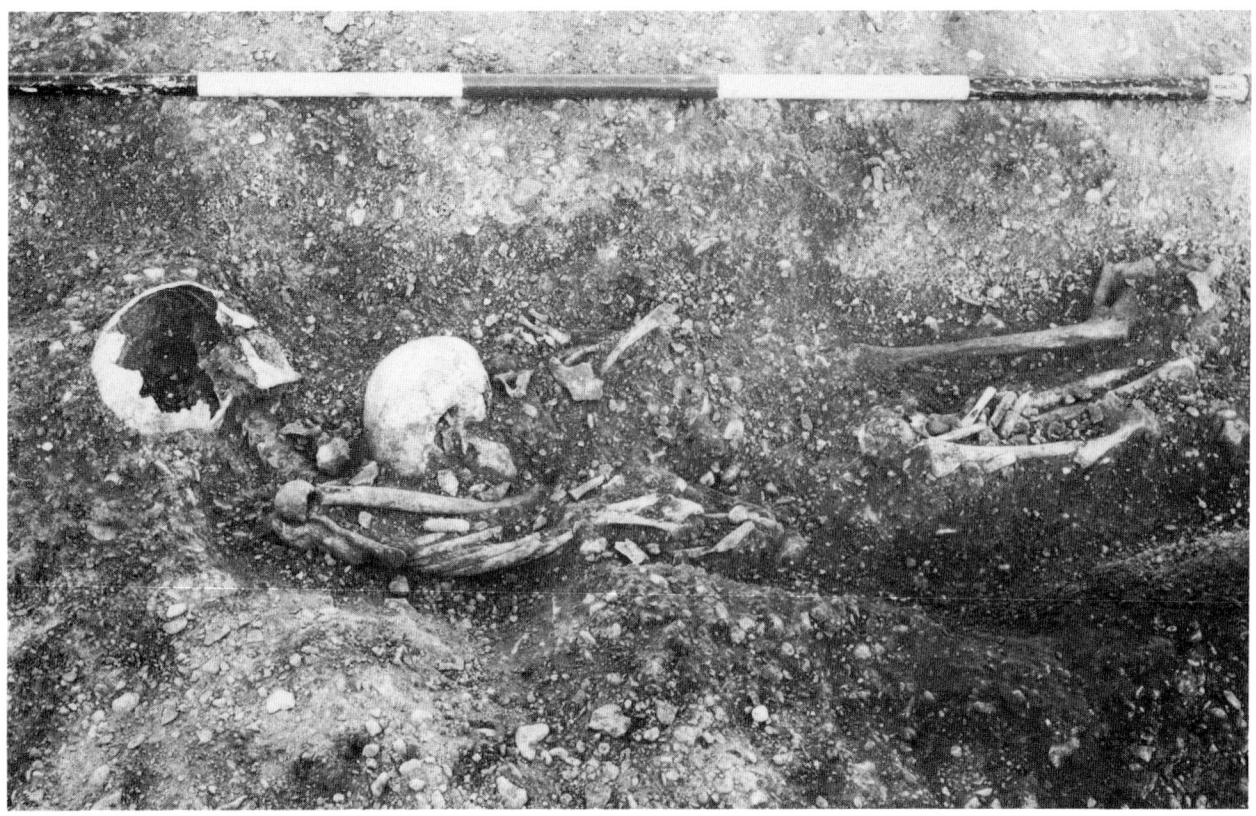

Figure 71 Late Roman double burial 584 in the northern enclosures, viewed from the south-west

Figure 72 Late Roman decapitated burial 894 from the north-east. Skeleton damaged by scraper

ditches, 608 was parallel to 584 further south-west. Part of an adult was also found in 584, suggesting either that there had been further burials on top or that this grave had been reused.

Within 825 graves 804 and 807 were in line, and 806 parallel to 804. These and 813 formed a tight group with 808 a little further off. Between 804 and 806 and parallel was a grave-shaped feature 805, and another 809 lay further south-east, also aligned north-west. No bones were recovered from either, but it seems likely that they were graves whose bodies had been scraped away, making seven graves in this enclosure. Just outside the north-west corner of 825 was another grave 782. None of these burials had any grave-goods. They were mostly in line with the axis of the later Roman enclosures, not with the much earlier enclosure 825.

IV.F.4.d Burials in the southern enclosure group and alongside the boundary ditch

In the southern enclosures grave 834 lay within ditch 833 on the alignment of the enclosure boundaries, 894 and 895 in the tops of ditches at the east end.

Three further burials lay alongside boundary ditch 959/960. 974 and 975 were apparently adjacent and were aligned parallel to the boundary ditch, 982 lay further north and was oriented north-west.

IV.F.4.e Other burials

Six burials were recorded by Miss B M Blackwood during construction of the Lechlade cattle market in 1928, west of the southern enclosure group (Fig. 69). Two were destroyed before she arrived. The other four were cut c 0.6 m into gravel, and were orientated with heads to the north, three lying parallel to one another, the fourth north of these. No bones were recovered for examination, but one is noted as a young female, and the flexed burial as an old woman. One of these burials was accompanied by a greyware 'olla'. Further human burials were destroyed without record when gravel quarrying began in the field immediately to the W (letter of 2nd July 1930 to E T Leeds at Ashmolean Museum). No further details are given.

One more burial 1700, which was oriented west-east, was recovered south of the excavated area at No. 18 Hambridge Lane in builders trenches (not on plan). I am indebted to S Palmer for information concerning this burial.

IV.F.4.f Points of interest

One burial from the northern enclosures and one from the southern ones, both middle-aged women, were decapitated and the head placed between the legs. Two burials, one alongside the boundary ditch 959/960 and the other 1700 south of the main excavations, were prone. Grave 975 alongside 959/960 contained a bracelet (Fig. 93 No. 11), and several graves contained sandal studs, notably 585 and 974.

For discussion of these burials see Ch. V.16 and Ch. VI.5.

IV.F.5 The northern enclosure group

Plan: Fig. 73; 138 on Fiche 1#44; Fiche 4#3, 9–12, 22–26, 36–40, 53–5, Sections: Figs. 139 on Fiche 1#45, 140 on Fiche 1#46, 141 on Fiche 1#47

IV.F.5.a Introduction

The earliest features were Neolithic pits (see Ch. II). At the north end of the area ditch 484 was probably Early Iron Age (Ch. III.B.1.a). Several adjacent circular pits 505–507 may also have been Iron Age, but produced no finds (see Fiche 4#3 and Fiche 4#10).

The first Romano-British feature was the north boundary ditch of the 'green lane'. This was overlaid by a succession of linked enclosures which were sub-rectangular, often sharing a common boundary on the north-east, and which were frequently recut. The enclosures in the middle of the group shifted their limits several times, and constant recutting makes dating and elucidation of a development very difficult.

Fig. 138 on Fiche 1#44 shows the excavated trenches. Only 20–25% of the ditches in the western half of the group were excavated, and only some 10–13% of the enclosure group as a whole. Discrete features were dealt with more fully, almost all being half-sectioned at the least. Most of these ie pits, silt pits, burials and ovens, have been described already (Ch. IV.F.1–Ch. IV.F.4).

IV.F.5.b The enclosure ditches

The first addition to the linear boundary (hereafter 532–4) was probably enclosure 825 (Fig. 73 Stage 2). which had a four-post structure in one corner. Lengths of ditch approximately parallel to 532–4 may have formed a narrow trackway behind it leading down to enclosure 825 (Stage 2). These ditches contained only 2nd century finds.

The earliest enclosures south-west of the boundary probably had straight sides with right-angled corners like 825. One enclosed a corndrier (Stage 3); its ditches were cut by early 3rd century features (see Stage 6). Subsequently these enclosures cut across 532–4, running up to a new boundary north-east of it (Stage 4).

Most of the features in these enclosures lay south-west of the former boundary 532–4, and the few pits and burials north-east of this were all 4th century (Ch. IV.F.3–Ch. IV.F.4), perhaps suggesting that activity areas were established early on, and did not move when the enclosures

102 *Roughground Farm, Lechlade, Gloucestershire: a prehistoric and Roman landscape*

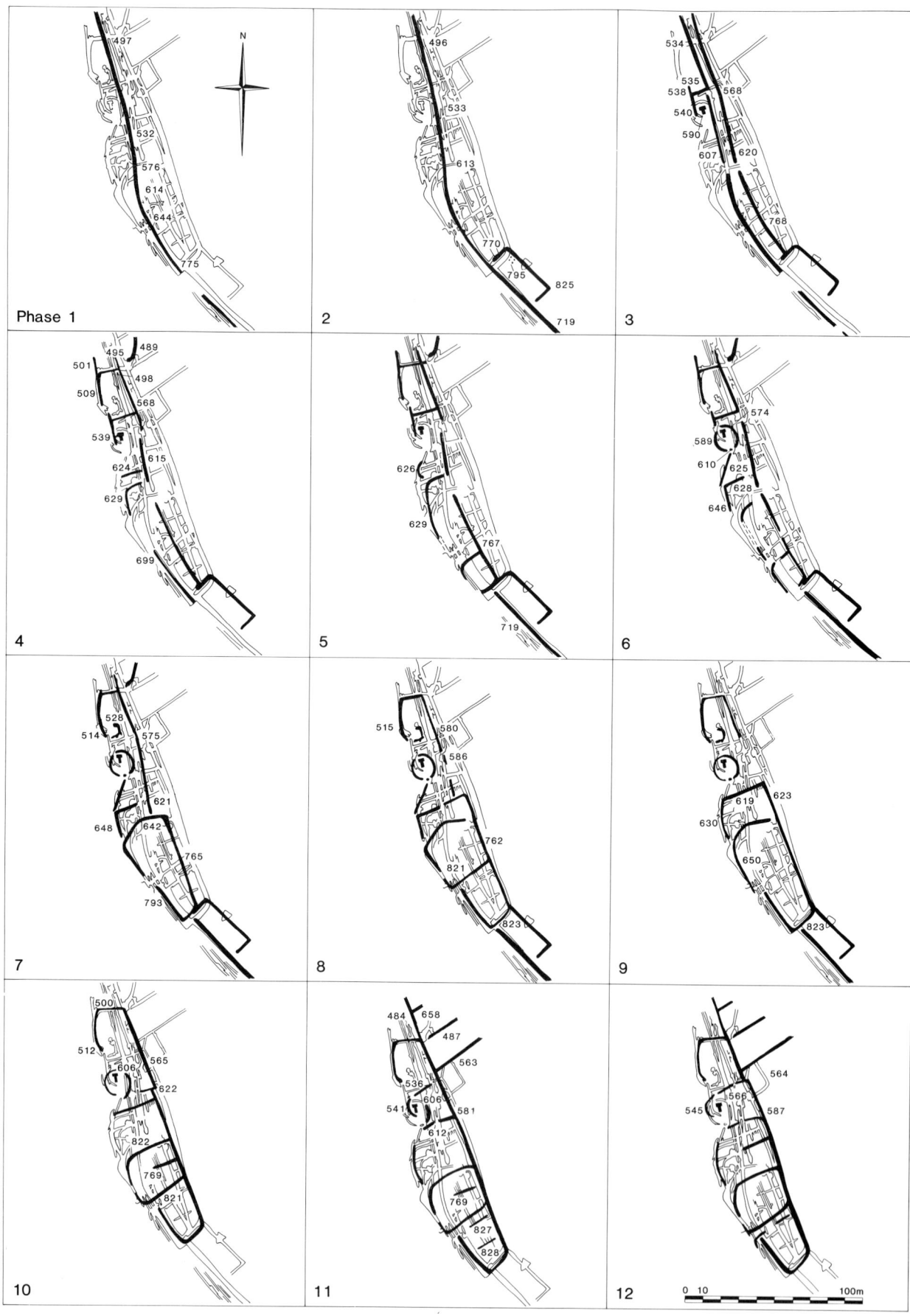

Figure 73 Development plan of northern enclosure group (2nd–4th centuries)

increased in size. However this difference could be due to different use of the rear part of these enclosures.

South-east of the corndrier ditched enclosures at this stage are few. Beyond 624 and 627 divisions, if present at all, were only delineated by narrow slight slots such as 698 and 824 (Stages 5 and 6). The northernmost enclosure 501 etc was frequently recut, the later cuts becoming deeper. The deep cuts can be dated to the later 3rd century AD. This enclosure contained three ovens, an assortment of small pits and postholes. At the back of the enclosure a partly articulated horse was buried in rectangular pit 573.

The T-shaped corndrier 590 was later enclosed by arcs of gully 574, 575 and 589, dating to the late 2nd/early 3rd century. 589 was cut by another curving gully 545 which contained late 3rd or 4th century material (see Stage 12). It is clear from the numerous gullies surrounding 590 that it had a long life. Clustered around it were many ovens (Fiche 4#24), which often intercut (see Ch. IV.F.2 above). This was probably a bakery.

At the southern end of the enclosure group the arrangement can only be inferred, as hardly any relationships were established. Ditches 765 and 642 (Stage 7) probably formed one large enclosure without subdivisions. Several pits which overlay earlier boundary ditches, among them a latrine-pit 771, may have been dug at this stage. This enclosure was enlarged again (Stage 8). The north-western boundary was probably an addition to 628, but was soon moved north (Stage 9). Within the enlarged enclosure groups of ovens were dug overlying the former boundary (see Fig. 64).

Following this came a major extension of the northern enclosures (Stage 10). At the back of the enclosure around the corndrier burials 584, 585 and 608 were cut into the earlier boundary ditches and large pits were dug (see Ch. IV.F.3 above).

825 was now used as a burial enclosure; seven graves were found within it and one just outside (Fig. 69 and Ch. IV.F.4). The southernmost enclosure was now divided by 821, with an entrance between 793 and 821. Both west and east of 821 shallow gullies sub-divided the enclosures; all these gullies belong to the late 3rd or 4th century AD. At the north end ditches 619 and 628 were cut into by silt-filled hollows 627 and 635 (Ch. IV.F.3).

The circular ditches around the corndrier were superseded; from 536 came a coin of 305–307 AD (Table 21). There were stones in the top of 541 and pit 544 adjacent, so possibly this area was surfaced with stone (cf 861 in the southern enclosures, Ch. IV.F.6 below). The stones were overlaid by an occupation soil, possibly Roman but more likely medieval. In the middle enclosures south of this there was a scatter of ovens (Fig. 64 and Ch. IV.F.2).

One or two more pits and short ditches were dug (Stage 12), but there is no dating evidence later than the mid-4th century.

IV.F.5.c Features behind the enclosures

Parallel ditches 487, 563 and 658 ran off north-east from 565 *c* 27 m apart. These were not at 90 degrees to 565, and were perhaps laid out from some other boundary. The distance between them was the same as the width of the rectangular cropmark enclosures immediately surrounding the villa buildings on the north and east (see Fig. 112 and Ch. IV.E above). Added onto the side of 563 was a small rectangular enclosure with an entrance at the south-west corner.

IV.F.6 The southern enclosure group

Plans: Fig. 74; 142 on Fiche 1#48; Fiche 4#71–4, 76–8, 86–7, 90–92.
Sections: Figs. 143 on Fiche 1#49; 144 on Fiche 1#50

IV.F.6.a Introduction

Small trial trenches were dug into this area before stripping (Fiche 4#91 and 92), and further sections afterwards, but this set of enclosures was much less thoroughly excavated than the northern group, and correspondingly fewer relationships were established. The stripped area comprised only one half of the enclosure group, which continued as cropmarks west of the Lechlade-Burford road (Fig. 1). The sequence was the same as in the northern group, a linear boundary later cut across by enclosures, which gradually expanded in size.

IV.F.6.b The enclosure ditches

The earliest features in this area were Later Bronze Age (Fig. 7; Fig. 119 on Fiche 1#19).

Ditch 1037 and ditches 978 and 979 were possibly the first ditches alongside a droveway, with entrances into the fields either side opposite one another (Fig. 74 Stage 1). This entrance was still apparently in use when 1036 replaced 1037 (Stage 2), but later 1036 was extended across this gap (Stage 3).

842 was probably a continuation of 1036. It was recut several times, always on the north side. 842 was traced west as a cropmark for *c* 70 m until it joined one of the ditches of the regular enclosures just east of the villa (Fig. 1 and Frontispiece). 843 contained Oxford colour-coated wares postdating 250 AD (Young 1977).

Ditches 842–3 were cut across by enclosures laid out from a new boundary 833 (Stage 3). Parallel to it was 843 and other lengths of ditch, 899 and later 849 (Stage 4), and cross-ditches 847 and 861 subdivided the enclosure into three. 833 was later replaced by 836 (Stage 5), which was recut several times. The cropmark of 836 continued west up to the regular enclosure ditch (Fig. 1 and Frontispiece), and possibly continued beyond it. The cross-ditches were modified, and 845 replaced 847 (Stage 5). These cross-

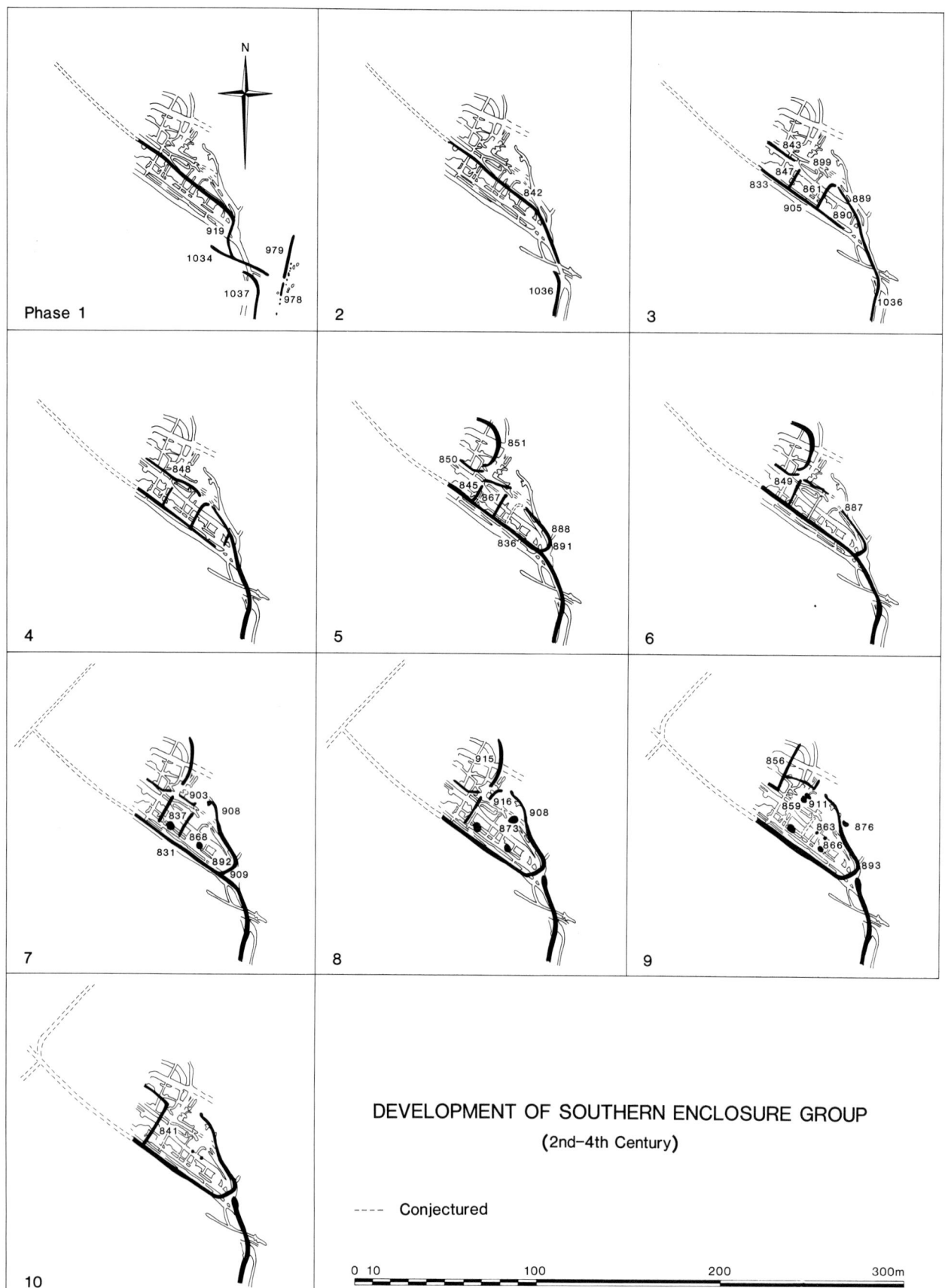

Figure 74 Development plan of southern enclosure group (2nd–4th centuries)

Figure 75 Northern enclosure group after stripping by machine, photographed by W A Baker in 1961

ditches contained no diagnostic sherds; 836 was cut by pit 837, and ditch 845 by pit 839. 849, 850 and 903 appear to have been yet more phases of the 848 boundary.

Ditches 889, 888 and 887 were the successive eastern ends of the enclosures. The ditches move progressively northwards, 889 cutting 843, 888 cutting 889 and 887 cutting 888 (Fig. 143 on Fiche 1#49), so that the enclosures were continually enlarged on this side. The relationship of 908, the northernmost boundary, to 887 or 888 was not established.

Soilmark ditches appear to join up the northern and southern enclosure boundaries, 891 linking 888 to 836 (Stage 5) and 909 later crossing 836 from 887 and 908 to 831 (Stage 7; see also Fig. 142 on Fiche 1#48; Fiche 4#92 and 73). 836 was cut by pits 837 and 868, 831 was not cut by later features, and the latest cross-ditch 841 ran beyond 836 up to 831 (Fiche 4#90 and 91). 831 was recut at least four times (Fig. 143 on Fiche 1#49), always on the south side, strengthening the hypothesis that the enclosures were continually enlarged (see Fig. 74). At the west end the cropmark of 831 curved to join the regular enclosure ditches, demonstrating that these were still in use into the 4th century.

One phase of 847 ran beyond 836 up to 905, so that 905 and 832 were probably intermediate in date between 836 and 831. The soilmarks suggest that the south side of individual enclosures may have been recut at different times, but were later subsumed into one continuous boundary 831, just as was formed by ditches 581 and 587 in the northern enclosure group. At the east end 903 and 848 cut through an oven 862 (Fiche 4#91; see also Ch. IV.F.2).

Ditch 861 was overlaid by 912, a dark occupation layer, and this was overlaid by two probable stone hearths, 863 and 866, and by further stone spreads (Fig. 143 on Fiche 1#49). To the north was a silt-filled pit 873 with pitched and flat stones 876 in its top (Fig. 143 on Fiche 1#49 and Ch. IV.F.3), and sealing 876 was layer 875, probably more of this occupation soil. Outside the features this soil lay directly upon gravel, indicating either topsoil stripping during the occupation or complete mixing of the occupation and topsoil by dense activity. This Late Roman occupation layer covered most of the interior of the easternmost enclosure except where destroyed by medieval furrows such as 864.

North of 848 and south of 851 was a cluster of small pits, gullies and an oven 853. Just east of 857 were two silt-filled pits 911 and 859 (Ch. IV.F.3.a). Like 873, 859 contained flat stones at both the top and bottom.

On the north side of the enclosures the greatest area was enclosed by ditch 908. This ended opposite ditch 858, with which it was probably contemporary. 858 appears to have run across 851 to join ditch 856 (Fig. 74 Stage 9).

Ditch 851 was a curving enclosure boundary north of the line of three rectangular enclosures. A parallel curving ditch just east of it was presumably another phase of boundary. These ditches demonstrate that the enclosures extended northwards, probably along the edge of the more regular layout just east of the villa.

The final phase of enclosure is represented by ditch 841, which turned a corner approximately in line with 858 (Fiche 4#77 and 90–91; Fig. 143 on Fiche 1#49). At the south end its broad soilmark ran as far as 832, and a narrower one continued into 831. 841 contained a Constantinian coin of AD 331–346 (Table 21 Ch. V.3). It was cut by silt-filled pit 855, which contained a coin dated AD 350–360. This was the latest feature from this enclosure group.

During salvage in 1990 ditches were observed in drainage trenches west of the Lechlade-Burford road. Three of these ran on a west-north-west alignment, another north-north-east at right angles to them. No finds were recovered from the exposed sections, but these ditches follow the alignment of the Southern enclosure group and are in line with 841, so are probably Roman.

Within this enclosure group there did not appear to be any specialised activity areas. Large pits (868) and possible wells (837) lay along the back of the enclosures, as in the northern group, and the ovens were fairly evenly distributed. Burials were placed in ditches towards the back and at the end of the enclosures (Fig. 69), which is also the pattern in the northern group.

IV.F.6.c Features behind the enclosures

Fiche 4#71–73; Fig. 115

South of the enclosure-group and west of 1036 were linear soilmarks on two slightly different alignments. Both sets may have been medieval furrows; one alignment was parallel to a medieval headland, but the other was parallel to boundaries 842 and 1054, and since these soilmarks were roughly 17m apart, may have been Roman, like ditches 487 and 563 beyond the northern enclosure-group. 882, the only one which was sectioned, had a V-profile and silt fill unlike a furrow, but was undated.

IV.F.7 Circular enclosure 481 and adjacent features

Plan and Section: Fig. 76, Fiche 4#36 and 37

Feature 481 lay at the centre of the open area where the trackways met, between the northern and southern enclosure groups (Fig. 66). It was a soilmark approximately 12.8 m in diameter consisting of a small central platform 3.45 m north-south by 3.2 m east-west surrounded by up to 14 successive ditch cuts. The ditches were excavated by trenches in spits, and cuts were rarely recognised within the upper levels of these, so that the sequence has had to be reconstructed from the sections. No attempt was made during excavation to link cuts around the feature, and in most cases they can only be traced for short lengths.

The innermost four cuts were shallow, and the outermost of these was almost invariably cut by a V-profiled deeper cut (Fig. 76). This deeper cut was recut up to ten times, usually towards the outside, though the very latest was often a little inside the outermost one or two cuts. The sections on the east and north-east are the most spread out, and so show the succession of cuts most clearly (Fig. 76 III and IV); those on the west and south are shorter, the ditch being recut on top of the previous cuts.

The central platform is not therefore central to the circumference of the whole feature, the centre of which lies towards the north-east of this platform. The circuit of one of the inner shallow cuts can be traced all the way round; this is roughly circular, and is centred upon the middle of the platform, while the innermost, and probably the earliest, deep cut is centred upon a point intermediate between the original centre and that of the circumference of the whole.

This suggests that the centre shifted gradually north-eastwards.

The shallow early cuts were filled with eroded clay subsoil and gravel. The deeper cuts became generally darker, the latest ones often having a grey silt fill, as in many 4th century features on the site. Finds also became more prolific as time went on. Limestone, often burnt, was common throughout the feature, as was tile. Both finds and stones were concentrated in Trench I along the latest cut; possibly this represents a final dump infilling the ditch. At various stages terminals or deeper scoops were evident in the gravel bottom (Fig. 76), but none were recognised during excavation. If these indicated entrances then their orientation varied, as they occurred on the south-west, south, south-east and north-east.

The deep cuts generally silted up right to the top before being recut, implying that each cut was open for at least 5–10 years. Spilling down the inner sides of the deep cuts were very gravelly layers which cannot have derived from the side, as these cuts were cut into earlier ditch fills on the inside, and must represent either backfilling or spill from upcast on the inside. In view of the tendency for ditches to be recut on the outside, upcast on the inner side seems more plausible.

If all the upcast was thrown out on the inside there would have been a mound inside the ditch. The volume of soil from one of the inner cuts would have covered the interior to a depth of 0.3 m. The spoil from the first deep cut added to this would have meant that its interior was covered at least 0.4 m deep, and with successive recuts the mound would have increased in depth. Evidence for spoil on the outer side of the ditch was largely removed by recutting, but where the outer side survived there was no strong evidence of upcast, and the outward progression of the cuts implies that there was little or no upcast on this side.

The fact that the cuts do not always progress outwards would suggest that spoil was not always dumped right up to

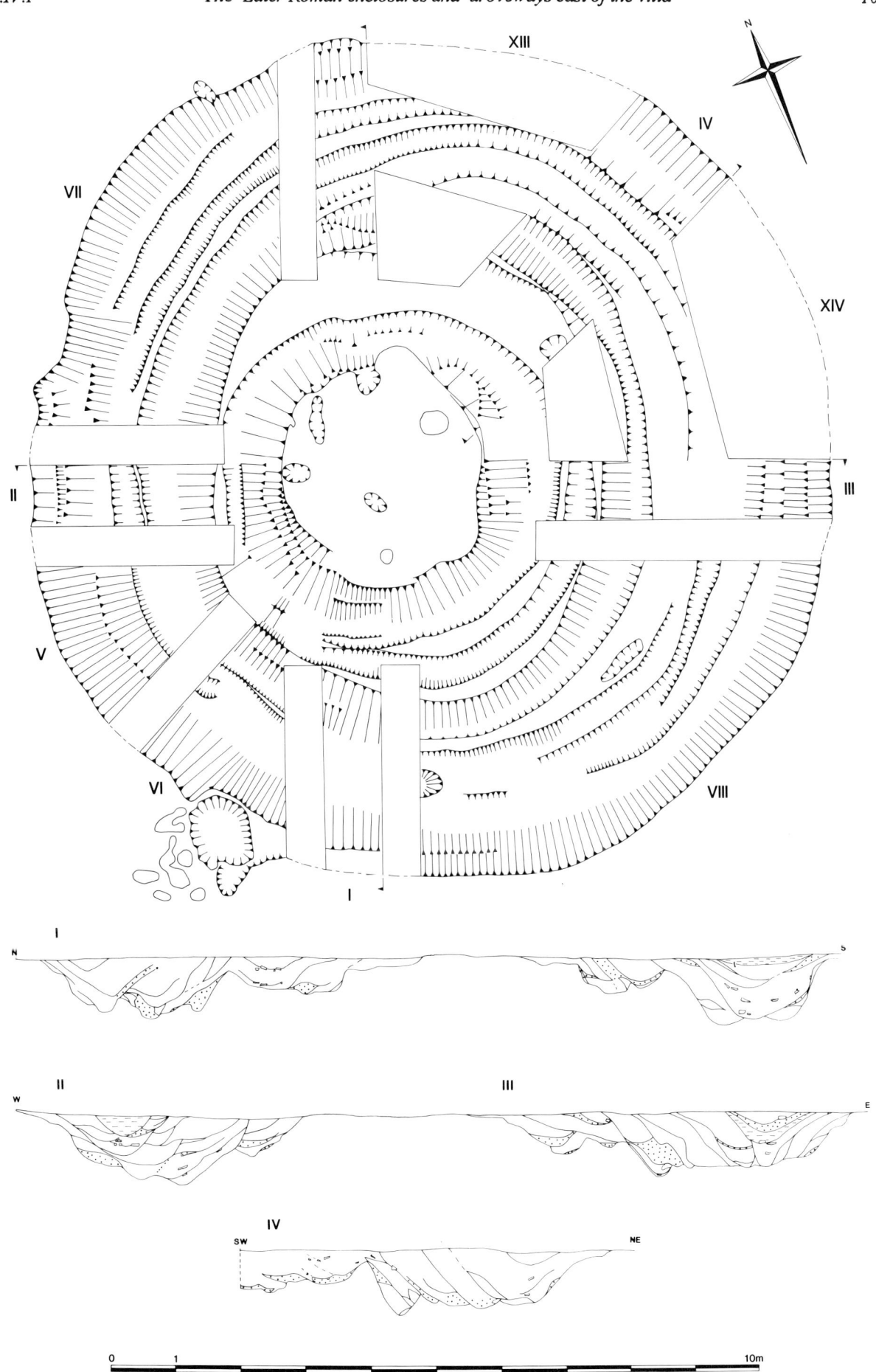

Figure 76 Circular enclosure 481, plans and sections

Figure 77 Circular enclosure 481 in the middle of the open area east of the villa, taken from the west

the edge of the ditch; one of the recuts of the inner shallow ditches lay slightly inside the original circuit, and the latest deep cuts up to 1 m inside the outermost. Because of this late shift inwards the mound was probably never more than 9 m in diameter. Since the outermost and innermost cuts cannot be related stratigraphically, it is possible that the outermost cuts predated or were contemporary with a whole succession of ones further in, creating a double-ditched monument. However, the fact that the outer and inner circuits were not concentric would argue otherwise, and the pottery also suggests that 481 had only one ditch in its later phases.

A mound would explain the shift in the centre of the ditch circuits, for as this spread it would obscure the original platform, and its differential settling would dictate the shape of further recuts. The central platform had only one stone-packed posthole and a scatter of irregularly-spaced and very shallow hollows in it. Most of the latter were probably due to animal disturbance. The one posthole is very close to the centre of the whole feature, and may have been a central marker in its last stages. There may have been other features, but if the interior was covered by a mound only those over 0.5 m deep would have penetrated gravel.

Precise dating is difficult; pottery ranges from the late 1st/early 2nd century to the late 3rd/ early 4th century, but the method of excavation and frequent recutting makes only a broad division into early, middle and late cuts possible. The few finds from the inner shallow cuts included Oxford colour-coated ware, apparently dating the deepening of the ditch after AD 250. None of the pottery was diagnostically 4th century, but the number of recuts suggests that the ditch was active until at least AD 325. On the basis of the number of ditch cuts, the origins of 481 ought to lie at least as far back as the early 3rd century; the pottery suggests a 2nd century date.

Just south of 481 was feature 482 (Fiche 4#36), only the north-east part of which had survived quarrying. Two ditch cuts surrounded an irregular shallow feature 483; the inner ended just north of 483, the outer ran out of the excavated area at both ends. The outer side of the outer ditch was gently sloping, the inner side of the inner cut nearly vertical. Both cuts contained dark gravelly silt with domestic rubbish and building material; 483 was filled with darker silt containing brown gravelly patches, which was possibly backfill. 483 was perhaps another silt-filled pit like 558–560, and included pottery of the last quarter of the 3rd century. Finds from 482 were less diagnostic.

It is uncertain what function 481 performed. A class of unusual enclosures of similar size have recently been recognised at the Roman settlement at Gravelly Guy, Stanton Harcourt, Oxon (Lambrick and Allen in prep.), with ditches recut many times, but the interior of these was always sunken below the surrounding ground level, and the spoil apparently piled in a bank on the outside. 481 could perhaps have been a burial mound but there was no trace of any burials, and it is unlikely that these would have lain entirely in the topsoil.

Possibly there was a structure on the mound, but if this was an original feature it would have been only *c* 3 m across and shallowly-bedded. There were not sufficient concentrations of rubbish to suggest domestic occupation within or immediately adjacent to it, nor deposits suggesting any more specialised building such as a temple. Nevertheless, the position of 481, in the middle of the open area between the two enclosure groups and at the meeting point of the trackways leading in from the east and the south, clearly made it a focal point. If it had a mound this would have been visible approaching the settlement down either droveway.

Its position between two sets of ancillary enclosures is reminiscent of circular structures which occupy focal positions in more classical layouts, as in the outer courtyards as at Winkel-Seeb or Darenth (JT Smith 1978, 154–8). These were interpreted as water-shrines; it is not suggested that there was such a structure inside 481, though this is possible, but that 481 acted as a landmark, possibly as a platform for overseeing culling, markets or estate meetings.

IV.F.8 The gravel-pit area

Plans: Fig. 66; Fiche 4#66, 79 and 80. Section: Fig. 145 on Fiche 1#51

Between the northern and southern groups of enclosures and just west of the long field boundary 959/960 was an irregular soilmark 70 m × 30 m in extent (Fig. 66). Part of this was destroyed without investigation, but sections were dug along the south-west side. These revealed a series of intercutting wide and shallow hollows (660–670), which had mostly been deliberately backfilled (Fig. 145 on Fiche 1#51). Primary fill was sometimes dark humic loam with charcoal, sometimes light and very sandy or gravelly, and this was overlaid by interleaved tips of gravelly soil and clean sand or gravel.

The latest fill in each group of hollows was a dark occupation soil containing abraded pottery and building materials.

Their dark primary fills suggest that these features were used for rubbish-dumping and possibly burning was carried out in them, though no evidence of in situ burning was found in the excavation area. The late occupation fill contained many abraded sherds and was probably backfill, possibly from a midden; joining sherds from separate hollows suggest that much of this occupation soil was dumped at one time.

The successive hollows or scoops were largely discrete, only intercutting at the edges. They were too extensive to be pits, and were not cut to a regular shape like the large hollow 409 (Fiche 4#48; 134 on Fiche 1#38) or even the silt-filled hollows (Fig. 68; Ch. IV.F.3.a). Their irregular edges suggest that they might have been gravel quarries.

There was however a high proportion of gravel and sand in the backfill, and these scoops are also shallow, cut only 0.5 m into gravel. A similar large area of Roman hollows was found at Ashville, Abingdon (Halpin 1983, 113–4).

Pottery from the hollows dates from the late first to the late 3rd century, and the vast majority is 2nd century. Even allowing for the abraded state of many sherds it seems likely that these quarries were in use from the mid 2nd century, and the very small numbers of Oxford colour-coated sherds suggests that the excavated area was largely disused by 250 AD. However surface finds from the eastern part of the soilmark apparently included 4th century mortaria sherds, so the quarrying may have shifted eastwards over time.

IV.F.9 The timber building, Building VI

Plan: Fig. 66; 78, Fiche 4#52 and 66

North of the gravel pit area and just west of the corner of 959/960 was a line of sub-rectangular pits 922 etc, running just east of south-north. These produced scraps of Early Iron Age pottery, and are described in Ch. III.B.1.c.

South of these pits were two lines of smaller pits or postholes between 0.45 m and 0.9 m in diameter. Most of these were spaced *c* 2.5 m apart, but there were also intermediates and at the north end they were only 1.5–1.8 m apart. These were aligned slightly more north-south than the rectangular pits, and most had a darker and more gravelly fill. Several had possible post-pipes or post-positions sunk into the bottom, but most contained homogeneous backfill.

Pits 939 and 940 had small postholes on their east sides with similar fill to those alongside the pits; 940 cut the posthole adjacent, and while the relationship between 939 and its posthole was not recorded, their markedly different fills suggest that they were not contemporary.

The two lines were parallel and of roughly the same length, with circular pits or postholes set at similar intervals. Only the more northerly features of the east line were excavated, but the size and fill of these was similar to those of the western line. 944 and 946 had possible post-positions, the others had all been backfilled.

Just west of these lines were further postholes, 951 and 950, and roughly parallel to the western line was a short length of gully 941 which contained two possible post-positions in its shallow fill. This gully lay 1.25m from the posthole line. There was also a possible rectangular outlier, 943, north of the eastern line.

From their similar size and positions the features in both lines were probably contemporary. There was very little dating evidence from either line, one Romano-British sherd from pit 953 and a scrap of Samian from 966=948. Their relationship to the rectangular pit alignment seems too close for coincidence, and despite the Iron Age pottery from 933 this alignment too may have been Romano-British, like the rectangular sumps at regular intervals along the bottom of shallow ditches at Watkins Farm, Northmoor, Oxon (Allen 1990, 18–19, 27 and 31).

The parallel lines of pits or postholes were 16.9 m long. The eastern line consisted of two parts, the northern (9m long) being 6.8 m from the western line, the southern only 6m away, and the gap between the ends of the two parts was larger than that between the other postholes (Fig. 78). Possibly these lines represent an aisled building, and 941 the only remaining length of the outer wall. The nave of such barns is generally between 6m and 7m wide, and the length *c* 18 m (Morris 1979, 196–8). The posts are not all evenly spaced, nor do the postholes in the two lines all form pairs, but neither is this the case in Building IV (see Ch. IV.C.6). It is possible that two separate buildings are represented, but the even spacing of the western line suggests strongly that all its postholes were laid out at one time. Posthole 950 is in line with those further south in the eastern line, and 953, 950 and 949 may perhaps have tied the two elements together in some way.

Alternatively these may not have been roofed structures, simply pens, but the absence of intermediate posts along the shorter sides makes this unlikely. Since the dating evidence for this group of features is so scant, it is also possible that they are post-Roman. The irregular form of the building is more like that of Anglo-Saxon or Early Medieval structures, but there is no evidence of occupation in either of these periods to substantiate this.

IV.F.10 Post-Roman use of the site

There is no good evidence of Anglo-Saxon occupation at Roughground Farm, although Building VI (Fig. 78) has similarities with timber halls of this period at Radley, Barrow Hills, Oxon (R A Chambers pers. comm.) and elsewhere. A fragment of a circular loomweight (Fig. 108 No. 142) and one bone pin (Fig. 102 No. 98) may also be Anglo-Saxon, but are probably derived from the settlement visible on cropmarks just east of Butler's Field, some 800 m to the south. Stones from the villa were being re-used in the cemetery of this settlement in the 6th century (Boyle *et al* forthcoming).

The eastern half of the site was ploughed in the medieval period; the villa site itself and the Roman fields west of it did not show any traces of ridge and furrow, and were probably pasture; probably the villa buildings themselves discouraged this and gave rise to the name Roughground.

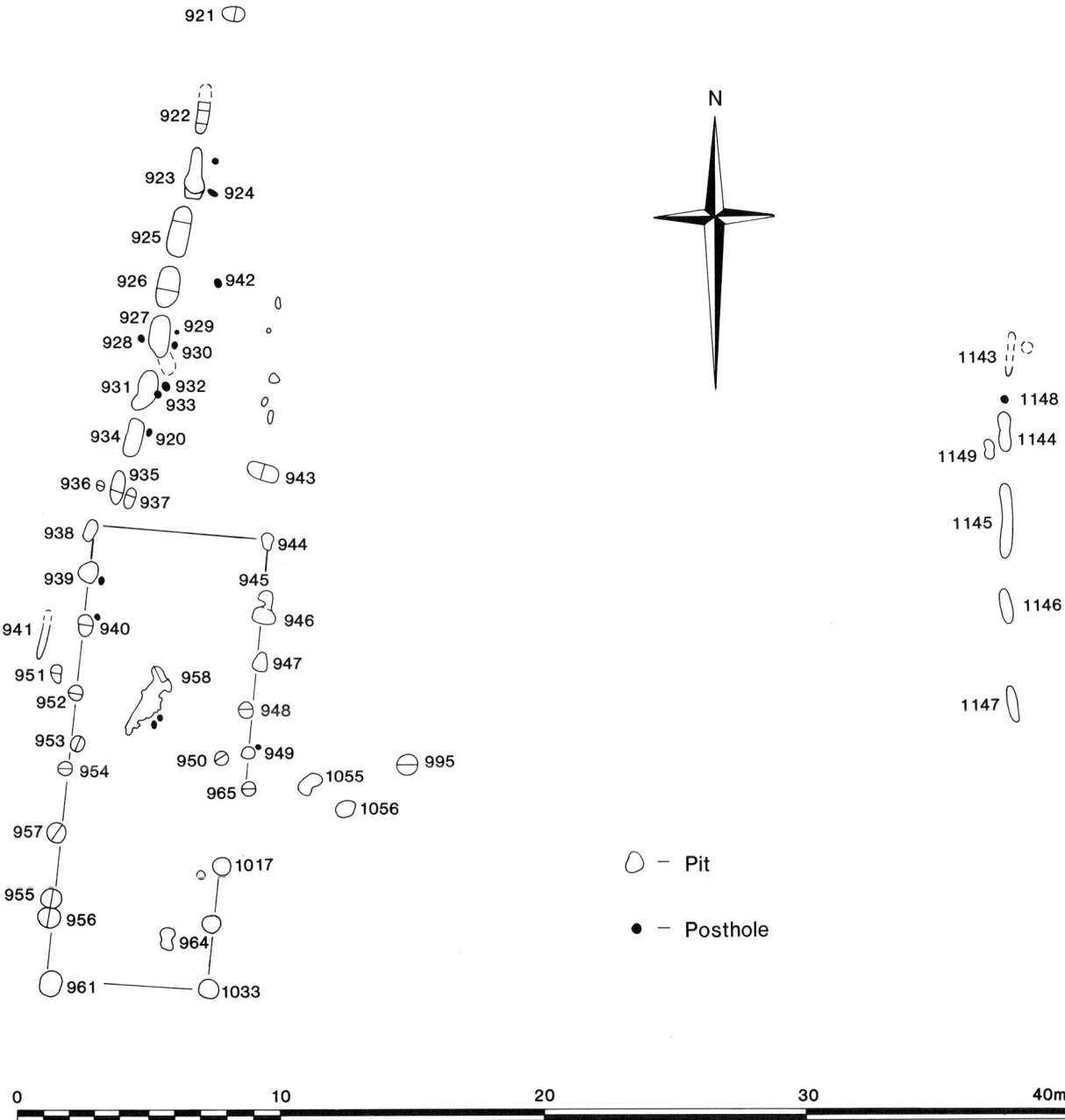

Figure 78 Plan of pit alignments and Building VI

Chapter V

The finds of the Roman and post-Roman periods

V.1 The organisation and phasing of the finds reports

The finds reports upon the material recovered from the 1957–65 and the 1981–82 excavations were already completed when renewed excavation began in 1990. For this reason the finds from the 1990 excavation are numbered separately from the rest, using the small finds numbers issued on site. For some categories of find, *eg* coins, the new discoveries have been integrated with the rest. For others, for instance the copper alloy and iron finds, the additional items have been integrated into the print catalogue, but illustrations will be found in a group following those from the previous excavations, in order to avoid re-paging. The Roman pottery and animal bone reports upon the 1990 finds immediately follow the reports upon the earlier material.

The report has been divided into five main periods as follows:

1. The Early Prehistoric, including Grooved Ware, Beaker and Early Bronze Age features and finds (see Ch. II).
2. The Later Prehistoric, covering Later Bronze Age and Iron Age occupation (see Ch. III).
3. Early Romano-British, from the 1st century AD until the villa was established in the middle of the 2nd century AD.
4. High Roman, from the mid-2nd century until the later 3rd century AD. This corresponds to the establishment of the villa and its surrounding field system.
5. Late Roman, from the late 3rd to the end of the 4th century AD.

The prehistoric features were grouped to provide larger assemblages for broad comparison of the animal bones. The chronological distinction between the Later Bronze Age and Early Iron Age features was not at that time apparent, but the broad distinction between these and the earlier prehistoric features remains valid.

Subdivisions within the Roman period into Early, High, and Late Roman were made to allow intra-site comparison of the animal bone assemblages and of the pottery. They were chosen on the basis of one event of major significance, the construction of the villa, which was fairly well-dated, and one clear chronological division within the pottery, the appearance of Oxford colour-coated wares. This latter division also appeared to correspond to the construction of a major new building, Building III, and to the emergence of the enclosure groups east of the villa. Subsequent analysis has suggested that the development of the settlement was more complex, but the major periods still correspond broadly to the change from the characteristic early Roman survival of Celtic economy, structures and practices to a fully romanised villa, and the shift in emphasis of the later Roman economy implied by changes in building materials, in imported pottery and by the influx of population to the enclosures and workshop areas east of the villa.

Because of the difficulties in defining the precise point of transition in various parts of the site or types of artefact the phase divisions have not been used throughout the finds reports, many of which use a looser 'earlier' or 'later' Roman framework, but will be found in the pottery and animal bone reports on the material from the 1957–65 excavations.

V.2 The Roman pottery

by Sarah Green and Paul Booth

V.2.a Introduction to the pottery recovered between 1957 and 1982

by Sarah Green

The bulk of the Roman pottery, from Margaret Jones' 1957–65 excavations and from the 1981 and 1982 trenches, was analysed by Sarah Green. The Roman pottery from the 1990 excavation was analysed by Paul Booth, and his report follows afterwards.

V.2.a.1 Excavation methodology

Initially all the pottery was kept, but many sherds from the 1957–59 sites were subsequently discarded (mostly body sherds) and only a summary record made in the finds notebooks. Because of the difficulty in correlating the fabrics and in some cases the forms thus described with those defined during the current study, it was not possible to compile a complete catalogue of the pottery originally recovered.

V.2.a.2 Post-excavation methodology

An initial decision was made not to base any analysis upon quantification, given the uncertainty about discarded pottery outlined above. All sherds were recorded (by sherd count and weight) on Oxford Archaeological Unit Roman pottery recording forms designed for this study. From these a catalogue was compiled for analysis, recording the presence of the fabric, form type, and rim form in a context and, where possible, dating information. Variations in diameter etc, were not included, although this information will be found on the recording forms. This catalogue was compiled using the sorting facilities of the Oxford University Computing Service VAX 11/780 computer; programs were written (using the SPITBOL programming language) to present the proportions of fabric and forms by phase in tabular form.

The methods used to define fabrics and forms are described below.

V.2.b Fabrics (for pottery recovered between 1957 and 1982)

V.2.b.1 Introduction

The pottery was examined and 'unknown' pottery was then examined macroscopically using a ×10 hand lens and, following the criteria suggested by D P S Peacock (Peacock 1977a), was divided into groups on the basis of inclusion and whether oxidised or reduced.

An attempt was made to relate the pottery found at Roughground Farm to that from other sites in the area. This was really only possible with material from Cirencester where a type series exists, although it had been created somewhat differently (Rigby 1982a, 153 ff and Rigby 1982a, mf 5 and 8). Pottery from older excavations has generally been published with descriptions of illustrated sherds but without recording all of the ceramic material. The same problems apply to any comparison of form types.

V.2.b.2 Summary list of fabrics

1. Amphora—Dressel 20 and Pelichet 47
2. Mortaria
2.1 Oxford white ware
2.2 Oxford white colour-coat
2.3 Oxford red/brown colour-coat
2.4 Lower Germany
2.5 Mancetter/Hartshill
2.6 Lower Nene Valley—Castor/Stibbington
2.7 S.Glos./N.Wilts—Cirencester
2.8 Verulamium region
3. Samian
4. Rhenish
5. Roughcast
6.1 Oxford red/brown colour-coat
6.2 Oxford Parchment ware
6.3 Oxford white colour-coat
7. New Forest
8. Nene Valley
9.1 White colour-coat oxidised—SWWS (South Western White Slip)
9.2 White colour-coat oxidised—SWWS (South Western White Slip) (coarser)
9.3 White colour-coat oxidised—SWWS
9.4 Red/brown colour-coat—SWBS (South Western Brown Slip)
10.1 White firing ware—fine
10.2 White firing ware—coarse
11.1 Black burnished 1 (Dorset)
11.2 Black burnished—wheelthrown
11.3 Black—fine
12.1 Reduced—fine
12.2 Reduced—less fine
12.3 Reduced—coarse—Savernake-type
12.4 Reduced—Savernake type
12.5 Reduced—with much quartz—Savernake type
12.6 Reduced—very fine, hard—imitation Gallo-Belgic
12.7 Reduced—fine—imitation Gallo-Belgic
12.8 Reduced—mica dusted
13.1 Oxidised—quartz tempered
13.2 Oxidised Severn Valley ware type—fine
13.3 Oxidised Severn Valley ware type—soapy
13.4 Oxidised Severn Valley ware type—vesicular
13.5 Oxidised Severn Valley ware type—grog + iron
14.1 Brown—fine burnished
14.2 Brown—less fine
14.3 Brown—coarser
14.4 Brown—grog etc—storage jar
14.5 Brown—sandy
15. Shell inclusions
16. Limestone inclusions
17. Oolite inclusions
(18. not used)
19. Chalk inclusions
20. Organic/grog inclusions
21. Flint inclusions
(22. —see Iron Age section)
23. Black
24. Oxidised—1 sherd only with unique decoration and form
25. Campanian
50. Medieval
99. Post-medieval

V.2.b.3 Amphorae

by David Williams

The amphorae sherds were classified by fabric and form and then weighed and counted. The types represented are Dressel 20 and Pelichet 47, together with two unassigned sherds. The proportions of these amphorae are summarised in Table 17. In Britain Dressel 20 amphorae date from the late pre-Roman Iron Age to the 3rd century AD and Pelichet 47 from the late 1st to the early 3rd century.

Fabric	Weight	% by weight	Total count	% by count
Dr. 20	2.05 kg	69.7%	17	53.1%
Pelichet 47	0.85 kg	28.9%	10	31.2%
Unassigned	0.04 kg	1.4%	5	15.6%
Total	2.94 kg		32	

Table 17 Proportions of amphora sherds by fabric

V.2.b.4 Mortaria

by Kay Hartley

At least 81 mortaria are represented in this sample. After c 140 AD the increasingly important and closely located Oxford potteries were the main suppliers at all periods of the occupation. 68 of the 78 (87.3%), which could be assigned to type, were made there and only 10 (12.6%) came from all other sources put together (Fig. 79). It is worth noting that 4 of the 10 were from an unlocated local workshop of some regional importance, producing flagons and mortaria (Fabric 2.7), which was probably situated in Gloucestershire or possibly north Wiltshire: Cirencester was its biggest known customer for mortaria. Two other mortaria were from Lower Germany and the lower Nene valley and any merchant supplying mortaria from these sources is likely to have been based in Gloucestershire since the best route was by coastal or river traffic; Roughground Farm is fairly typical of sites in the south-west in having such mortaria.

The earliest mortarium in the group is from context 132/8, dated AD 80–120, which was made in the Verulamium region potteries (including workshops at Brockley Hill, Radlett, Verulamium etc); these potteries were especially important in the Flavian and Trajanic periods. The largest number were used in the period AD 240–300 and perhaps in the period AD 300–350. The fourth-century mortaria cannot be dated closely enough to give a clear indication of the terminal date.

For a description of the mortarium fabrics see the microfiche report Ch. 5.2.d on Fiche 2#8.

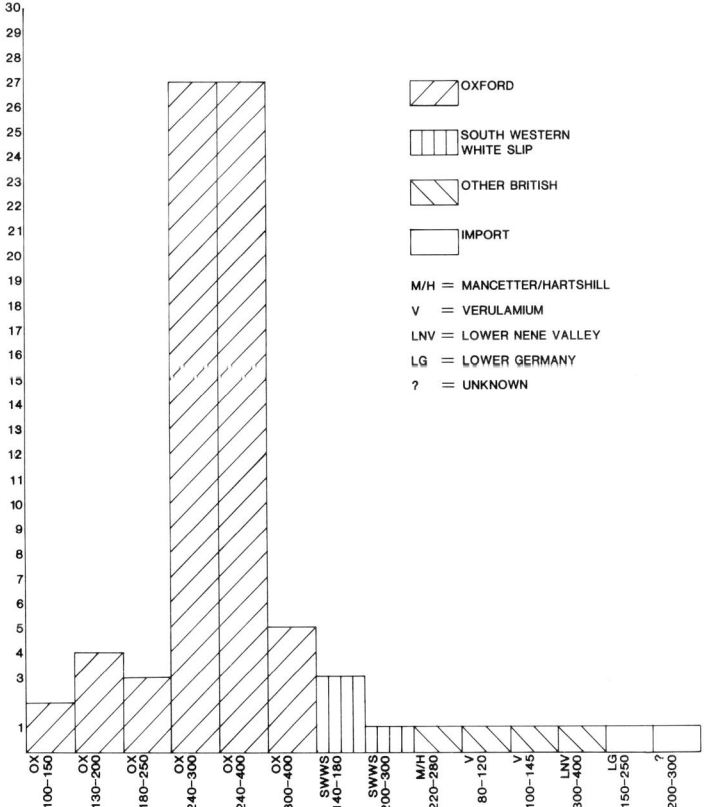

Figure 79 Roman pottery: histogram showing number of mortaria present on site

V.2.b.5 Samian ware

by Grace Simpson

Of the 523 ceramic contexts 270 contained samian; it would appear that very little if any samian was discarded. It is interesting when considering residuality to note that the Late Roman period (Period 5) had the greatest percentage and number of contexts producing samian (Table 18).

Period	3	3/4	4	4/5	5	Unstratified
Number of sherds	18	1	68	10	117	30
Percentage of samian	7.37	0.40	27.86	4.09	47.95	12.29
Percentage of pottery assemblage	4.21	3.84	7.47	9.25	5.64	8.74

Table 18 Quantity of samian by site period (excluding 1990 finds)

A detailed catalogue of the samian can be found in Table 42 on Fiche 2#2: the context catalogue lists forms and provenance where possible.

Most of the samian from the site is 2nd century, mainly Hadrianic to early Antonine. There are however two early vessels, Neronian or Vespasianic, a Drag. 27 and a Curle 11. Slightly later South Gaulish forms include Drs. 18, 15/17, 27, 29, 36 and 37. Many of the sherds are very small, with few large groups, but contexts 132/2 and 132/3 contain large parts of several Hadrianic to early Antonine vessels including applique black samian (Fig. 80.4). There is ample evidence of repair in the form of lead rivets or rivet holes (as in Fig. 81.11) and reuse of vessels to form lids. Rare forms are numerous and include Curle 11, Curle 15, Curle 21, Drs. 15/17, 38, 42, 44, Dechelette 72 and 74, Walters 79 and two Ludowici forms TL and Tf. Two globular vases, one plain-walled and one incised, and a barrel-shaped beaker (from the 1990 excavation, see Ch. V.2.g.1 below) are also rare forms, all of which indicate well-chosen purchases.

The sherds commented on below were selected either as being of importance to site interpretation or because of their intrinsic interest.

Fig. 80.1 132/2. Drag. 37 stamped ALBVCI. One-third of a large bowl, and one of the sherds is burnt black. A good example of the work of ALBVCIVS. For similar figure-types on his bowls cf. Stanfield & Simpson 1958, pls. 120–122. Venus D. 177=0.288 or 288A, and the large cupid 0.376A, have not been previously recorded on his signed bowls. Period of production, *c* 140–170 AD.

Fig. 80.2 320/1. Large Curle 11, like Oswald & Pryce 1920, pl. LXXI No. 131 with flat flange. Neronian to Vespasianic. Repaired with rivets. Possibly an heirloom, especially since other pieces from the same level could date half a century later.

Fig. 80.3 132/2. Drag. 37. A large bowl in the style of Criciro. For Hercules with the snakes D.464=O.783, see the bowl signed CRICIRO from London (Stanfield & Simpson 1958, 10, Pl. 117), which has similar rosettes on the borders and similar pairs of birds. The ovolo is his ovolo 2 (Stanfield & Simpson 1958, Fig. 33, 205). *c* 140–165 AD.

Fig. 80.4 132/2. Dechelette Form 74. Originally a two-handled vase with applied plaques and rouletted ornament; but only one handle, with a groove down its outer side, and one plaque have survived, together with part of the lower band of rouletting. The plaque is a copy of the moulded type D. 16=0.19 of a Triton. The face is unusually distinct. It is better work than some of the copies from moulded figure-types illustrated in Simpson 1957, 29–42, on this class of samian ware, *eg* Nos. 31 and 32. The vase is red inside, and dark silvery-grey outside. It was fired in an inverted position and has thus retained the ferric colouration inside. Hadrianic.

Fig. 81.5 193/2. A small Drag. 37 badly damaged during manufacture, because the ovolo is obscured. This is probably an 'apprentice-bowl'. A second sherd was found in context 1010, and is also illustrated. Probably Hadrianic.

Fig. 81.6 528. Ovolo close to Rogers B47. Early Antonine.

Fig. 81.7 532. The large ovolo Rogers B89. Late 2nd century.

Fig. 81.8 82. Drag. 42 rim with en barbotine decoration, see Oswald & Pryce 1920, 195, pl. liv 1–5. Antonine.

Fig. 81.9 200. Drag. 37 ovolo resembling CRICIRO, ovolo 2 = Rogers B47. *c* 140–165 AD.

Fig. 81.10 400. Drag. 37 with a very fine wavy line above and below the ovolo. AD 100–120.

Fig. 81.11 534 and 1507. Large Drag. 37 in the style of potter X-6 with several unusual figure types: the squirrel and small lion to left (neither in Oswald 1936 7), lion looking backwards see Stanfield & Simpson 1958, pl.76, 23. From the left is the cupid O.504, small boar O.1642, Hercules O.760B, small lion to right O.1404A, large lion O.1450, gladiator O.1002, Hercules and lion O.796. Most remarkable is the bear (Anubis) like a Drag. 37 at Tongeren (Vanvinckenroye 1989, pl. 5, no. 50). *c* 125–150 AD. Mended with lead rivets.

Fig. 81.12 200. Drag. 30 with part of the column Rogers P68. Hadrianic to Antonine.

Fig. 81.13 661. Drag. 37 in the style of PATERNVS II, seabull O.52A, seahorse O.33, leaf Rogers H77. *c* 160–190 AD.

Fig. 81.14 54/6 joins 160. Drag. 18/31 base, stamped OFNIG [. For NIGER see Oswald 1931, 219, 410. Stamps by the same potter have been found at Bath, Cirencester and Usk. *c* 60–85 AD.

Fig. 81.15 169. Drag. 33 base stamped NAMILI[ANUS], Oswald 1931, 215. Antonine.

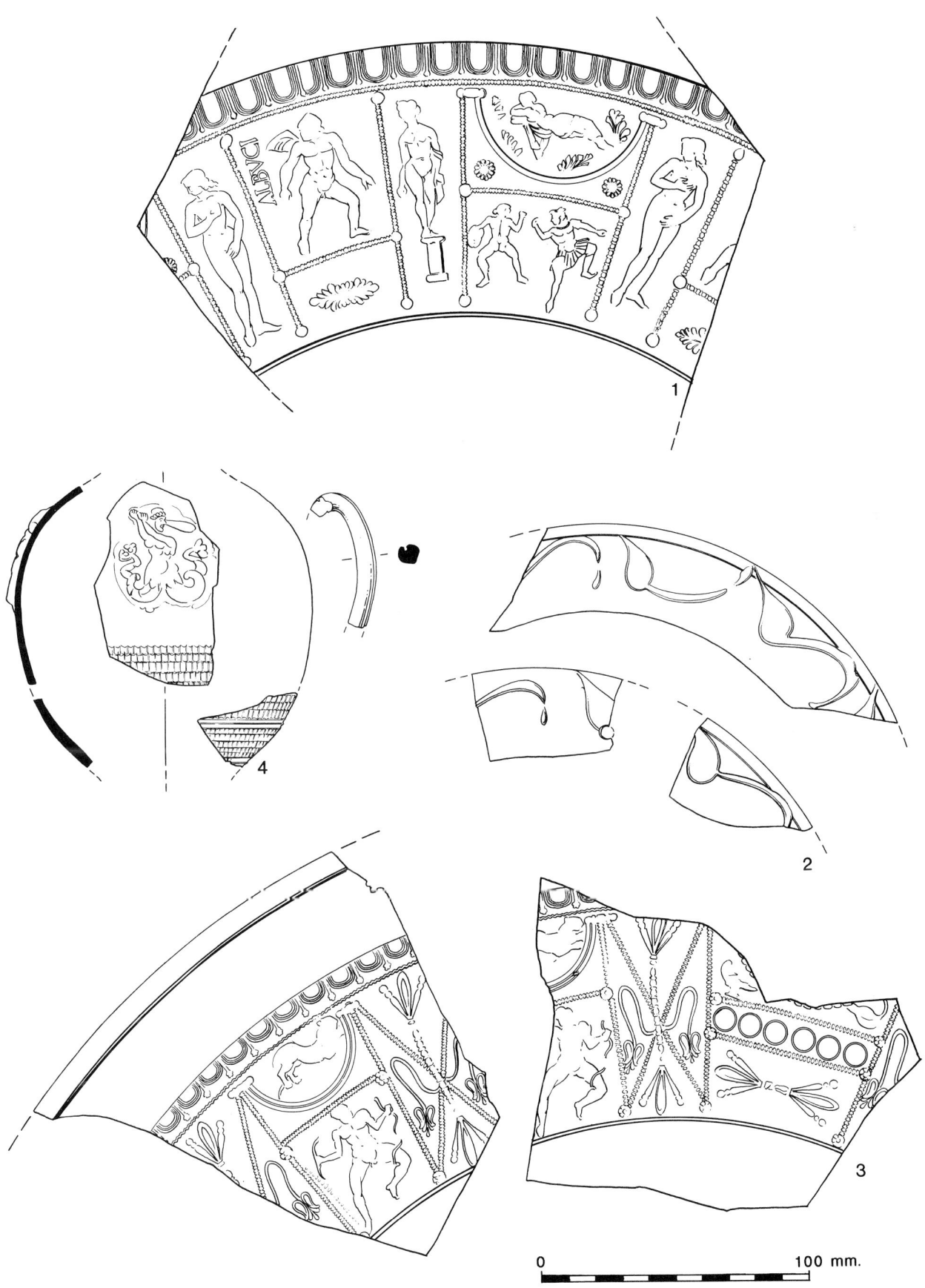

Figure 80 Roman pottery: illustrated samian Nos. 1–4

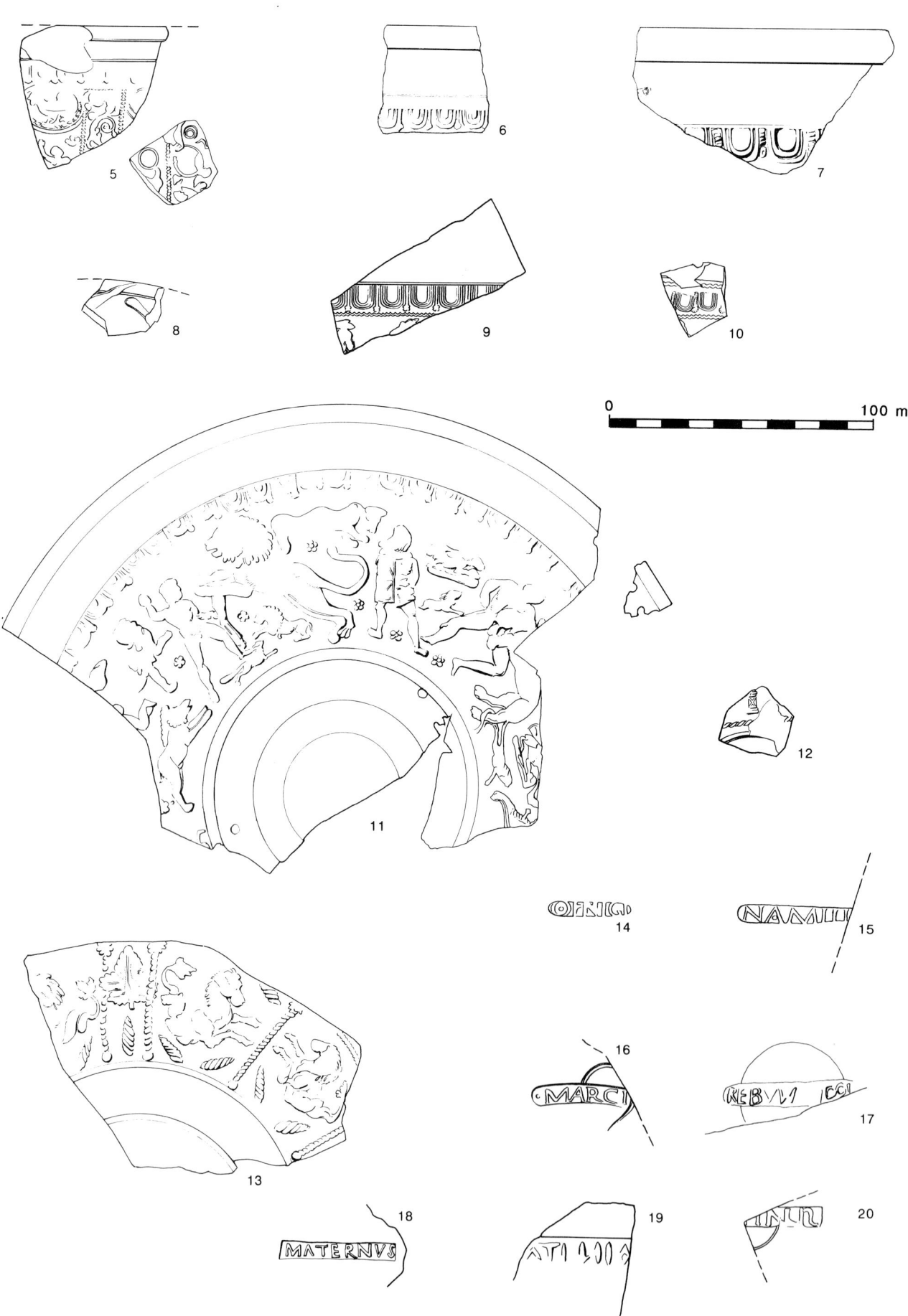

Figure 81 Roman pottery: illustrated samian Nos. 5–20

Fig. 81.16 132/2. Drag. 53 complete section stamped MARCI[. See Oswald 1931, 185–6, 401. Another longer stamp with this name was found on a Drag. 33 (see Oswald 1931, 184–5). Antonine.

Fig. 81.17 830. Drag. 33 base stamped REBV[RR]IOF, Oswald 1931, 259. Antonine.

Fig. 81.18 559. Drag. 18/31 base stamped MATERNVS, Oswald 1931, 194. Antonine.

Fig. 81.19 868/1. Form uncertain, stamped ATTILIM, very fine fabric and good red gloss. Oswald 1931, 28, 354. Antonine.

Fig. 81.20 200. Drag. 33 base with part of a stamp]INIS. 2nd century.

Fig. 80.1, 3, and 4 and Fig. 81.16 are part of a large group from enclosure ditch 132 between Buildings I and II, dated AD 150–165. Fig. 81.11 shows two joining fragments, one of which came from Building III, the other from the northern enclosure group over 200 m away. Such cross-joins support the argument for a close association between these two areas (see also Discussion in Ch. VI.3).

V.2.c Forms (for pottery recovered between 1957 and 1982)

V.2.c.1 Introduction

A general form series was devised, initially divided into twelve major forms, and subdivided within the major form into types different in detail, but all conforming to its general specification. This system is designed to facilitate the recognition of similarities and relationships between fabric types and production centres (eg the imitation of BB forms in various grey wares). The basic form definitions are give below and the possible variations, based on pottery types commonly found on sites in Roman Britain, are shown in microfiche figures Fig. 147 on Fiche 2#20 and 148 on Fiche 2#21. The criteria for each sub-division are described and illustrated in the vessel catalogue. A full numerical description of a particular vessel is given thus: *eg* 3.2/41, where '3' is the major vessel type, '2' the subdivision, and '/41' the numerical code for the rim. In some cases the major code and rim form only are given: this occurs when all that can be recognised of vessel is its general type and rim form because the sherd is too small or too damaged to give further unambiguous information about body shape. Handles and bases were also coded as listed in Table 43 on Fiche 2#18 and Table 44 on Fiche 2#18. Rim forms were defined separately and are illustrated in Fig. 149 on Fiche 2#22; they were given arbitrary numerical classification as each new type was recognised. Decoration types were similarly coded (see Table 45 on Fiche 2#18).

While this system follows the conventional one of classifying forms in order from closed to open vessel types, it departs from it in that neither the rim forms nor the subdivisions of the vessel types within the major categories are arranged with any ideas of traditional typological order. It was felt that too great an emphasis on typological development added little to a description of the pottery. As far as possible preconceptions based upon functional interpretation have been avoided, form types being defined by their proportions. The cut off points between types are arbitrary, as, for instance, between jars and beakers where the form description is similar, size being the important distinction. However, the common names used for these forms were in most cases based upon traditional terminology, which, it is suggested by Millett 1979a, 37, provide a generally consistent classification.

The proportion of different forms (according to the presence of a form in a context) is illustrated in Fig. 150 on Fiche 2#23. This is not intended as a precise quantification but does give a useful general view of the relative numbers of each form in use during the whole of the period.

A formal vessel catalogue is given in Figs. 83–90. The illustrated vessels represent the range of basic forms, rim variations and decoration. Wares which are already well known are not illustrated but are included in the series with references to published corpora. The vessel catalogue includes a list of fabrics (see Ch. V.2.c.3) in which the forms occur.

V.2.c.2 Major form definitions

1. **Flagons** A closed vessel with a long narrow neck, wide diameter body, and one or more handles.
2. **Jugs** A closed vessel with a long narrow neck, wide diameter body, one or more handles and a pouring lip.
3. **Jars** A vessel which can be closed or open (see form subdivisions). Its height is arbitrarily defined as being 150 mm or more and is as great or greater than its body diameter.
4. **Beakers** A closed vessel whose height is less than 150 mm. Its height is as great or greater than its rim diameter which is less than its body diameter. The rim diameter is 100 mm or less. It has no handle.
5. **Cups** An open vessel with no neck, whose rim diameter is as great or greater than the body diameter. It has one or more handles.
6. **Bowls** An open vessel whose height is less than its rim diameter. The proportion of height: diameter can vary from 3:8 up to, but not including 1:1.
7. **Dishes** An open vessel whose proportions of height to diameter are less than 1:4 but more than 1:8.
8. **Plates** An open vessel whose proportions of height to diameter are less than 1:8.
9. **Lids** An open vessel whose height diameter is less than 1:2 and which has a 'handle' or knob with which to hold the vessel in the centre of the base exterior. These vessels appear unstable if drawn as bowls.

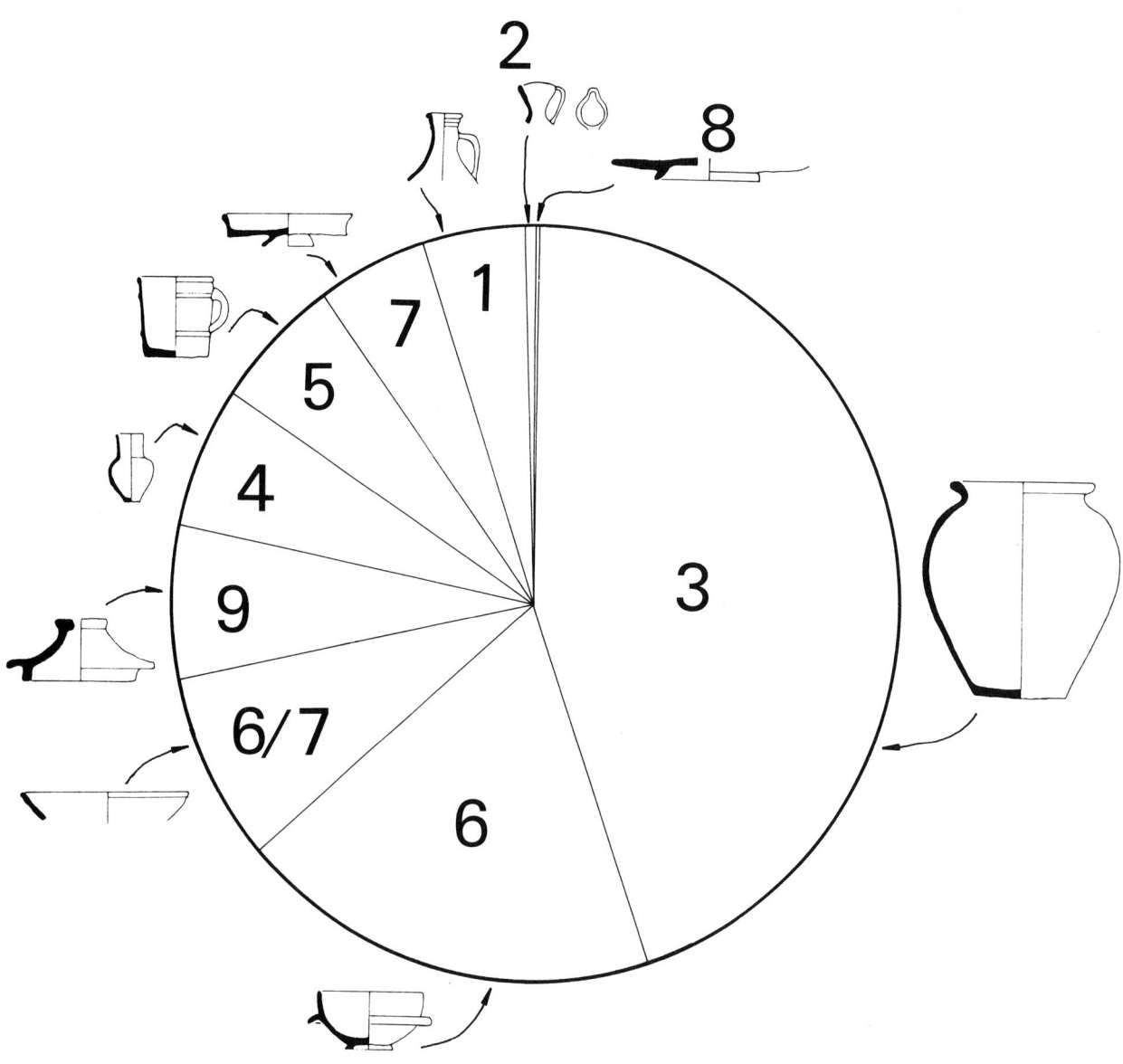

Figure 82 Roman pottery: pie diagram showing proportions of major forms

Ch. V *The finds of the Roman and post-Roman periods* 121

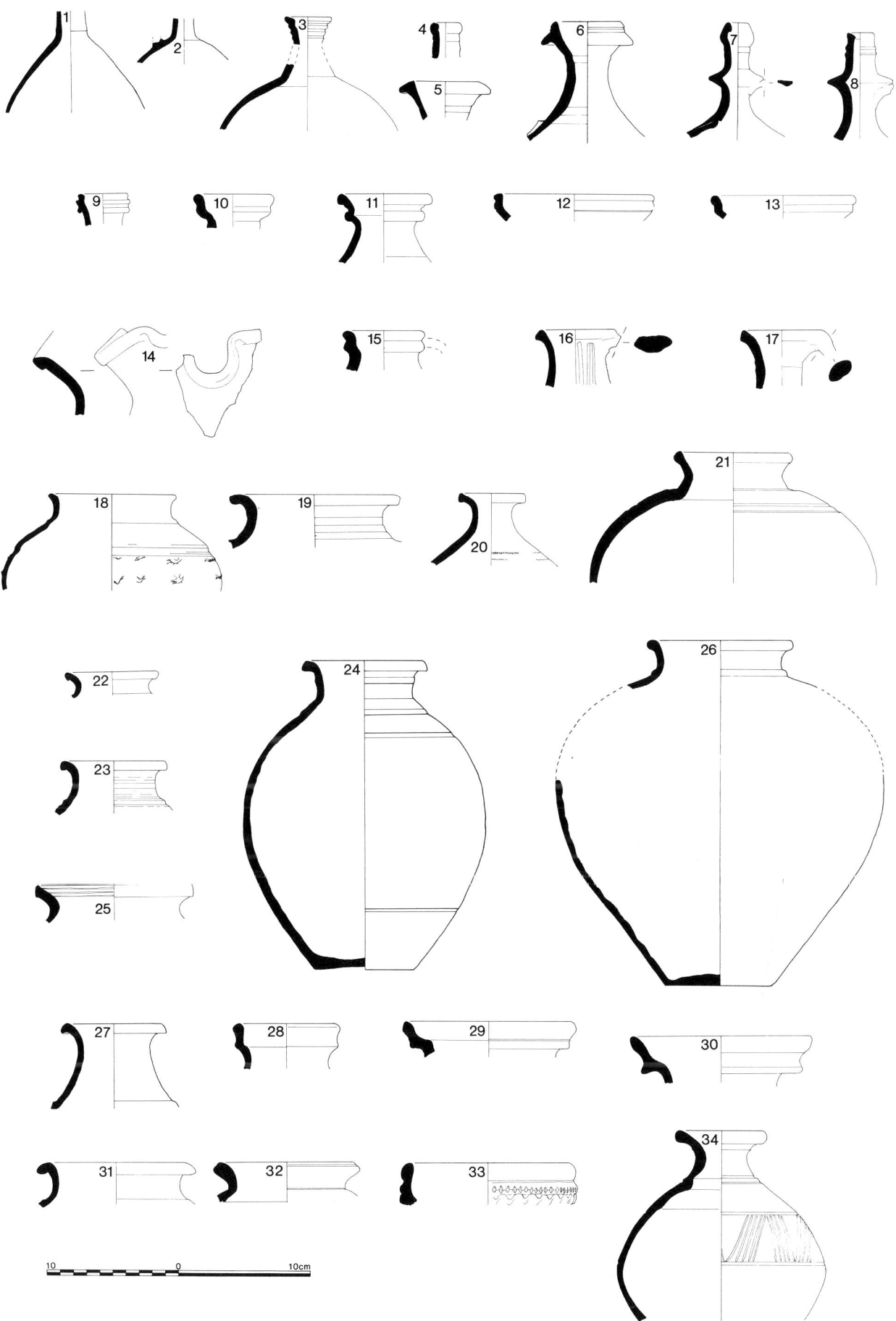

Figure 83 Roman pottery: Form Corpus Types 1 to 3.2

V.2.c.3 *Form corpus*

Type 1 Flagons.
The sub-divisions based on the major differences in rim and neck forms are illustrated below; where vessels occur in different fabrics to those of the illustrated example the fabrics are given in brackets. Since the pottery was classified according to a theoretical framework, there are missing numbers in this form series, *eg* there is no form 1.2 in the Roughground Farm pottery; however, this form has been found elsewhere. Where appropriate, cross reference is made to Young's classification (Young 1977).

1 Fabric 13.2. Fig. 83.1 and 2. Although these vessels have no rims, they are included as being good examples of wide bodied, long necked, vessels with handles.
1.1 Fabric 12.2. Fig. 83.3. (Not illustrated 13.1).
1.3 Fabric 8. Fig. 83.4.
1.4 Fabric 9.2. Fig. 83.5. (Not illustrated 13.1).
1.5 Fabric 9.1. Fig. 83.6.
1.6 Fabric 6.1. Fig. 83.7 and 8. Young 1977, C8, p. 148, Fig. 53.
1.7 Fabric 9.4. Fig. 83.9.
1.8 Fabric 10.1. Fig. 83.10 and 11.
1.9 Fabric 10.1. Fig. 83.12 and 13.

Type 2 Jugs
Two variations are illustrated, only one of which, 2.1, was found at Roughground Farm.

2.1 Fabric 6.1. Fig. 83.14. Young 1977, C12, p. 150, Fig. 54

Type 3 Jars
The sub-divisions within this form are based upon differences in body shape. Descriptions and illustrations are given below. The rim forms are illustrated in the microfiche Fig. 149 on Fiche 2#22.

3.1 A narrow necked jar with one or more handles.
3.1/65 Fabric 12.1. Fig. 83.16 and 17. (Not illustrated Fabric 6.1, Young 1977, 150, Fig. 54.)
3.1/36 Fabric 10.1. Fig. 83.15. Young 1977, W29
3.1/89 Fabric 6.1. Not illustrated. Young 1977, 150, Fig. 54.
3.2 A narrow necked jar, otherwise corresponding to the general definition given for jars.
3.2/2 Fabric 12.2. Fig. 83.18, rusticated, late 1st/early 2nd century form, almost the only example of rusticated decoration recovered from this site.
3.2/4 Fabric 11.2. Fig. 83.19. (Not illustrated Fabric 12.3).
3.2/6 Fabric 12.3, 14.1. Not illustrated.
3.2/8 Fabric 12.2. Fig. 83.20. (Not illustrated 12.1).
3.2/10 Fabric 12.1. Fig. 83.21.
3.2/15 Fabric 12.1. Fig. 83.25.
3.2/19 Fabric 12.2. Fig. 83.26.
3.2/24 Fabric 12.1. Not illustrated.
3.2/27 Fabric 12.1. Fig. 83.27.
3.2/30 Fabric 12.1, 6.1. Fig. 83.23 and 24.
3.2/33 Fabric 6.3. Not illustrated. Young 1977, WC2, 120, Fig. 38.
3.2/34 Fabric 6.1. Not illustrated. Young 1977, C16, p 150, Fig. 54
3.2/37 Fabric 12.1. Fig. 83.28.
3.2/41 Fabric 12.1. Not illustrated.
3.2/43 Fabric 12.1. Not illustrated.
3.2/45 Fabric 12.7. Not illustrated.
3.2/46 Fabric 13.5. Not illustrated.
3.2/56 Fabric 12.1. Fig. 83.22. (Not illustrated 12.2).
3.2/57 Fabric 12.1. Fig. 83.31.
3.2/59 Fabric 12.1. Fig. 83.33. Young 1977, R9 and 10, p. 209, Fig. 74.
3.2/60 Fabric 12.1. Fig. 83.29 and 30.
3.2/64 Fabric 13.1. Fig. 83.34. (Not illustrated 12.7, 12.1).
3.2/65 Fabric 12.1. Fig. 83.32.

3.3 Jars with a distinct carination were fragmentary. There were no complete or even semi-complete profiles.
3.3 Fabric 12.1 Fig. 84.1. (Not illustrated 13.1, 13.4, 13.5, 14.2).
3.4 This sub-division is defined as wide mouthed jars in which the diameter of the mouth is the same or a little less than that of the body. Those vessels, for which only the general type and rim form could be recognised and so have numerical descriptions of the form 3/5 without sub-division of the vessel type, are included here because, although they were fragmentary, they appeared to be wide mouthed.
3/5 Fabric 6.3. Fig. 84.6.
3/27 Fabric 13.5. Fig. 84.29. (Not illustrated 12.1).
3/40 Fabric 10.1. Fig. 84.2.
3/42 Fabric 11.2. Not illustrated.
3/45 Fabric 12.1. Fig. 84.5.
3/46 Fabric 10.2. Fig. 84.4. (Not illustrated 12.1).
3/71 Fabric 13.5. Fig. 84.7.
3/82 Fabric 12.1. Fig. 84.3.
3.4/2 Fabric 13.1. Fig. 84.8. This vessel has small patches of lead glaze on its rim and shoulder. It is suggested that it is a product of the N. Wilts kilns which produced lead glazed pottery. Fabric 11.2. Fig. 84.10. Fabric 12.1. Fig. 84.11, grooved on shoulder. (Not illustrated 10.2, 11.1, 12.3, 12.4, 12.7, 13.5, 13.6, 14.3, 15, 20).
3.4/3 Fabric 12.1. Fig. 84.13. (Not illustrated 10.2, 11.1, 11.2, 12.2, 12.3, 15).
3.4/4 Fabric 12.1. Fig. 84.20. (Not illustrated 12.3).
3.4/5 Fabric 17. Fig. 84.21.
3.4/6 Fabric 12.1. Fig. 84.26. (Not illustrated 11.2, 12.3, 14.2, 14.4, 15).
3.4/7 Fabric 12.1. Fig. 84.27.

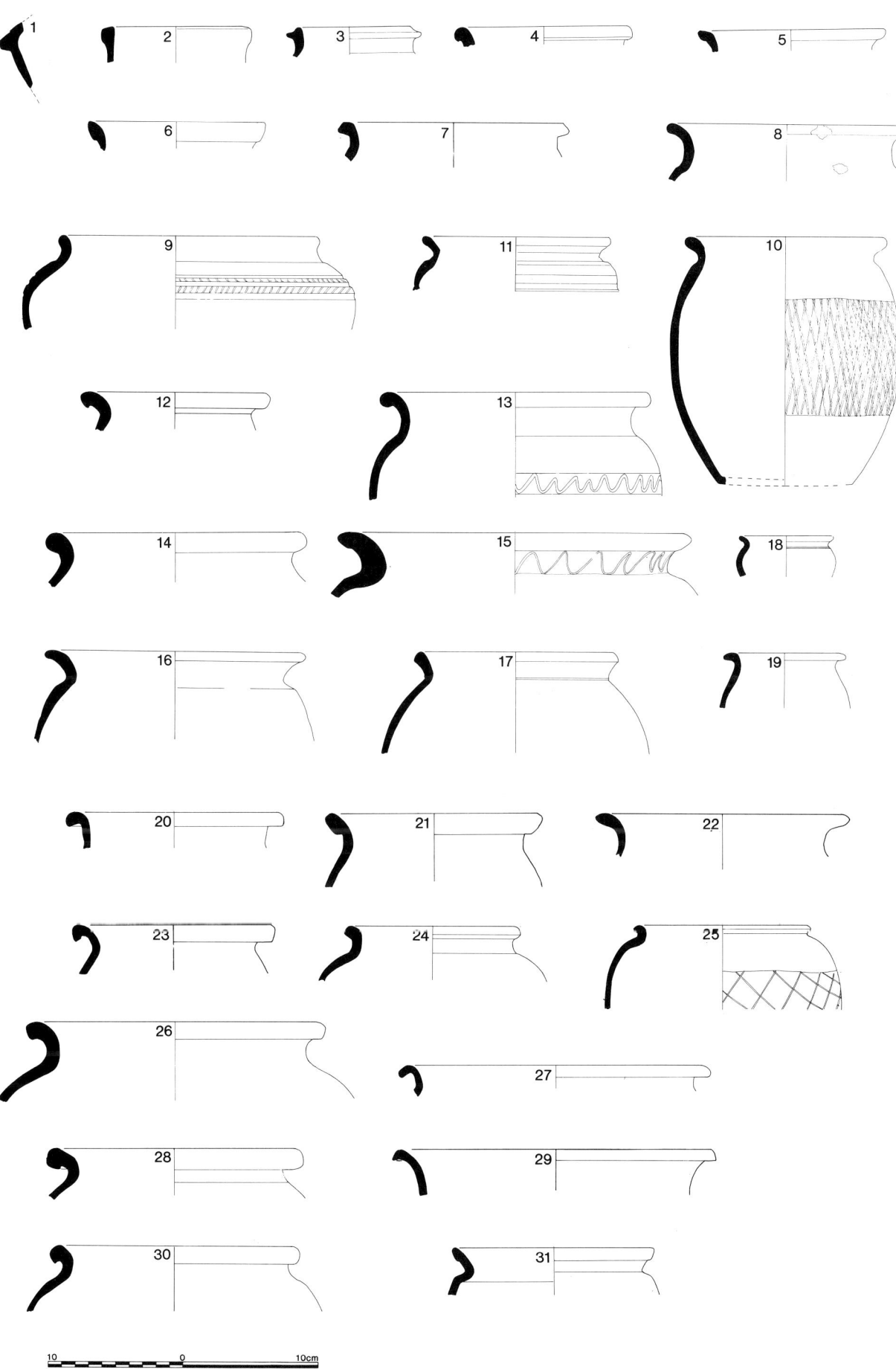

Figure 84 Roman pottery: Form Corpus Type 3.3 to 3.4

3.4/8 Fabric 12.1. Fig. 84.24. (Not illustrated 12.3, 15, 20, 21)
3.4/10 Fabric 12.1. Fig. 84.17. (Not illustrated 15).
3.4/11 Fabric 11.1. Fig. 84.25.
3.4/12 Fabric 12.1. Fig. 84.9. (Not illustrated 12.3).
3.4/13 Fabrics 12.1, 12.3, 12.4. Not illustrated.
3.4/14 Fabric 12.1. Not illustrated.
3.4/19 Fabric 12.1. Fig. 84.14. (Not illustrated 11.2, 12.3, 14.1).
3.4/21 Fabric 11.2. Fig. 84.23. (Not illustrated 12.1, 12.3).
3.4/24 Not illustrated
3.4/28 Fabric 12.2. Fig. 84.31. (Not illustrated 12.1)
3.4/30 Fabric 12.3. Fig. 84.30. (Not illustrated 12.1, 12.4).
3.4/36 Fabric 11.2, 12.1. Fig. 85.5 and 6.
3.4/42 Fabric 12.1. Not illustrated
3.4/43 Fabric 11.1. Fig. 84.22. (Not illustrated 11.2, 12.1, 12.3, 13.5).
3.4/45 Fabric 12.3. Not illustrated
3.4/46 Fabric 12.3 Not illustrated
3.4/49 Fabric 20. Not illustrated
3.4/52 Fabric 11.1. Fig. 84.15 and 16. (Not illustrated 11.2, 12.1, 12.2, 12.3, 12.4).
3.4/55 Fabric 12.1. Fig. 84.18. (Not illustrated 11.1, 12.2, 13.1).
3.4/56 Fabric 11.2. Fig. 84.12. (Not illustrated 10.2, 12.1/22, 12.3, 12.4, 13.1, 15).
3.4/57 Fabric 12.1. Fig. 85.8. (Not illustrated 12.3, 15).
3.4/62 Fabric 12.3. Not illustrated.
3.4/64 Fabric 13.1. Fig. 84.19. (Not illustrated 12.1, 12.3, 12.4, 15).

3.4/66 Fabric 12.3. Fig. 85.4.
3.4/67 Fabric 12.3. Fig. 85.7.
3.4/68 Fabric 12.3 (variation). Fig. 85.3. This form and fabric are paralleled at Claydon Pike, Fairford, Glos. (Green in Miles and Palmer in prep), Churchill Hospital Kilns, Oxford (Green and Young in prep), Wanborough (Janet Richardson pers. comm.), Cirencester (J Richardson), Tiddington and Alchester (Paul Booth pers. comm.). More complete vessels take the form of a large globular storage jar. All these examples appear to be of 3rd to 4th century date.
3.4/69 Fabric 12.3, 12.4. Fig. 85.1 and 2.
3.4/73 Fabric 12.2. Not illustrated.
3.4/80 Fabric 20. Fig. 84.28.
3.5 This division forms a distinct vessel type with a curved neck, a high shoulder, and body walls tapering to a relatively narrow, often foot-ring, base.
3.5/2 Fabric 20. Fig. 85.9. (Not illustrated 11.5, 12.1, 12.3, 13.5, 14.3).
3.5/3 Fabric 12.1. Fig. 85.12. (Not illustrated 12.7, 14.3 cf. Young 1977, R38, p. 220, Fig. 80).
3.5/4 Fabric 12.1. Not illustrated.

3.5/56 Fabric 12.1. Not illustrated.
3.5/64 Fabric 12.1. Fig. 85.11.
3.5/81 Fabric 20. Fig. 85.10. (Not illustrated 19).
3.5/82 Fabric 20. Not illustrated.
3.6 This definition is very similar to that of 3.4, the important difference is that the diameter of the rim is greater than that of the body.
3.6/2 Fabric 11.2. Fig. 85.20.
3.6/3 Fabric 12.1. Fig. 85.17.
3.6/6 Fabric 13.1, 12.1. Not illustrated.
3.6/16 Fabric 12.1. Not illustrated.
3.6/27 Fabric 13.5. Fig. 85.13.
3.6/30 Fabric 13.5. Fig. 85.14 and 15.
3.6/36 Fabric 12.1. Not illustrated.
3.6/43 Fabric 11.1. Fig. 85.19.
3.6/51 Fabric 12.1. Fig. 85.16.
3.6/52 Fabric 11.2. Fig. 85.18. (Not illustrated 16).
3.6/56 Fabric 12.1. Not illustrated.
3.6/64 Fabric 13.5. Fig. 85.21.

3.7 Jars with globular bodies and very little or no neck. The rim diameter is less than that of the body.
3.7/12 Fabric 12.3, 12.5. Fig. 86.6 and 7. (Not illustrated 12.6, 15, 20, 21).
3.7/38 Fabric 12.3, 15. Fig. 86.1 and 2. (Not illustrated 17).
3.7/55 Fabric 11.2. Fig. 86.8.
3.7/77 Fabric 16. Fig. 86.3.
3.7/84 Fabric 11.3. Fig. 86.9.
3.8 Jars with relatively uncurved body walls close to vertical and everted rims whose diameter may be greater or less than the body.
3.8/12 Fabric 16. Fig. 86.10.
3.8/55 Fabric 16. Fig. 86.4 and 11; fabric 20, Fig. 86.5.
3.8/76 Fabric 16. Fig. 86.12.
3.8/78 Fabric 16. Fig. 86.13.
3.8/79 Fabric 15. Fig. 86.14.

Type 4 Beakers
Most of the specimens from Roughground Farm were fragmentary and it was difficult to define them further than major type with differentiated rims.

4/1 Fabric 6.1. Not illustrated.
4/2 Fabric 6.1. Not illustrated.
4/3 Fabric 12.1. Not illustrated.
4/12 Fabric 11.1. Fig. 86.15.
4/14 Fabric 11.1. Fig. 86.16. (Not illustrated 6.1).
4/22 Fabric 6.1. Not illustrated Young 1977, Form C22, p. 152, Fig. 55.
4/25 Fabric 12.1. Fig. 86.23. (Not illustrated 5 and 8).
4/26 Fabric 8. Not illustrated.
4/35 Fabric 12.1, 11.2 Fig. 86.25 and 26.
4/44 Fabric 6.1. Not illustrated.
4/45 Fabric 6.1. Not illustrated.

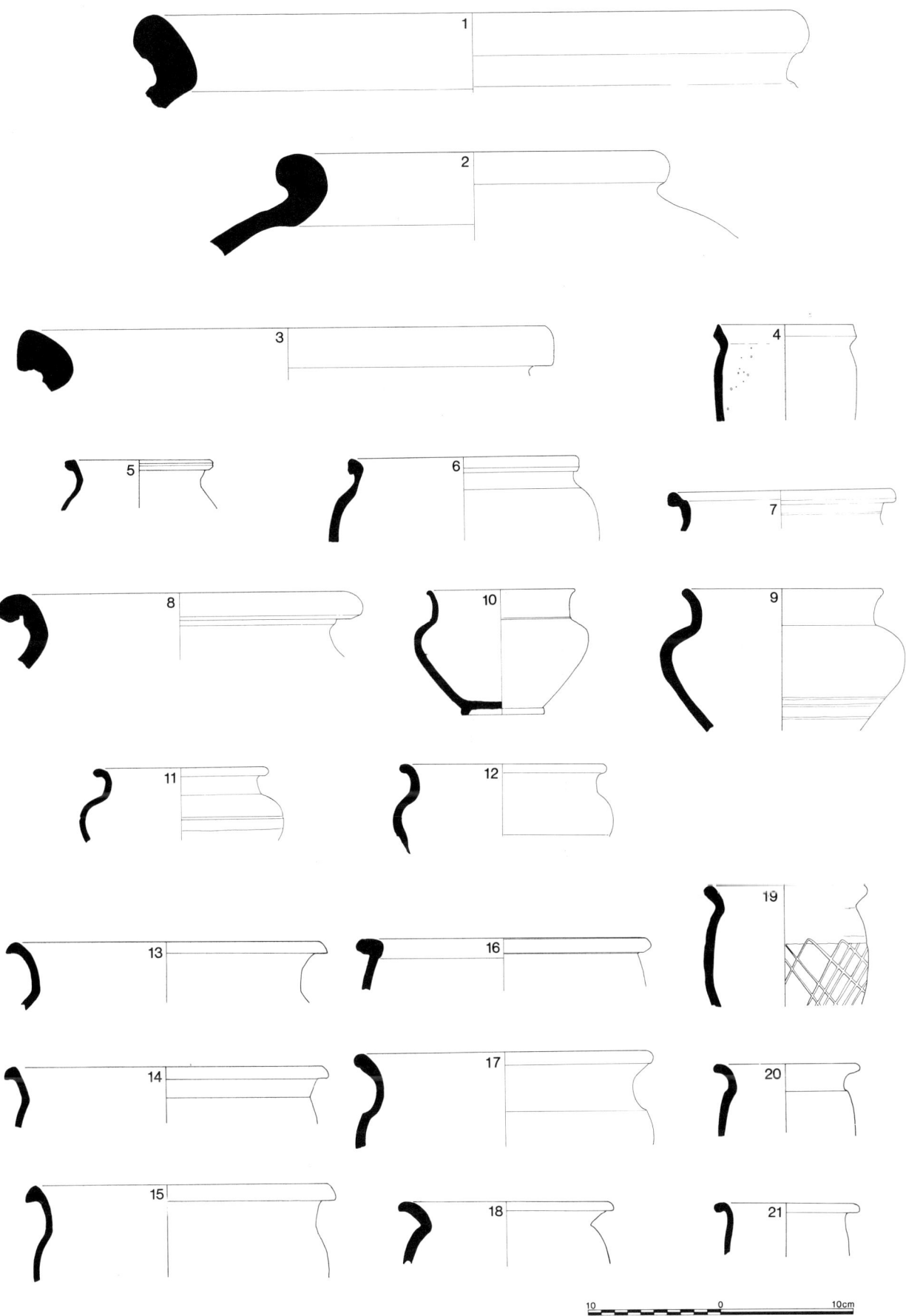

Figure 85 Roman pottery: Form Corpus Types 3.4 (cont.) to 3.6

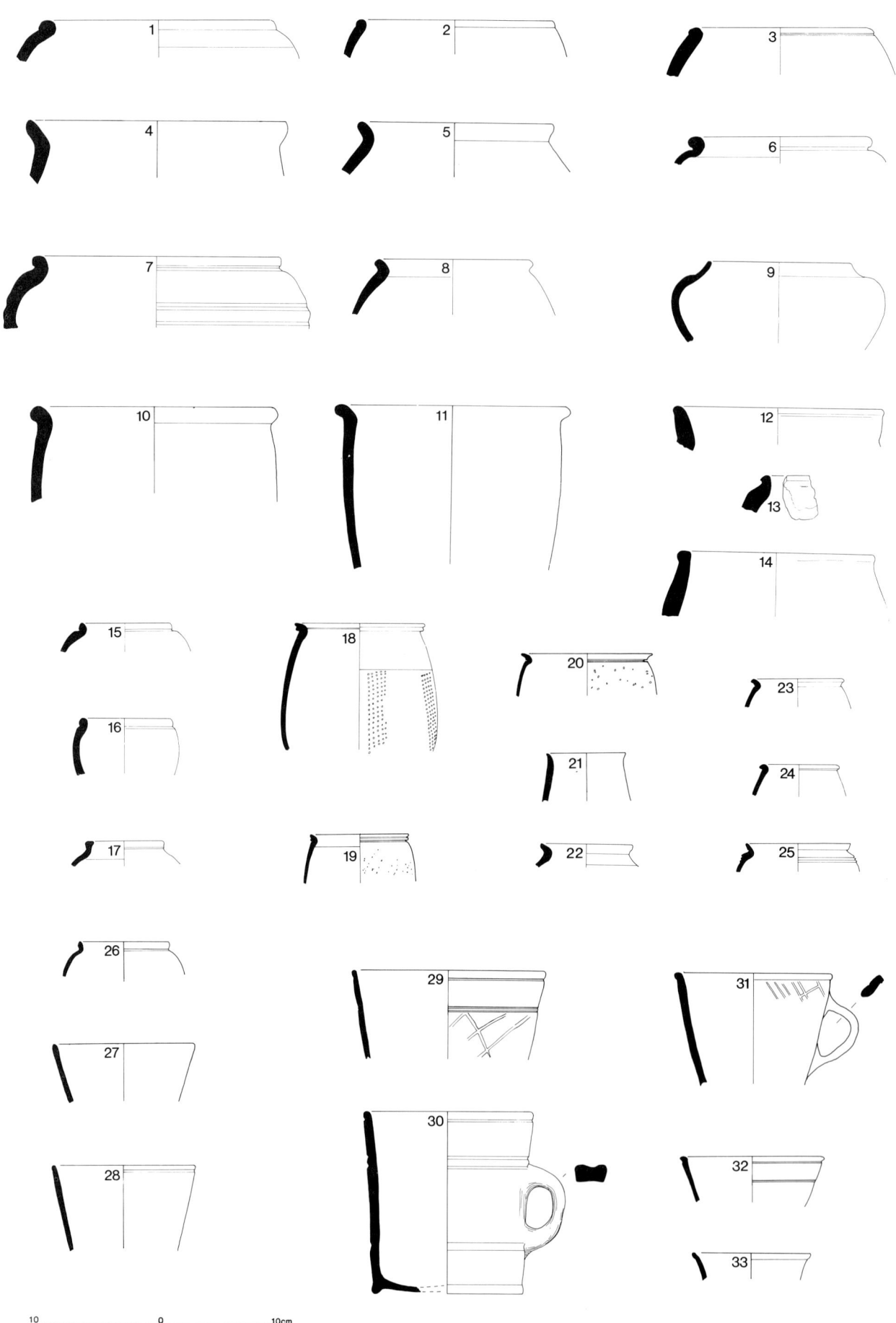

Figure 86 Roman pottery: Form Corpus Types 3.7 to 5

4/46 Fabric 10.1. Fig. 86.24.
4/55 Fabric 12.1. Fig. 86.22.
4/70 Fabric 12.1. Fig. 86.21.
4/77 Fabric 12.1. Fig. 86.17.
4.1/25 Fabric 5. Fig. 86.20.
4.1/26 Fabric 5. Fig. 86.18.
4.1/39 Fabric 5. Fig. 86.19. (Not illustrated 12.1).
4.3 Fabric 7, Fulford type 39, not illustrated Fulford 1975.
4.3/19 Fabric 6.1. Not illustrated. Young 1977, C27, p. 154, Fig. 56.
4.6 Fabric 6.1. Not illustrated. Young 1977, C20, p. 152, Fig. 55. Fabric 8, 13.1, 5, 7. Not illustrated.

Type 5 Cups
As with the other major forms subdivisions are made according to differences in body shape.
Only the major form number is given for fragmentary sherds; these are ordered by rim number.

5/14 This rim type was the most common (see catalogues for actual figures) Fabric 13.1. Fig. 86.28 and 32. (Not illustrated 12.1, 13.5).
5.2 This subdivision is defined as having more or less straight, vertical sides
5.2/1 Fabric 13.1. Fig. 86.27. (Not illustrated 12.2).
5.2/14 Fabric 13.1, 13.5. Fig. 86.29, 30 and 31. (Not illustrated 12.1).
5.3 This type differs from the above in that the sides of the vessel curve outwards away from the vertical.
5.3/1 Fabric 12.1. Not illustrated.
5.3/14 Fabric 13.1. Fig. 86.33. (Not illustrated Fabric 12.1).

Type 6 Bowls
The major subdivisions with variations in rim form are described below. The more common imitation samian forms have been given separate numbers under this scheme.

6.1 This form corresponds to the general description above but is differentiated from others under this heading by its incurving sides.
6.1/1 Fabric 11.2. Fig. 87.4. Note parallel lines of burnishing. (Not illustrated 6.1 Young 1977, C41, p. 156, Fig. 57).
6.1/2 Fabric
6.1/4 Fabric 10.1. Fig. 87.17. (Not illustrated 12.8).
6.1/16 Fabric 12.1. Fig. 87.18.
6.1/17 Fabric 13.5. Fig. 87.8 and 9.
6.1/19 Fabric 12.1. Fig. 87.6.
6.1/20 Fabric 10.1. Fig. 87.23. This vessel is decorated with orange painted crosses on the upper flange. Similar in form to Oxford white ware bowl W50 Young 1977, 106, Fig. 32.
6.1/22 Fabric 12.1. Fig. 87.7. (Not illustrated 11.2).
6.1/23 Fabric 11.2. Fig. 87.11.
6.1/29 Fabric 12.1. Fig. 87.16. (Not illustrated 11.2).
6.1/42 Fabric 11.2. Fig. 87.5.
6.1/47 Fabric 9.2. Fig. 87.3.
6.1/51 Fabric 10.2. Fig. 87.15.
6.1/53 Fabric 11.2. Fig. 87.12. (Not illustrated 12.1).
6.1/54 Fabric 11.2. Not illustrated.
6/58 Fabric 12.1. Not illustrated.
6.1/62 Fabric 12.1. Fig. 87.14.
6.1/63 Fabric 15. Fig. 87.10.
6.1/65 Fabric 14.2. Not illustrated.
6.1/70 Fabric 13.2. Not illustrated.
6.1/72 Fabric 13.5. Fig. 87.19 and 20.
6.1/74 Fabric 13.6. Fig. 87.21. Upstanding part of rim damaged.
6.1/75 Fabric 14.2. Fig. 87.22.
6.1/88 Fabric 11.2. Fig. 87.13.
6.1/90 Fabric 12.1, 16. Fig. 87.1 and 2. The coarse storage vessels in fabric 16 are placed in the category of bowls because close parallels from other sites are of this form, viz. Claydon Pike, Fairford, Glos. (Miles and Palmer in prep), Poston, Herefordshire (Anthony 1958, Fig. 7, p. 33), Sutton Walls (Kenyon 1953, Fig. 18, 5), Frocester (pers. comm. S Trow), North Cerney, Glos (Trow 1982) and Beckford, Glos. (pers. comm. H Rees). In all cases these vessels, like the examples illustrated here, appear to be tempered with palaeozoic limestone of probable Cotswold origin.
6.2 A sub-division made on the basis of the straight walls of these vessels, while still corresponding to the general form description.

6.2/1 Fabric 15. Fig. 88.1. (Not illustrated 11.1, 11.2, 12.1).
6.2/3 Fabric 12.1. Fig. 88.18.
6.2/14 Fabric 13.2 Fig. 88.10. (Not illustrated 12.1).
6.2/16 Fabric 11.1. Fig. 88.11 and 12. (Not illustrated 11.2, 12.1, 12.7).
6.2/20 Fabric 11.2. Fig. 88.14.
6.2/23 Fabric 12.1. Fig. 88.9.
6.2/29 Fabric 9.4. Fig. 88.17.
6.2/34 Fabric 11.3. Fig. 88.3.
6.2/41 Fabric 11.1, 11.2, Fig. 88.15 and 16. (Not illustrated 6.1 Young 1977, C93, p. 173, Fig. 66, 12.1, 14.1).
6.2/42 Fabric 11.2. Fig. 88.5.
6.3/47 Fabric 11.1. Fig. 88.2 and 6.
6.2/52 Fabric 11.1. Not illustrated.
6.2/53 Fabric 11.1, 12.1. Not illustrated.
6.2/54 Fabric 11.2. Fig. 88.8. (Not illustrated 11.1).
6.2/58 Fabric 12.1. Fig. 88.4.
6.2/59 Not illustrated
6.2/61 Fabric 11.1. Fig. 88.7. (Not illustrated 12.1).
6.2/62 Fabric 12.3. Not illustrated.
6.2/82 Fabric 11.2. Fig. 88.13.
6.3 This vessel type corresponds to the general criteria for bowls outlined at the beginning of this section. Its

128 *Roughground Farm, Lechlade, Gloucestershire: a prehistoric and Roman landscape*

Figure 87 Roman pottery: Form Corpus Type 6.1

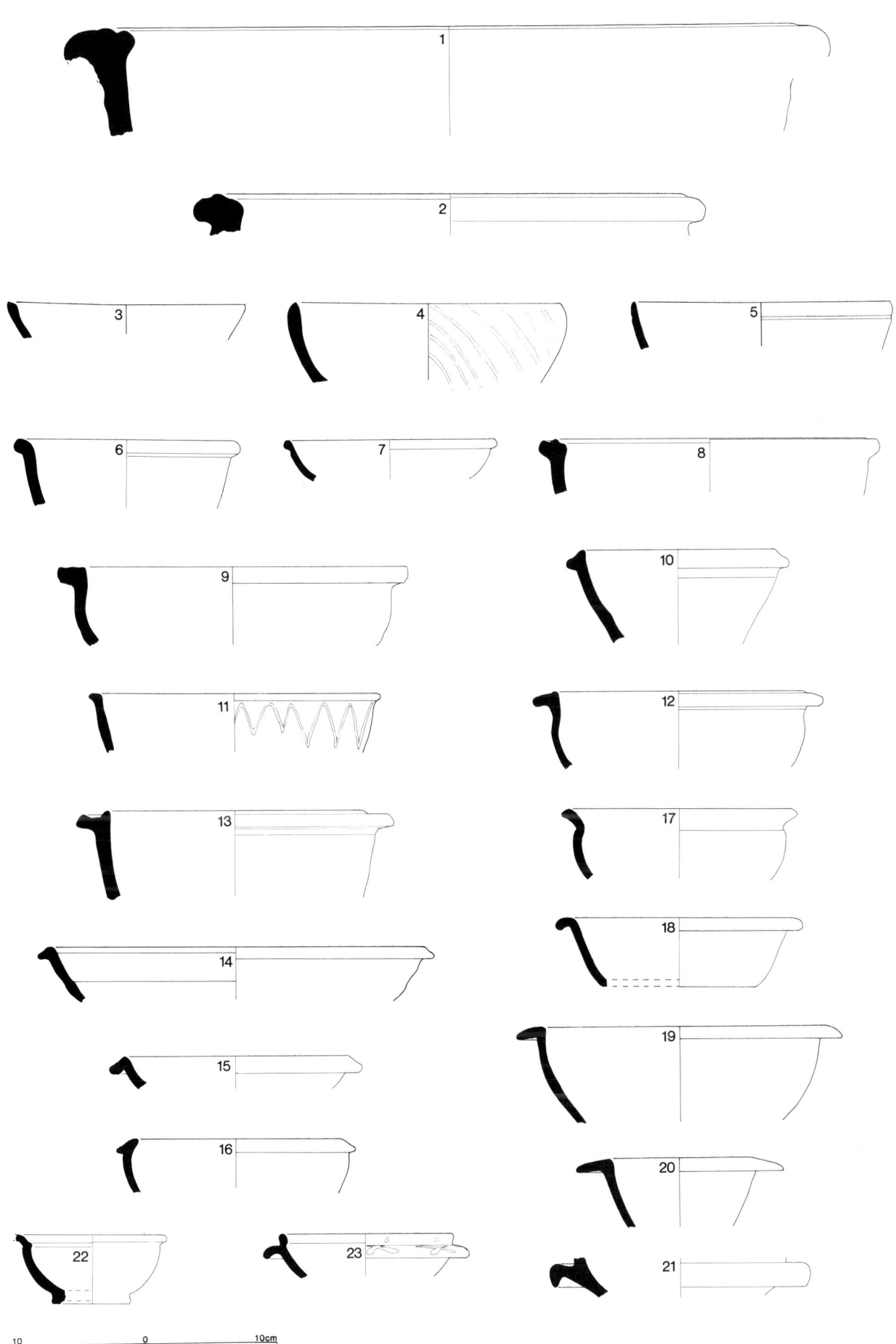

Figure 88 Roman pottery: Form Corpus Types 6.2 to 6.11

distinguishing characteristics are its angular profile and carination. Only one example has been recognised from Roughground Farm.

6.3/14 Fabric 13.5. Fig. 88.25. Highly burnished, cf. Webster 1976.

6.4 A bowl with numerous holes pierced in the base before firing to allow drainage, viz., a colander. No vessels with rims were found, that illustrated being the most complete example. Fabrics 12.1. Fig. 88.19. (Not illustrated 13.1, 11.2).

6.5 Bowl imitating samian form Drag. 31 This form only definitely occurred in Fabric 6.1. Young 1977, 158, Fig. 58, C45 and C46. Fig. 88.22. This example was chosen for illustration because of its complete profile and illiterate stamp.

6.6 A bowl imitating samian form Drag. 27 One example only from this site, Fabric 12.1, not illustrated. Young 1977, R62.1, p. 224, Fig. 83. The dating is given as second century.

6.7 A bowl with a chamfered base.

6.7/16 Fabric 11.1. Fig. 88.20 and 21. (Not illustrated 12.1).

6.7/18 Fabric 12.7. Fig. 88.23.

6.7/53 Fabric 12.1. Not illustrated.

6.7/63 Fabric 12.1. Fig. 88.26.

6.8 Bowl copying samian form Drag. 36 and Curle 15.

6.8/85 Fabric 6.1. Not illustrated. Young 1977, C47 and C48, p. 158, Fig. 58

6.8/86 Fabric 13.6. Fig. 88.27. (Not illustrated 6.1, Young 1977, p. 158, Fig. 58).

6.9 Bowl copying samian form Dr 38. (Not illustrated 6.1, Young 1977, C51 and Young 1977, C52, p. 160, Fig. 59).

6.10 Bowl form copying Drag. 37 Fabric 6.1. Fig. 88.24. Young 1977, C55, C73, C75, C81, C84, C86, pp. 160, 164, 166, 170. Figs. 60, 61, 62, 64, 65.

6.11 Bowl form with wall sides. Not illustrated. Fabrics 6.2, 6.3, Young 1977, 24, 87, Fig. 27, and 120, Fig. 38.

Type 6–7 Bowl or dish

Vessels were given this classification when a positive identification as either 'bowl' or 'dish' was impossible. The two forms illustrated below were picked to extend the range of decoration illustrated rather than for rim form.

6–7/1 Fabric 11.2. Fig. 89.1. (Not illustrated 11.1, 12.1)
6–7/14 Fabric 11.2. Fig. 89.5. (Not illustrated 11.1).

Type 7 Dishes

Four sub-divisions are described below. The commoner rim forms which are also to be found with Form 6 are catalogued but not illustrated.

7.1 A dish with straight sides and flat base.
7/1 Fabric 8. Not illustrated.

7.1/1 Fabrics 11.1, 11.2, 13.1, 15. Not illustrated.
7.1/14 Fabric 13.1. Fig. 89.6.
7.1/16 Fabric 11.1. Fig. 89.7.
7.1/19 Fabric 12.1. Not illustrated.
7.1/42 Fabric 12.1. Not illustrated.
7.1/47 Fabric 11.1. Not illustrated.
7.1/58 Fabric 12.1. Not illustrated.

7.2 A sub-division corresponding to the major form type but being distinguished by its having one or more handles. The vessel may be oval or circular in plan.

7.2/1 Fabric 11.1. Fig. 89.2. Only one fragment of a vessel corresponding to the above description was found.

7.4 A vessel type following the major form description above but with a shallow wall, or 'hammerhead' rim. Fabric 6.1. Not illustrated. Young 1977, C41, p. 156 for description.

7.5 This sub-division is distinguished by its small footing base and outward sloping straight or slightly convex sides. Fabric 14.5, 11.2, Fig. 89.3, and 4.

Type 8 Plates

8 The sherd illustrated apparently corresponds to this type, but the walls have been ground down, possibly indicating re-use as a lid. Traces of red colouring occurred on both sides. Fabric 10.1. Fig. 89.8. (Not illustrated 12.1, 12.3).

Type 9 Lids

Differences in rim types formed the basis for sub-dividing this type.

9.1 A lid with plain rim. Fabric 12.1, 11.2. Fig. 89.9 and 10. (Not illustrated 12.3, 11.2).

9.2 Lid with slightly everted pointed rim. Fabric 11.2. Fig. 89.11. Fabric 12.1. Fig. 89.12 and 13.

9.4 Lid with rim square in section with groove. Fabric 12.1. Fig. 89.14 and 15.

9.5 Lid with inturned rim projected outwards at right angles to body. Fabric 13.6. Fig. 89.16. (Not illustrated 12.1, 13.5).

9.6 Lid with everted rounded rim. Fabric 11.2. Fig. 89.17. (Not illustrated Fabrics 12.1, 13.5, 13.6).

9.7 Lid with inturned angular rim. Fabric 12.2. Fig. 89.18. (Not illustrated 12.4, 14.3).

9.8 Lid with inturned rim, similar to 9.5 but without projection. Fabric 13.1. Fig. 89.19 and 20.

Type 10 Mortaria

by Kay Hartley and Sarah Green

See specialist report Ch. V.2.b.4.

10.1 Mortarium with roll rim turned under at its tip and bead which is lower than the highest point of the rim.

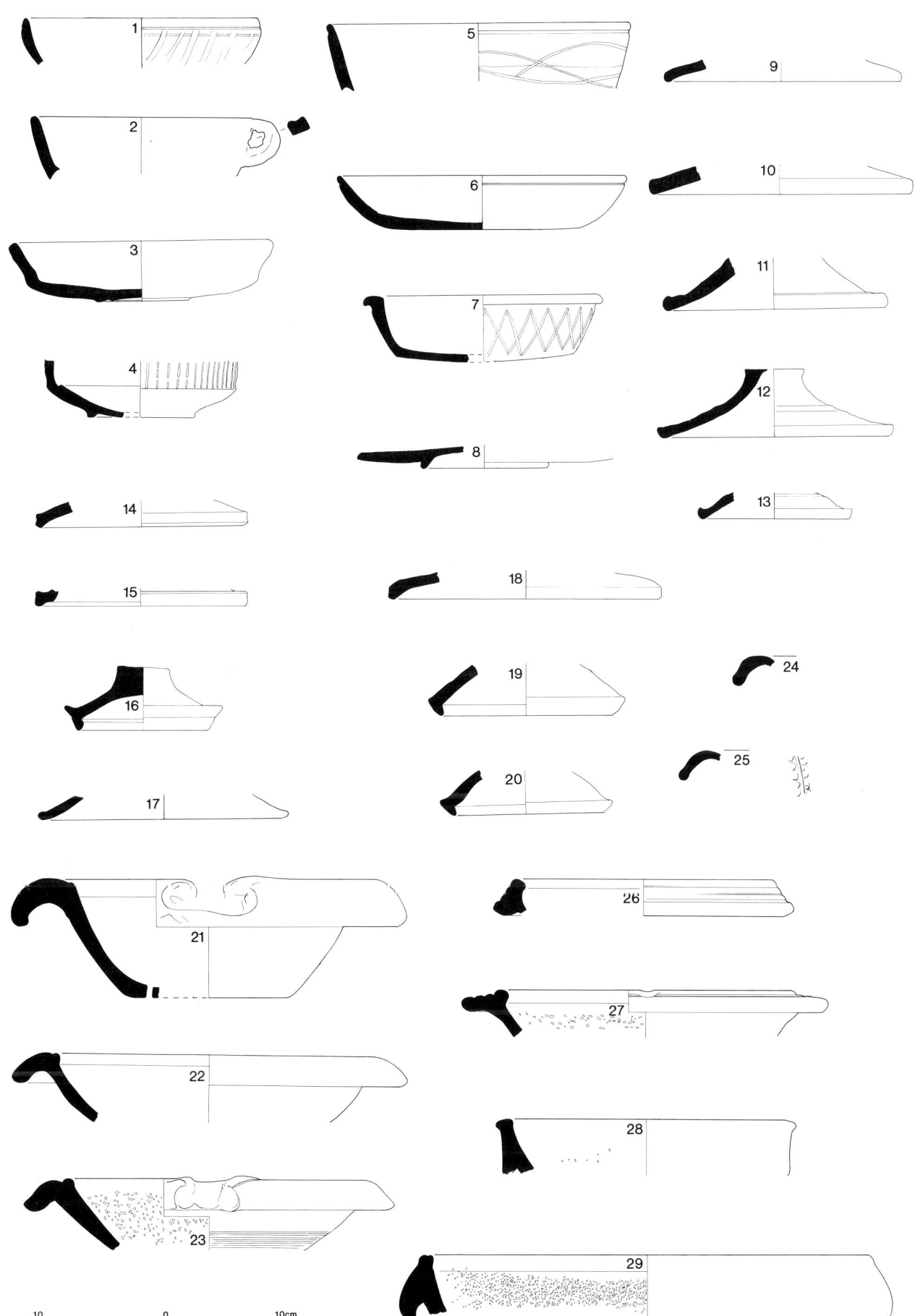

Figure 89 Roman pottery: Form Corpus Types 6–7 to 10.11

Fabric 2.8. Not illustrated. Verulamium 110–145 AD. Fabric 2.1. Not illustrated Oxford M1 100–150 AD Young 1977, 68.

10.2 Mortaria with roll rim and internal bead which is lower than the highest part of the rim. Fabric 2.8. Fig. 89.21. Verulamium 80–120 AD. Fabric 2.1. Fig. 89.24 and 25. Both of the illustrated sherds may come from the same vessel. Oxford M2 100–170 AD Young 1977, 68.

10.3 Mortaria with roll rim and bead which is the highest point of the rim. Fabric 2.1. Not illustrated. Oxford M3 140–200 AD Young 1977, 68.

10.4 Fabric 2.7. Fig. 89.22. Cirencester 140–180 AD. Fabric 2.7. Fig. 89.23. Cirencester 140–180 AD.

10.5 Mortarium with thick downward pointing grooved flange. Fabric 2.5. Fig. 89.26. Mancetter/Hartshill 220–280 AD. Fabric 2.9. Not illustrated Unknown source 200–300 AD.

10.6 Mortarium with upright rim and downward pointing hooked flange. Fabric 2.4. Fig. 89.29. Lower Germany 150–250 AD. Fabric 2.1. Not illustrated Oxford White Ware M11 Young 1977, 70 180–240 AD

10.7 Wall sided mortarium. Fabric 2.7. Fig. 89.28. Glos./N.Wilts 200–300 AD. Fabric 2.1. Not illustrated Oxford White Ware M14 Young 1977, 72. Fabric 2.2. Not illustrated Oxford Red/brown CC C97 Young 1977, 174, Fig. 67.

10.8 Mortarium with upstanding rim, wide flat hooked flange and spout formed by turning the rim out across the flange. Fabric 2.1. Not illustrated Oxford White Ware M17 Young 1977, 72, Fig. 21. 240–300 AD Fabric 2.2. Not illustrated Oxford White CC Ware, WC4 Young 1977, 120, Fig. 38 240–300 AD.

10.9 Similar to above but with closed hook. Fabric 2.1. Not illustrated Oxford White Ware M18 Young 1977, 72, Fig. 21. 240–300 AD

10.10 Mortarium with upstanding rim, sometimes grooved, and wide thick inbent flange. Fabric 2.1. Not illustrated Oxford White Ware M19 Young 1977, 76, Fig. 22 240–300 AD.

10.11 Mortarium with slight bead on a straight, slightly downsloping grooved flange. Fabric 2.6. Fig. 89.27. Lower Nene Valley 300–400 AD.

10.12 Mortarium with downward pointing angular flange hooked sharply back. Fabric 2.1. Not illustrated Oxford White Ware M21 Young 1977, 76, Fig. 22 240–300 AD.

10.13 Mortarium with upstanding rim and squat flange folded over quite close to body. Fabric 2.1. Not illustrated Oxford White Ware M22 Young 1977, 77, Fig. 23 240–400AD. Fabric 2.2. Not illustrated Oxford white colour-coat WC7 Young 1977, 122, Fig. 38 240–400AD. Fabric 2.3. Not illustrated Oxford red/brown colour-coat C100 Young 1977, 174, Fig. 67 300–400AD.

Type 11 Amphorae

See the specialist report above (Ch. V.2.b.3). Because of the fragmentary nature of the sherds the only drawing is of a name stamp from the handle of a Dressel 20 (Fig. 90.1). Two amphora types were identified.

11.1 Dressel 20, used for transportation of olive oil, from southern spain. Globular shape but short neck and thick double handles. Mainly first to second century but continued into third century.

11.2 Pelichet 47, used for transportation of wine, probably from southern France. Dated from last half of first century to beginning of third century.

Type 12 Miscellaneous vessel types

12.1 Not illustrated. Castor Box or its lid. Nene Valley coated ware (see Hartley 1972, Fig. 4, 17–18) and Howe et al 1980).

12.2 Fabric 12.6, two body sherds possibly from a butt beaker made in an imitation *Terra nigra* fabric. Vertical and diagonal combing in groups of four between zones of rouletting. Fig. 90.2.

12.3 Fabric 23, a miniature dolium in fine hard dark grey fabric. Fig. 90.3.

12.4 Fabric 9.4, a cylindrical two handled flagon-like vessel with rough horizontal grooves round its neck and shoulder. Fig. 90.4.

12.5 Fabric 12.2, a cylindrical vessel of vaguely chimney like appearance with pronounced flange around lower neck. Fig. 90.5.

12.6 Fabric 20, pedestal base. Fig. 90.7

12.7 Fabric 16, base, pierced after firing, fulfilling some straining function. Parallels from Barton Court (Miles 1986), Stanton Harcourt (Grimes 1943 44) and Frilford (Bradford & Goodchild 1939). Fig. 90.8.

12.8 Convex base from jug or flagon. See report on Fabric 25. Fig. 90.9

12.9 Fabric 12.1, Body sherd of vessel with deeply fluted sides in fine grey fabric. cf. 'Salmonsbury vase'. (See Discussion below for further details). Fig. 90.6.

12.10 Fabric 24, A single body sherd probably from a jar. The decoration consists of regularly spaced square stamps impressed onto the body and the applied semi-circular lug handle (?) of the vessel. Fig. 90.11)

Type 13 Re-used sherds

Spindle whorls made out of bases of Oxford red/brown colour-coated vessels (Fig. 90.12 and 13). Other re-used sherds (not illustrated) included a grey ware body sherd roughly rectangular in shape (c 70 mm long) with all four corners rounded off and its sides smoothed. A similar sized sherd of BB1 had one side filed off and rounded in the same way. As has already been noted at least one samian vessel had been re-shaped for use as a lid.

Ch. V.   *The finds of the Roman and post-Roman periods*   133

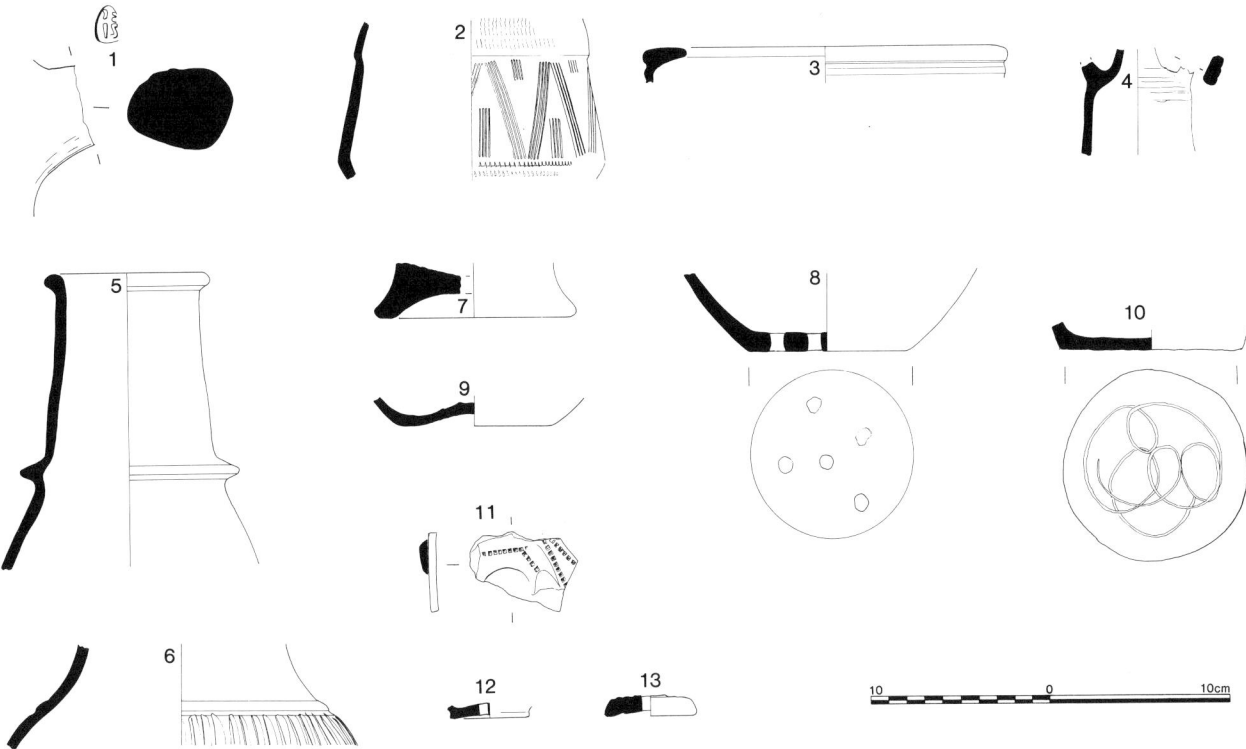

Figure 90 Roman pottery: Form Corpus Types 11 to 13

V.2.d Discussion of pottery recovered between 1957 and 1982

V.2.d.1 Introduction

The criteria used for phasing within the Roman period have already been discussed (Ch. V.1). Problems with using the pottery for dating included a scarcity of good stratified deposits, residuality, and contamination.

A major problem was the lack of published dated sequences of comparable material from the area, a problem partially allayed at a late stage of the analysis by the publication of the early Cirencester sites (Wacher & McWhirr 1982). Examination of the pottery from Fairford, Claydon Pike (in prep) which is some 3 km from Roughground Farm) also provided useful stratified sequences. The local coarse wares of presumably limited distribution (such as many of the grey wares, *eg* fabrics 12.1, 12.2) were particularly problematical but an effort was made to define their distribution if only by noting their absence at other sites. Parallels from Bagendon have been sought where relevant, with the redating suggested by Swan (Clifford 1961; Swan 1975).

A series of pie-diagrams (Fig. 150 on Fiche 2#23) attempts to show the changing proportions of fabric during the Roman phases of the site. Intermediate phases were introduced when the available evidence did not allow greater accuracy.

V.2.d.2 Non-local fabrics

Imported types form a small proportion of the ceramic assemblages of the earliest phases of the site. South Gaulish samian, including a few Neronian and Flavian sherds, forms the bulk of these imports but the quantity is very small in comparison to the later, mainly Central Gaulish samian which continues to be the major long distance import throughout the second century. Occasional sherds of early imported fine wares occur residually, for instance, the flagon base of 'black sand' fabric (Fig. 90.9). Rhenish and imported rough-cast wares are poorly represented.

Of the major Romano-British colour-coat industries Oxford wares are the most important with Nene Valley and New Forest types coming a poor second and third respectively. The other colour-coated pottery (Fabric 9) forms a relatively large proportion due to its more local nature and will be considered below.

No amphorae occur in the first site period and the majority of sherds appear to be residual examples of first and second century Spanish imports. Single specimens of mortaria from several well known industries occur, the majority, however, are third and fourth century Oxford types (see Fig. 79 for a detailed breakdown of types).

The dividing line between local and non-local is arbitrary and certain coarse ware fabrics of unknown provenance are difficult to ascribe satisfactorily. Some fabrics which are poorly represented on the site (eg Fabrics 13.2–13.5) show attributes characteristic of Severn Valley Wares. Others however, some of the sandy grey wares for example, are considered local because of their relative abundance, their absence from assemblages from relatively similar sites (with the proviso noted at the beginning of this section), and the assumption that coarse grey or black wares are unlikely to have been imported from a great distance. Black-burnished 1, although anomalous by these criteria, is considered with its imitations under the second category of local fabrics.

V.2.d.3 Local fabrics

This category contains both fine and coarse wares. Finer wares are well represented in the earliest phases of the site; generally these are local copies of Gallo-Belgic type, the butt beaker (Fig. 86) being a good example of this class. Other Gallo-Belgic inspired forms include a small number of dishes and platters with shallow foot-ring base, paralleled at Bagendon etc. One sherd (Fig. 90.6) appears to have much in common with a vessel from Salmonsbury (Greene, in Dunning 1976, 103, pl.IX) in a fine grey fabric with similar deeply fluted sides, cordon and curved neck. The vessel from Salmonsbury was considered to be of probable Claudian date. A comparison of the fabrics would establish whether the unstratified example from Roughground Farm is an import or a high quality local imitation of *Terra nigra*.

Fabric 20 is one of the most distinctive, found in large quantities in the early phases of the site. It has a wide distribution, being found at Claydon Pike, Lechlade and Cirencester (Fabric 3) up to the end of the first century, and in second century levels at Gloucester (TF2 and variants) as well as at Bagendon. The most characteristic form in this fabric, the necked bowl form 3.5, is exactly paralleled at Langford Downs (Harding 1972, 10). As at Langford Downs, the form appears associated with the handmade inverted rim, slack profiled jar of 'Iron Age B' type. The published description of the fabrics suggests that these too resemble those from Roughground Farm, but it is debatable whether this represents pre-Roman occupation as is suggested at Langford Downs. The dating of similar forms from Bagendon must be considered in the light of Swan's redating of the site (Swan 1975), the significant point of this being that 'almost the entire assemblage of excavated material from Bagendon probably reached there after 43 AD'. It is possible that 'native' forms continued in use up to the end of the first century AD with more Romanised forms and fabrics being slowly adopted outside the area immediately under the new Roman influence.

The area excavated at Roughground Farm produced none of the vessel types considered typical of a military presence, *eg* Hofheim type flagons, fine Arretine or Lezoux table ware, or early imported mortaria as at Cirencester.

The ceramic assemblage is dominated in all periods by BB1, its wheelthrown imitations and the grey wares. The grey ware (Fabric group 12.1–2) probably contains fabrics of different provenance but a finer division was not attempted. It seems likely that material from Swindon is represented as well as

Oxford and other sources as yet unknown; grey wares predominate in the phase 1 assemblage, and Savernake types gradually decline in favour of the black burnished wares, especially after the end of the second century. A smaller but still significant group are the local colour coats which most frequently appear as flagons or mortaria (Fabric 2.7). This fabric is commonly known as South Western White Slip or SWWS with a wide distribution centring on the South Glos./North Wilts/Cirencester region.

In conclusion, the local and non-local fabric types appear to be of roughly equal importance, although the finer table wares, especially in the latest site phase, are generally imports, as are the mortaria and amphorae.

V.2.d.4 Form analysis

Taking the eleven basic groups of vessels and assessing their relative importance over time produced the following results. The range of types represented during phase III is wide, but the newly introduced Romanised types are far fewer than 'native' types, and jar forms predominate. The range of forms within the basic groups increases with time; the last site phase sees the introduction of the jug, the colander and a wide range of colour-coated table wares. Two factors should be borne in mind when assessing these results: one is the residual survival (or in the case of samian, use or re-use), in later phases of obviously early forms, the other is the original excavation strategy, in that partial excavation in the area of the villa buildings has produced a bias in favour of later material.

V.2.e Conclusions from the pottery recovered between 1957 and 1982

If the quantity and quality of fine tablewares can be taken as an indication of status, the site appears to be somewhere in the middle range of affluence in its first phases, having a reasonable quantity and number of samian forms, although no glazed or colour-coated pre-Flavian finewares have been recorded, and the quantity of second and third century fine ware imports is exceedingly small. The scarcity of amphorae possibly suggests that its long-range trading contacts for the more 'civilized' commodities were limited. A possible indication that the site was prospering in the latest period is suggested by the number and variety of colour-coated and parchment wares, mainly from the Oxford region but with Nene Valley types well represented.

In the earlier Roman phases the site's westerly contacts appear important: there are reeded-rim jars of first century date from Herefordshire and Gloucestershire, Severn Valley and Gloucester types including tankards and mica dusted vessels and the local colour-coated wares of the second and third centuries. This influence declines in importance throughout the third and fourth centuries and is superseded by pottery sources to the east, reflecting the increased predominance of the major Oxford and Nene Valley Romano-British pottery industries.

V.2.f Introduction to the pottery from the 1990 excavation

by Paul Booth

The 1990 excavation produced a further 2168 sherds of Iron Age and Roman pottery. This material was treated differently from that from the earlier excavations. Since the assemblage was small and as the pottery from the main excavation was not quantified in detail (see above), making close comparisons impossible, no detailed quantification of the 1990 material was undertaken.

Accordingly some aspects of the pottery were treated in summary fashion, particularly as regards attribution to precise fabrics and vessel forms. Sherds were assigned to a series of major ware groups:

S samian
F finewares (including mica-gilt and colour-coated wares)
A amphorae
M mortaria
W white wares
Q white-slipped wares
E 'Belgic type' (usually grog-tempered) fabrics
O oxidised coarse wares
R reduced coarse wares
B black-burnished wares
C calcareous tempered fabrics

The first six of these were grouped under the heading of 'fine and specialist' wares; sherds within these ware groups were assigned where possible to specific fabrics. A few basic subdivisions were recorded within the remaining major ware groups. The correlation between the ware groups used here and the fabrics identified among the earlier material is shown in Table 46 on Fiche 2#24.

Vessel types, like fabrics, were recorded at a fairly broad level and details of rim and base forms and decoration were only recorded where they seemed to be particularly significant. Recording at this level was intended to give as much information as possible within the limited resources available, while providing data which would still be directly comparable at a general level with that from the fully recorded assemblages. Quantification was by sherd count (Table 19), weight and EVEs (Table 20), though the discussion that follows is based principally on the figures for sherd count and EVEs.

Fabric	Number	Fabric group total	
		Number	%
Samian ware		75	3.5
Finewares		72	3.3
F31	1		
F44	5		
F51	52		
F52	4		
F55	3		
F60	2		
F61	5		
Amphorae		17	0.8
A11	6		
A13	8		
A21	2		
A31	1		
Mortaria		24	1.1
M21	3		
M22	15		
M31	2		
M41	4		
White wares		18	0.8
Unspec.	1		
W10	1		
W12	3		
W21	1		
W22	8		
W23	3		
W30	1		
White-slipped wares		14	0.6
Q20	3		
Q22	8		
Q24	2		
Q30	1		
'Belgic Type' wares		15	0.7
Unspec.	15		
Oxidised coarse wares		115	5.3
Unspec.	32		
O30	52		
O40	27		
O80	4		
Reduced coarse wares		1291	59.5
Unspec.	910		
R10	29		
R20	34		
R30	2		
R50	154		
R90	162		
Black burnished wares		466	21.5
B11	457		
B20	6		
B30	3		
Calcareous tempered wares		51	2.4
Unspec.	1		
C10	11		
C11	39		
'Prehistoric' (Middle Iron Age) fabrics		10	0.5
Unspec.	10		
Total		2168	

Table 19 Fabric sherd totals of Roman pottery from the 1990 excavation

	FLAGONS				JARS					BEAKERS				CUPS			TANKARDS		BOWLS				BOWL/DISH			DISHES			MORTARIA				LIDS	UNKNOWN	TOTAL EVES	
Fabric	BA	BB	B	CD	CH	CK	CL	CM	CN	C	EC	EH	E	FB	FC	F	GA	G	HA	HB	HC	H	IA	IB	I	JA	JB	J	KA	KD	KE	K	L	Z	Number	%
S	0.21	0.28												0.04	0.37	0.41				0.12	1.17	1.33			0.07		0.25	0.25							2.08	6.5
F51	0.21		0.21									0.73							0.02		0.39	0.56		0.05	0.05										1.55	
F52												0.16																							0.16	
F55											0.09	0.09																							0.09	
F61												0.18																							0.18	
F Total	0.21		0.21								0.09	1.16							0.02		0.39	0.56		0.05	0.05										1.98	6.2
M21																													0.23			0.23			0.23	
M22																														0.10	0.31	0.41			0.41	
M41																															0.16	0.16			0.16	
M Total																													0.23	0.26	0.31	0.80			0.80	2.5
W00										0.04												0.04													0.04	
W22																						0.04													0.04	
W Total										0.04												0.04													0.08	0.2
Q22	0.28	0.28																																	0.28	0.9
E																						0.07													0.07	0.2
O00										0.12		0.05	0.05				0.07	0.22							0.02										0.14	
O30										0.09								0.04							0.03										0.46	
O40								0.55		0.73																									0.77	
O80										0.03																									0.03	
O Total								0.55		0.97		0.05	0.05				0.07	0.26				0.07			0.05										1.40	4.4
R00				1.19		0.59	0.53		0.07	9.79	0.21	0.28					0.02	0.02	0.14	0.08	0.09	0.40	0.08	0.64		0.18		0.18					0.50	0.29	21.10	
R10												0.10	0.10						0.95			0.95													1.05	
R20										0.61								0.12			0.12	0.12	0.11	0.21	0.21								0.11	0.03	1.20	
R30										0.04																									0.04	
R50			0.59	0.10						1.26																									1.61	
R90			0.76						0.04	1.38													0.15	0.21									0.07	0.07	1.38	
R Total			2.54	0.10		0.59	0.53		0.11	12.97	0.21	0.38					0.02	0.14	1.09	0.08	0.09	1.47	0.19	1.06	0.18	0.18		0.18					0.68	0.39	17.38	54.1
B11						2.74				2.74										0.81		0.83	0.54	0.59		1.86		1.86							5.79	
B20																				0.93		0.93		0.12											1.05	
B30										0.05																									0.05	
B Total						2.74				2.79										1.74		1.76	0.54	0.71		1.86		1.86							7.12	22.2
C10					0.34	0.31				0.07																									0.07	
C11					0.34	0.31				0.79																									0.79	
C Total					0.34	0.31				0.79																									0.86	2.7
P																																			0.05	0.2
Total	0.21	0.28	2.88	0.10	3.64	0.53	0.55	0.11	17.79	0.09	0.36	1.59	0.04	0.37	0.41	0.09	0.40	1.11	1.94	1.65	5.30	0.73	0.15	1.94	2.04	0.25	2.29	0.23	0.26	0.31	0.80	0.68	0.39	32.10	
Major type total		0.49						0.55		17.79						0.41																				
%	0.7	0.9	1.5	9.0	0.3	11.3	1.7	1.7	0.3	55.4	0.3	1.1	5.0	0.1	1.2	1.3	0.3	1.2	3.5	6.0	4.8	16.6	2.3	6.0	6.4	0.8	7.1	0.7	0.8	1.0	2.5	2.1	1.2		

Table 20 Fabric by vessel types (EVEs) for Roman pottery from the 1990 excavation

V.2.g Fabrics of the pottery recovered in 1990

V.2.g.1 Samian ware
(incorporating identifications and comments by Grace Simpson)

The majority of the 75 sherds of samian ware was from Lezoux and dated from the Hadrianic period onwards. There were only two South Gaulish sherds (both Flavian) and four sherds from Les Martres-de-Veyre. The Lezoux material demonstrated a fairly wide chronological spread. While many of the sherds were probably of Antonine date they were by no means all late in the period.

Only seven sherds were decorated, although at least two plain rims may have been from Drag. 37 bowls. All the decorated sherds were probably from this form, In addition there was a single sherd from a beaker with 'cut glass' decoration. While most of the vessels were common types the diversity of the samian assemblage, evidenced also in the material from the earlier excavations, is illustrated by some less usual forms. These included Curle 21, Drag. 44 and most notably the base of a barrel-shaped beaker with a ribbed body (cf. Stanfield 1929, 133–134 Nos. 30–32).

A list of the samian ware from all of the excavations can be found in the Microfiche (Table 42 on Fiche 2#2).

V.2.g.2 Other pottery

Of the 2093 sherds (discounting samian ware) ten, in sand and shell-tempered fabrics, were residual Iron Age sherds. One of these was a rim sherd, of uncertain form. The remainder of the pottery was of Roman date, although 15 sherds were assigned to the 'Belgic type' (E) ware group, not all of which need have been of post-conquest date.

The 'fine and specialist' wares totalled 10.1% of the total sherds from the site (but 16.3% of the vessels based on EVEs). Of these, samian ware (3.5% sherds) and fine wares (3.3% sherds) were the most important components. The samian was mainly Central Gaulish, with only two 1st century pieces noted. Fine wares were dominated by Oxfordshire colour-coated products (F51, 72.2% of F sherds), though there may have been some confusion between some of these and sherds of more local origin (Fabric F61 — 9.4), which were relatively poorly represented. The other fine wares were Nene Valley and possibly Colchester products, and sherds of a 'Rhenish' (Trier?) indented and rouletted beaker (F44) also occurred.

There was a single sherd of a mica-gilt fabric, possibly local.

Amphorae were relatively scarce, but the likely sources were the same as those identified from the rest of the site; Southern Spain, Southern France and possibly also Campania. Of these Fabric A13, used for forms such as Pelichet 47, was the most common here.

Mortaria, like the fine wares, were dominated by Oxfordshire products. The only two non-Oxfordshire sherds were from a single vessel, probably from the Verulamium region (Fig. 91.3). Oxfordshire white wares were the principal fabric (M22), though white-slipped (M31) and red-slipped (M41) sherds (Young (1977) Fabrics C and WC) were also present. White wares were more diverse, though again most (14 out of 17 sherds) were probably from the Oxfordshire industry, including three sherds of ?Burnt White Ware (W23). White slipped (non-mortarium) wares, however, were dominated by more local fabrics, particularly Q22 (9.1), probably of south Gloucestershire/north Wiltshire origin. The only rim sherd in this ware group was a flagon in Fabric Q22. Oxfordshire fabric WC seems not to have been represented here, though three sherds with oxidised bodies may possibly have been of Oxfordshire origin.

Oxidised coarse wares constituted 5.3% of the assemblage. Of these, almost half (52 sherds) were probably from the relatively local North Wiltshire potteries situated in the Swindon area (O30). A further 27 were probably products of the Severn Valley ware kilns (O40). The most common vessels in Severn Valley wares were wide mouthed jars; the characteristic tankard was rare, and seems to have been more common in the North Wiltshire fabrics (see below). The remaining oxidised sherds were from uncertain sources and included no diagnostic rim types.

Reduced coarse wares (R) made up the bulk of the assemblage (59.5% of sherds, 54.1% EVEs). Most of this material was not differentiated, but some sub-groups were defined. A group of coarse-tempered fabrics was designated R90. They constituted 12.8% of all the R sherds. They were used exclusively for jars, most of which were probably storage vessels. This group included probable Savernake fabrics (12.3–12.5). Grey sherds with black surfaces (R50) totalled 11.9% of the reduced wares. These, like the R90 group, probably included products from a variety of sources. Twenty-nine sherds (23 from a single vessel) were assigned to a 'fine' subgroup (R10). Most were probably Oxfordshire products in the 'London ware' tradition. A group of sand-tempered sherds were designated R20, but were not readily distinguishable from the rest of the undifferentiated material. The remaining reduced wares did not have distinctive superficial characteristics.

Many of the R and R20 sherds were probably of local origin, the North Wiltshire potteries again being one likely source (cf. comments on Fabric 12.1 above). These fabrics were current throughout the Roman period (from the later 1st century onwards?) and were used for a wide range of vessel types.

Black-burnished wares, 21.5% of the total sherds, were the second largest group after reduced coarse wares. The large majority of the black-burnished ware appeared to be handmade BB1 probably of Dorset origin (Fabric B11).

Fairly fine, wheelthrown fabrics (B20 and B30) were also recorded, but these were comparatively much less significant than the wheelthrown Fabrics 11.2 and 11.3 recorded elsewhere at Roughground Farm, the former in some quantity. The reasons for this difference are not clear. The sources of Fabrics B20 and B30 are unknown: they are not BB2 wares.

Sherds of the final major ware group, calcareous tempered (C) wares, amounted to only 2.4% of the site total. All of these were shell-tempered. Three-quarters of these belonged to the standard late-Roman fabric of East Midlands origin (C11), but since there was also a local tradition of shell-tempered wares in the Iron Age and early-Roman periods confident attribution of small body sherds to the late-Roman fabric was not always possible. The C10 group (11 sherds) included those sherds about which there was most doubt (cf. the discussion of Fabric 15 above). While the existence of early and late forms of the fabric was noted, the division of the two was not attempted.

V.2.h Vessel types of the pottery recovered in 1990

Fourteen principal groupings of vessel types have been identified, of which three (amphorae, jars/bowls and miscellaneous) were not represented by rims in this assemblage. The groupings are much the same as those adopted in the earlier report, with the differences that a) jugs are grouped together with flagons and platters are grouped with dishes (though there were no jugs or platters in this assemblage), and b) amphorae, mortaria, jars/bowls, cups, miscellaneous and uncertain types are all recorded as separate categories.

Some 338 vessels were represented by rim sherds, which totalled 32.10 EVEs (Table 20). A few of the rim sherds in different contexts may have belonged to the same vessel, but other vessels occurred which were not represented by rims. The relative proportions of the major ware groups expressed as percentages of EVEs and rim sherd counts were broadly similar, suggesting that the rim sherd count gives a reasonably accurate impression of the relative proportions of the major ware groups and vessel types.

Jars were the most common vessel type, amounting to 55.4% of the total EVEs. Over half of the jars were of types not further specified. For the rest, about one fifth (ie 11.3% of all vessels) were of the 'cooking-pot' type exemplified by black-burnished ware, and a further fifth were of general medium-mouthed types. The remainder included a single bead rim jar, two storage jar types, and wide-mouthed jars, the latter occurring exclusively in Severn Valley ware. Jars amounted to 70% of the vessels in oxidised coarse wares, and 74.6% of the reduced coarse ware vessels. The latter accounted for 72.9% of all the jars on the site. Black-burnished ware 'cooking-pot' types were a further 15.4% of the jar total, oxidised and calcareous-tempered fabrics accounting for the rest. Jars were the only vessel type to occur in shell-tempered wares.

Bowls (16.6%) were the next most important vessel type. Straight sided bowls, almost entirely in black-burnished ware, were most common, but curving sided types were also popular. These were mainly samian ware forms such as Drag. 31 and 38 (there was also a substantial portion of a Drag. 44) and, less frequently, the imitations of these forms in Oxfordshire colour-coated ware. Carinated bowls were generally rare and occurred mainly in reduced coarse wares. Although amounting to 3.5% of the total EVEs this figure derived mainly from a single well-preserved vessel (Fig. 91.5). Unspecified types amounted to 13.5% of all the bowls.

Dishes, principally straight sided types, most of which were in black-burnished ware, were less common than bowls (7.1%). There were similar quantities of the uncertain bowls/dishes type (6.0%) (vessels of which insufficient survived to allow attribution to one or the other category). These, like bowls and dishes, occurred in black-burnished ware, but the majority (54.6%) were in reduced fabrics, with rare occurrences in Oxfordshire colour-coated and oxidised coarsewares.

Beakers were the only other major vessel type to amount to 5% or more of the total vessels. About three quarters of these were in fineware fabrics, with the remainder (small vessels of 'jar beaker' type) in reduced coarsewares. The fineware beaker rims were generally small and could not be assigned to specific types, apart from a single example of a bag-shaped beaker in Fabric F55 (Fig. 92.17); this, with a cornice rim and roughcast decoration, was probably the earliest beaker in the assemblage. Other types, an indented beaker with rouletted decoration (Fabric F44) and part of a hunt cup (Fabric F51, Fig. 92.16) occurred as body sherds only.

The remaining vessel types were only found in small quantities. There were only two flagons, although these constituted 1.5% of the total EVEs. Cups (1.3%) consisted entirely of samian forms 27 and 33, and tankards were found in reduced and oxidised coarseware fabrics. Oxidised tankards were more common in Wiltshire fabrics (eg Fig. 91.6) than in Severn Valley wares. It is unclear why this should have been so; it is possible that the rims in O30 fabrics identified as tankards were of other types, the sherds concerned being generally quite small.

Mortaria were mainly of late-Roman types. The only 2nd century type represented was the sole non-Oxfordshire vessel in the group (Fig. 91.3). The other vessels were of Young's (1977) types M14, M17, M18 and M22 (the latter being surprisingly rare) and C97.

Finally, lids (2.1% of EVEs) and unidentifiable types (1.2%) were found exclusively in reduced coarsewares. The lid forms were all extremely simple. The unidentifiable types were more numerous than the figures would suggest, since these were mainly small sherds.

V.2.i Chronology derived from the pottery recovered in 1990

While the date range of the pottery extended from the Early or Middle Iron Age to the Late Roman period very little pottery was recovered dating from before the early 2nd century. Only one sherd each of fabrics assigned to the Middle Iron Age and the Late Iron Age/Early Roman period occurred in contemporary contexts (together 1.2% of the total sherds from the site). This is probably because there was not time to investigate the pre-building levels.

The pottery assemblage was too small to allow a meaningful breakdown by building phases, but was divided between 'early' and 'late' phases, the former consisting of pottery from pre-building contexts and from the first two phases of the life of Building IV. Even so this only amounted to 24.1% of the total sherds from the site (26.1% EVEs).

A comparison of the fabric proportions in the 'early' and 'late' groups (Table 47 on Fiche 2#25; Table 48 on Fiche 2#26) shows trends which would have been expected, most significantly the domination of the early group by reduced coarsewares (72.8% as opposed to 55.4% of the later group). Black-burnished and oxidised wares were less important in the earlier group (12.4% and 4.0%) and among the latter Severn Valley wares hardly occurred at all. Calcareous-tempered wares were also less common earlier than later, and only three sherds of possible 'Late Roman' shell-tempered ware occurred in the early group. There was only a single fine ware sherd (of the mica-gilt Fabric F31) in the early group, and amphorae and white-slipped wares were less common than later, while samian and white wares were better represented.

Comparison of the representation of vessel types between the early and late groups is rendered dubious by the small total of EVEs (8.38) for the early group. Jars were less common in this early group than later, contrary to expectation, since jars are generally more common in earlier than later Roman assemblages (eg Millett 1979a, 37–39). While this may be partly explained by the increased importance of black-burnished ware vessels in the later group, jars were more common in the later than the earlier group even among the reduced coarsewares (respectively 81.5% and 60.8% of all vessels in R fabrics). It is unclear whether these facts reveal significant characteristics of the pottery supply to Roughground Farm or arise from the inadequacy of the data. Broadly speaking, cups, tankards, bowls, dishes and lids were all better represented earlier, and beakers were more common in the later group. Some uncommon types such as flagons were not represented at all in the early group.

The dating of the individual contexts within the early group suggests that Building IV was probably constructed before the middle of the 2nd century AD and that its first two phases may have lasted into the 3rd century, though diagnostic 3rd century groups were rare. The dating of the early building phases relies more on pottery from features adjacent to the building than on material from within the structure. The groups from the phase 2 ditch 2429 were the most significant from the 1990 excavation. An early fill of this ditch (2429/A/9) contained a sherd of Antonine samian ware, and the pottery from the upper fills was no later in date than this. If this feature was in contemporary use with the second phase of the building (see above) the latter need not have extended beyond the end of the 2nd century.

The 'late' group consisted of contexts dated primarily from the mid-3rd to mid-4th century, and there were few groups among these which need have been particularly late. There was for example an absence of any of the Oxfordshire types dated exclusively to the later part of the 4th century and, as noted above, even M22, the characteristic 4th century mortarium type, was rare. The relative absence of the white-slipped mortarium fabric (M31, Young's Fabric WC) may also be significant. Other typical late-Roman form and fabric combinations, such as bowls and dishes in shell-tempered and Nene Valley wares, were also absent. The ceramic evidence is therefore consistent in suggesting that while activity in this part of the site probably extended after the mid 4th century there was no deposition of pottery in the last quarter of the century.

V.2.i.1 Catalogue of the illustrated vessels (Figs. 91 and 92)

Samian ware

Fig. 91.1. 2008/A. Base of Drag. 18/31, Central Gaulish, with stamp of TEDDILLVS of Lezoux (Die 4a). This stamp occurs on forms 18/31 and 27. Despite the lack of good site evidence the likely date is c 140–155 AD. (This identification was kindly supplied by Brenda Dickinson.

Fig. 91.2. 2429/A. Drag. 37, Lezoux. The double-bordered ovolo is close to Rogers B228 but appears to be damaged: there is a flaw on one side of the outer border. Probably Hadrianic to early Antonine.

Other pottery: 'early' groups

Fig. 91.3. 2419/A/1 (and 2429/A/1). Fabric M21.
Fig. 91.4. 2403/D/1. Fabric O30.
Fig. 91.5. 2029/C/4. Fabric R10.
Fig. 91.6. 2429/A/1. Fabric O30.
Fig. 91.7. 2429/A/1. Fabric O40.
Fig. 91.8. 2429/A. Fabric R.
Fig. 91.9. 2429/A. Fabric R.
Fig. 91.10. 2429/A. Fabric R.
Fig. 91.11. 2429/A. Fabric R.
Fig. 91.12. 2428. Fabric R90.
Fig. 91.13. 2429/A/1. Fabric B11.
Fig. 91.14. 2429/A/1. Fabric B11.
Fig. 91.15. 2428. Fabric B11.

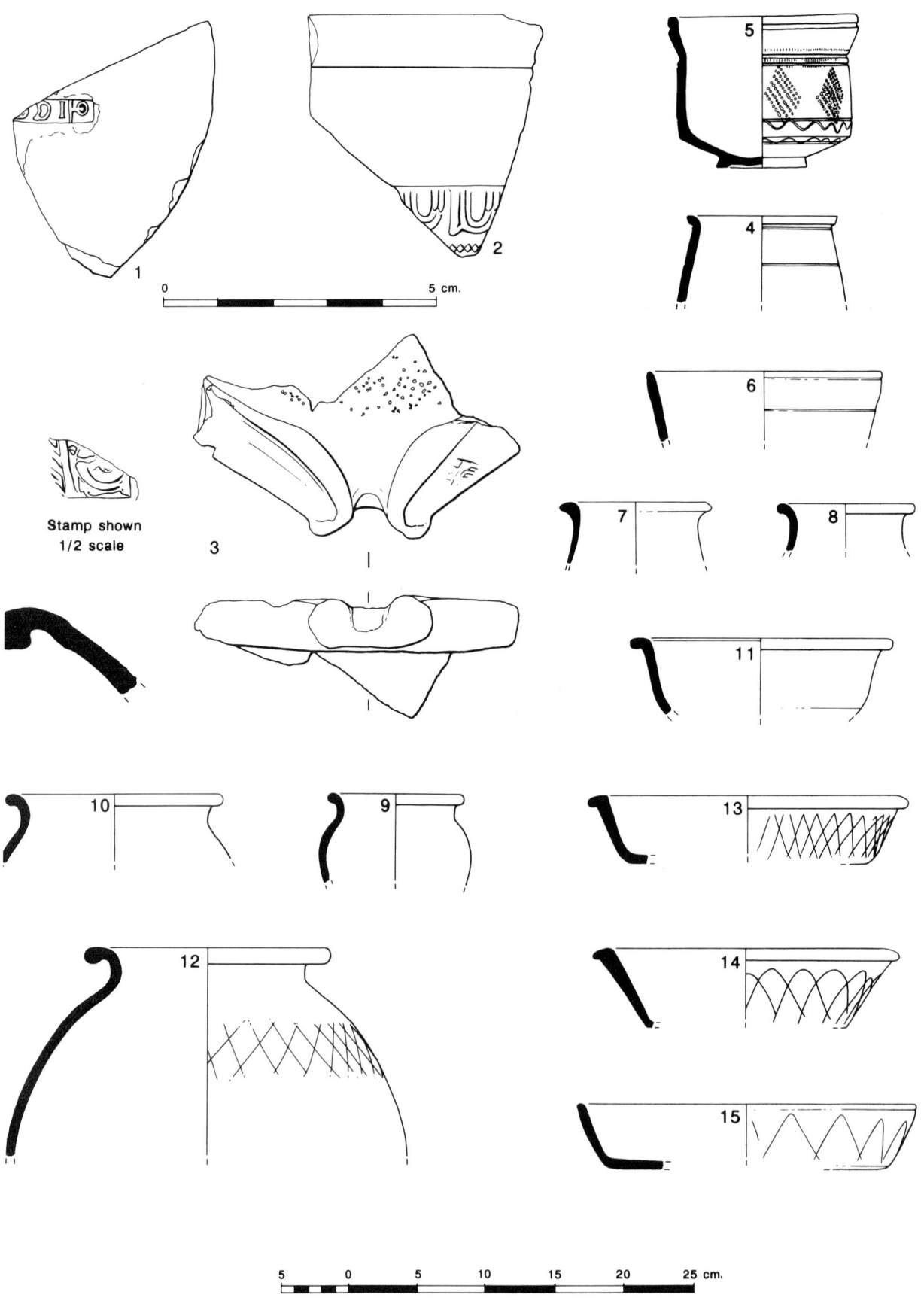

Figure 91 Roman pottery: illustrated vessels from the 1990 excavations. Samian and 'early' groups.

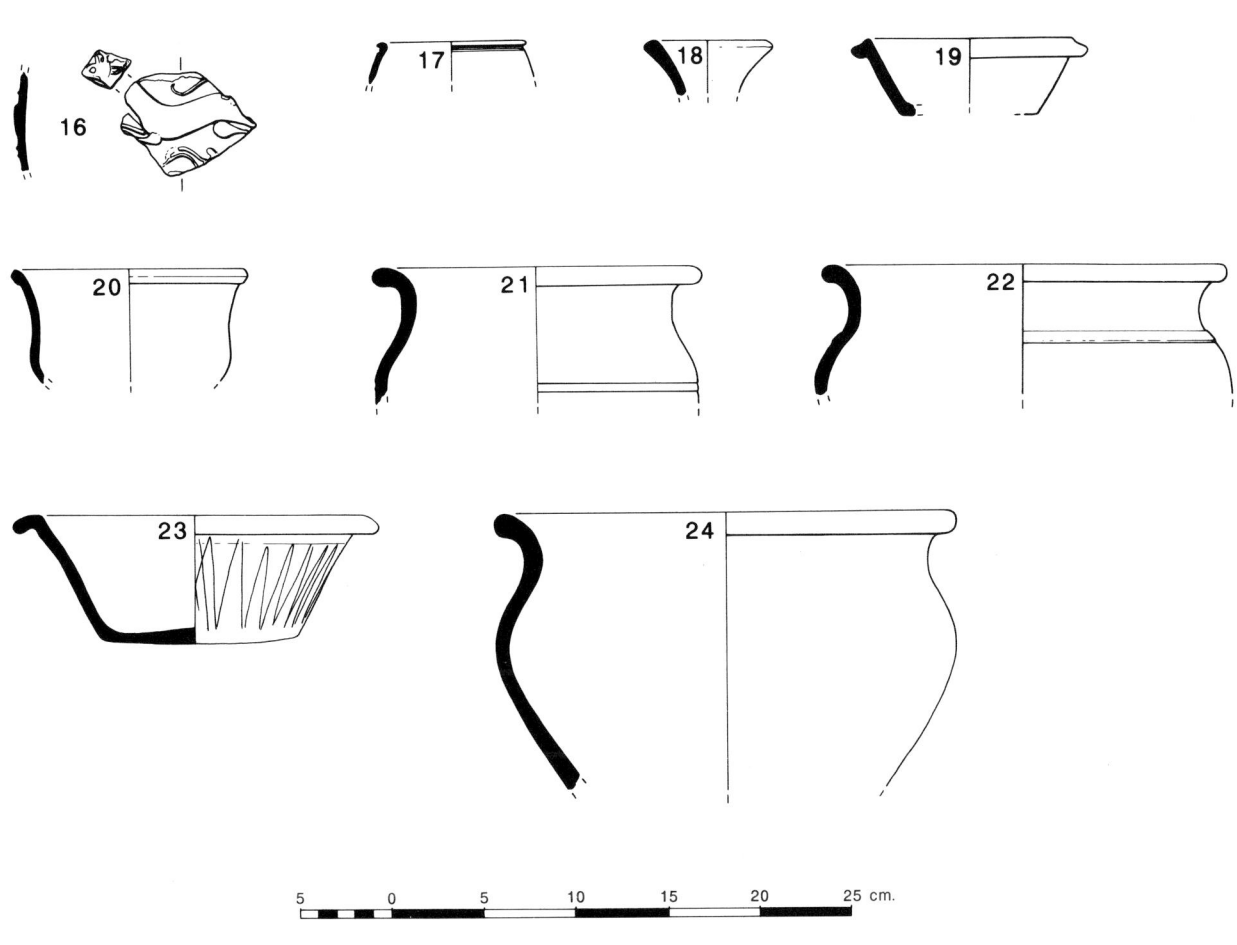

Figure 92 Roman pottery: illustrated vessels from the 1990 excavations. 'Late' groups.

Other pottery: 'late' groups

Fig. 92.16. 2410/B/1 and 2410/C/1. Fabric F51.
Fig. 92.17. 2421/G. Fabric F55.
Fig. 92.18. 2436/A/1. Fabric Q22.
Fig. 92.19. 2415/D/3. Fabric R20.
Fig. 92.20. 2436/B. Fabric R10.
Fig. 92.21. 2030. Fabric R50.
Fig. 92.22. 2483. Fabric R.
Fig. 92.23. 2013/B. Fabric B20.
Fig. 92.24. 2008/B/7. Fabric C11.

V.2.j Discussion

This assemblage was broadly comparable to that from the rest of the site. However, detailed comparison with the earlier material was not possible because of the quantification problems of the latter. The 2nd century assemblage was dominated by reduced coarsewares and had a 'fine and specialist ware' component of 7.3% (sherd total). In the later 3rd to 4th century group reduced wares were of lesser importance, though still the principal ware group. Black-burnished wares increased markedly in significance and the proportion of fine and specialist wares rose to 11.1% (owing principally to the appearance of Oxfordshire colour-coated wares, though the increase follows a widely observable trend). For the earlier excavations the equivalent figure in the late-Roman Period 5 was about 30%, but this figure is considerably inflated by the discard of coarseware sherds on site by the excavator. It is therefore uncertain if there were genuine differences in the nature of the assemblage from the 1990 excavation and of that from the earlier work.

Few villa excavations in the region have produced data which are adequate to demonstrate comparable or contradictory trends. The nearest and most directly relevant site is Claydon Pike, Fairford, only 2.5 km to the south-west. The data here are not directly comparable (Green, in Miles and Palmer in prep), but the fine and specialist ware component (excluding samian ware and amphorae, and expressed as percentages of weight rather than sherd count) was c 7.7% in the 'early Roman' period and 15.4% in the 'late Roman' period. Claydon Pike is most closely comparable to Roughground Farm (in site terms) in the late period, since its character in the 2nd century seems to have been rather unusual, which may have had consequences for the nature of the associated pottery assemblage.

The fine and specialist ware component of the late 4th century assemblage at Barnsley Park was c 7.5% (figures based on Webster & Smith 1982, 168; as at Claydon Pike this figure omits samian ware and amphorae, for which data were not provided), but this was for phases dated after 360 AD only, since the earlier material was not quantified in the same way (Webster 1981, 63–77). There are no usable data from Shakenoak (Brodribb *et al* 1968 etc) and the fabric categories employed at Barton Court Farm do not permit a breakdown in terms of fine and specialist wares since oxidised coarsewares are grouped with other Oxfordshire products such as colour-coated wares and mortaria (Miles 1986 fiche V.4.2). The status of Roughground Farm (as indicated by ceramic evidence) cannot, however, be determined from the 1990 evidence in isolation. The Late Roman figure for fine and specialist wares (11.1%) may be somewhat below the expected average for sites of this type in the region. The diversity of material from the earlier excavations might suggest, therefore, that the area excavated in 1990 was not representative of the whole site. On present evidence the figures suggest that this is at least a middling status assemblage.

The range of vessel types in the 1990 assemblage sheds little light on the function of this part of the site. In any case the limited extent of excavation may mean that any rubbish removed and dumped from Building IV lay outside the excavated area. There were no abnormal concentrations of particular vessel types although certain types are notable for their relative absence. These include amphorae and flagons, and also large storage jars. In this context the complete absence of pink grogged ware (Booth & Green 1989), found elsewhere on the site and included in Fabric 12.3 above, may be significant.

V.3 Roman and later coins

by Cathy King

Forty-seven coins were recovered from the excavations at Roughground Farm, and one further coin (No. 29, now lost) was found on the surface before excavation began. One of these (No. 20) is a post-medieval token. The Roman coins which have been seen and listed date from the mid-second century to the late fourth century (Table 21).

Although the number of coins is too small to yield a reliable statistical picture of either the chronological or geographical distribution, it nonetheless conforms generally with the usual pattern of coin loss in Roman Britain. There are two bronzes of the 1st to 2nd century, nine radiates dating from c 260–284, five 4th century folles of 305–330; twelve bronzes (or copies) datable to c 330–348, eleven bronzes (nine of which are imitations) of the years 348–360 and one undatable 4th century piece. No coins of the House of Valentinian (364–378) were recovered from the excavations, but a surface find made by A J Baxter in 1931 in the field containing the villa buildings, Table 21 coin No. 29, was identified as Valentinian I or Valens, dateable to c 364–378.

The clipped siliqua is the latest coin which was found and was minted in the late fourth or early fifth century. Clipped siliquae are often found in late fourth century British silver hoards and have also been recovered from villa sites (see for instance Brodribb *et al* 1968 onwards). Their distribution outside towns appears, however, to be limited to sites in Oxfordshire and Gloucestershire (Fulford 1989, 199). Although it seems clear that the coins were clipped at some stage after they were minted, precisely how long after remains problematical. A conservative estimate would date these pieces to about 410.

The token is a 16th century Nuremburg jeton with the Lion of St Mark on the obverse, made for use in Venice. The inscriptions are meaningless lettering. This jeton was probably made by Hans Krauwinckel between 1580 and 1610 AD (identification by the Ashmolean Museum).

Context No.	Coin No.	Obverse	Reverse	Denom.	Mint	Date	Cat. Ref.
2413	1453	Illegible	Illegible	Dp	Rome	1st–2nd C	
212	1	ANTONINVS AVG PIVS PP PMTRP COS III	[ANNO]NA A[VG SC]	Sest	Rome	140–44	
1504	24	GALLIENVS AVG	SECVRITAS [AVG]	ANT	—	260–68	
2415	1566	Claudius II	AEQVITAS AVG	IMIT ANT	—	c 268–84	
2417	1416	IMP C CLAVDIVS AVG	AEQVITAS AVG	ANT	Rome	268–70	
361	2	Claudius II	[MARS V]LTOR	ANT	Rome	268–70	
271	3	Claudius II	ANNONA AVG	?IMIT ANT	—	c 268–84	
291	4	Tetricus I	[SPES PV]BLICA	IMIT ANT	—	c 270–84	
2410	1411	Tetricus II	[SPES P]VBLICA	ANT	Gaul	270–74	
868	5	Tetricus II	?Pax	?IMIT ANT	—	c 270–84	
u/s	1014	Tetricus II	Pax	IMIT ANT	—	c 270–84	
536	6	IMP MAXIMIANVS PF AVG	GENIO POPVLI ROMANI	Follis	Lon	305–07	RIC 52b
1602/3	25	IMP CONSTANTINVS P AVG	SOLI INVICTO COMITI	Follis	Lon T/F//PLN	310–12	RIC 121a
u/s	1404	CONSTANTINVS AVG	BEATA TRANQVILLITAS VOTIS XX	Follis	Trier ST[R]	320–25	
551	8	CRISPVS NOB CAES	BEATA TRANQVILLITAS VOTIS XX	Follis	Lyons PLG	322–25	
361	9	CONSTANTINVS AVG	PROVIDENTIAE AVGG	Follis	Trier PTRE	325–30	RIC 504
1504	27	VRBS ROMA	WOLF AND TWINS	Follis	Lug. PLG	330–35	LRBC 190
361	10	CONSTANTINVS IVN NOBC	GLORIA EXERCITVS (2 STANS.)	Follis	Trier TRS	330–35	RIC 527
641	11	CONSTANTIVS NOB CAES	GLORIA EXERCITVS (2 STANS.)	Follis	Illegible	330–35	
763	18	CONSTANTINOPOLIS	Victory on Prow	Follis	Trier TRS	330–35	RIC VII, 543
u/s?	26	CONSTANTINVS [IVN] NOBC	GLORIA EXERCITVS (2 STANS.)	?Irreg.	Lug. PLG	330–35	cf. LRBC 187
582	12	VRBS ROMA	WOLF AND TWINS	Imit. Follis	Illegible	330–48	
2454/–/1	1442	Illegible	Illegible	Imit. Follis	—	c 330–48	
2005/1	1021	Illegible	GLORIA EXERCITVS (1 STAN.)	Follis	Illegible	335–41	
291	14	Constantius	GLORIA EXERCITVS (1 STAN.)	Follis	Illegible	335–41	
560	13	CONSTANTIVS PF AVG	GLORIA EXERCITVS (1 STAN.)	Follis	Aquileia AQ[P]	335–41	cf.LRBC 692b
764	19	Constantius II	GLORIA EXERCITVS (1 STAN.)	Follis	Illegible	335–41	
u/s	1400	Illegible	GLORIA EXERCITVS (1 STAN.)	Follis	Illegible	335–41	
2000/A/1	1000	Illegible	GLORIA EXERCITVS (1 STAN.)	Imit. Follis	Illegible	c 335–48	
2004/B/1	1002	FL MAX THEODORAE AVG	PIETAS ROMANI	Follis	—	c 337–41	
841	15	CONSTANS PF AVG	VICTORIAE DD AVGG Q NN	Follis	Trier M/TRP	341–48	LRBC 138
2034	1018	CONSTANS PF AVG	VICTORIAE DD AVGG Q NN	Follis	Lyons [ ]//PLG	341–48	
u/s	1415	Illegible	[VICTORIAE DD AUGG Q NN]	Imit. Follis	Illegible	c 341–48	
2459/C/2	1438	Illegible	FEL TEMP REPARATIO (fh)	Imit. Follis	Illegible	c 348–60	
2413	1414	Illegible	FEL TEMP REPARATIO (fh)	Imit. Follis	Illegible	c 348–60	
u/s	1401	Illegible	FEL TEMP REPARATIO (fh)	Imit. Follis	Illegible	c 348–60	
u/s	1402	CONSTANS PF AVG	FEL TEMP REPARATIO (fh)	Imit. Follis	Illegible	c 348–60	
2434	1469	Illegible	FEL TEMP REPARATIO (fh)	Follis	Illegible	348–60	
u/s	1405	Illegible	FEL TEMP REPARATIO (fh)	Follis	Illegible	348–60	
136	7	Magnentius or Decentius	VICTORIAE DD NN AVG.ET CAES	Imit. Follis	Lyons PLG	c 350–60	
1408	23	Magnentius	Illegible	Imit. Follis	Illegible	c 350–60	
1503	28	Illegible	FELTEMP REPARATIO (fh)	Imit. Follis	Illegible	c 355–60	
1385	21	Illegible	FELTEMP REPARATIO (fh)	Imit. Follis	Illegible	c 355–60	
855	17	Illegible	FELTEMP REPARATIO (fh)	Imit. Follis	Illegible	c 355–60	
u/s	29	Valentinian I or Valens	GLORIA ROMANORVM	Nummus	—	364–78	
271	16	Arcadius or Honorius	VIRTVS ROMANORVM	Clipped Siliqua	?Milan	c 395–405	Wt. 0.60g.
1414	22	Illegible	Illegible	—	—	4th cent.	
400	20	Lion of St. Mark	—	Jeton	Nuremburg	1580–1610	

Table 21 Coin List

V.4 Copper alloy objects

by Tim Allen, Sarnia Butcher and Robin Brunner-Ellis
Figs. 93, 94, 95, 96. Table 22

V.4.a Summary catalogue

There were 91 Romano-British copper alloy finds, including 11 fibulae or parts thereof. Initial identifications of the 1957–9 finds were made by M R Hull; Miss Sarnia Butcher has updated the Brooch report and included the brooch found in 1982, and Martin Henig has commented upon the other finds. The finds from the villa and its immediate surroundings are described first, then those from the late Roman enclosures to the east. A comparison of these assemblages is given in Table 22. Each assemblage is described in full in the Microfiche report in the order of the table. An analysis of the metals of some of the other objects by Justine Bayley is also included in the Microfiche report.

Table 22 Copper alloy objects

Villa and Environs			Late Roman Enclosures to the East		
Context	Type (Small Find No.)	Fig. No.	Context	Type	Fig. No.
Dress articles			**Dress articles**		
299	Brooch	93.1			
324	Brooch	93.2			
307	Brooch	93.3			
1438	Brooch	93.4			
21	Brooch	93.5			
48	Brooch	93.6			
150	Brooch	93.7			
89	Brooch	93.8			
360	Brooch				
2428	Brooch (SF 1421)				
2001	Brooch (SF 1565)	95.1565			
2429	Pin (SF 1445)	95.1445			
2040	Pin (SF 1016)	95.1016			
2413	Pin (SF 1418)				
2426	Pin (SF 1431)				
109	Bracelet end	93.9	764	Bracelet	
2030	Wire bracelet (SF 1012)		612	Bracelet	93.10
2008	Wire bracelet (SF 1019)		528	?Bracelet, plain band	
2410	Bracelet (SF 1412)	95.1412	582	Child's bracelet	93.11
2509	Bracelet (SF 1564)	95.1564	480	Child's bracelet	93.12
2427	Bracelet (SF 1420)		975	Child's bracelet	94.13
			582	Strip bracelet	
			582	Strip bracelet, plain	94.14
			858	Wire bracelet	94.15
2426	Ring (SF 1458)		629	?Wire earring	
Toilet articles			**Toilet articles**		
299+307	Tweezers	94.16	837	Tweezers	94.20
360	Nail cleaner	94.17			
409	?Ligula				
2004	Ligula (SF 1004)				
419	Mirror of white bronze	94.18			
201	Mirror (or spoon)				
193/2	Mirror (or spoon)				
361	Small link chain	94.19			
Domestic utensils			**Domestic utensils**		
2429	Key (SF 1562)				
?	Bowl rim fragment (SF 1020)	95.1020			
U/S	Collander base (SF 1403)				
U/S	Bowl (SF 1481)				
2413	Spoon bowl (SF 1417)	95.1417			
2402	Bowl or box fragment (SF 1407)				
Casket fittings			**Casket fittings**		
1414	Knob	94.21			
1432	Conical stud	94.22			
187	Small boss/stud	94.23			

Copper alloy objects (Table 22 continued)

Villa and Environs			Late Roman Enclosures to the East		
Context	Type (Small Find No.)	Fig. No.	Context	Type	Fig. No.
82/4	Stud with solder				
272	Conical stud	94.24			
2413	Stud (SF 1441)				
Casket/harness rings			**Casket/harness rings**		
89	Ring		1100	Ring (?modern)	
2460	Horse terret (SF 1441)	100.1441			
Decorative mounts			**Decorative mounts**		
299	Triangular mount	94.25	511	Votive leaf	94.26
151	Scrap				
2402	?Box fitting (SF 1406)				
2004	?Box fitting (SF 1001)				
204	×3 Split pins/rivets for leather				
2486	Bar mount (medieval) (SF 1408)	95.1408			
2401	?Stud (SF 1413)				
2001	Scabbard mount? (SF 1568)	95.1568			
2434	Leather rivet (cf. 204) (SF 1432)				
2454	Leather rivet (cf. 204) (SF 1465)				
Bindings			**Bindings**		
271	Curved with holes				
271	Strip without holes				
336	Curved, iron rivets				
Tubing			**Tubing**		
132/2	×4	96.27	774	Decorated at end (?binding)	96.31
		96.28			
82		96.29			
120		96.30			
2008	(SF 1022)				
Cast fragments			**Cast fragments**		
1414	Waste?				
72	Waste?				
119	Waste?				
Strips			**Strips**		
207	Cast		841	×2 Riveted	
36	Curving, ?brooch				
Sheet bronze			**Sheet bronze**		
109	2 fragments				
53	—				
203	?Mount fragment				
212	×3 Mount fragment				
Post-Roman and miscellaneous					
38	Decayed fragments				
1503	Disc + cogs or ratchet, ?modern				
1506	Material 2-piece clasping ring, ?modern				
272	Spectacle-Buckle	96.32			
272	Brass ring				
2000	Thimble				
1240	Button				
2000	Colander (SF 1403)				
2000	Bowl (SF 1481)				
838	D-shaped buckle				
830	Silvered button				

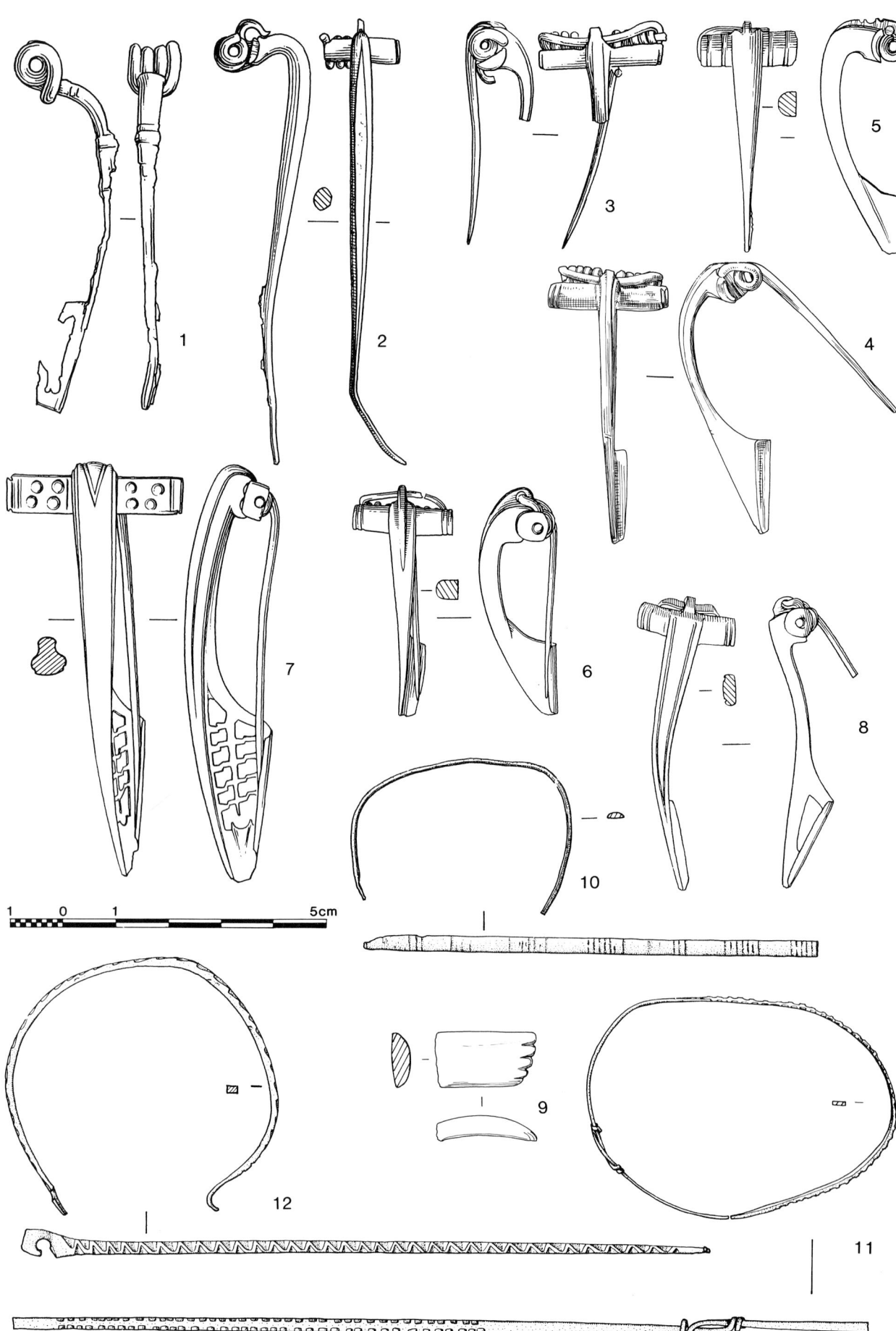

Figure 93 Copper alloy objects: Nos. 1–8 brooches; Nos. 9–12 bracelets.

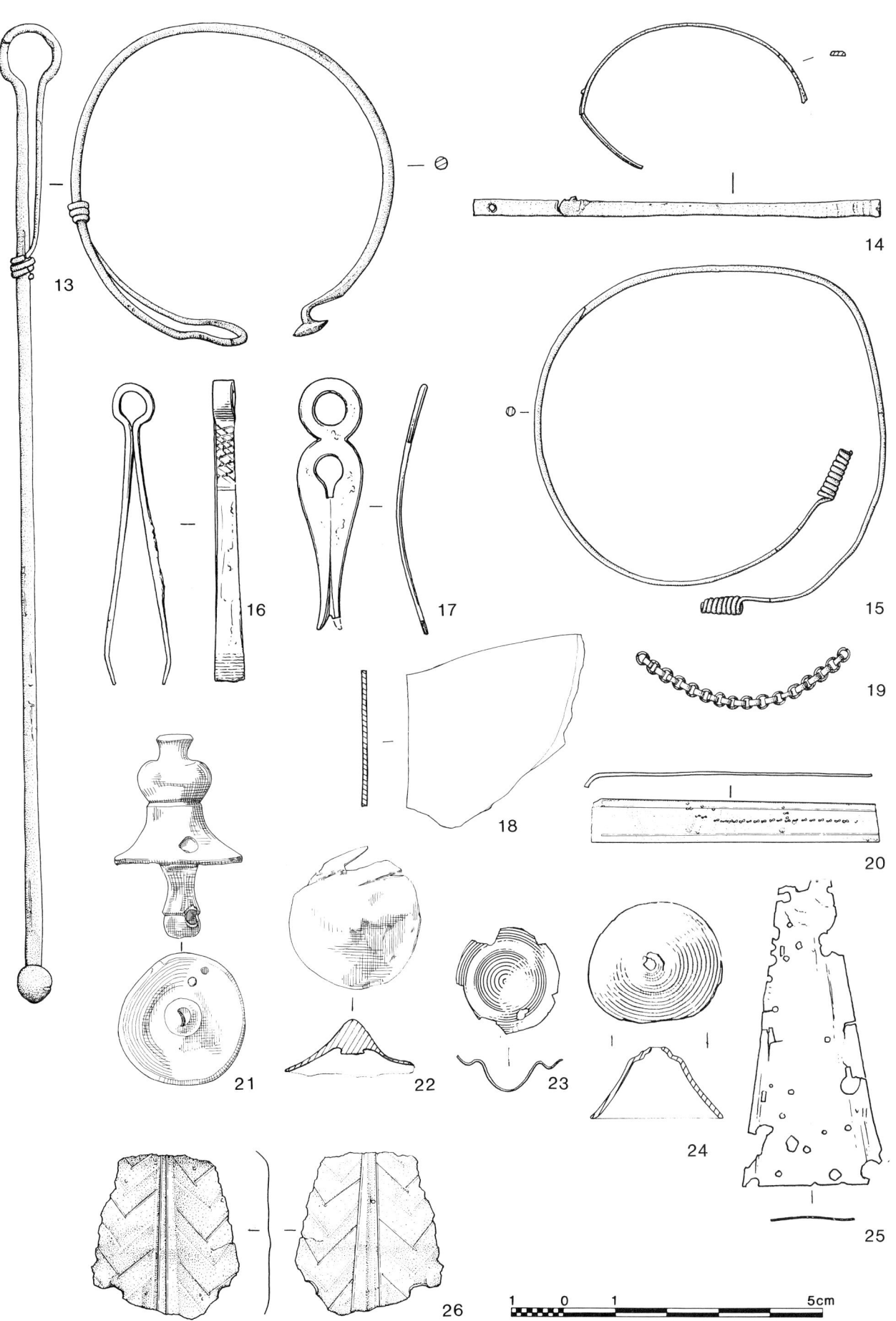

Figure 94 Copper alloy objects: Nos. 13–15 bracelets; Nos. 16 & 20 tweezers; No. 17 ligula; No. 18 mirror; No. 19 chain; Nos. 21–24 studs; No. 25 mount; No. 26 votive leaf.

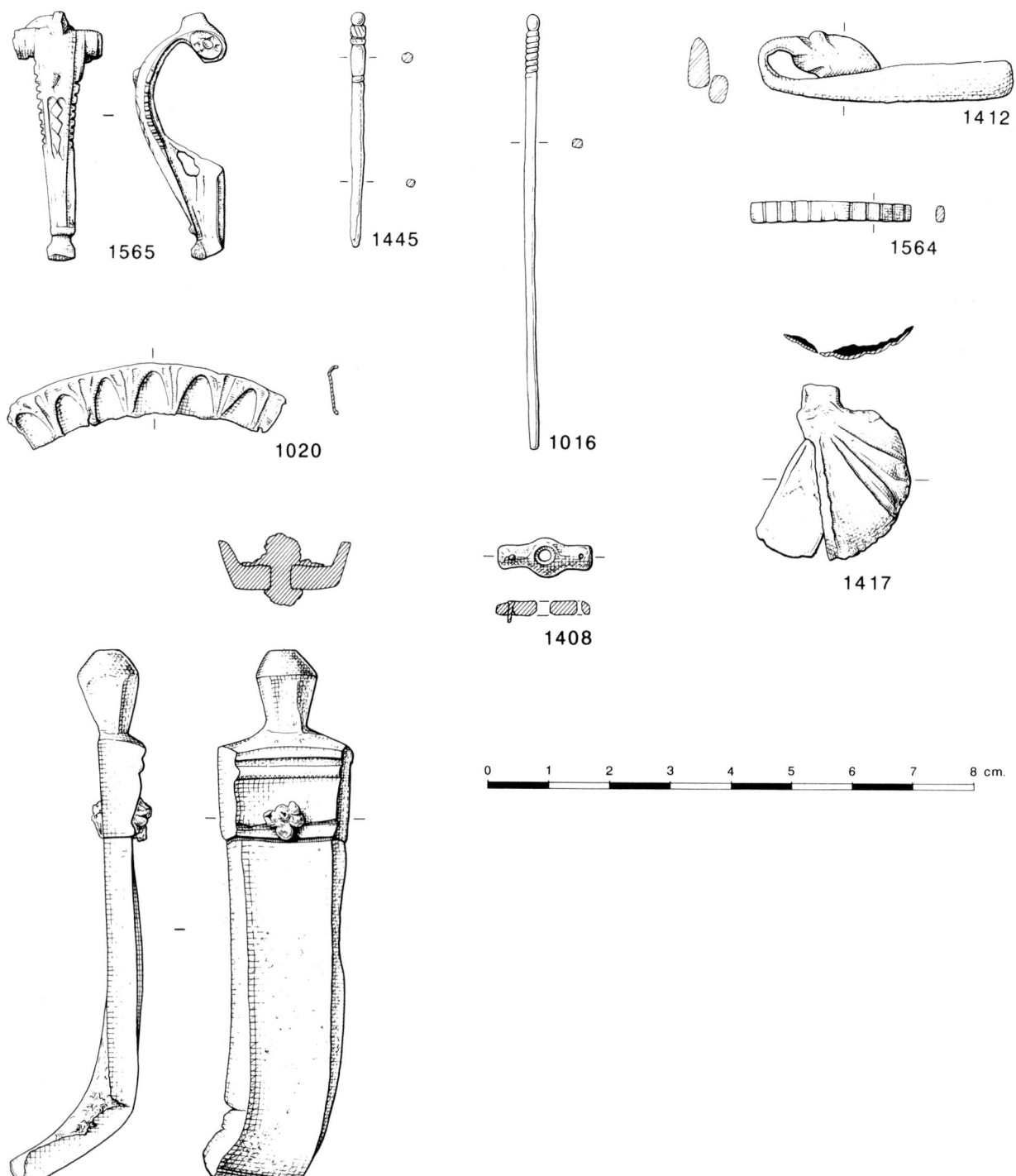

Figure 95 Copper alloy objects: No. 1565 brooch; Nos. 1016 and 1445 pins; Nos. 1412 & 1564 bracelets; No. 1020 bowl rim; No. 1417 spoon bowl; No. 1408 bar mount; No. 1568 ?scabbard mount.

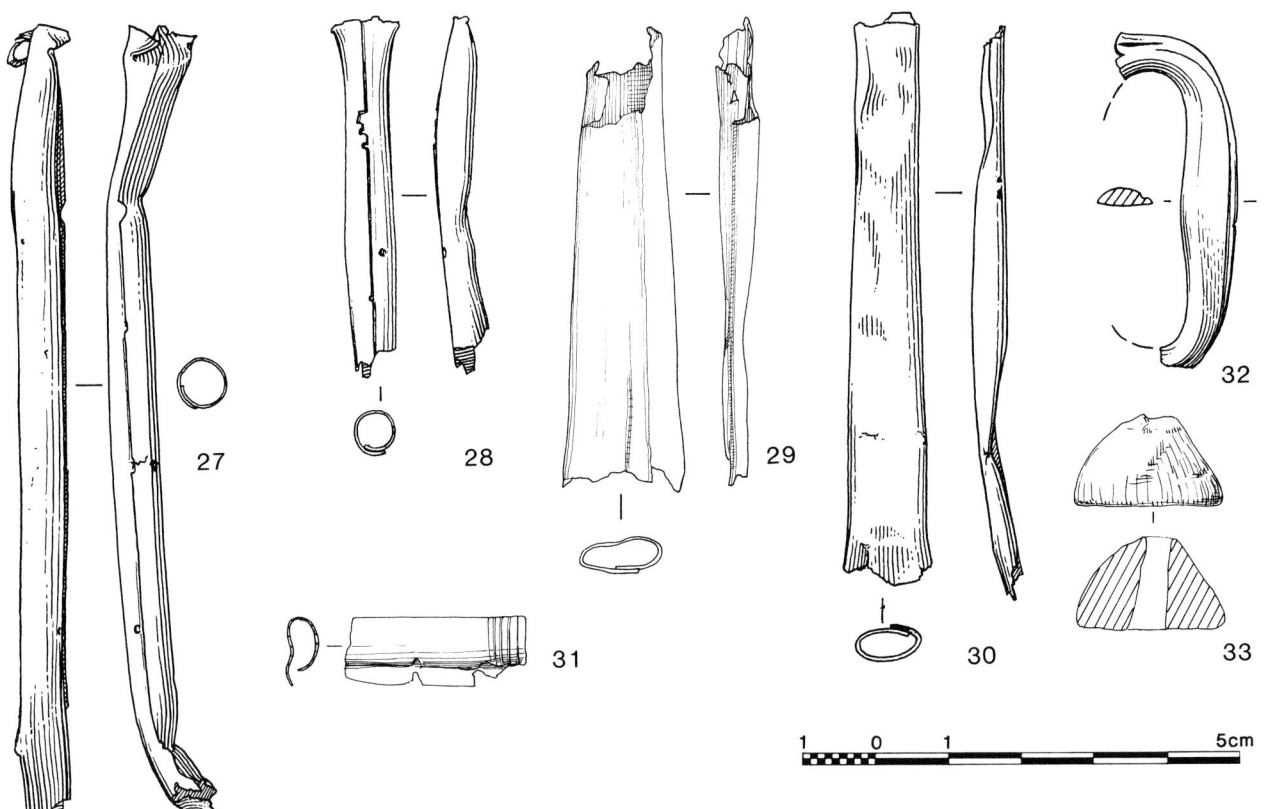

Figure 96 Copper alloy objects: Nos. 27–31 tubing; No. 32 spectacle buckle. Lead object: No. 33 weight

V.4.b Discussion

This small assemblage represents a standard range of domestic and decorative items from a villa of modest pretensions; compare Shakenoak (Brodribb *et al* 1971 onwards) and Barton Court Farm (Miles 1986). The character of the finds from the villa and from the enclosures to its east differs, reflecting disparities both in date and status. Fibulae, which are more common in the early Roman period, are confined to the villa area, while the late bracelets occur in both the area of the villa and the eastern enclosures. Toilet articles and casket fittings are commoner around the villa, again reflecting its greater wealth and domestic emphasis.

The enclosures east of the villa produced a small but varied collection of bracelets, including two worn by children and one from a burial. Such bracelets are common on late Roman rural sites. Fig. 94.26 is part of a votive leaf or plaque, which are found almost exclusively on religious sites; locally examples have been found at the temple at Woodeaton in Oxfordshire (Toynbee 1964, 328–331). This fragment comes from the northernmost enclosure in the northern enclosure group, and may indicate that there was a shrine in the vicinity. (Thanks are due to Pamela Irving for drawing our attention to this object).

Scrap bronze and cast waste came only from the villa area. This is most likely debris from robbing and stripping down furnishings, although it is alternatively possible that the reworking of scrap was carried out close to the villa (see Ch. IV.C.5) rather than in the enclosures further east.

V.5 Lead objects

by Tim Allen and Robin Brunner-Ellis

Fig. 96

There were 22 lead finds, including one conical weight of 20 grams, Fig. 96 No. 33, one junction collar or seal, two square-sectioned rivets and two fishing weights made from tightly rolled sheeting and twelve fragments of sheet. Just over half of these finds come from late Roman enclosures to the east. Two fragments from the mortar make-up of the floor in Building I, (87), were clearly offcuts left over in construction; two more offcuts were recovered in 1990 from Building IV. Another fragment from the area of the supposed destroyed hypocaust (see Ch. IV.C.4) was part of the inside lining of a container; it had iron and mortar staining on the outside, and limescale on the inner surface, so this was perhaps a small tank. For a full list see the Microfiche report.

V.6 Iron objects

by Tim Allen and Robin Brunner-Ellis
Figs. 97, 98, 99 and 100 and Table 23

There were 126 iron objects (excluding a large number of nails and sandal studs) from the villa and its immediate vicinity and from the Later Roman enclosures east of this. Table 23 below gives a summary catalogue of these. The full catalogue, which is in the Microfiche report, is arranged according to the order in the Table, except that all the finds from the villa are described first, and those from the eastern enclosures afterwards. The nails are also described in the Microfiche report.

Table 23: Iron objects

Villa and Environs			Late Roman Enclosures to the East		
Context	Type (Small Find No.)	Fig. No.	Context	Type	Fig. No.
Dress articles			**Dress articles**		
182/1	Brooch	97.34			
41/1	Brooch	97.35			
49	Brooch				
2016	Brooch spring (SF 1503)				
361	Belt-fitting	97.36	959/960	Buckle	
361	Shoe-plate	97.37	533	Shoe-plate	
361	Shoe-plate	97.38	628	Shoe-plate	
70	Shoe-plate		836	Shoe-plate	97.39
			894	Shoe-plate	97.40
Building materials			**Building materials**		
201	Water pipe-collar (or nave-hoop?)	97.41			
164	?Water-pipe collar fragment		837	six large cleats or joiners dogs	97.43
160	Angle-iron or cleat		868/1	Angle iron	
114	Washer or rove	97.42	666	Washer or rove	97.44
299	Washer or rove		830	?Washer or rove	
132/2	?Washer or rove		876	Washer or rove	
			978	?Washer or rove	
2004	Collar (SF 1548)				
Household fittings			**Household fittings**		
270	Lever-lock key	98.45	582	?Key shank	
364	Padlock key		559	Plate and spring-plate from a lock	98.48
			U/S	Barrel-padlock. Modern?	
28/1	?Latch-lifter	98.46	868/1	?Latch-lifter	98.49
1431	?Ring-headed pin	98.47	873	Ring-headed pin	
361	Wall-hook		559	Wall-hook	98.50
200	Trivet or pot-stand	98.52			
2414	Hinge/spring (SF 1492)				
2429	?Latch-lifter (SF 1427)				
2434	Peg (SF 1433)				
2465	Split pin and ring (SF 1447)	100.1447			
Furniture fittings			**Furniture fittings**		
132/2	Casket handle	98.51	500	?Drop-handle/mount	98.53
161	?Reinforcing strip		865	Handle	98.54
2460	Casket-ring or terret (SF 1441)	100.1441			
Tools — Knives			**Tools — Knives**		
			868/1	Knife with loop handle	99.55
1413	Knife		868/1	Knife	99.56
169	?Knife		660	?Knife	
361	?Knife tang		1010	Knife	
2004	Knife (SF 1007)				
2001	Clasp-knife (SF 1437)	100.1437			
Other tools			**Other tools**		
361	?Spearhead		865	?Drill or twisted handle	99.57
1511	?Chisel tip		559	Chisel or punch	99.58
2008	Tongs (SF 1027)	100.1027			

Iron objects (Table 23 continued)

Villa and Environs			Late Roman Enclosures to the East		
Context	*Type (Small Find No.)*	*Fig. No.*	*Context*	*Type*	*Fig. No.*
2413	Bone and iron ?tool (SF 1490)				
2429/A/2	Spoon bit (SF 1425)	100.1425			
2481	Pointing trowel (SF 1462)	100.1462			
			764	Sheep shears	99.59
			764	Socket of tool	99.60
			528	Goad	99.61
			509	Goad	
			669	?Goad	
			868/1	?Goad	
			865	?Spatula	99.62
			481	Trident or fork	99.63
			830	Cooper's croze	99.64
2485	Chisel or stylus (SF 1535)	100.1535	903	Chisel or stylus	99.65
			526	?Punch	99.66
Horse-gear, rings, etc			**Horse-gear, rings, etc**		
1421	?Harness-loop				
1506	Ring				
337/1	Ring fragment				
2014	D-ring (SF 1559)				
2410	Ring (SF 1446)				
2413	Ring (SF 1424)				
Straps			**Straps**		
271/2	S-curve		550	Curving	
264			669/4	×3	
271/2			558		
132/2			582		
272/2			841	×3	
163	?Collar		868		
2004/D	Strip (SF 1006)		664		
2028	Strip (SF 1006)				
Sheet iron			**Sheet iron**		
210	Tapered binding		868		
109	Ridged		500	Folded	
210					
2429/A/2	Window catch? (SF 1478)				
Miscellaneous			**Miscellaneous**		
			579	Spike or nail	
190	Bar — riveted		665	Spike or nail	
135	Bar		481/1	Rod or bar	
132/2	Bar		873	Thin rod	
109	Lumps				
132/2	Large lump				
Post-Roman					
190	Decorated handle or harness (?cast)	99.67			
2001	?Bowl rim (modern)		2000	Knife, not Roman	
2004/C	Collar		2000	Stirrup	
2400	(SF 1481)		2000	Stirrups & harness-chain	

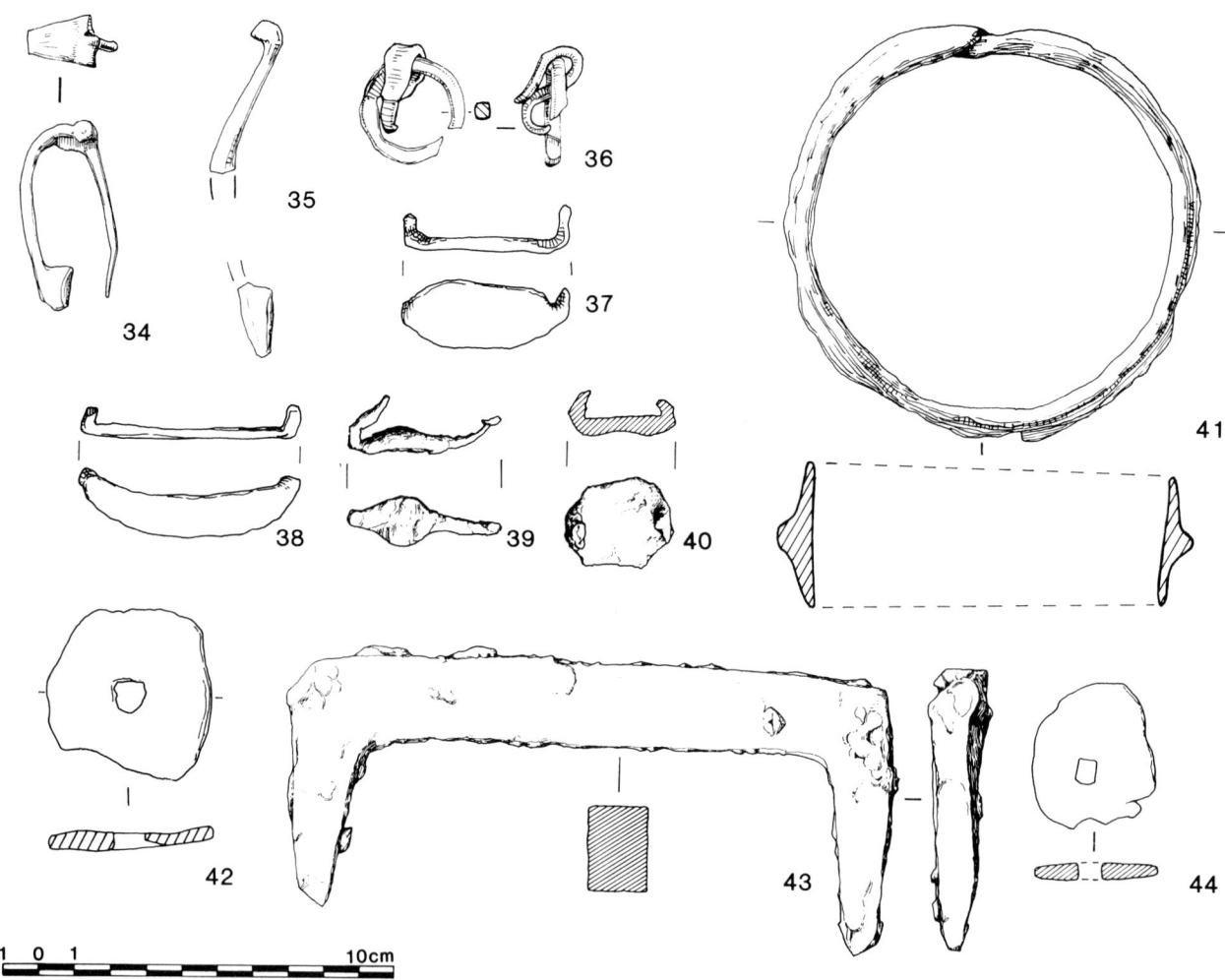

Figure 97 Iron objects: Nos. 34–35 brooches; No. 36 belt-fitting; No. 37–40 shoe-plates; No. 40 pipe collar; No. 41 pipe-collar; Nos. 42 & 44; No. 43 joiners dog.

V.6.a Discussion

The iron finds demonstrate the range of domestic and agricultural items common to most villas. Considering the partial nature of excavation, the mechanical stripping and post-Roman disturbance of much of the site the assemblage is comparable to that at Shakenoak. That the vast majority of tools come from the eastern enclosures suggests that the villa area was primarily residential, while the eastern enclosures performed the agricultural and semi-industrial functions of the estate. Those few tools which do come from the villa are essentially those associated with building activities, such as the trowel and spoon-bit.

The cattle-goads and sheep shears suggest a mixed pastoral element in the site's economy that is shared by Shakenoak (Brodribb *et al* 1978, 195–6). Cattle-droving is also suggested on the evidence of numerous cattle-goads at Barnsley Park, Glos. (Webster & Smith 1982, 116 Fig. 25.37) and keeping sheep for wool at Ditchley and Barton Court Farm, where sheep shears were also found (Miles 1986, IV. 2.1.1).

The group of joiner's dogs or masonry cramps, probably unused stock, are also informative. No trace of a building suitable for these was found in the eastern enclosures; they were presumably intended for use in the villa. They may have been made in the enclosure group itself; considerably more smithing slag was found in the southern group of enclosures, from which the cleats came, than in the northern ones. In neither case was the quantity large, and need only have come from 10 or 12 uses of a smithing hearth, but nevertheless possibly iron-smithing was carried out primarily in the southern enclosures, at least in the latest stages of the occupation (see Ch. 5.15.c on Fiche 2#84).

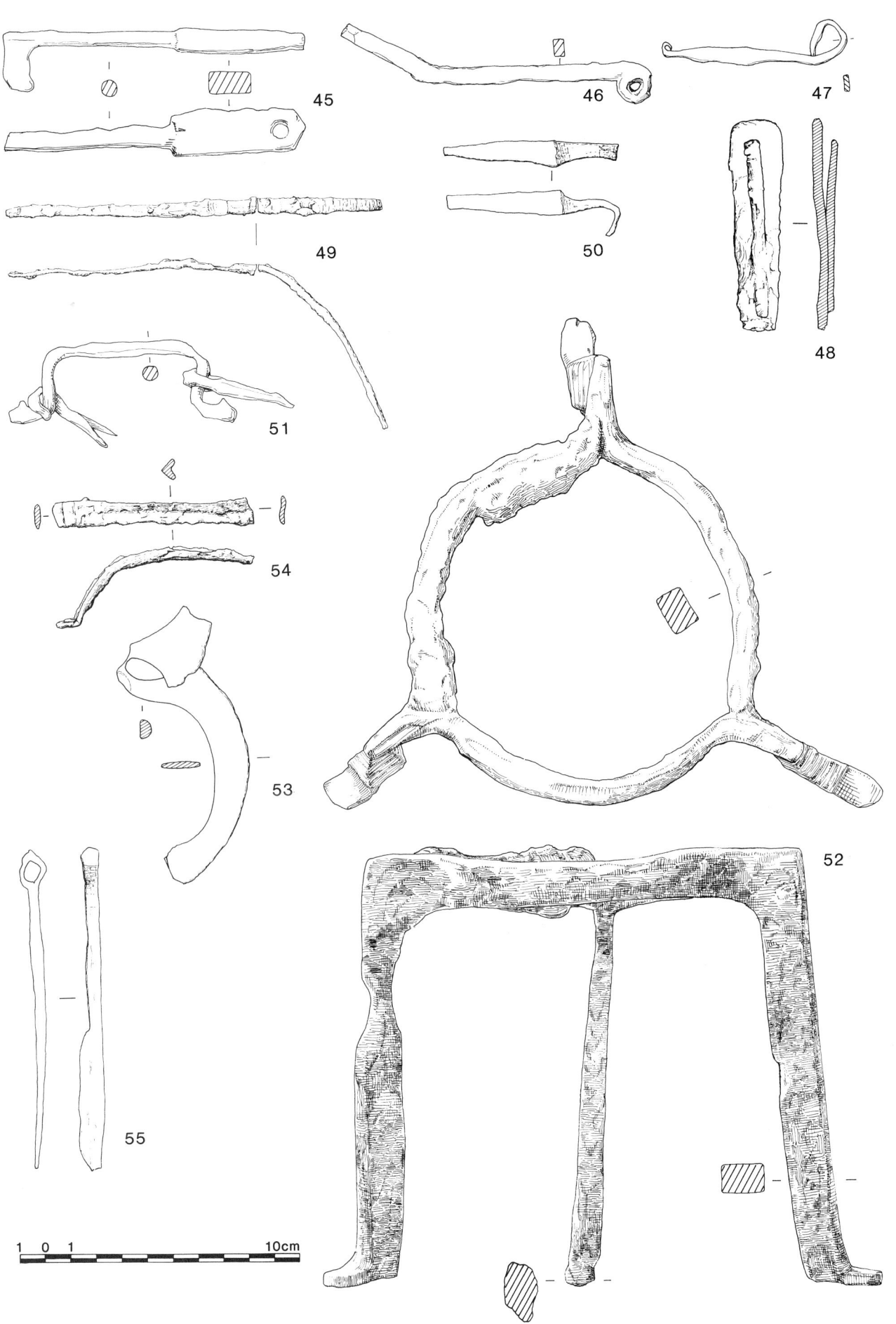

Figure 98 Iron objects: Nos. 45 lever-lock key; No. 46 & 49 latch-lifters; No. 47 ring-headed pin; No. 48 lock spring-plate; No. 50 wall-hook; Nos. 51, 53 & 54 handles; No. 52 trivet; No. 55 knife.

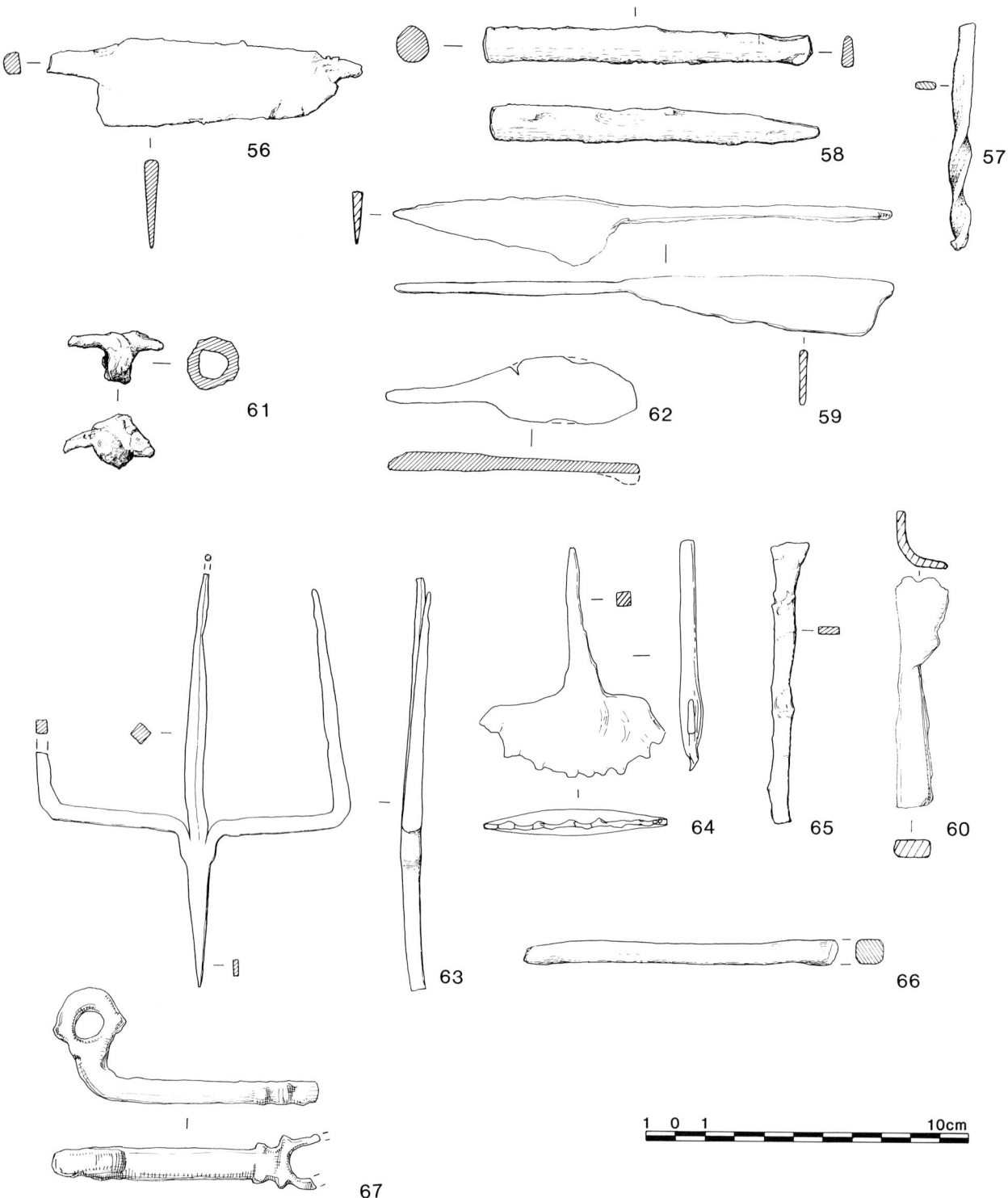

Figure 99 Iron objects: No. 56 knife; No. 57 drill; No. 58 ?punch; No. 59 shears; No. 60 socketed tool; No. 61 goad; No. 62 spatula; No. 63 fork; No. 64 cooper's croze; No. 65 chisel; No. 66 ?punch; No. 67 harness.

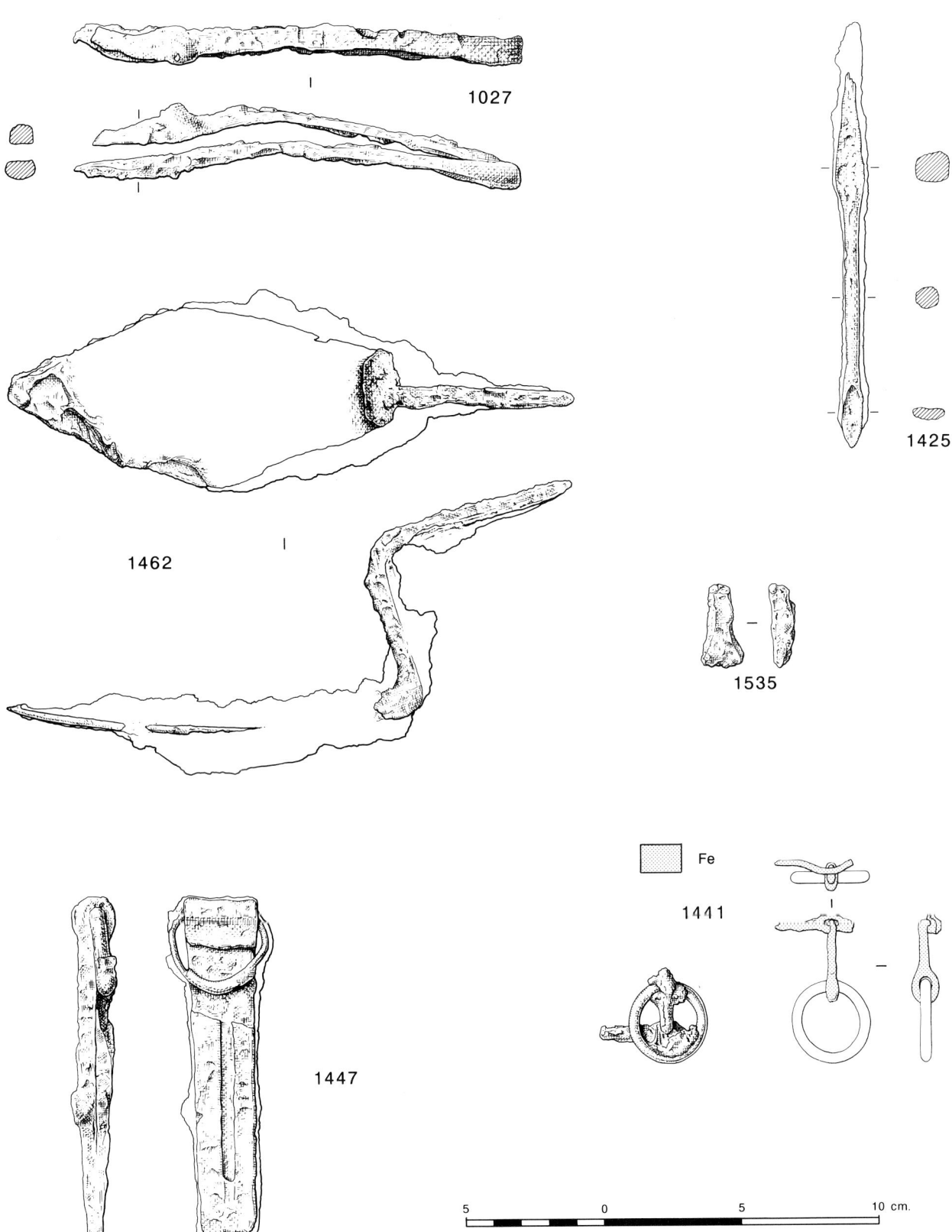

Figure 100 Iron objects: No. 1027 tongs; No. 1425 spoon bit; No. 1441 terret; No. 1447 split pin and ring; No. 1462 trowel; No. 1535 chisel tip.

V.7 Glass objects

by John Shepherd and Cecily Cropper

V.7.a Analysis

327 fragments of glass were retrieved. 257 were of Roman date: of these 216 are from vessels, 37 are window glass, and 4 are indeterminate. The remaining 70 fragments are post-medieval. A summary catalogue of the illustrated fragments is given below; for the full catalogue see the Microfiche. For illustrations see Fig. 101.

V.7.b Catalogue of illustrated fragments

Fig. 101.68 Cat. No. 1. Context 271. Rim of a jar or bowl of free-blown, pale amber glass. Rim thickened and fire-rounded.

Fig. 101.69 Cat. No. 2. Context 560. Base and side of a bulbous-bodied flask or jar of free-blown, greenish-blue glass. First to mid-second century AD.

Fig. 101.70 Cat. No. 67. Context 132/2. Rim and side of a bowl of free-blown, colourless glass with a greenish tint. Thickened and fire-rounded rim, with horizontal trailed and marvered rib of the same metal below.

Fig. 101.71 Cat. No. 68. Context 132/2. Rim of a bowl or beaker of free-blown, colourless glass with a greenish tint. Thickened, fire-rounded and outsplayed rim.

Fig. 101.72 Cat. No. 69. Context 132/2. Rim of a bowl or beaker of free-blown, colourless glass. Thickened and fire-rounded rim, with an applied horizontal trail of the same metal at the base of the neck.

Fig. 101.73 Cat. No. 70. Context 132/2. Solid foot-ring base of a bowl of thick colourless glass.

Fig. 101.74 Cat. No. 71. Context 132/2. Fragment from a base of thick colourless glass decorated with incised grooves. Probably from the same vessel as No. 6.

Fig. 101.75 Cat. No. 72. Context 132/2. Base of a bowl or beaker of free-blown, colourless glass. The side is decorated with horizontal wheel-cut lines.

Fig. 101.76 Cat. No. 73. Context 132/2. Side of a beaker of free-blown, colourless glass, with a horizontal rib, trailed and marvered, of the same metal.

Fig. 101.77 Cat. No. 74. Context 132/2. Side of a very thin-walled vessel of free-blown, colourless glass decorated with bands of horizontal wheel-cut lines.

Fig. 101.78 Cat. No. 82. Context 134. Rim and side of a beaker or bowl of free-blown, colourless glass with a faint greenish tint. Knocked-off, rough rim.

Fig. 101.79 Cat. No. 83. Context 134. Base of a bowl or beaker of free-blown, colourless glass with a faint greenish tint.

Fig. 101.80 Cat. No. 84. Context 133. Rim of a bowl or beaker of free-blown, colourless glass. Knocked-off, rough rim.

Fig. 101.81 Cat. No. 85. Context 133. Side of a beaker or bowl of free-blown, colourless glass with a greenish tint. Decorated with a trailed and marvered rib and dot of the same metal.

Fig. 101.82 Cat. No. 100. Context 1478. Rim of a bowl or beaker of free-blown, colourless glass. Thickened and fire-rounded rim.

Fig. 101.83 Cat. No. 101. Context 1451. Rim and side of a small bowl or beaker of free-blown, colourless glass with thickened and fire-rounded rim. Possibly the bowl of No. 102 below.

Fig. 101.84 Cat. No. 102. Context 1451. Base of a small stemmed goblet of free-blown, colourless glass with a faint greenish tint. The centre of the base is thickened and the pontil scar has been ground smooth. The foot has a thickened and fire-rounded lip, and a trail of the same metal has been applied at the bottom of the stem.

Fig. 101.85 Cat. No. 104. Context 285. Side and part of the base of a bowl or beaker of free-blown, colourless glass with a trail of the same metal around the base.

Fig. 101.86 Cat. No. 105. Context 271. Rim of a funnel-shaped beaker of free-blown, poor colourless glass. Knocked-off, rough rim.

Fig. 101.87 Cat. No. 106. Context 285. Rim of a beaker of very thin free-blown, colourless glass. Knocked-off, rough rim, with two bands of horizontal incised lines.

Fig. 101.88 Cat. No. 111. Context 60. Base of an unguentarium of free-blown, greenish colourless glass.

Fig. 101.89 Cat. No. 117. Context 830. Base of a footed beaker of free-blown, colourless glass. Pushed-in base with flattened hollow tubular section.

Fig. 101.90 Cat. No. 119. Context 582. Rim of a beaker of free-blown colourless glass. Knocked-off, rough rim with wheel-cut horizontal lines.

Fig. 101.91 Cat. No. 158. Context 774. Now missing; described from the illustration. Probably from the rim of a small unguentarium or flask, but just possibly from the base of a small stemmed goblet. Natural self-coloured greenish-blue glass.

Fig. 101.1435 Cat. No. 1435. Context 2434/B. Three fragments of base of a thin-walled bowl or flask with a hollow tubular footing in a colourless, free-blown glass. Approximate diameter of the foot-ring is 60 mm.

Fig. 101.1448 Cat. No. 1448. Context 2429/A/1. Fragment of rim and body of a vessel of colourless, slightly blue-tinted, free-blown glass. Rim is hollow and tubular with the lip rolled over to the inside and flattened. Diameter is between 60–70 mm.

V.7.c Discussion

All numbers referred to are catalogue numbers

Overall, the assemblage of Roman glass can be dated to the late 2nd to 4th centuries. The exceptions are No. 2 and No. 1440, a fragment from a hexagonal sided bottle, that can be attributed to the late 1st to early 2nd centuries (compare the glass from Woodchester, Shepherd 1982).

The assemblage is composed, primarily, of well-attested forms, especially bowls and beakers (Nos. 1, 67–72, 82–4 and 100–101), but the absence of distinctive late 4th century metals (ie poor quality greenish colourless glasses) and the thin walls of the vessels with knocked-off rims suggests that these vessels may have been produced before this late period. (For an assemblage which contains similar forms to these, but dated to the late 3rd and 4th centuries see Frocester Court; Price 1979, 37–46, especially Nos. 11, 24, 26, 27).

Of particular interest are the bowl fragments (No. 67) and the goblet (No. 102) of which No. 101 is probably the bowl. The former is most unusual. In form and decoration it is similar to the two-handled stemmed cups of the 1st century (Isings 1957, 53f, form 38) but its size, metal and context (a later 2nd century ditch; see also Ch. V.2.b.5) makes this interpretation unlikely. Similarly enigmatic is the stemmed goblet (No. 102). Isings (1957, 139f) notes that this form is unique to the mediterranean and more common in such areas from the late 4th century onwards. That here we have a stemmed goblet suggests the limited production of such vessels in the north-west provinces at an earlier date. Since only a small part of the villa was excavated, to find two such unusual vessel types in a small assemblage may be an indication of the quality of glassware

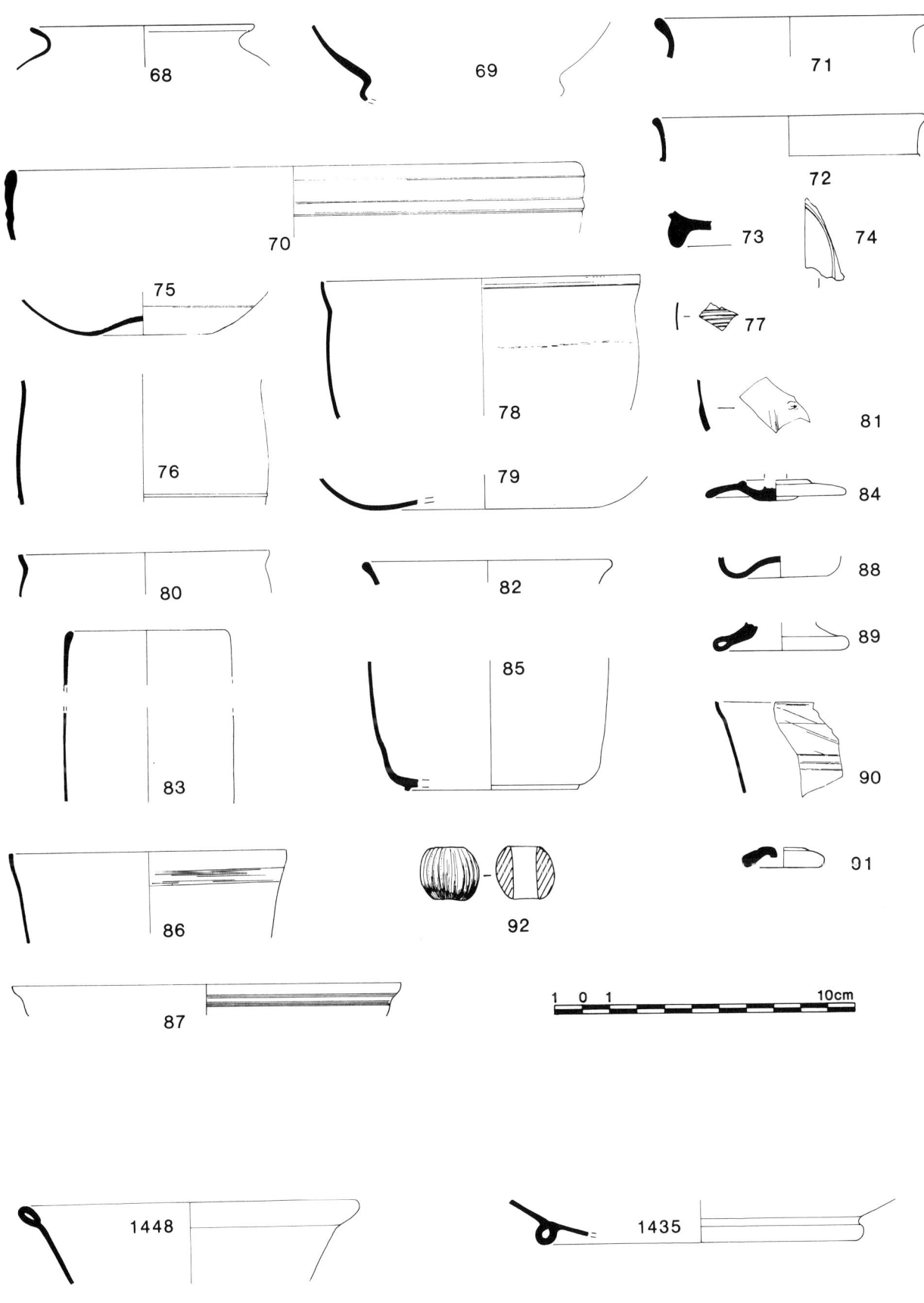

Figure 101 Glass vessels: Nos. 68–91, 1435, & 1448; and faience melon bead: No. 92.

being used there in the later 2nd and 3rd centuries.

In the later 3rd to mid-4th centuries all the forms are common, all but one of colourless glass, and a high proportion were very thin-walled (cf. J Price in Webster & Smith 1982, 177, No. 13 ff). The absence of late 4th century metals supports coin and pottery evidence suggesting that the villa was in decline by the 360s AD (Ch. VII).

Apart from the mould-blown square-sectioned bottles (Nos. 5–37), which may well have still been produced, almost certainly employed, in the late 2nd and early 3rd centuries, most of the glassware is fine tableware.

Only 25 fragments came from the enclosures east of the villa; a few common late forms are illustrated. This fits the interpretation of these areas as ancillary and largely agricultural. Window fragments perhaps suggest that there were buildings here, despite the absence of structural evidence.

V.7.d Faience and other glass beads

Fig. 101.92

Half of a turquoise-blue faience melon-bead of 20 mm diameter came from context 214. This had a hole 9 mm in diameter through it. The design had been incised on the unperforated sphere and the hole made afterwards, as was evident from the fact that it lay slightly askew to the decoration. Margaret Guido has listed some 65 examples from Romano-British sites in Britain, and believes that they were current only in the 1st and 2nd centuries AD. (Guido 1978, 100).

A small bead of blue glass also came from the site, but is now lost. From a surviving drawing this was cylindrical, 8–9 mm long, and was slightly thicker at one end (maximum diameter 10 mm). The bead was made by winding a broad trail of glass around a rod of circular cross-section 4 mm in diameter. The overlapping join has not been ground smooth, and is still visible.

V.8 Worked bone and ivory objects

by Tim Allen and Robin Brunner-Ellis

Fig. 102

There were 11 pins or needles, a clasp-knife handle and another knife handle, a polished ivory disc and 5 other artefacts, including a tool made from a nail driven into a cow's metatarsal. A complete catalogue will be found in the Microfiche report.

There were also five sawn pieces of bone, the identifiable pieces being horse or red deer antler; there were several other finds of antler that may have been kept for bone-working. Two other pieces showed marks from either skinning or working (for full list see archive). The deer skull found in a late ditch (419) west of the villa was probably kitchen debris, the antlers having been taken elsewhere for working. Bone working debris was found in the southern group of enclosures and also probably in the northern, in both cases in only one or two instances. A little also came from the yard area close to Building IV.

All the artefacts come from contexts belonging to the villa phase of the occupation, most coming from the area of the buildings themselves. The worked debris seems also to belong with the villa phase. Of these a fragment from 1467 may, however, be earlier. One of the pins, Fig. 102.98, is much more akin to Anglo-Saxon than to Romano-British types: it comes from Late Roman pit 763.

Of particular interest is the decorated bone handle of an iron clasp knife, handsomely carved in the shape of a panther springing from a calyx of stylized acanthus leaves Fig. 102.1437). There are several examples extant of this type of decorated clasp knife (Toynbee 1964, 360), a particularly close parallel coming from an early 2nd century context at Wroxeter (Bushe-Fox 1913, Pl. 22, Fig. 10). It shows a tiger emerging from a cup of leaves in the act of eating something between its forepaws, a carved piece which Toynbee suggested was of continental origin. Martin Henig believes that the floral calyx motif could be seen as a stylized representation of life. Possibly the springing beast/calyx of life is a metaphor for the springing action of the knife blade — a visual talisman for the knife's owner, as one might say.

V.9 Jet and shale objects

by Tim Allen

Fig. 103

Three jet objects were recovered, a fragment of decorative inlay (Fig. 103.103) and the shank of a pin (Fig. 103.104) from the villa area and the head of another pin (Fig. 103.105) from the southern enclosure group east of the villa. A shale spindle whorl (Fig. 103.1567) was found unstratified in the area of Building III. For a full description see Microfiche report.

The nearest source for jet is the Whitby area of north-east Yorkshire; the shale is probably derived from Dorset.

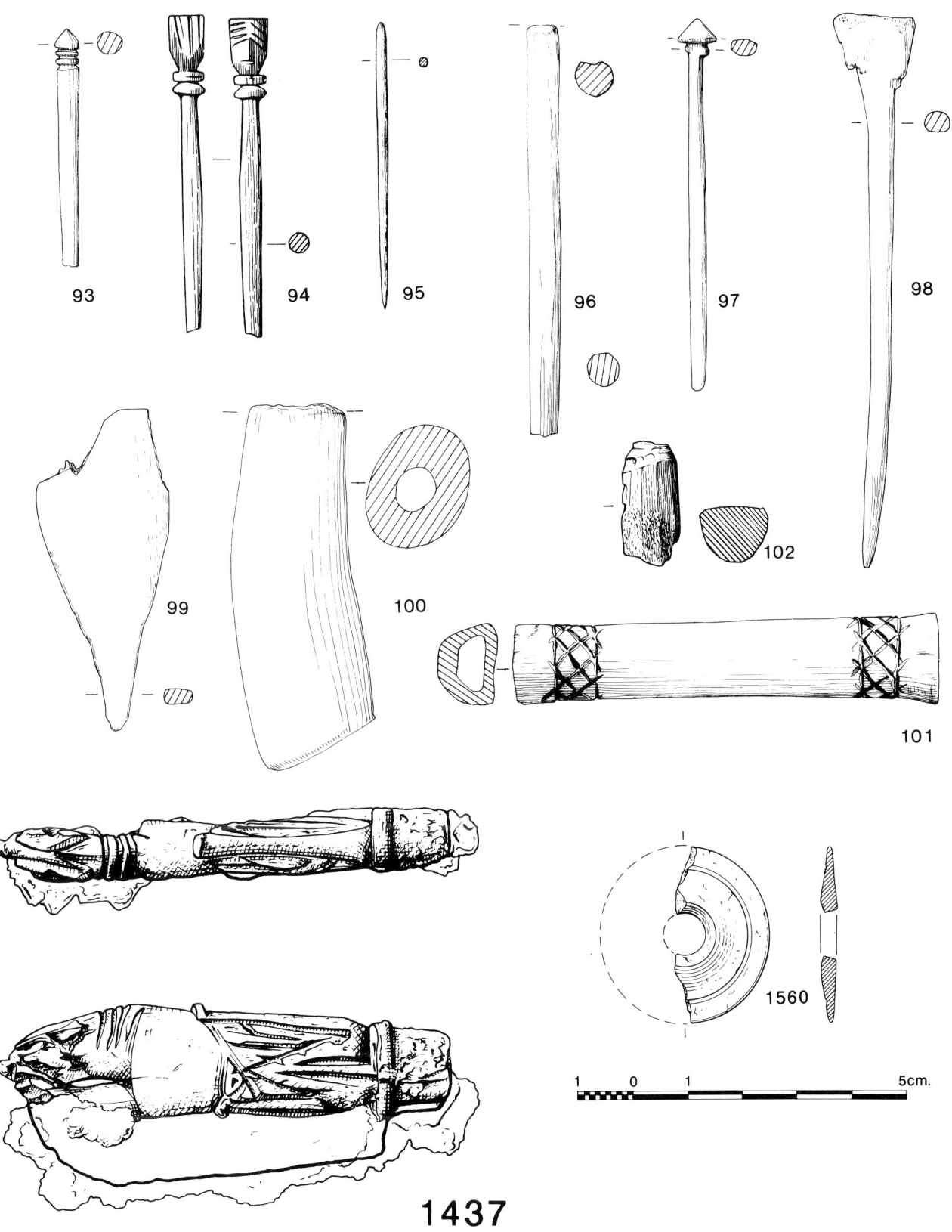

Figure 102 Bone objects: Nos. 93–98 pins; No. 99 spatula; No. 100–101 handles; No. 102 waste; No. 1437 clasp-knife. Ivory object: No. 1560 disc.

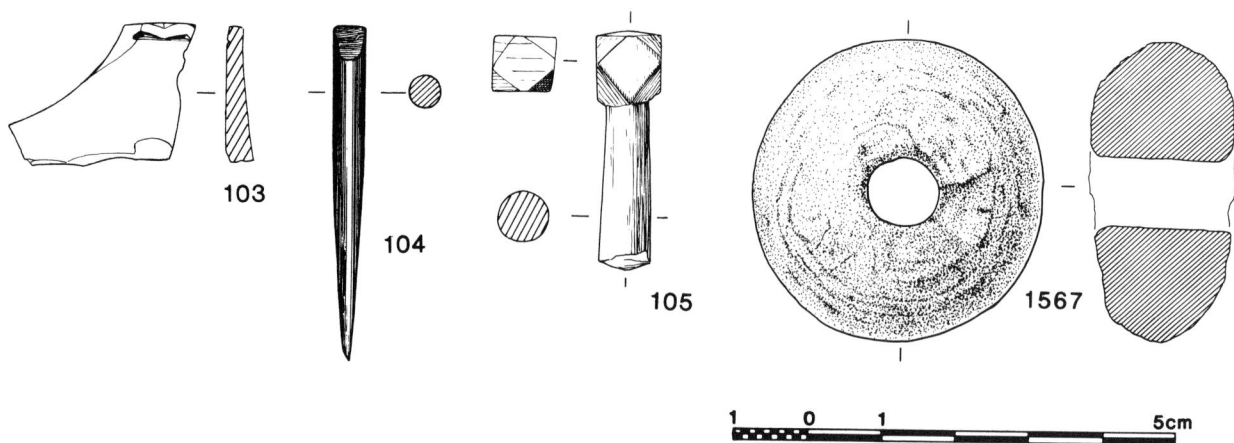

Figure 103 Jet objects: No. 103 inlay; Nos. 104–105 pins. Shale object: No. 1567 spindle whorl.

V.10 Stone objects

by Tim Allen

Figs. 104–107, Tables 25 and 24

Fragments of eighty one stone objects, including a fragment of stone statuary, were found, of which two are now missing. These comprised both saddle and rotary querns, quern-rubbers or pounding stones, whetstones and sharpening slabs, spindle whorls and loomweights, oven or cooking bases, a small selection of building fragments and a variety of troughs, mortars, gate pivot stones and hollowed stones. For a full catalogue of the Stone Objects and descriptions see Table 51 on Fiche 2#58. A table of the incidence of these types indicating their geographical and chronological position is given in Table 25.

Five fragments from 4 saddle querns, 8 possible 'rubbers', one complete lower stone and thirty four fragments from a minimum of 27 rotary querns were found. Table 24 shows the frequency of each rock type and the date of the contexts in which they occurred.

Of the Lower Greensand querns the saddle quern is clearly residual in a Late Roman context. If the other fragment is from a rotary quern this is likely to be an early type because of its thickness, but this fragment too may instead come from a saddle quern. Both querns therefore belong with the earlier rather than the later group. Although clearly a rotary quern, the type and therefore the date of the Italian lava quern is unknown. When these types are discounted, it becomes clear that there is not only a significant shift in the source of querns between the early and later periods, but also a marked predominance of two specific sources, Millstone Grit and Coarse Quartzitic Conglomerate. This may reflect greater specialisation in quern production and marketing in the later period, or, since the changeover coincides broadly with the establishment of the villa, bulk trade on a much greater scale than before.

	43–150 AD	150 AD–360 AD	Totals
Sarsen	2S	—	2
Felspathic Sandstone	1S + 3R	—	4
Coarse conglomerate	2R	7R	9
Lower Greensand	—	1S + 1?R	2
Millstone Grit	—	17R	17
?Millstone grit	—	2R	2
Italian Lava	—	1R	1
Unidentified	—	1R	1
	3S+5R = 8	1S+28R+1?R = 30	38

S = Saddle quern ; R = Rotary quern

Table 24 Querns by source and date

The stones from the Early Roman settlement are unexceptional for a rural site. Early quern types such as Fig. 105 Nos 106 and 107 have been dated to the pre-

Boudiccan period at Colchester (Crummy 1983, Fig. 78 Nos. 2071 and 2075). Saddle quern fragments and rubbers (Fig. 104.111–113) are not generally considered to continue in use into the Early Roman period in the Upper Thames Valley, being found only as residual items on site with previous Iron Age occupation. These finds may therefore indicate a greater level of Iron Age activity in this area than is demonstrated by the known features; alternatively they may have been brought in as rubble from elsewhere (see Ch. VII). A collection of querns and 'gate-pivots' (Fig. 105.122 and Fig. 106.124) in pits 464/465 and 414 perhaps provides evidence of the major reorganisation of the mid-2nd century, old boundaries and buildings being swept away to make way for the villa and its field system. Some of these objects were still usable, and their deposition in the pits may have some special, perhaps propitiatory, significance.

Thorough robbing has left very few architectural fragments (Fig. 105.118–120). Greensand chippings from the final dressing of Building III (Ch. IV.C.8.e) and blocks of Bathstone shows that good-quality stone was imported; but the rest of the stone is local Taynton stone, probably from the Burford area only 5–10 km away. Two fragments found close to the site, the upper part of a small figure, Fig. 105.121, and a small altar from an Anglo-Saxon grave at Butler's Field (Miles & Palmer 1986, 13), probably come from the villa, and give glimpses of the missing dimension, but both are of poor workmanship and local limestone. The overall impression is that the villa was not architecturally sumptuous.

Almost all the whetstones, querns and troughs of late 2nd century or later date came from the enclosures east of the villa, bearing out their use as agricultural and semi-industrial areas in contrast to the area of the villa buildings. Querns with a lower stone of conical profile continue in use (Fig. 104.114), and thin flat querns with flat tops and wide central eye are introduced (Fig. 105.115). One probable millstone (Fig. 105.116) with an estimated diameter of 0.63m was found.

A group of stone objects in pit 876 may represent a reorganisation; like those in an earlier pit 464, they were not found dumped with other stones as rubble, and some were still usable when deposited. Lamps, troughs and mortars (Fig. 105.123, Fig. 106.125–8) were found in the 'silt-filled hollows' 550, 558, 560 etc. These stone objects were of a different character to those in pits; they were associated with much pottery and other rubbish including small quantities of tesserae and wallplaster, so may be specialised robbing from a building.

Three unusual Stonesfield slates were found, two from the enclosures east of the villa, and one from the villa. The edges of all three had been chamfered. The first two were 320 and 340 mm in diameter; Fig. 106.131. was found *in situ* covering the bottom of a small oven, whose sides were also lined with slates. The example from the villa was only 100 mm in diameter and was probably used as a pot-lid. These slates were probably quarried from large cigar-shaped lumps of slate which occur naturally, and which can easily be split up into roughly circular slates (information from George Swinford, Filkins Museum, Glos.).

	Saddle querns	Rotary querns	Pestles/ rubbers	Whetstones	Architectural fragments	Gate-pivots	Mortars/ troughs etc.	Oven bases/ potlids	Spindle whorls	Dished slabs	Totals
Pre-villa 1st-mid 2nd century	3	6	2(2)	2	—	3	—	—	1	—	19
Villa late 2nd to 4th centuries	—	7+1	2	2	2	—	—	1	1	—	16
Eastern enclosures late 2nd to 4th centuries	(1)	14+5	1(1)	8(1)	1	—	2	2	—	2	38
Silt-filled pits 4th century	—	1	—	1	—	—	5	—	—	—	7
Totals	3(1) 4	28+6 34	5(3) 8	13(1) 14	3 3	3 3	7 7	3 3	2 2	2 2	80

Table 25 Stone objects: types and distribution. Numbers given in brackets are only tentatively identified. In some instances the rotary querns have been divided into two groups, to distinguish first the minimum number and second other fragments.

162 *Roughground Farm, Lechlade, Gloucestershire: a prehistoric and Roman landscape*

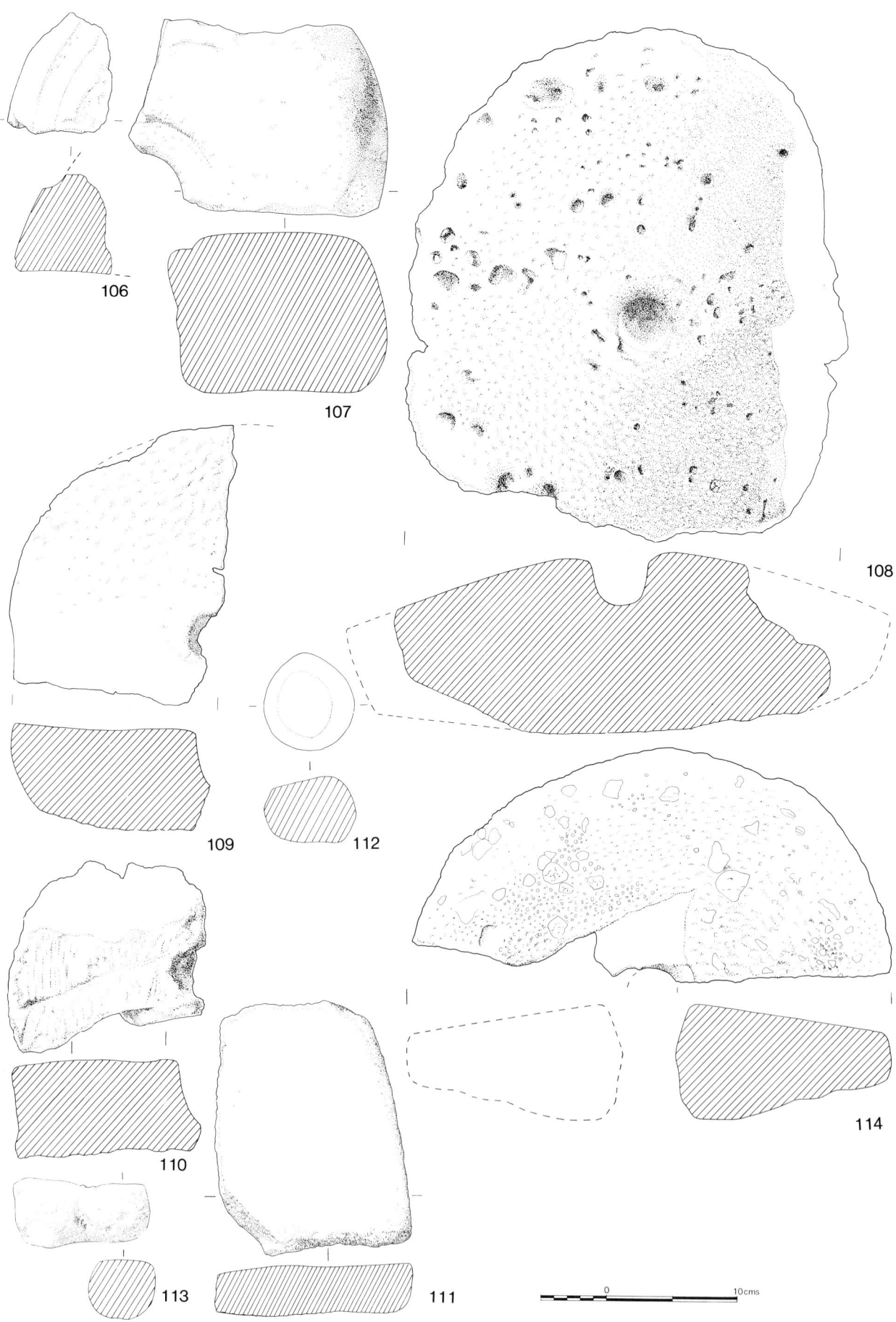

Figure 104 Stone objects: Nos. 106–110 & 114 rotary querns; No. 111 saddle quern; Nos. 112–113 rubbers or pounders.

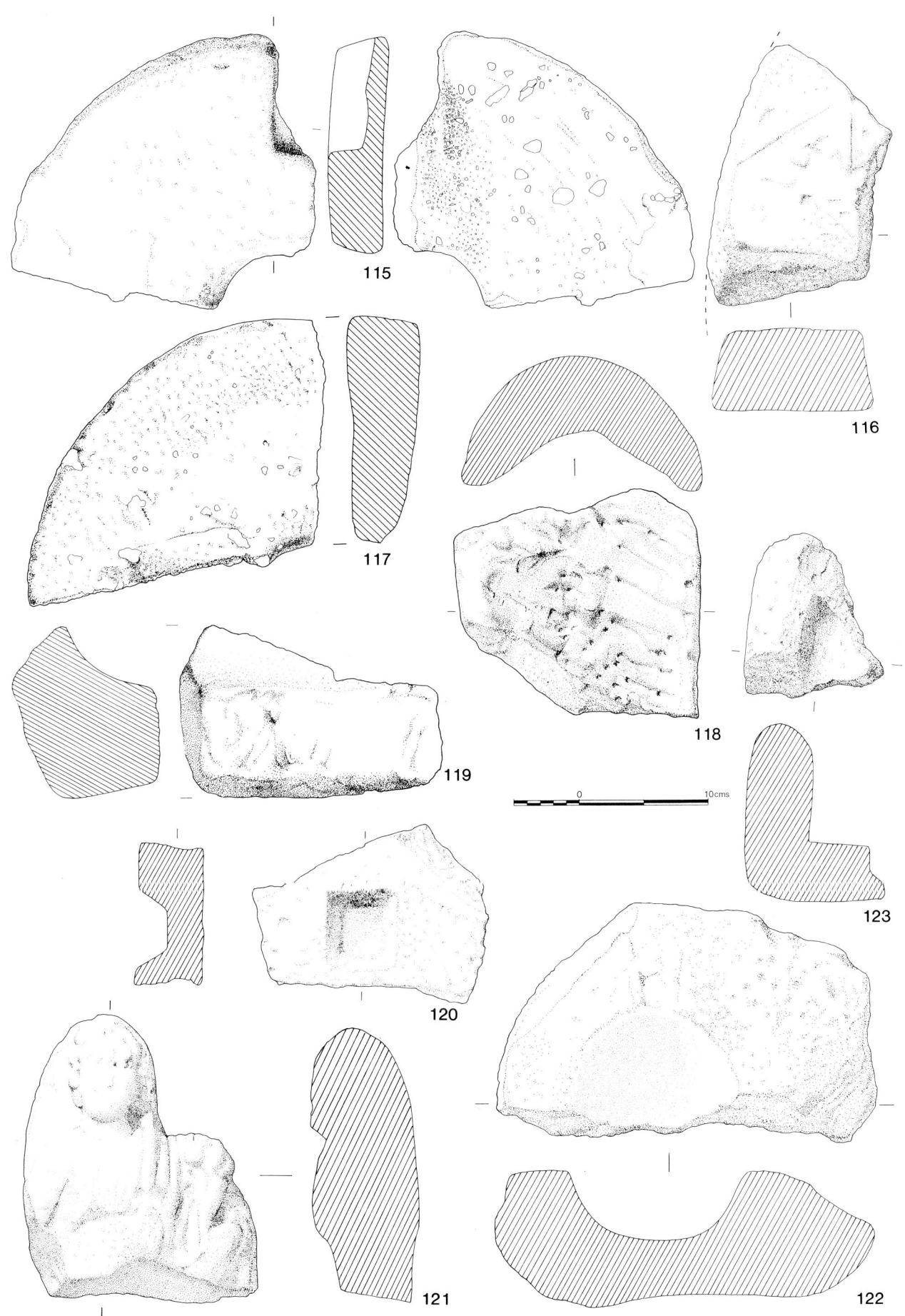

Figure 105 Stone objects: Nos. 115–117 querns; No. 118 roof ridge; No. 119 architectural fragment; No. 120 socket; No. 121 figurine; No. 122 gate pivot; No. 123 trough.

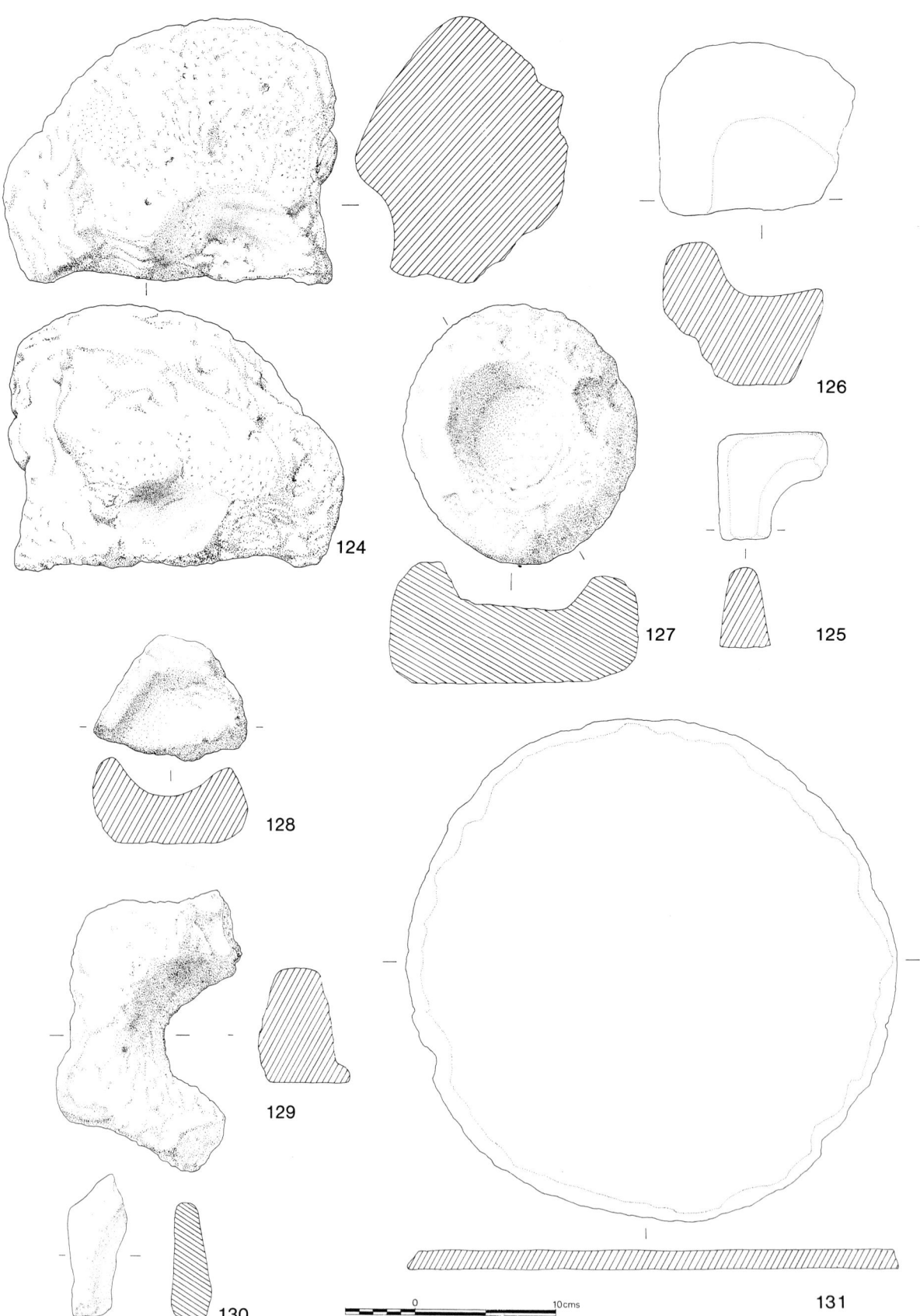

Figure 106 Stone objects: Nos. 124 gate pivot; Nos. 125–6, 129–30 troughs or basins; Nos. 127–128 lamps; No. 131 oven base

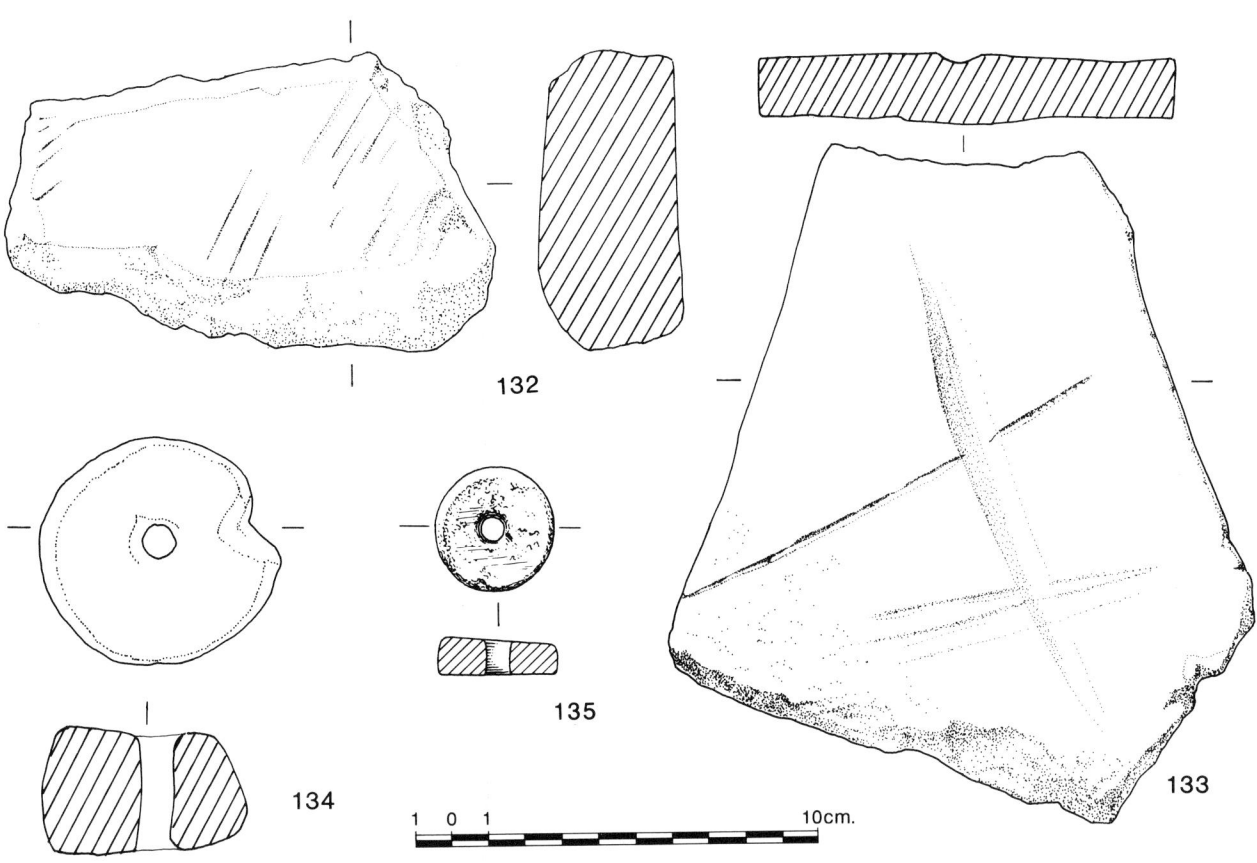

Figure 107 Stone objects: Nos. 132–3 whetstones; Nos. 134–5 spindle whorls.

V.11 Fired clay objects

by Alan Palmer and Tim Allen

Fig. 108

In total 8718 gms. of fired clay from Roman contexts were kept. The site drawings and records suggest that most fragments from the enclosures north-east of the villa, which were largely from collapsed ovens, were discarded, but in contrast fired clay from the sites closer to the villa was kept.

Fourteen fabrics were identified which can be grouped as follows:

A Mixed streaky clays
B Mixed streaky clays and quartz
C Organic inclusions
D Calcareous inclusions
E Rounded quartz (iron-rich) and some organic inclusions
F Angular quartz (iron-rich)

For a full description see Ch. 5.11 on Fiche 2#62. Three fabric groups were common, A, D and E. The types of object are listed with their fabrics in Table 53 on Fiche 2#66. There is some correlation between fabric and function. Objects are generally made from the dense group A fabric, solid clay oven structure from E, and the wide range of fabrics used for daubing material suggests and indiscriminate use of whatever material was available.

Three clay pellets are illustrated (Fig. 108.136–8). Cynthia Poole has suggested (Poole in Cunliffe 1984, (Vol II), 398) that their use might be determined by their size and weight: larger pellets used in warfare, as in the Late Iron Age phase at Danebury, smaller pellets such as those from Glastonbury or All Cannings Cross more probably for gaming. The pellets from Roughground Farm correspond approximately to the smaller category.

Triangular loomweight fragments came from areas with very little evidence of Iron Age activity, and may genuinely reflect their use up until the 2nd century AD. A circular weight from context 798 (Fig. 108.142) is unusual in an Iron Age/Roman context, being more typically Saxon (Hoffman 1964). A similar weight was found at Winterton (Stead 1976, 226–7) although that example was considerably larger.

Fragments from a triangular crucible (cf. Wainwright 1979, 132 Fig. 99) were found in pit 190. No trace of metal residue was present. The fabric included large fragments of hammerscale from iron-smithing. Pit 190 contained a large deposit of iron slag (Ch. V.15) and much charcoal, and was

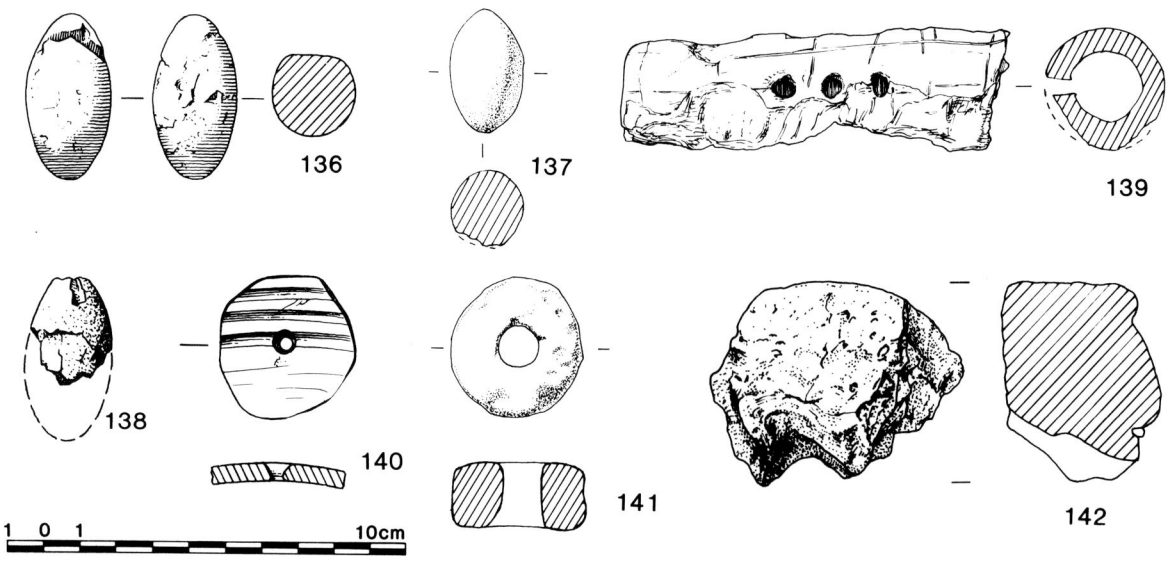

Figure 108 Fired clay objects: Nos. 136–8 clay pellets; Nos. 139 'flute'; Nos. 140–1 spindle whorls; No. 142 circular loomweight

probably adjacent to an iron-working area; the crucible was probably manufactured and used in the same area.

One end of a highly-fired hollowed cylindrical object is also illustrated (Fig. 108.139). The clay was probably wrapped round a forme, and before firing three small holes were made through one side in line, about 7 mm apart. The external surface was scored in a pattern of squares. Much of the exterior is deeply scarred by spalling; some of this heating occurred after breakage. Margaret Jones interpreted this object as a pottery flute or whistle, but it could only have been played by a child, as the holes are too close together for adult fingers, and with this wide a bore could only have produced quarter-tones or closer intervals. The diameter of the bore would also necessitate the complete instrument being three times the surviving length to produce effective notes. If an instrument, it would thus have been long and flute-like with clusters of holes at intervals, providing modulations around two or more notes. Alternatively the object might have been a bellows-nozzle or tuyere. Since simple bellows both expel and suck in air through the nozzle, the three holes might have been to let in cold air when filling the bellows, rather than taking in entirely hot air from the furnace, or having to remove the bellows from the nozzle between blasts. (I am indebted to Andy Parkinson for this suggestion). It has however been objected that the presence of scored decoration makes this interpretation unlikely. No close parallels are known to the writer.

The ovens are described in Ch. IV.F.2. Oven superstructures have been divided into two types:

Type 1 solid clay
Type 2 clay daubed onto a wattle framework

The identifiable fragments from type 1 are listed in microfiche; all but one were of fabric E, from the early Roman occupation area, concentrated in enclosure 56. The one fragment from a later Roman context, a pedestal plate support from pit 560, was also the only fragment of Fabric group D. This is also the fabric used for the later wattle ovens, suggesting a change both in oven manufacture and in clay fabric from the early Roman period. The only oven from which samples were kept is 781, located in the later Roman enclosures to the east of the villa. The fragments suggest a dome-roofed structure over a wattle framework.

V.12 Building materials: flooring

V.12.a Mosaic fragments

by Elizabeth MacRobert and Tim Allen

In all 417 tesserae were recovered, comprising 184 individual pieces and 42 groups from tessellated floors. Others were recorded in the notebooks but were discarded. They were of three sizes and were made of white or grey limestone, red tile or blue-grey lias. For a breakdown of the colours and sizes see microfiche Table 55 on Fiche 2#69. The tesserae were set in mortar surfaced with *opus signinum*.

V.12.a.1 Designs
Fig. 151 on Fiche 2#71

These show lines of different colours, corners including some triangular tesserae and curving bands, possibly part of a guilloche motif. Most of the surviving groups of tesserae come from Building III, and almost all of these from Room 2, but lines of different colours including the only light grey tesserae (No. 16) and some very small tesserae from Building I suggest that there were also mosaic designs there.

V.12.a.2 Distribution

Most of the tesserae came from Building III, but at least 37 from Building I. A handful were found in Buildings II and IV, but too few to suggest that there were tessellated floors within them. Almost all of the large white tesserae were from Building III, but the few large red tesserae were not from this building. Large tesserae were usually used for borders or for single-colour tessellated floors. The absence of large red tesserae from Building III may reflect a chronological change, as other villa buildings were first erected in the mid-2nd century AD. By the later 3rd century, when the major enlargement of Building III took place, tile production was apparently much reduced (M. Stone pers. comm.), hence increasing shortage of tiles and so a change to local white limestone tesserae for covering large areas. A shift from ceramic tiles to limestone slates is also possible in the roofing materials on site (see Ch. V.14 below).

The surviving fragments of mosaic do not suggest anything more complicated than geometric designs, and the range of surviving colours is also small. Only parts of the domestic buildings were, however, excavated and these had been heavily robbed.

V.12.b *Opus signinum* and mortar flooring

by Tim Allen

Only a small number of samples were kept, mostly from Building III, and none were in situ. Some samples were not labelled, making their attribution to specific buildings dependant upon references in the notebooks, which are often imprecise (see also the microfiche Ch. 5.12.a on Fiche 2#69).

The mortars were examined macroscopically according to type and size of inclusion, colour and hardness or density; no mortar analysis has been done. For details see the microfiche report.

Quarter-round mouldings were found in Building III, Room 1, from Building II or B and from the robbing of Building IV. These were made of variants of *opus signinum*. Two dense mortar fragments from pits east of the villa had their surface coated with light blue and blue-black paint, and most likely came from a bath; *opus signinum* is not normally painted except in baths, where blue was frequently employed, for instance at Rockbourne, Hants and at Sparsholt (Johnston 1979, 17–19).

V.13 Building materials: walls and ceilings

V.13.a Painted plaster

by Elizabeth MacRobert (1990 report by Robin Brunner-Ellis

A total of 1289 fragments were kept from the excavations in 1957–65 and in 1981–82. A detailed account of the analysis with a full catalogue will be found in the microfiche. A set of colour slides illustrating the designs is available on request.

The majority of the plaster came from Building III. The range of colours and designs from this building was very varied, and it is clear that it was decorated throughout. Dadoes seem to have been spattered with paint in several colours in imitation of marbling, and above this large panels, often of a single colour, were bordered by multicoloured rows of stripes. The panels were sometimes elaborated by diagonal striping and the borders by sinuous motifs or cable designs. Less abstract panels with floral designs were also common. Frilled curves along the edge of borders may represent drapery. Hints of more sophisticated wall-paintings are provided by what appears to be a fragment of a column painted with perspective, and some fragments of finely-painted and complicated design with a particularly large range of colours that are similar to the finest design from Shakenoak (Brodribb *et al* 1971, 94–7). Moulded plaster fragments were also found, showing that some panels were outlined in relief. Fragments of wall-plaster from the earlier phase of Building III were few, but suggest that it was decorated more simply, largely in single colours.

Little plaster was kept from the other buildings, and the range of colours and designs is correspondingly smaller. However fragments of representational painting were found in Building I, as well as painted pilasters like those in Building III. The mortars used in the plaster from Buildings I, II and IV were generally distinct from those in Building III, possibly reflecting the chronological gap between the construction of the former in the 2nd century and of Building III in the later 3rd. Other fragments of plaster from west and east of the villa buildings are most similar to those from Buildings I, II and IV, but include other colours than those from the excavated parts of these buildings. This suggests that there were further painted rooms in the earlier villa.

Several fragments of painted plaster were coated with a smooth thin film of limescale. These were fragments of dense *opus signinum*, and may have come from plunge baths. Although no bathhouse was positively identified on the site, this is one of a number of indicators that one existed (see Ch. VI.2).

A further 119 fragments of painted plaster were recovered from the 1990 excavation, 90 coming from Building III and 29 from Building IV. These all fell within the range of colours and designs represented in the assemblage from the earlier excavations.

V.13.b Other plaster and Tufa

by Tim Allen

Fragments of light, white mortars bearing lath or wattle impressions came from Buildings II and III and from pits east of the villa. These were probably from ceilings; they were undecorated, suggesting that these ceilings were left plain.

One fragment of sawn tufa was kept, and others were recorded west of the villa buildings. Tufa was often used in ceilings because of its light weight; blocks were found at Shakenoak in the debris of Building C and of part of the bath-suite of Rooms VI and VII in Building A (Brodribb *et al* 1971, 25; 1973, 24). Tufa is common in hard-water springs in the Upper Thames (Brodribb *et al* 1972, 153).

All the tufa found at Shakenoak came from the roofs of bath-houses, as do tufa blocks from Fawler, Oxon (Allen 1988, 310); the fragments from Roughground Farm may be further evidence of a bath-house on this site. Norman Davey (Davey 1961, 201–3 and Fig. 114 B) refers to specially-shaped tufa blocks used for the construction of hollow vaults in bath-houses, and at Sparsholt there were tufa voussoirs in the apse-vault (Johnston 1978, 79–82 and Fig. 24).

V.14 Building materials: roofing slates and roofing and other tiles

by Tim Allen

Hexagonal and diamond-shaped slates of Forest Marble or Stonesfield slate occurred in great quantity around Building III and in smaller numbers around Buildings I, II and IV. Building III was certainly roofed with these, and possibly also part of Building I, although tiles were much more common from this building. Roof slates were also found in the enclosures east of the villa, but not in sufficient numbers to indicate roofs; slates were commonly reused here in ovens and in pitched and flat stone floors.

Part of a roof-ridge of local Great Oolite is illustrated (Fig. 105.118).

V.14.a Ceramic tiles

by Tim Allen (with comments by Mike Stone)

Very few tiles from the excavations prior to 1990 were kept, less than 150 identifiable fragments in all. These included tegulae and imbrices, pilae and box-flue tiles and floor tiles which may have been used on the sub-floor or as bridging tiles in hypocausts. Fabric analysis identified products from the Minety kilns and from Shore Farm near Swindon, and some grog-tempered tiles similar to ones found at Barnsley Park, Glos. Tiles of all types occur in all fabrics; a summary of types by fabric groups is given in Table 56 on Fiche 2#81 in the microfiche report.

The 1990 excavation produced 32.5 kg of tile comprising 328 fragments, 226 of which were classifiable to type. In general the same range of tile types were present, the proportions of which are given in Table 57 on Fiche 2#81. A few examples of semicircular tile-signatures on tegulae were present, and one imbrex fragment had been combed on the outside.

One further fragment is of a type not previously recognised; this is illustrated (Fig. 109.143). This fragment was blackened by soot, which may indicate that it was part of the heating system. Gerald Brodribb, who kindly examined this fragment, was unable to categorise it firmly, but felt that the scoring and blackening was consistent with box flue tiles. He tentatively suggested that it might have been from a double box flue tile. An unusual alternative is that it may have been part of a hexagonal or octagonal window frame. In the latter case the thin ridge might have acted as a stop for the glass on one side, also possibly explaining why the ridge is slightly offset from the middle of the inside edge of the tile.

Nine fabrics were distinguished (see Table 58 on Fiche 2#81), Minety products (Fabrics 2 and 3) accounting for over 66% of the tiles. Quartz-tempered tiles from Shore Farm (Fabric 1) were also well-represented, as were tiles with calcareous inclusions, Fabric 4. One tile in a related fabric, Fabric 5, was stamped RPG, which is the mark of the Gloucester tilery (Clifford 1955, 68). This may be the source of the calcareous fabrics. Heavily grog-tempered tiles were very few; small amounts of grog occur regularly in tiles from Minety, and are included in Fabric 3. Fabric 8 is represented only by a single tile, but this distinctive fabric is very common at Redlands Farm, Stanwick and elsewhere in Northamptonshire (Keevill in prep).

Roof-tiles came from Buildings I–IV, and all of these buildings were probably roofed in part with tile. Many of the tiles from Building IV and Building III were however reused, and in both these buildings stone roof-slates were more numerous. This could indicate increased use of stone slates in the later Roman period.

One imbrex fragment had preserved the paw-print of a dog of medium size, identified by Leslie Cram.

V.15 Metalworking debris

by Tim Allen (with comments by Chris Salter)

In all 6.39 kg of slag were kept, only a sample of that from the villa being retained. One sample from the villa (Sample 1419 from context 2413) was probably from bronze-working; all of the remainder was smithing slag, and clay furnace lining suggests the use of bowl furnaces at ground level. A more detailed account will be found in the Microfiche report (see Ch. 5.15 on Fiche 2#82).

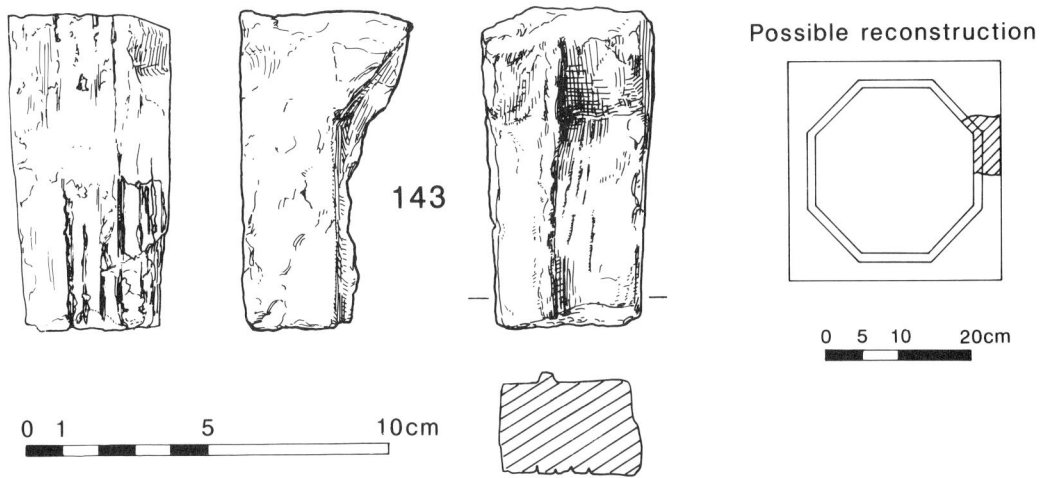

Figure 109 Tile: No. 143

V.16 Human bones

by Mary Harman

V.16.a Introduction

All the bones were examined. Most of the skeletons had previously been seen and described: those from the first three years of the excavation (Contexts 96, 188, 206, 343 and 478) by Miss R Powers of the British Museum (Natural History) and those from the later years by Miss J Bayley at the Ancient Monuments laboratory of the Department of the Environment. Those from contexts 1215, 1275 and 1279, found in 1965, had not been looked at before, and for the sake of consistency in the compilation of this report all the skeletons were examined by the author. No serious disagreements with other workers occurred, except in the observation of osteo-arthritis; where I was inclined to see none or slight evidence only, Miss Bayley described the same bones as slightly or moderately affected.

V.16.b Methodology

The condition of the bone generally was good though many bones were broken; some skeletons were poorly preserved. The sex of the skeletons was decided, where possible, from the size and general physique of the bones and from the relevant characters of the skull and pelvic girdle, while the age of juveniles was decided on the basis of the state of the tooth eruption and epiphyseal fusion, and the length of the diaphyses, using the criteria published by Ferembach, Schwidetzky and Stloukal (1980, 527–532) and a chart prepared by Miss R Powers (pers. comm.). The age of the adults was assessed from wear on the teeth, by comparison with the chart produced by Miles (1962, 884). Height was calculated from the length of the long bones using the formula of Trotter and Gleser, as published by Brothwell (1981, 101).

The details of the skeletal analysis, comprising the age, sex and height of each individual, where possible, along with some notes on the amount of bone recovered, any evidence of disease or injury, and other comments, will be found in Microfiche Table 64 on Fiche 2#84, and the state of dental health, noted in accordance with the method recommended by Brothwell (1981, 53), in Microfiche Table 65 on Fiche 2#87. Table 26 below summarises the skeletal data from the Roman burials, together with the circumstances of burial.

Three inhumations 1157, 1215 and 1275 were crouched or contracted burials, and were probably prehistoric. A calibrated radiocarbon date of 1160–940 cal. BC (to 1 sigma) was obtained from bone from 1157, and one of 350–40 cal. BC (to 1 sigma) from 1215. Cremation 1279 is also probably prehistoric, but produced no dating evidence (see Fig. 26 for location). The burial from context 1700 was a casual discovery made during building works south of the site, and is included here as a probable outlier of the Roman settlement (see Ch. IV.F.4.e).

V.16.c Decapitation

Two skeletons, both of middle aged women, are recorded as having been decapitated: 894 was buried with the head face down between the thighs (see Fig. 72), and 806 was buried with the head between the knees, facing the left knee. 894 has the back of the head and all the cervical vertebrae missing; since the head was face down the back of it was probably removed during topsoil removal, and possibly the cervical vertebrae too. Some vertebrae at least were probably attached to the severed head; there are no cuts visible on the first thoracic vertebra or any other bones.

Context	Orientation	Position	Grave goods	Parts present	Sex	Age	Comments
1140			pot			Adult	Cremation
Courtyard							
206	WSW	S	?	LC	F	40+	OA in back & L elbow. Healed fracture of R ulna.
Northern Enclosure							
Group 1 — NW end							
584	NW	FL		LC	?	16–18	
584	NW	FL		LC	?	12–13	
585	NW	S	coffin nail	P	F	40+	
608	NW	S		P	M	Adult	OA in back
Group 2 — SE end							
782	NW	L		LC	F	20–25	Healed fracture L clavicle
804	NW	S		P	M	Adult	
806	NW	S		LC	F?	40–50	OA in back & R foot. Decapitated, head between knees
807	NW	S		LC	F	35+	OA in back & arms
808	N	S		LC	?	7–8	
813	SW	S	coffin nail	LC	F	35–40	OA in back
Southern Enclosure							
834	W	S		LC	F?	16–18	
894	NE	S	shoe-plate	LC	F	40+	OA in back & joints. Decapitated, head between thighs
895	SW	S?		P	?	?	No bones recovered
Boundary Ditch 959/960							
974	N	S	sandal stud	LC	M	40+	
975	N?		?bracelet	P	?	Adult	
982	NW	P		LC	M	30–40	
Cattle Market							
1	N				F	18–30	No bones recovered
2	N				F	40+	
3	N				?	?	
4	N				?	?	
5	—				?	?	
6	—				?	?	
South of Excavation							
1700	W	P		P	M	20–30	

KEY

Position: S=Supine, P=Prone, F=Flexed, L=L side, R=R side
Parts present: LC=Largely complete — missing some ribs, vertebrae, hands and feet, P=Part only
Comments: OA=Osteo-arthritis

Totals: 5 male; 9 female; 9 uncertain
1 child; 3 adolescents; 15 adults; 5 uncertain

Table 26 Summary of details of human burials of Roman date

806 has the lower five cervical vertebrae missing, and most of the thoracic vertebrae, though the absence of some of these is probably due to deterioration of the bones, the vertebrae and ribs being rather poorly preserved. There are two probable cuts on the bones, one on the mandible and one on the axis. The gonion on the left side of the mandible is broken off, but this break appears to have originated with a cut into the lower edge of the horizontal ramus. The axis appears to have suffered an oblique cut which has removed part of the neural arch and the inferior articular facet, on the left side. Neither cut is clearly defined, mainly because of the poor condition of the bone, but the two together and the presence of both atlas and axis, presumably buried with the head, combined with the absence of the rest of the cervical vertebrae, suggest fairly convincingly that the head was removed by a cut in the upper part of the neck, probably from the left side.

V.16.d Conclusions

The infant burials, complete and disturbed, are unexceptional on a site of this type.

Decapitated burials are not uncommon in this part of the country in the late Romano-British period. Details of other examples in the south midlands and the south-west are given in a recent survey (Harman et al 1981, 159–188) and the burials from Lechlade are unremarkable within this group, except possibly for two aspects of 894; if the neck was really severed just above the first thoracic vertebra, it would be a remarkably low point, previously observed only at Meon Hill and Poundbury. However, the absence of all the cervical vertebrae is not conclusive evidence for the position of the cut. The position of the head is slightly unusual, as it tends to be between the knees or somewhere about the lower legs, as in the case of 806. It is between or beside the femora in only about 10% of the recorded cases. Unfortunately, the examples from Lechlade do not seem to throw any further light on the reasons for this form of burial.

V.17 Animal bones

by Gillian Jones and Bruce Levitan

V.17.a The nature of the assemblage recovered between 1957 and 1982

by Gillian Jones

The material of Romano-British date is summarised in Table 27; it was grouped as follows:

1. The 1982 excavations from Building IV and from the courtyard between it and Building III

2. The 1957–59 excavations of villa buildings I, II and III. This sample had been studied during excavation by Mr Baxter, the Lechlade vet. With the exception of sample 2a, the bones were not kept.

2a. Two boxes of the bones were studied by Professor Higgs, and these were also recorded in the present study.

3. The 1961–65 excavations, of trackways, field ditches and enclosures to the east of the villa (see Figs. 73 and 74; Fig. 1).

All the bone fragments found in the 1982 excavations (carried out by hand digging) were collected. Bone was also collected with reasonable care from the 1961–65 sites. There were no sieved samples. The four main domesticates were present, in varying proportions, bones of other species being rare.

The collecting of bone during 1957–59 may have been less rigorous, which means that the percentages given in Table 27 for assemblage 2 must be viewed circumspectly. However, the sample was of moderate size and suggests that cattle were more numerous than sheep or goat and that both pig and horse were important. Mr Baxter noted that there was a considerable range in the size of cattle. The horse bones were generally of mature animals (he noted only one bone from a young horse). In a pair of red deer frontal bones the antlers had been sawn off. Probable disease was noted in an adult horse humerus, and the lower part of a cattle humerus indicated injury during life. Most of the larger bones were broken up and several shank bones 'had cross marks suggesting that they had been used to cut something on', possibly evidence of butchery. In sample 2a, the writer's identifications and Mr Baxter's were nearly unanimous; four cattle bones (three of them phalanges) were misidentified as pig, and the proportion of pig bones in sample 2 may thus be slightly overestimated.

V.17.b Overall results (bones recovered between 1957 and 1982)

The material from excavations in 1982 dated from the 1st to 4th centuries. Very few bones were found from the earliest phase, but the assemblages from phase 4 (mid-2nd to mid-3rd century AD) and 5 (late 3rd to 4th century AD) were larger and show an increase in cattle over sheep, the proportion of pig bones remaining constant. Oyster shells appeared in phase 5, and were quite common.

Sample 3 from the enclosures east of the villa contained lower proportions of sheep and pig bones than villa sample 1. It is possible that varying policies on collection of bones influences the figures. However, the proportion of mandibles, and of long bones with more than half of the proximal end, the shaft or the distal end present (ie excluding small pieces) shows the same difference. Most of the features east of the villa were later Roman, and, as both sample 1 and results from other sites (King 1978)

		N	Percentages				Deer	Other	Percentage identified
			Cattle	Sheep	Pig	Horse			
1	Building IV	263	37	44	14	3	—	dog*, fox*, fowl**, oyster	52
2	Buildings I–III	396	48	26	12	13	1	—	
2a		61	52	23	5	15	red 5		91
3	Enclosures east of villa	263	59	22	6	10	red 2, roe*	dog*, hare*, water vole**, oyster**	71
Total 1 & 3		526	48	33	10	6	1	other species 2	60

N — number of identified bones
* — species represented by a single bone (** — two bones).
Oyster and water vole are not included in the total number of bones.

Table 27 Animal bones from the 1957–82 excavations: percentages of species from different groups (see Ch. V.17.a).

show, cattle tend to become more important in the later Roman period.

Sample 3 consisted of bones from two sets of enclosures to the north and south of an apparently open area east of the villa buildings, and from gravel pits in between. Bones from the southern enclosures and the gravel pits were too few for useful comparison with those from the northern enclosures, due to the small scale of excavation. Within the northern enclosures comparisons were made between the bone collections from the silt-filled hollows (559, 560 etc) and from the pits, and between those from pits and those from ditches, but no significant differences were found. Worked bones do not show any concentration of bone working.

V.17.c Cattle bones (recovered between 1957 and 1982)

Bones of all parts of the skeleton were present. Mandibles and cannon bones were proportionately more numerous in sample 3. The overall proportions of bones from the head, body and feet was very similar in samples 1 and 3; one might perhaps have expected a greater concentration of meat-bearing bones close to the villa. The bones were mostly fragmented but the finding of several nearly complete cannon bones showed that the bones were not always exploited for secondary products such as marrow, glue, grease or for bone working.

Most of the cattle represented had died when five years old or more. These would have been breeding, dairy and draught stock. The amount of meat available from young animals, and their age of slaughter, must have depended largely on breeding success and provisions of winter fodder. The small sample here suggests that more young animals were slaughtered in the first few months than between one and five years. These may have been natural deaths or animals culled due to poor health. Alternatively some surplus animals may have been slaughtered to minimise the number kept over winter.

The age at death of cattle was calculated from mandibles and loose teeth (Table 67 on Fiche 2#90). Jaws were grouped into six stages (defined in Bourdillon & Coy 1980). The figures show the minimum number of individuals (mandibles) at each stage, with additional data from loose teeth shown in brackets (*eg* there were two left stage 1 mandibles and a deciduous third premolar showing enamel wear only, from three different areas of the site). In eight out of the 15 individuals, the third molar was in full wear. Evidence from long bone fusion was consistent with the above (46 epiphyses, 89% fused; and two bones from calves). No data on the sex of the bones was available.

The measurements suggest a good size of cattle, larger than those found on local Iron Age sites (Wilson 1978, Fig. 19) and of similar size to Romano-British cattle from Barton Court Farm, Abingdon (Wilson in Miles 1986, VI.2.3.5.). Their estimated shoulder height was 1.10 to 1.27 m (mean 1.177 m, N 12) (method of Fock in Driesch & Boessneck 1974). Greatest lengths: metacarpals: (1st to 4th century) 183, 187; (3rd to 4th century) 193, 200; metatarsals: (3rd to 4th century) range 203–233, mean 216.6, N 8. Greatest lateral length of astragalus: (2nd to 3rd century) 59; (3rd to 4th century) 62, 65, 69, 70.

V.17.d Sheep/goat bones (recovered between 1957 and 1982)

The caprine bones are mostly from sheep. One horn core fragment was definitely from a sheep and no other bones bore features characteristic of the goat, which has only rarely been found on Romano-British sites in the Upper Thames (Wilson, pers. comm.). One skull fragment was from a polled animal. Hornless sheep are found somewhat more commonly on Roman than earlier sites (*eg* Roman Tripontium and Frocester, Noddle 1973 and 1979), which gives some support to the hypothesis that some new stock was introduced into Britain.

Fig. 152 on Fiche 2#90 shows the stages of development of the mandibles, following the method of Grant (1975). A greater proportion of adult jaws were recovered, especially in sample 3, than is general on sites of the period (*eg* Wilson 1978, 132). The sample suggests that most lambs of both sexes were kept into adulthood, and therefore that wool production was important. However other factors may be involved, eg a recovery bias against younger, fragile jaws in the sites east of the villa or movement of surplus lambs away from the site.

The few measurable bones suggest that the sheep were of average size for the period.

V.17.e   Pig bones (recovered between 1957 and 1982)

Pig bones formed about a tenth of the overall Romano-British sample. No difference in the proportion of pig was observed over time, but pig bones were commoner on the villa sites.

Upper and lower jaws of at least eight pigs were recovered, all from pigs which had overwintered at least once, and two of these were from adult pigs of about two years old (third molar partly in wear, Silver 1969). Occasional slaughter of younger pigs is shown by the presence of an immature pelvis. The age structure is similar to that discussed by Maltby (1981) for Roman sites, where although most porkmeat was from immature animals, rather little of it was from the lean carcass of a piglet. The need for lard and the use of pigs in clearing ground may have been significant factors in pig husbandry.

A bone pin made from the fibula of a pig is described in Ch. V.8.

V.17.f   Horse bones (recovered between 1957 and 1982)

Horse bones occurred in small numbers in many deposits, including those near the villa. They were often associated with bones of other species, and are therefore probably also food waste. The bones were less fragmented than those of cattle. The only intentional marks seen were on a metacarpal, which is a naturally pointed bone sometimes worked into a bone tool.

Measurements of long bones give an estimated size range of 11.5 to 14.5 hands (N 7, range 1.12–1.46 m, mean 1.318 m, method of Kiesewalter in Driesch & Boessneck 1974) (greatest lateral lengths: radius 291 mm; metacarpal 185, 197, 219 mm: metatarsal 263, 274 mm). In the enclosures east of the villa two horse-skulls and one partial skeleton had been buried. Only one of the skulls survived for examination. Photographs and notes show that the skeleton from 573 consisted of the vertebral column from the axis to the sacrum plus the pelvis, one femur and a few ribs, found articulated. A few loose incisors were all that remained of the skull. Since the surviving bones were quite well preserved and the pit had not been recut, the absence of the rest of the skeleton was probably genuine. It was noted on excavation that a long bone split, among the fragments, suggests that the carcass was 'used for food'. Whether the horse had partially decayed before burial, or whether the long bones had been removed with the meat, is not known.

One skull was that of an adult, and was buried in a pit by itself; the other was of a horse that had died at about one year old (first molar in wear on the first cusp), and was associated with cattle and sheep bones. There were three other bones from immature horses. The presence of young horses is of note and suggests that they were being bred at the site. Remains of young horses have also been found in the Upper Thames valley at Roman sites at Barton Court Farm and Farmoor (Wilson 1979).

The sawn-off lower ends of a metacarpal and a tibia show that horse bone was used in bone working. No cattle bones were sawn.

V.17.g   Bones of other species (recovered between 1957 and 1982)

Two dog-bones were found. Three bones of domestic fowl came from the 1982 excavation near the villa, and oyster shells (19 valves) from 3rd/4th century deposits in the same area. Two bones of water vole may be intrusive.

Remains of hunted species were few (Table 27), suggesting that hunting provided an insignificant part of the diet, but red deer were apparently important for their antlers, which were both collected from the ground and sawn from the skull. Three of the four antler specimens were sawn.

For details of the pathology see Microfiche report.

V.17.h   Introduction to the bones recovered in 1990

by Bruce Levitan

This assemblage of 764 bones (found by hand digging) is from an adjacent area to those reported on above; the two reports are analyses of different portions of the same overall assemblage. Not surprisingly, therefore, the range and taxa represented in the present analysis is almost identical to that found by Gillian Jones.

The assemblage can be subdivided into:

pre/early villa 140 bones (48);
late villa 623 bones (233).

Numbers in brackets are bones identified to taxon. The early phase is roughly equivalent to 2nd to mid 3rd century AD and the late phase is late 3rd and 4th centuries (with, perhaps, a small element of residuality).

The bones can also be divided between Buildings III and IV, though only about 35% of the bones relate directly to these two buildings, and some of these come from robber trenches (the majority of the bones in fact come from ditches):

Building III 116 bones (43)
Building IV 150 bones (42)

The assemblage is small, so the conclusions that can be drawn from it should therefore be regarded with circumspection.

V.17.i Taxa represented in the bones from 1990

Table 28 summarises the identifications. The majority of the bones were not identified to taxon because of their fragmentary and weathered nature. As with the bones from the earlier excavations there was a restricted range of taxa (only three or four non-domestic taxa are present) and the major mammalian domesticates predominated. This is typical of Roman villa assemblages; hunting was not an important activity, and even on Roman sites where sieving is undertaken small mammal, bird or fish bones are rare. The rabbit bone is very probably intrusive as rabbit is thought not to have been present in Britain at this time.

	p/e villa		l/p villa		total	
	N	%	N	%	N	%
Cattle	19	40	90	40	109	40
Sheep/goat	10	21	81	36	91	33
Pig	15	32	39	17	54	20
Horse	2	4	7	3	9	3
Dog			4	2	4	1
Cat			1	<1	1	<1
Rabbit			1	<1	1	<1
Red deer			2	1	2	1
Field vole	1	2			1	<1
Sub-total	47	34	225	36	272	36
Domestic fowl	1	100	7	88	8	89
Duck			1	13	1	11
Sub-total	1	1	8	1	9	1
Unidentified:						
Large mammal	43	47	239	61	282	59
Medium mammal	47	51	147	38	194	40
Small mammal			1	<1	1	<1
Bird	1	1	3	1	4	1
Fish	1	1			1	<1
Sub-total	92	66	390	63	482	63
Total	140	18	623	82	763	

p/e villa — pre/early villa; l/p villa — late/post-villa.
1 human bone from l/p villa; 14 sheep from l/p villa

Table 28 Summary of vertebrate remains from the 1990 excavation

All of the sheep/goat bones that could be identified to species are sheep. Horse, dog and cat all occur in the later phase, but only horse in the earlier phase. However the numbers of bones are very small indeed and in all probability these taxa were simply not very common. The two red deer bones (a metacarpal and a first phalanx) imply that hunting may have occurred very occasionally. The field vole bone may well be intrusive.

Two bird taxa are present: domestic fowl and duck (probably domestic). Both are commonly found on similar sites in small numbers. Domestic fowl was probably much more numerous than these results imply, but their bones are far more likely to have been destroyed during meals and by scavenging than any of the mammalian taxa. The single fish bone is a portion of dentary from a small-sized fish.

V.17.j Lateral variation in the bones from 1990

Table 69 on Fiche 2#91 summarises the taxa from Buildings III and IV. Building IV was an aisled building with several ovens, possibly used as a kitchen; Building III was a domestic building containing hypocausts and living rooms. There is very little difference in sheep/goat representation between the two buildings, but cattle are much more common in Building III than IV, and for pig the reverse is the case. The numbers of bones from each building may be related to their different functions, but in any case, the major refuse deposits would not have been in the buildings themselves but in pits and ditches some distance away (see Introduction above).

V.17.k Cattle bones from the 1990 excavation

The skeletal element representation of cattle bones and bones of the other major taxa agrees with the results from the earlier excavations. The majority of the ageable cattle bones were from adults. A few of the early fusing long bones had unfused epiphyses (and at least two were very young), but most were fused, and similarly with the later fusing bones. Two mandibles had teeth present, one with a third molar in wear (state k of Grant's scheme Grant 1983), and one with a permanent fourth premolar at state e. Three loose third molars were all in wear, ranging from state h to k. No deciduous teeth were found.

A large proportion of the cattle bones bore butchery markings (especially if the large mammal ribs are counted as cattle). Most parts of the skeleton bore some evidence of butchery, ranging from superficial cuts to deep gouges and chops and one or two bones with sawing marks. No unusual butchery was noted.

A metatarsal with extreme modification of the proximal end (exostoses, eburnation, erosion of the joint surface) was the only pathological specimen.

Measurements were obtained for only three bones, but these, and the general size of the other bones, indicate that the cattle were of average size for the period.

V.17.1 Sheep/goat bones from the 1990 excavation

No juvenile or younger sheep were indicated by the epiphysial fusion evidence, but two mandibles show that there were lambs (one with first molar at state a and second molar not erupted, and one with a deciduous fourth premolar at state g). Most of the mandibles/loose teeth, however, are of adults (though at the younger end of the age: mandibles/loose teeth with third molar wear states: a, d (2) and g.

Only 3 sheep bones bore any butchery marks, but the deposit was typical of butchered remains. However sheep undergo less intensive butchery than cattle and this might partially explain the lack of direct evidence. One of the butchered bones (a metatarsal) was also worked with a hole drilled into the proximal end and at the posterior of the proximal end.

A pair of lower hind limbs were found which come from one individual, the left metatarsal of which measured 143.3 mm in length. Some sheep measurements are given in Ch. 5.17.b on Fiche 2#91.

V.17.m Pig bones from the 1990 excavation

In contrast to sheep/goat, most of the pig bones were from young animals (*eg* only two out of seven metapodials had fused distal epiphyses). This is typical for pig on such sites. As with sheep/goat, very few pig bones had butchery marks. The interpretation is the same as for sheep/goat.

Eight of the bones from the pre/early villa are from a foetal skeleton (skull, left humerus, both femora, right tibia, two ribs and a metapodial.

V.18 Charred plant and molluscan remains

by John Letts and Mark Robinson

V.18.a Introduction

Five flotation samples containing charred and mineralized plant remains recovered during the 1990 excavation were submitted for analysis. Only haphazard environmental sampling had been carried out during previous excavations at the site (see Ch. 5.18 on Fiche 2#92). All of the 1990 samples derived from 2nd to 3rd century features associated with an aisled Roman building, Building IV. Samples 1016, 1014 and 1000 were from ovens within the central nave of the building, samples 1001 and 1017 came from an adjacent boundary ditch.

Sampling for plant remains was prompted by assessment of a sample which contained free-threshing bread-type wheat (*Triticum aestivum s.l.*) — an uncommon find on Roman sites in Britain. The small number of samples available and their poor preservation limited analysis to documenting the presence of bread-type wheat and outlining the restricted range of weed taxa that was recovered.

V.18.b Results

Table 70 on Fiche 2#92

Taxa were identified by comparison with modern reference specimens, and plant nomenclature follows that of Clapham, Tutin and Moore (1989).

Sample 1000 contained no cultigen or weed seed remains. Within the wood charcoal which dominated the sample twiggy material was common, in addition to frequent specimens of 10–20 mm diameter branches, some of which appeared to be thickened stem bases possibly cut from coppiced stumps. One specimen was tentatively identified as ash (*Fraxinus excelsior*), but a range of woody taxa is likely to be present.

Samples 1016 and 1014 contained few remains of cereal grain or chaff. The cereal grains were very poorly preserved and could not be identified even to generic level. Two fragments of oat (*Avena sp.*) awn were recovered from sample 1016. Both samples contained small numbers of grass (*Gramineae*) seed, as well as a range of charred seeds of herbaceous annuals that are common to open grassy and disturbed habitats including arable fields.

Sample 1014 presented the richest assortment of weed species of the 5 samples. It contained 92 mineralized and charred achenes of spikerush (*Eleocharis sp.* — probably *E. palustris* L. Roem. and Schult.) and sedge (*Carex sp.*) — both native, rhizomatous and herbaceous perennials common throughout the British Isles, and which frequent damp to wet places, including poorly drained and infertile arable fields. 77 of the spikerush specimens were mineralized — a result of silica deposits in the epidermal cells of the seed fusing during heating under oxidizing conditions. This commonly occurs in members of the family Cyperaceae, as well as in the Boraginaceae as evidenced by the single specimen of corn gromwell (*Lithospermum arvense*) also recovered in a mineralized state. Under oxidizing conditions, grain and most weed seeds would be burnt away. The 15 remaining spikerush seeds had been charred in the absence of oxygen.

Interesting identifications include a probable specimen of restharrow (*Ononis sp.*), a small, procumbent and spiny shrub characteristic of rough open grassland, and a single specimen of purging flax (*Linum catharticum*), also native and common to short grassland throughout the British Isles.

Cereals were particularly abundant and much better preserved in sample 1001. Oat (*Avena sp.*) is attested by the presence of two small fragments of awn. Barley is represented by 9 grains, one lateral grain being from a 6-row hulled form (*Hordeum vulgare sbsp. hexastichum*). The presence of 6-row barley is supported by a rachis fragment. 7 additional barley grains could not be characterized further.

Sample 1001 also revealed 12 short, plump, free-threshing grains of wheat similar to that commonly found on Saxon and Medieval sites in southern Britain. Although shorter than modern hexaploid bread wheats (*Triticum aestivum s. l.*), they are almost certainly of this type. Only one wheat specimen showed the distinctive lateral grooves characteristic of a hulled wheat — most probably of spelt (*Triticum spelta*).

A further 215 wheat grains could not be identified beyond generic level, although most are probably of the free-threshing bread-type form. The numerous poorly preserved cereal fragments present were taken to represent 41 individual grains.

The weed flora of both 1001 and 1017 is dominated by a number of small annual species characteristic of open habitat and arable fields.

Sample 1017 also contained relatively well preserved cereal remains, including 2 median and 1 distinctly lateral grains of barley, two of the previously described bread-type wheat, 7 wheat grains identifiable only to generic level, and one spikelet fork and two glume bases from a hulled wheat (probably spelt *T. spelta*).

V.18.c   Discussion and conclusions

The oven samples contained few charred seeds, but the weed seeds present were dominated by species of grassy and damp places. The abundance of silicified seeds in sample 1014 suggests that many other plant remains had burnt away. The two ditch samples 1001 and 1017, on the other hand, contained a greater number of cultigen remains but fewer weed seeds.

The cereal remains in the ditch fill samples (1001 and 1017) may be derived from one disposal or charring event, and could relate to the cleaning of the ovens in the aisled building, while the oven samples more likely reflect fuel waste. Weeds were undoubtedly being carried onto the site in harvested crops, and it is likely that crop residues, old thatching, and anything else than could be burned (in addition to coppice wood and scrub) was used as fuel for the ovens.

The presence of bread wheat in a well-dated Roman context is significant; although it has been identified in archaeobotanical assemblages dating from Neolithic date onwards, bread wheat is an uncommon cereal on British sites until the Saxon period. A large quantity of bread-type wheat was identified from a late Iron Age pit at Barton Court Farm, Abingdon (Oxon), and a little bread wheat was also present in Roman samples from the site, although spelt wheat dominated the cereal remains from these later assemblages (Jones in Miles 1986).

Although bread wheat may have been imported into Britain during the Roman Period, it is just as likely that it was grown in small quantities for restricted use — possibly by the more prosperous segment of Romano-British society that inhabited villas such as at Roughground Farm.

Romanists have traditionally asserted that bread wheat replaced the staple emmer wheat in the central Roman provinces during first century AD due to simple flavour preference and a desire for wheat with improved baking qualities (Moritz 1958). Hulled wheats produce high quality flour, however, although their baking quality is usually somewhat reduced by the parching process that is required to free the grains from their indurate glumes. Others have suggested that hulled wheats were simply more difficult to process and transport than naked wheats, and that economic forces encouraged the shift to free-threshing bread wheats (Jasny 1946). Hulled wheats, however, almost certainly provided more reliable yields that were less prone to damage by birds, insects or mould both in the field or in storage, while the early Roman bread wheats are believed to have required richer and drier soils than contemporary hulled forms in order to produce equivalent yields (Spurr 1986). In Roman Italy, farmers were careful to tailor crop species and varieties to soil conditions. Both specialized farms growing one crop type or variety of wheat and mixed crop farms growing a range of cultigens and wheat varieties were common.

An unsubstantiated possibility is that two principle forms of wheat were grown in Britain from the Roman period through to the late Medieval period; a short-strawed free-threshing hexaploid bread wheat grown primarily for specialized food purposes, and a long-strawed variety (initially hulled emmer or spelt, and in the later Saxon period a naked tetraploid (*T. turgidum*) grown for industrial purposes (thatching, fodder) as well as providing grain for human consumption (Robinson pers. comm.).

Overall, the large number of bread-type grains recovered from the ditch samples indicates that free-threshing bread wheat (*Triticum aestivum s.l.*) was probably grown as a minor food crop in its own right in 2nd to 3rd century Roman Gloucestershire, rather than simply having been imported or maintained as a volunteer contaminant of other cereal crops.

V.18.d   Molluscan and other charred remains

For the report on molluscan and other charred remains see the Microfiche report Ch. 5.18 on Fiche 2#92.

V.19   Coal

by Tim Allen, with identifications by R Neves and G Clayton

Samples of coal from twenty seven contexts, both from around the villa and from the enclosure groups and gravel-pit further east, were examined by the Ancient Monuments Laboratory. All, with the possible exception of that from feature 409 west of the villa, were characteristic of surface coal deposits in the Forest of Dean. The composition of those samples examined under the microscope will be found in the Microfiche report. There is no further information about the sample from 409.

No quantification of the coal was undertaken, but most pieces were described as 'scraps'. Four separate samples however came from the black fill in the top of ditch 132, and some of the finds from this layer were also coated with coal-dust. Several samples also came from the black fills of pits 54 and 55 not far north of this. The infill of ditch 313 below Building III contained coal, which may indicate that the extensive black layer adjacent to it beneath the building was in part derived from coal-dust, but there were no further samples from this, and no explanation for the blackness is offered in the notebooks. Similarly the black fill of pit 409 and ditch 420 adjacent could have been coal-derived. A substantial layer including coal chips and dust was found just E of Building III (2029/B/4), contemporary with the use of the building. This may have been used in the hypocausts adjacent.

The coal all came from contexts dating after the mid-2nd century, that is, to the villa phases of occupation. Its concentration in extensive black layers close to the main domestic buildings on this site perhaps suggests that it was used in the hypocausts. Coal was officially supplied to the forts on Hadrian's Wall for this purpose, and many villas in Gloucestershire, Somerset and Wiltshire were also supplied with it (Frere 1976, 279). The common use of coal in this area reflects the easy availability of local outcrops in the Severn basin.

Samples also came from a wide range of pits, ditches, gullies and silt-filled hollows in the enclosure groups further east. Almost all these contexts belonged to the late 3rd to 4th century. Its ubiquity here perhaps suggests that coal was also used for semi-industrial and domestic hearths in the Late Roman period.

Chapter VI
Discussion of the Romano-British occupation

VI.1 The Early Roman occupation

Evidence of 1st century and early to mid 2nd century occupation was found over a large area west of the Lechlade-Burford road (Fig. 33). The settlement lay a little way north-west of the junction of two droveways between 20 m and 30 m wide. These droveways were probably first defined by ditches in the 2nd century AD, but appear to be of much greater antiquity (see Ch. III.B.1.a and Ch. III.B.8). One ran south-east parallel to the river Leach down to the floodplain just above its junction with the river Thames, the other headed south towards the low-lying first terrace and the floodplain of the Thames (Fig. 4; Fig. 110).

Only a part of this settlement was investigated, but occupation seems to have been entirely native in character. The only probable domestic structure excavated was that within enclosure 56 (Fig. 34). In contrast to the circular gullies of the Iron Age, house sites of this period are characterised by oval or sub-rectangular ditched enclosures with occupation debris in their terminals, as at Vicarage Field, Stanton Harcourt, Oxon (Case & Whittle 1982, 104 Fig. 59 and 115–6) and Smithsfield, Hardwick, Oxon (Allen 1981, 30–31). Circular enclosures are found, but no longer appear to represent house-sites (see also below). Enclosure 56 appears to show the transition from a circular to a sub-rectangular enclosure, although the progression cannot be closely dated. Traces of the houses themselves rarely survive, perhaps indicating a mass-wall construction like that of the conquest period houses at Hod Hill (Richmond 1968, 19–23 and Figs. 10b, 12 and 13), where oval and horseshoe-shaped buildings were excavated.

Related to the house was a cluster of pits. As at other sites of the 1st century AD these were of very varied shape and size; none were as regular as Iron Age storage pits and few of classic U or beehive shape. Nevertheless some of those at the 1st century AD settlement at Barton Court Farm, Abingdon (Miles 1986, 8, Fig. 5) had apparently been used for grain-storage, and this was also possibly true at Roughground Farm. Pit-storage is abandoned by the end of the 1st century at Barton Court, but may have persisted until the mid-2nd century here.

Adjacent to 56 were short lengths of slot enclosing an area c 14 m square (internal area c 190 sq. m), dating to the late 1st century or early 2nd century. This was more likely a fenced pen than the outline of a building. Rectangular pens of similar size are a common element of contemporary settlements, for instance Gravelly Guy, Stanton Harcourt, Oxon (Lambrick 1986, 113) and Barton Court Farm (see below).

The house, pits and pen were at one stage contained within a ditched compound c 40 m square. In this phase the arrangement was very similar to that of the Late Iron Age enclosure at Barton Court Farm, Abingdon (Miles 1986, 5–8 and Fig. 5), which had a cluster of pits and a rectangular enclosure (internal area 180 sq. m) adjacent to the house. Apart from open areas for livestock, these three elements constituted virtually all of the farmstead of this phase at Barton Court Farm, suggesting that the compound at Roughground Farm should be seen as one complete farming unit within the settlement.

The compound ditches are dated to the end of the 1st century, and are clearly a secondary development of what was previously a more 'open' settlement similar to the earliest phase at Claydon Pike and Thornhill Farm (S. Palmer pers. comm.), where functional areas are less rigidly defined and individual stock and occupation enclosures are protected by deep ditches to keep animals in or out. Ditches 42, 65, 68 etc (Fig. 34) and 456/457 (Fiche 4#62) indicate that there was at least one further compound adjacent on the south.

Other features were scattered larger storage pits and several sizeable ditches recut on numerous occasions, some of which may have formed stock enclosures; heavily recut enclosures 12–20 m across with equally few finds have been excavated at Claydon Pike and Thornhill Farm, Fairford nearby (Miles 1984, 199). There they belonged to 1st century AD Late Iron Age and Early Roman settlements that were superseded before the 2nd century. The smaller circular gullies 66 and 67 (Fig. 34) are of more typically Iron Age form, but can also be paralleled with Early Roman circular enclosures at Eagle Farm, Standlake, Oxon (Allen & Moore 1987, 96–7) and at Smithsfield, Hardwick, Oxon (Allen 1981, 29). At these sites they were shallow and contained few finds, and were not apparently domestic; similar circular enclosures at Claydon Pike have been interpreted as surrounding hayricks (Miles pers. comm).

Lines of postholes, one of which lay beneath the floor of Building I, may indicate an early timber building

Figure 110 Vertical aerial view of Roughground Farm and the area to the south, showing the continuations of the Early Iron Age boundary ditches and the Romano-British trackways, the Bronze Age ring-ditches and the settlement to the south-west of the villa (Fairey Survey 1961 No. 11 023)

beneath the villa, but in the absence of occupation layers have plausibly been interpreted as scaffolding holes (see Ch. IV.C.2). Margaret Jones has suggested that the so-called 'early house' at Ditchley (Ralegh Radford 1936, 19–23) might be similarly re-interpreted.

The Early Roman settlement covered an area of at least 80 m by 140 m, most of which was probably occupied contemporaneously. At Claydon Pike the settlement nucleus was c 60 m square, but was surrounded by stock enclosures and other features (S. Palmer pers. comm.). Roughground Farm may originally have been similarly organised, as the features at the south end mostly contained few finds and were probably peripheral. Nevertheless the occupation area suggests that there was more than one domestic focus like 56, and the settlement probably consisted of a hamlet of several such farming units (see also below).

The pottery of this phase included very few fine wares, showing little evidence of wealth and only gradual Roman influence. The assemblage is in this respect comparable to such sites as Gravelly Guy, Stanton Harcourt, Oxon or Smithsfield, Hardwick, Oxon, where native fabrics and forms continued until the end of the 1st century (Green in Lambrick and Allen in prep; Allen in prep). Other finds include saddle and rotary querns, triangular loomweights and spindlewhorls, fired clay from ovens and possibly bone-working debris. A possible tuyere may also indicate metalworking, but there is no other evidence to support this (Ch. V.11) These are the activities typical of a largely self-sufficient farm of the Late Iron Age and early Romano-British period, comparable to the sites at Langford Downs (Williams 1947, 44–59) and the first phase at Barton Court Farm (Miles 1986, 6–8). The discovery of triangular loomweights, which are not generally considered to continue into the Roman period, perhaps demonstrates the conservatism of the settlement.

The evidence suggests that mixed farming was practised. Storage pits and querns suggest arable, while the droveways, the layout of the settlement and the deep-ditched enclosures imply pastoral farming. The bone sample represents a typically Late Iron Age/Early Roman mixture of livestock comparable to those of the sites already mentioned. Overall the picture is of a conservative settlement gradually adopting Romano-British technology and practices during the first century of the Roman occupation.

A dump of pottery of the 1st half of the 2nd century came from pit 320 beneath Building III (Fig. 53; Fig. 130 on Fiche 1#34). This includes fineware imports and is of higher quality than pottery associated with 56. This assemblage may predate the construction of the villa, in which case it hints at another domestic building in the Early Roman settlement, and one of higher status than that within 56. On the analogy of other villas such as Latimer (Branigan 1971, 81–2) and Park Street (O'Neil 1947, 24–5) there may have been an earlier house below the west end of villa building I in the area destroyed without record. This would clearly have important implications for the general conclusions offered about the wealth and status of the site.

VI.2 The villa buildings

VI.2.a The aisled buildings

This class of building is well-known from Roman Britain, and examples are most commonly found on villa sites. The date and area of origin of this form of construction have been much discussed (JT Smith 1963; Stead 1976, 94; Morris 1979, 55–6); excavations at Gorhambury (Neal *et al* 1990, 32–5 and 91–2) have recently revealed a sequence of these buildings starting at least as early as the mid-1st century AD, showing that the design was either already familiar to the Romans at the conquest or more likely was developed in Late Iron Age Britain.

In the Upper Thames valley the earliest examples, two at Claydon Pike, Fairford, Glos. (buildings B1 and B3, Miles 1984, 199–201) one at Neigh Bridge, Somerford Keynes, Glos. (Palmer 1988a), have all been dated to the end of the 1st century AD. The larger two of these were purely of timber construction, the aisle posts surrounded by outer walls bedded on timber sills, the third had outer walls of stone. All these buildings remained in use until the later 2nd century.

Two aisled buildings were identified at Roughground Farm, Building IV within the main villa-building complex, Building VI further east at the junction of the south and south-east droveways (Fig. 42 and Fig. 78).

Building VI, which was represented only by postholes and a length of slot, appears to have been constructed entirely of timber like the larger aisled building at Claydon Pike or that at Wakerley, Northants (Jackson & Ambrose 1978, 138–140). In the Wakerley report the excavators suggested that the ratio of overall length to width (including aisles) is usually about 2:1, and Building VI also fits this specification. At both sites the aisle is narrow when compared to the average ratio between nave and aisle width in such buildings.

Dating evidence from the postholes is very slight, but suggests 2nd century construction at the earliest. A 2nd century or later date is also implied by its position alongside the droveway ditches, which were probably not dug before the early 2nd century (see Ch. IV.F.5.a). The change in width between the lines of postholes halfway along may indicate that two buildings are involved, or that an originally shorter structure was later extended. In its situation Building VI is similar to aisled buildings P and Q at Winterton (Goodburn 1978, 95–100); building Q in particular offers parallels for the less regular construction and possible stock function of Building VI.

Building IV has a more complex history. It was constructed in the first half of the 2nd century AD in the south-east corner of the villa enclosure, adjacent to a trackway. The aisles consisted of rows of posts; it is suggested (see Fig. 43) that the outside walls were originally stone sills supporting a timber superstructure, similar to the smaller aisled building at Claydon Pike nearby. There is little information about the overall dimensions of this building or of its internal arrangements, but it can be inferred that the surviving part was not subdivided to a significant degree. Hadman (1978, 189–190) states that the simple timber examples without elaboration are usually twice as long as wide, which would indicate a length of around 23 m externally, but the proportions of nave to aisles, which he also claims is usually 2:1, is not found in either of the Roughground Farm examples.

It is possible that a timber structure (directly overlain by the later Room 5) was attached to the N side, similar to building B2 added to the larger aisled building B1 at Claydon Pike (Miles 1984, 199–201). At Claydon Pike B2 was interpreted as domestic accommodation, the aisled building reserved for storage. Miles has argued that the finds at Claydon Pike (and at Neigh Bridge) demonstrate links with the military, the sites perhaps acting as official storage depots, and the size and construction of B2 has been compared with military buildings of the period. No such evidence has been found at Roughground Farm, and it seems possible that this is an example of the copying of military construction by a civilian settlement nearby. This arrangement is otherwise also found at Great Casterton (Morris 1979, Fig. 37 g and h).

The outer walls were soon rebuilt in masonry, slightly enlarging the building. Fig. 43 suggests that the aisle posts were replaced by continuous slots at the same time, but since few of the postholes were excavated and the slots were completely robbed their construction date is uncertain. It is possible that the aisle posts continued in use contemporary with the masonry walls, as for instance in building D at Winterton in the late 2nd century (Stead 1976, 39–49), but the fact that the westernmost pair of aisle posts lie immediately adjacent to a stone wall makes this unlikely.

Aisled buildings are commonly subdivided into an upper and lower end, the west end of an east-west building generally being preferred (Morris 1979, 56). Subdivision usually occurs along the length of the nave and aisles, creating large central rooms and smaller side chambers and maintaining the structural continuity of the building. It is much less common to have a narrow central room and wide side rooms as at the west end in Building IV; where this arrangement is found elsewhere, principally at Norton Disney and Mansfield Woodhouse, it occurs at the lower end of the building and the narrow area between the side rooms is seen as a passage giving access to the outside. A passageway is also the preferred interpretation for Room 2 in Building IV, but here it leads into the apsidal room on the west end of the building. In size this room compares favourably with the principal room found within the nave of most other aisled buildings, and is architecturally rather more sophisticated. Its width is very slightly greater than that of the nave, but the similarity to these central rooms in other aisled buildings seems clear.

One function performed by an external end room may have been to buttress the gable end of the aisled building against linear instability; at Winterton aisled buildings B and D both had one end wall significantly more massive than the side walls, and this was also the case at Denton (Stead 1976, 88). Having a principal room outside the west end of the main structure is a rare feature paralleled at Landwade, near Exning, Suffolk and at Castlefield, Andover, Hants. (JT Smith 1963, 5–8), both second century examples. Other possible examples are Clanville and Carisbrooke in their first phases (Morris 1979, Fig. 35), both without evidence of other subdivisions, but the excavations are 19th century, and at Clanville in particular the principal rooms may in fact have been internal.

Large apsidal rooms are found in only a few Romano-British villas (for instance see Eagleton, Staffs; DJ Smith 1978, 124–5 for Lullingstone, Kent and Neal 1978, 45 for Gorhambury, Herts), and are usually of high status, containing mosaic floors as at Frampton, Dorset and Littlecote Park, Wilts (illustrated by DJ Smith 1978, 132–3) or occupying a focal position in the domestic range as in Building G, Winterton, Lincs (Stead 1976, 83). They are sometimes interpreted as triclinia, sometimes simply as the principal reception room. The large apsed room recently discovered at Bulls Lodge Quarry, Boreham, Essex, is compared to the *principia* at Stonea in Cambridgeshire and interpreted as the headquarters building of an Imperial estate (Frere 1991)! Floors in the apsidal room of Building IV were largely destroyed, but there was no indication in the surrounding features or overlying ploughsoil that this room had ever had more than a mortar floor surface. In view of the proximity of the ovens and hearths in the aisled hall it is tempting to interpret the apsidal room as a triclinium, and this might perhaps have been the function of the principal rooms in other aisled buildings, but this close association of ?kitchen and dining room is not usual in the main domestic ranges on other villa sites.

The apsidal room was apparently later surrounded by a parallel wall 2452=2454, probably creating a peristyle or ambulatory around it. The foundation trench was of similar dimensions to those of the main walls, but unlike that of the inner apse was separate from those of the main building, and presumably this wall buttressed the original apse; it may only have been a dwarf verandah wall, but the foundations suggest not. This ambulatory is an unique feature in Romano-British architecture, and it is alternatively possible that 2452=2452 replaced 2420. This would, however, be a very large room indeed by the standards of Romano-British villas, and the scale of the foundations are not commensurate with this.

Professor Frere has suggested that this might have been a 'sun-parlour' or 'view-room', and that possibly the addition of a peristyle was to compensate for the loss of the view when Building III was erected, replacing the 'view' with a series of sunlit arches or trabeated openings. Certainly there would have been an unrestricted view to the west when Building IV phase 2 was in use, but whether Building III can be dated early enough to support his suggestion is uncertain. Building III phase 1 may predate Building IV phase 4, but is dated to the 2nd quarter of the 3rd century, while the addition of the peristyle to Building IV is tentatively dated to the late 2nd century. The dating evidence for the peristyle is, however, indirect, and could accommodate this later date.

Nothing of the superstructure of Building IV remains, but some tentative suggestions as to the missing third dimension are offered based upon the plan. There has been some debate as to whether these aisled buildings were covered by a single roof and lit only through the outer walls, or whether the central area was higher than the aisles and was lit by a clerestory. Smith (1963, 26–7) supported the former interpretation, but the recent excavation of the fallen south-eastern gable end of the aisled building at Shavards Farm, Meonstoke, Hants (King & Potter 1990, 196–204) has proven that at least some buildings of this type had a clerestory. For the suggested reconstructions (Fig. 111) the minimum height of the outer aisle walls has been taken to be c 1.8 m, sufficient for an adult to stand upright just inside the building. The height of the clerestory is taken to be 1.5 m, similar to that calculated from the fallen wall of the Meonstoke building.

Tile roofs, which are usually simply held in place by the weight of the tiles, require a shallow roof pitch; recent excavation of the fallen gable of a villa building at Redlands Farm, Stanwick, Northants (Keevill 1990, 7; Keevill pers. comm.), has indicated a pitch between 20 and 25 degrees. Slate roofs, which are pegged in place, can have a pitch of 35 degrees or more; at Meonstoke the roof pitch was apparently 47.5 degrees (King & Potter 1990, 200–202 Figs. 4–6). The roof of Building IV was probably of slate, or possibly thatch, which also requires a pitch of 45–50 degrees, and a pitch of 45 degrees has been adopted in the reconstructions.

The simplest reconstruction of Building IV involves a single roof covering both nave and aisles (Fig. 111 A); the aisle slots will presumably have supported a series of arches, and the amount of light will have been governed by the height of the side walls. If a clerestory is adopted then Rooms 1–3 at the west end, whose walls do not correspond to those of the aisles, have to be treated as a separate structural unit. These can then be roofed as a continuation of the pitch of the aisles (Fig. 111 B). In this case the addition of a peristyle to the apse in phase 3 simply extends the sweep of the aisle roof around the west end of the building (Fig. 111 C). This, however, will have meant that Room 4 was only lit indirectly through the outer walls of the peristyle, and alternatively this may have had its own clerestory. It is then possible that a single roof was employed as in A, but that the aisles, and hence the height of the whole building, was higher (Fig. 111 D). The main aisled block might also have had a clerestory as in B, but this would have made the building 11 m high.

It is alternatively possible that the pitch of aisle and peristyle roofs was lower than that of the main building, allowing for a clerestory without the need of additional height. However, since the rooms of the central block (Rooms 1–3) do not correspond to the breadth of the nave and aisles, this block has to be roofed in a single pitch, and may thus have protruded above the line of the apse and main aisled block (Fig. 111 E), providing a high gable wall for the apse. It may even have been roofed at a gentler pitch, and have stood up like a tower or transept (Fig. 111 F).

Because the foundations of the outer apsidal wall were dug separately, whereas those of the inner apse were integral with the main building, it is believed that the outer apse was secondary, and the incorporation of the eastern parts of this outer apse wall into the two rooms that replace the apse suggests that this was not simply a dwarf-wall for a verandah. It remains possible, however, that the two walls were after all contemporary, and that the outer wall was simply for a peristyle, and this is also shown on the last reconstruction (Fig. 111 F).

At Denton the presence of both ceramic tiles and stone slates in the backfilled postholes of the aisled building led to the suggestion that the nave had a steeply pitched roof of slates, the aisles tiled roofs of a shallower pitch (JT Smith 1963, 25). Excavation at Meonstoke demonstrated that the pitch of the central nave and of the aisles was different, and that the aisles were less steeply pitched than the nave (King & Potter 1990, 202 Fig. 6), and this is the preferred interpretation here.

VI.2.b Dating of the villa buildings

The earliest securely dated building is Building IV, which overlies contexts of the late 1st and early 2nd centuries, and is respected by ditches containing mid-2nd century assemblages. A construction date of 130–150 AD best fits this evidence. Aisled farmhouses do occur as the only building on some villa sites (eg Stroud), or at least predate the emergence of other domestic buildings as at Sparsholt (DJ Smith 1978, 126), but in view of the slight evidence of domestic occupation from Building IV it seems likely that Building I, which also overlies early 2nd century features, was also erected at the same time. A dump of high-quality glassware and large parts of several Samian vessels in ditch 132 adjacent, which very probably derived from the building, is dated to 150–165 AD (see Ch. V.2.b and Ch. V.7).

184 *Roughground Farm, Lechlade, Gloucestershire: a prehistoric and Roman landscape*

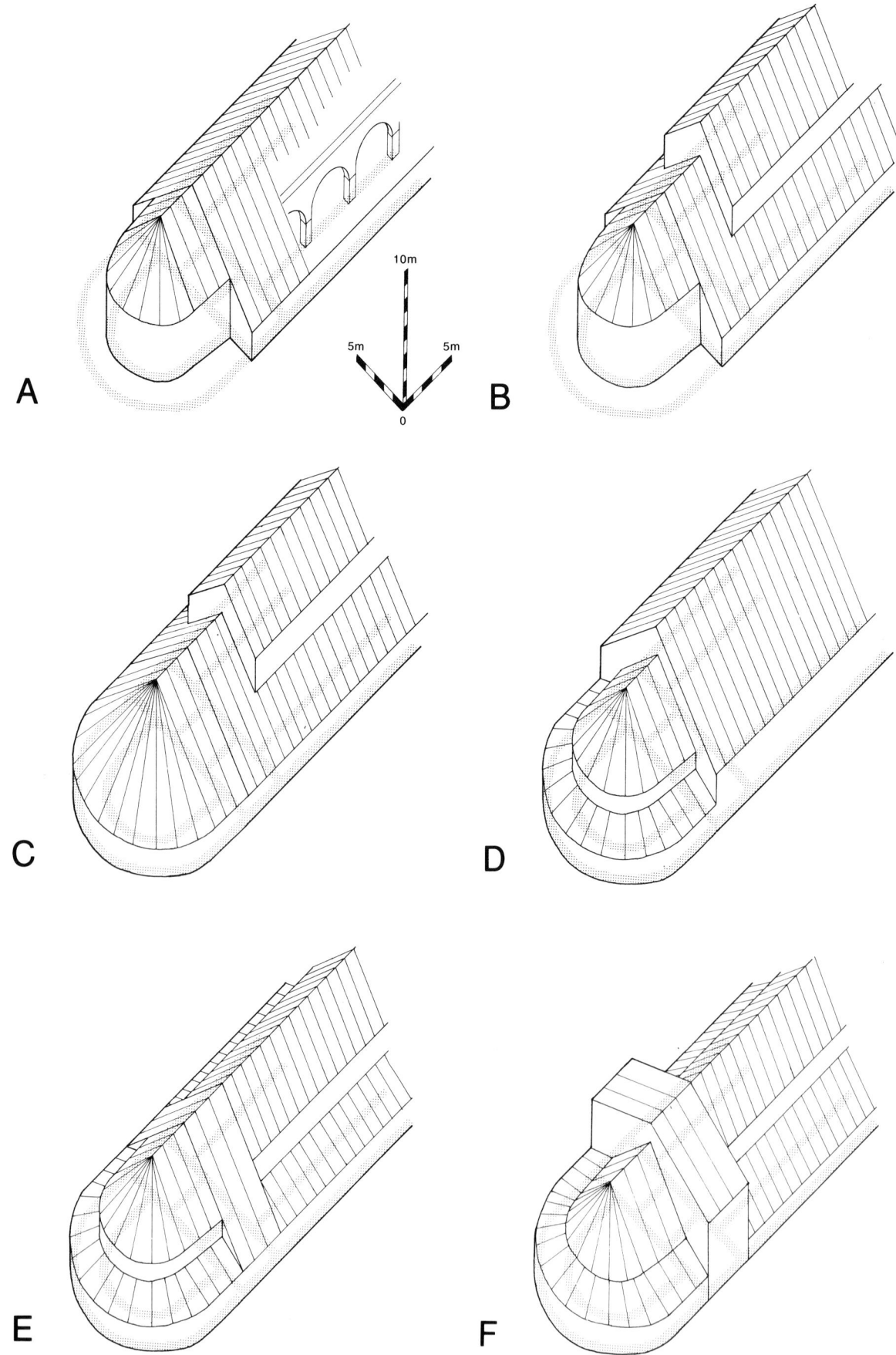

Figure 111 Possible reconstructions of Building IV

The full extent of Building I was not established, but fieldwalking in 1957 established that a slight mound extended north-west for some distance, and a dark rectangular cropmark in line with the east end of Building I is very possibly a hypocaust at its west end (see Frontispiece, Fig. 3, and Fig. 115).

The putative Building V, of which only a small length of wall was found, probably also belongs in the 2nd century.

Adjacent to Building I on the east was ditch 132, which contained a large assemblage of glass and finewares dating to the Antonine period. This ditch apparently curved NW and may have joined one of the broad soilmark ditches seen from the air just N of Building I (Fig. 3), in effect forming an enclosure around the north-east and north sides of the villa (Fig. 114). 132 is very similar in proportions and date to ditch 2429 south of Building IV (Figs. 42 and 55), which ends almost opposite it and appears to have performed a similar function on the south-east and south sides of the villa. It therefore seems possible that these may be the north and south terminals of a single villa enclosure ditch.

The wide gap between these terminals and the position of Building IV straddling their line would suggest that there was no physical barrier between the villa enclosure and the area to the east, which may also have been enclosed by continuations of the north and south boundary ditches (see Ch. IV.C.6). The terminals may, however, delineate a social or functional barrier between the domestic and agricultural buildings; the apsed room and adjoining rooms in Building IV lay west of the ditch terminals with Building I, while the aisled hall and the ovens lay to the east. In support of this hypothesis, the much later eastern villa boundary wall, 153=2496=2517, followed this same line across Building IV, incorporating the former rooms at the west end but excluding the aisled area.

Access to the villa courtyard was probably on the east side, facing onto the open area upon which the estate was focussed. Ditches and later enclosure walls on the south were continuous, and the soilmark ditches visible north of Building I appear to be similarly unbroken, though these are undated. A succession of large ditches are visible as cropmarks to the west, though these cannot be traced as far as the point where they might have met the excavated ditches on the south. During the second century there may have been gaps for access on this side, and for a brief period in the 3rd century there seems to have been direct access to the small ditched enclosures on the north-west (see Ch. IV.D.2 and Fig. 59).

In the courtyard no obvious access roads like those at Frocester Court (Branigan 1977, 75 Fig. 33) were identified, but varying surfaces of stone, gravel and loamy soil perhaps suggest garden beds and hard standings. Close-packed stone areas in the yard at Claydon Pike nearby were usually without covering structures, but at Barnsley Park such areas lay inside drystone-walled buildings (Webster & Smith 1982, 80 and 89) Possibly layers of clay and stones outside Buildings II and IV (Fig. 37), which would have been treacherous in wet weather, were covered by lean-tos of slight construction.

The area south of Building I was not investigated, but where Building III was later to be built the subsoil was disturbed by pits and hollows. An extensive black layer here, 299, may indicate use of an hypocaust nearby, presumably in the unexcavated area beneath the north part of Building III, but could alternatively represent charcoal-burning or some other semi-industrial activity. Local reports have spoken of another hypocausted building south of this, found on the edge of the quarry in the 1930s (A J Baxter pers. comm.), but in view of the presence of the villa enclosure ditch along this side this is unlikely. It is, however, possible that this report refers to the southern continuation of Building V.

In the first half of the 3rd century Building III was constructed south of I and west of IV. This building was over 15 m wide. Domestic buildings are commonly of this order of width; most are rectangular blocks three rooms deep, with a wide central range of rooms flanked on either side by narrower corridors or ranges, and the surviving part of Building III would fit such a plan. The east wall of Building III was, however, slight in its first phase, and the main structure may only have been two rooms deep (between 240 and 295), with an internal corridor on the east and passage on the west.

In this early phase the building seems to have had slight mortar floors and little decoration; there was very little destruction material when it was rebuilt in the later 3rd century, and it was probably a plain thatched building ancillary to buildings I and IV. Part of it was divided up into small rooms some of which were also unchanged in the 2nd phase. These rooms were clearly domestic in the later phase, so were probably also domestic in the first phase.

Building III was rebuilt later in the 3rd century. The east wall was made more substantial and the eastern rooms wider, so that the main structure was now fully 3 rooms deep, over 16 m wide and at least 33 m long, with the passage in addition on the west side. Containing a range of hypocausted rooms, a tessellated floor and a wide range of painted designs it is comparable to the principal residences at Ditchley (Ralegh Radford 1936, 29–44 and Fig. 9), Shakenoak (Brodribb et al 1971, Building B) or Barnsley Park (Webster & Smith 1982, 97–103). Only part of the plan of Building III was recovered, but its width combined with the modest nature of the original floor and wall-decoration may indicate that it too began as an aisled basilican building (from which in general the rectangular block plan described above probably developed). The conversion of basilican buildings from an ancillary role to domestic residence is common on Romano-British villas (see for example Shakenoak Farm (Brodribb et al 1971, 14–27) and

Sparsholt, Hants (Johnston in Todd 1978, 80–81 and Fig. 25).

There is no clear evidence that Building I had gone out of use by this time. Plaster and tesserae were found in ditches west of Building I dating to the late 3rd or early 4th century. They probably came from Building I, and may imply demolition, but charcoal, coal and ash in the long hollow 409 show that an hypocaust, most likely at the west end of Building I, was still in use into the 4th century. The plaster and tesserae need only represent alterations.

It thus appears that in the late 3rd and early 4th centuries there were domestic ranges on the south-west and north and a large aisled building on the south-east with rooms at the west end and to the north, grouped around a villa courtyard bounded by a wall on the south side (Figs. 113, 114 and 115). If Building III did originate as an aisled building, the arrangement is particularly reminiscent of that at Winterton in the 3rd century (Stead 1976, 82). Large deep ditches 416, 419 and 1604=2008 formed a ditched enclosure around the villa buildings, as was the case at Claydon Pike (Miles 1984, 200–202) and at Barton Court Farm (Miles 1986, 11–12) in the later 3rd and 4th centuries.

Construction mortar from the second phase of Building III extended some 7 m east into the courtyard, as happened adjacent to Building A at Shakenoak (Brodribb et al 1973, Fig. 7). At Roughground Farm this was levelled off and covered with stone paving, and was possibly enclosed by a wall. Also in the 3rd century an extension was built on the west side of Building IV Room 5 out into the courtyard. This was without foundations and of fairly short duration, being overlaid by further courtyard surfaces in the 4th century.

During the 4th century, if not before, Building II was constructed in the north-east part of the villa courtyard, and the south and east sides of the yard were enclosed by a further wall. Some of the rooms at the west end of Building IV may have been retained, and were probably linked to Building III by a portico along the south side. Access to the villa courtyard on the east side was maintained through a gap just north of Building II. Hypocausted Building B was probably in use at this time, to judge from the charcoal in the top of ditch 132. At least two domestic ranges, Buildings II and III, were in use, and possibly Building I as well. The gradual appearance of an enclosure wall seems to reflect a greater division between the domestic and agricultural functions of the villa, and the development of a true courtyard rather than farmyard (see also Morris 1979, 53–4).

A bath-house would be expected on the site, but none was positively identified. No obvious stream-course has been found closer than the river Leach, and there is no low-lying area close to the centre of the villa. Water may have been channelled via a leat from the river, or the baths may have been supplied by an internal well as at Shakenoak Farm (Brodribb et al 1973, 23). It has also been suggested (Miles pers. comm.) that an hypocaust at Claydon Pike functioned as a bath-house without a large water-supply, providing dry-heat sauna of the 'Spartan' type (Johnston 1979, 17).

Some of the rooms in Building III could perhaps have been part of a bath-suite, but the plan was not sufficiently clear to clarify this. Another possibility is the hypocausted Building B, whose charcoal rake-out overlay ditch 132 between Buildings I and II (Figs. 36 and 37). It was favourably situated close to two of the domestic buildings, and was active in the 4th century, but the fills of 132 from the late 2nd century do not include hypocaust ash, so this building was presumably constructed after this, and the bath-house must have been elsewhere in the 2nd century.

It is possible that a bath-suite was incorporated in the missing east end of Building IV, indeed 'Building V' may have been part of this, if the reports of an hypocausted building destroyed by quarrying in the 1930s are correct. Bath-suites are commonly found in aisled buildings, usually at the 'lower' end opposite to the domestic rooms (Morris 1979, 56), and at Sparsholt, Brading and Clanville there were never any baths in the main dwelling house, only in the aisled building (DJ Smith 1978, 126–7). In the 2nd and early 3rd centuries this may also have been the arrangement at Roughground Farm, and Building 'B' may then have been a 4th century replacement.

Other stone buildings include the rectangle at C and the 'subterranean' building at A (Fig. 1; RCHM(E) Glos. 1976, 73). There are no details for either, but the building at C was not apparently ornate and was presumably ancillary, perhaps a workshop. Agricultural buildings are commonly found outside the domestic courtyard, for instance the hall and possible barn at Sparsholt (Johnston 1978, 80–81) or the workers hall and other buildings in the outer courtyard at Gorhambury (Neal 1983, 116). The building at A presumably had hypocausts, and may have been a detached bath-house for the use of the farm-labourers, as has been suggested at Gorhambury. There is no dating evidence for either building.

The overall impression is that the villa was of middle size and status, more extensive than Shakenoak but not as prestigious as such villas as Winterton, Lincs (Stead 1979) or true courtyard villas as defined by Branigan (Branigan 1977, 52–3). No stone architectural fragments like the columns from Ditchley (Ralegh Radford 1936, 42) or Claydon Pike (Miles and Palmer in prep) were recovered, but the unstratified sculpture in the round (Fig. 105.121) and the altar and other stones from the Anglo-Saxon cemetery at Butler's Field 500 m to the south suggest that their absence is due to thorough robbing and only partial excavation.

VI.3 The field system and enclosures around the villa

Fig. 110, Fig. 112, Fig. 115

An interim plan of this was published by Margaret Jones (Jones in Bowen & Fowler 1978, 171–2).

The fields consisted of several elements covering at least 15 hectares. These were:

1. Wide droveways and large open fields of at least 2 hectares on the south-east.
2. Narrower trackways and rectilinear fields of between 0.5 and 1 hectare on the north-west, also incorporating some small enclosures or pens.
3. A grid of rectangular enclosures immediately north and east of the villa, based upon a unit size of 17 m by 27 m.
4. Longer strips of the same width (17 m) south and north of the southern and northern enclosure groups (see 5 below) respectively.
5. Two lines of sub-rectangular enclosures (the northern and southern enclosure groups) *c* 150 m apart facing one another across the open area east of the villa, and containing a 'corndrier', ovens, pits, burials and hollows.

1. The droveways were 20–30 m wide, and are distinguished from other trackways on account of their greater width (Hinchcliffe & Thomas 1980, 68–9). They were first defined by ditches in the 2nd century AD, but appear to have been of much greater antiquity (see Ch. III.B.8), and form the pre-existing landscape into which the villa was fitted. The early Roman settlement was set a little way back from the junction of the droveways leaving a wide-open space between the outer droveway boundaries, originally 2–3 hectares in extent. Settlements at the confluence of trackways incorporating a 'green'-like area are common in the region; another possible such site lay only 1 km south-west at Butler's Field (Fig. 4) and a closely parallel layout was excavated at Appleford (Hinchcliffe & Thomas 1980, 12–16), where the droveways were also between 20 and 30 m wide and the 'green' just under 2 hectares in area. As at Roughground Farm there were few gaps in the droveway ditches, which were interpreted as channeling stock through rather than into the settlement, with the 'green' acting as a collecting area for livestock and the areas either side of the droveways as arable (Hinchcliffe & Thomas 1980, 68–9). This was possibly also the original arrangement at Roughground Farm, though no boundary such as existed at Appleford was seen dividing the open area off from the early Roman settlement.

There may also have been a trackway running in from the south-west, as a cropmark shows a trackway leading from the nearby 'green' site towards Roughground Farm. These trackway ditches were sectioned some way from the enclosure at Butler's Field (Fig. 4; Miles & Palmer 1986, 5), but did not produce any clear dating evidence.

The subsequent uses of the 'green' at Roughground Farm seem to have been varied. At Appleford the flanking enclosures were added behind the droveway boundaries and respected them, without apparent access to the droveways, but at Roughground Farm groups of smaller enclosures (see 5 above) straddled the linear boundaries and opened onto the 'green', while gravel pits also encroached upon it (Fig. 66; Fig. 115). Nevertheless an area of just over 1 hectare was left untouched until well into the 4th century, and the circular mound occupying the middle of this open area may well have been an elevated platform from which stock-collecting or even a market was overseen.

2. and 3. These enclosures and fields were probably all laid out in the later 2nd century, and shared both a common alignment and the basic unit of measurement (Fig. 112). The smallest enclosures, 17 m by 27 m, are too small to have been anything but paddocks or garden plots, and even the multiples twice or four times that size are not as large as the majority of 'Celtic' fields, which range from 0.33 of an acre (roughly 2,000 sq m) to 1.5 acres (roughly 9,500 sq m) (Rivet 1969, 26–27). The length of these small enclosures, approximately 27 m, is a standard found at other Romano-British villas (McWhirr 1981, 99–101), apparently including enclosures at Barnsley Park, although this is not mentioned in the final excavation report (Webster *et al* 1985, 73–82). A regular grid of similar-sized enclosures surrounded the villa at Maddle Farm on the Berkshire Downs (S Ford pers. comm.).

Small ditched enclosures laid out on a regular grid and associated with 2nd century occupation were excavated at Brockworth, Glos. (Rawes 1981, 45–77). A number of sizes of enclosure were represented, most of which did not correspond to the measurements at Roughground Farm, but the earliest parallel ditches were 27 m apart. The excavator suggested that the grid there was associated with centuriation, but the context of this relatively small excavation was not established. There is no indication that the layout at Roughground Farm was part of a larger grid.

Similar-sized enclosures at Barnsley Park are interpreted as paddocks (Webster *et al* 1985, 73–77), and the limited excavation of the small enclosure ditches at Roughground Farm showed that they were filled with fine silt, which does not suggest that their interiors were ploughed or dug over, and they were most likely under grass. If the suggestion that the 'green' east of the villa was used for collecting livestock is correct, it would also make sense to have paddocks and pens alongside it. Two of these enclosures had a circular dark cropmark inside them, possibly a well for watering animals (Fig. 2).

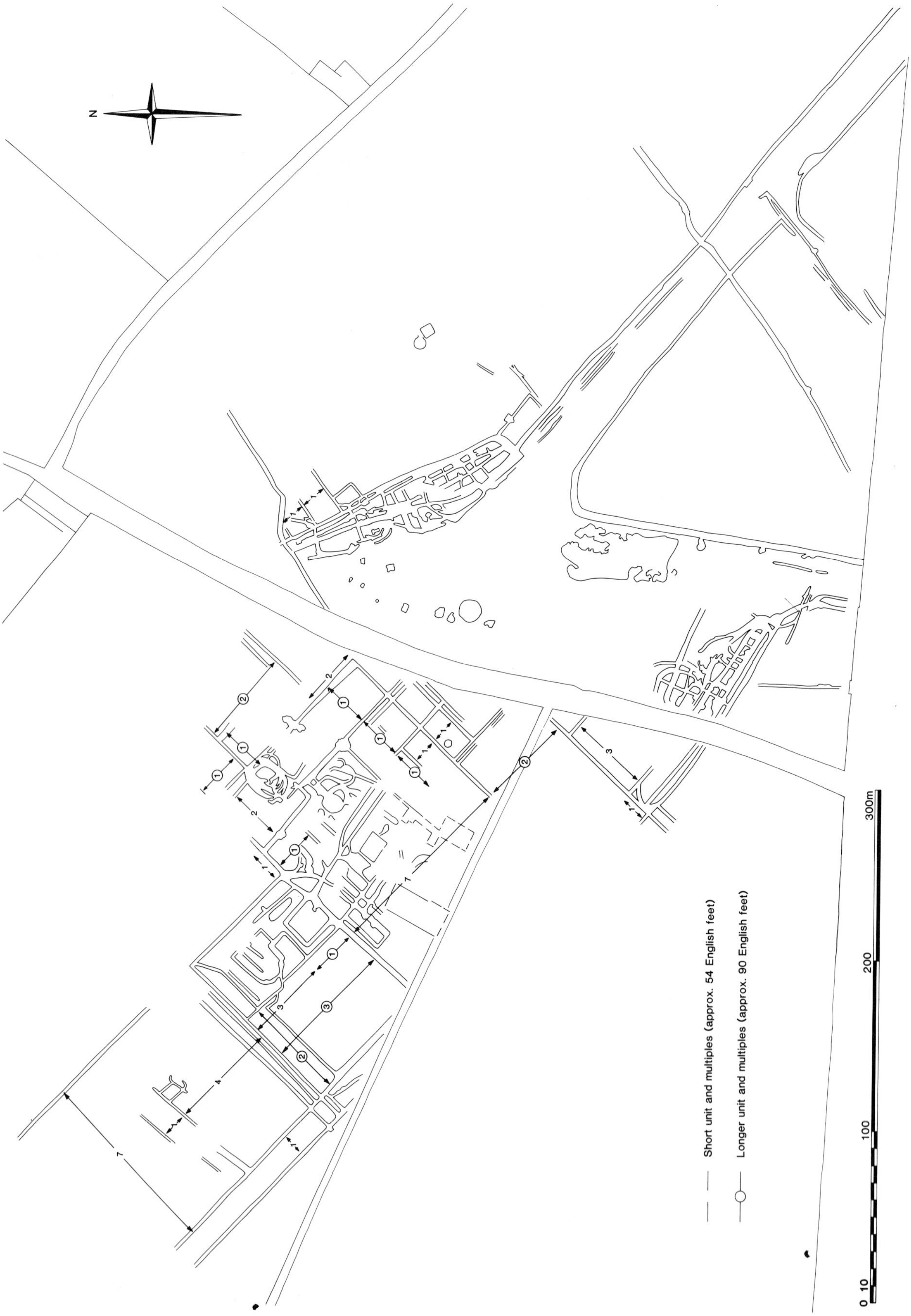

188 Roughground Farm, Lechlade, Gloucestershire: a prehistoric and Roman landscape

Figure 112 Roman field system showing standard measurements of layout

The larger enclosures west of the villa with their adjoining narrow trackways reveal a no less organised layout. Comparable trackways and fields have been excavated at Winterton (Goodburn 1978, 98–9) and are visible as cropmarks around other villas such as Cromwell, Northants (Frere & St. Joseph 1983, 199–200 and Fig. 121). Their use is not known, but many of their surrounding ditches had fairly homogeneous clay loam and gravel fills, in contrast to the silting of the paddock ditches east of the villa. Such an even mix of soil and gravel is characteristic of ploughsoils, and at 0.5–1.0 hectares (5,000–10,000 sq m) in extent these fields are of the same order of size as 'Celtic' fields (see above). They may, therefore, have been for arable. The very small pens or enclosures along the north side of the field nearest to the villa may have been used seasonally for animals, or alternatively may have been haystack enclosures or fodder stores for the winter.

One problem that has not been answered is why the villa buildings and their enclosure ditches are not on the same alignment as the surrounding field system. The first villa buildings, Buildings I and IV, were erected between AD 130 and 150, and appear to have a common orientation. The dating evidence for the field-system west of the villa, though limited, indicates that the system was laid out soon after, in the later 2nd century. Few of the small enclosures north of the villa buildings were investigated, and excavation only demonstrated that one phase of these is later than the early Roman house-enclosure 56, that is, after the mid-2nd century. Their orientation is, however, the same as that of the fields west of the villa, and they were probably contemporary. Even allowing for slight inaccuracy in plotting the cropmarks north and east of the villa, there is a difference of around 10 degrees between the buildings and their enclosing ditches and the excavated fields west of the villa.

Aerial photographs of the cropmarks and stripped soilmarks (see Figs. 2 and 3) show that there were two distinct alignments for the small enclosures on the north and east, one of which corresponds much more closely to the orientation of the early Roman ditches such as 40 and to that of Buildings I and IV. None of the ditches of this system were excavated, and it is possible that this was the original field layout, restricted to a group of small enclosures on the north and east sides of the villa enclosure.

Despite the limited scale of excavation of the early Roman settlement, it is evident that the villa buildings directly overlay its core, and that the boundaries of the earlier settlement were very closely mirrored by those of the villa, at least on the west and the south. There is some evidence that the alignment of boundary ditches belonging to the early Roman settlement such as 40 and 42 was followed when laying out the later field systems. Possibly the later orientation, which extended west of the villa as well, was based upon different pre-existing boundaries on the west side of the villa, or other features in the wider landscape that are no longer visible. The villa building area was incorporated within this layout, but was not the controlling factor in its orientation.

The orientation of the later Building III, which is close to that of I and IV, reflects the greater influence of the villa courtyard itself than of the surrounding landscape, but the 4th century enclosure wall and the plan of Building II appears to represent an attempt to correct the orientation to match that of the field system (see Figs. 36 and 115).

4. East of the villa and attached to the north side of the northern group of irregular enclosures were two strips delineated by ditches a standard 17 m apart but at least 70 m long. These were contemporary with the latest phases of the enclosure group, demonstrating that this unit of measurement was in use from the late 2nd until the 4th century AD. The northern limits of these strips was not established, and it is possible that these represent long strips of the sort suggested at Lye Hole (Fowler 1975, 127). South of the southern enclosures a series of soilmarks which were parallel to the enclosure boundaries and were also roughly 17 m apart are suggested to have been others, and were at least 70 m long. The only one of these sectioned had a silt fill, which does not suggest that these strips were ploughed; despite their similar width to the medieval strips in the same area their use appears to have been different.

5. Overlying the northern and southern boundaries to the 'green' there grew up strings of small enclosures facing inwards and opening onto it, often with a common boundary at the back. The earliest of the northern group were of regular rectangular shape, and included both 825 which contained a four-post structure and 535 etc enclosing the 'corndrier'. The regular shape of these suggests that they too were part of an organised villa layout.

Since 825 lay behind the droveway boundary and was possibly approached by a separate trackway running down its north side its use was perhaps unconnected with that of the green. The four-post structure within 825 may imply a connection with grain storage or haystacks (Gent 1983, 249–252; Reynolds 1979), so possibly this enclosure indicates that there was arable north of the droveway.

The 'T-shaped corndrier' is the common type in the south-west of Britain (Morris 1979, 20), and this example can be closely paralleled at Barton Court Farm, Abingdon, Oxon (Miles 1986, 15–16) and Farmoor, Oxon (Lambrick & Robinson 1979, 32–34). Experiments to test the hypothesis that 'corndriers' were used to dry grain for storage have demonstrated that only small quantities can be processed at one time (Reynolds 1981, 37–43) and other interpretations such as parching grain stored in the husk or ear prior to threshing (Jones in Lambrick & Robinson 1979, 104) or to malt soaked grain for brewing (Reynolds 1981, 41–43) seem more plausible. In view of the numerous

190 *Roughground Farm, Lechlade, Gloucestershire: a prehistoric and Roman landscape*

Figure 113 Phase plan of the late 2nd/early 3rd century villa

Figure 114 Phase plan of the late 3rd/4th century villa

ovens around the 'corndrier' its use to help threshing as part of a bakery is very attractive, providing sufficient grain for the day-to-day needs of a small community. Whether bakery or brewery it was probably the first structure built upon the green to serve the community that used it, and perhaps encouraged the growth of settlement in enclosures around it.

It has been suggested that parallel lines of postholes adjacent to ditch 959/960 where the more northerly droveway enters the green formed a timber building, Building VI (Figs. 66 and 78). The staggered eastern line of postholes is, however, not matched among Romano-British aisled buildings, and architecturally would necessitate fitting together two wall-plates of different height under one roof. Alternatively two roof-pitches may have been employed, and the posthole lines have represented the walls of less ambitious structures. While large aisled barns are often characterised by accurately-spaced postholes, as at Claydon Pike and Somerford Keynes (Miles and Palmer in prep), the postholes of Building IV on this site were not, and few lesser agricultural buildings have been excavated in the fields around villas (pace Winterton). It must also be remembered that not all the features of the structure at Roughground Farm were fully cleared or excavated. The use of this building, situated at the edge of the 'green', is likely to have been as a cattle-shed and hay-barn.

The subsequent expansion of both the northern and southern enclosure groups in the 3rd century may have involved an influx of population. While no buildings were identified in either set of enclosures, the profuse pottery, the glass vessels and the groups of burials scattered throughout imply that the occupation was domestic. Houses may have been of timber ground-sill construction, examples of which have been found locally at Claydon Pike (Miles & Palmer 1983, 94). The plentiful hand-operated querns also suggest activity on the household scale, and these, unlike the ovens, were equally represented in both enclosure groups. The concentration of ovens in one set of enclosures suggests that the two groups were interdependent, not entirely separate units. There is no excavated evidence of the whereabouts of the workforce that served the villa before the mid-3rd century, and they may have lived in settlements roundabout before these enclosures developed. Alternatively, however, the uninvestigated areas south and north of the villa buildings may have contained evidence of this.

There is, however, no doubt that a range of agricultural and semi-industrial activities such as smithing, sheep-shearing and bucket-making or coopering were carried out within these enclosures. Moreover their positions and their proximity to the villa suggests that they were directly involved in the villa's agricultural functions rather than simply housing part of its labour force.

Similar relationships between groups of enclosures and adjacent villas have been proposed at other sites. At Appleford the enclosures around the green were seen as largely agricultural, but large deposits of pottery were taken to imply some domestic occupation within them, and a close relationship between this 'native' settlement and a probable Roman villa at Penn Copse some 400 m away was suggested. Excavations of enclosures at Wakerley, Northants recovered a range of structures similar to that in the enclosure groups at Roughground Farm, for instance a 'corndrier', numerous ovens, a small cemetery and plenty of pottery, and the excavators suggested a link with stone-built buildings of a possible villa some 600 m distant (Jackson & Ambrose 1978, 172-3). The small quantities of animal bone, however, led them to believe that the enclosures had not been lived-in.

At Roughground Farm the enclosure groups are much closer to the villa buildings, an integrated part of the 'villa rustica'. The distinction between the 'pars urbana' and 'pars agraria' drawn by Agache (Agache 1978, 320) is clearly illustrated in the great Gallic villas such as Anthee, Namur, Belgium or Warfusee-Abancourt (Nord) (Percival 1976, 78–81), where the owner's house (the pars or villa urbana) lay within an inner court some 150 m by 100 m, separate from the vast farmyard and industrial enclosure (the pars agraria or villa rustica) beyond. Within the latter parallel rows of agricultural and industrial buildings, some of them also occupied by estate workers, faced each other across a courtyard over 100 m wide. The two roughly parallel enclosure groups at Roughground Farm are reminiscent of this arrangement. It is obviously not suggested that a comparable range of activities was carried out here, but that a similar centralisation of estate management may have been practised, with the distinction between 'pars urbana' and 'pars agraria' adapted to the pre-existing landscape.

VI.4 The villa economy

The villa economy appears, like its predecessor, to have been mixed farming, on the basis on the one hand of the droveways and paddocks, the mammal and bird bones, the shears and ox-goads and on the other of the carbonised remains, the fields, the 'corndrier', ovens and querns. This is the usual picture, the ditch-digging and settlement reorganisation of the Roman period representing labour investment in technical improvements rather than a radical change in the basic agricultural system. One innovation was the use of bread wheat as well as spelt wheat, oats and barley, and it is suggested in the environmental report that this was a specialised crop grown only on the wealthier villa sites (Ch. V.18.c). Charcoal from probable hypocaust debris and from ovens in Building IV suggests that hazel was being coppiced in the Later Roman period, but the low incidence of deer probably implies that there was scant unmanaged woodland near to the site.

Domestic fowl were kept (a relatively recent introduction to Britain) and probably also domestic duck. Horses were probably reared; horses may have been reared on specialised low-lying pastoral sites in the Middle Iron Age (Allen and Robinson forthcoming), and the droveways at Roughground Farm leading down onto the floodplains of the rivers Leach and Thames suggest a continuing emphasis upon grazing in the Roman period.

There was an increase in the importance of cattle in the Later Roman period, which is common over much of Southern Britain, but as is usual there was no evidence of large-scale butchery or of secondary processing such as tanning at the site; recent butchery deposits from the suburbs of towns such as York and Exeter suggests that cattle were driven to towns for butchery, thus avoiding the problems of transporting processed carcasses and other animal products. There are no large towns close to the Roughground Farm villa, but livestock was possibly taken to Wanborough (near Swindon) or Cricklade, or even possibly to Cirencester.

VI.5 Burials

VI.5.a Early Roman burials

The only early burial was 1140, a cremation within a square-ditched enclosure (Fig. 30; Fig. 35), of a type rare in Britain. Very close parallels come from the Champagne region of France, where several 1st century AD cemeteries have been excavated (Brisson & Hatt 1955). Along the east coast of Britain examples of this type of burial are growing, from the square barrows of East Yorkshire and Lincolnshire (Whimster 1981, 122–6) to the enclosures with single cremations excavated at Mucking (Jones pers. comm.), all indicating continental influence in the Iron Age.

In the Upper Thames there are no other square-ditched enclosure burials; the only possible links with this tradition are a four-post structure within a small circular enclosure at Appleford, dated to the later Iron Age (Hinchcliffe & Thomas 1980, 41–5 and Fig. 25), and a four-post structure within a rectangular enclosure at Smithsfield, Hardwick, dated to the mid-1st century AD (Allen in prep.). There are no parallels for the Appleford structure in the Marnian Region, and its attribution to this tradition is tenuous; the Hardwick example can be closely paralleled, but no human burials were found.

The postholes inside the ditch at Roughground Farm are similarly not matched on other sites, except for a square of four over the central burial, the sides of which were, however, normally oriented parallel to the surrounding ditch. Brisson and Hatt consider that there was a four-post roofed shrine of the dead person, a sort of heroon, upstanding over such burials. Possibly there was an oval fence around such a four-post structure here. Alternatively the oval of posts may have revetted a mound. Since the enclosure was eroded by ploughing it is possible that there were other shallower burials in this area, but the absence of other enclosures as well as of other burials suggests that it was an isolated occurrence, reflecting the preferred burial rite of one individual rather than the whole community.

The association with the circular post-setting 1100 is unparalleled, but seems hardly likely to have been coincidental, as no other circular post settings were found in the large area examined around it. There was a little abraded Early Iron Age pottery in one or two of these postholes, but little surrounding evidence of Iron Age settlement, and it is uncertain whether this was an Iron Age roundhouse. If the sherds were not residual, it may have been a funerary structure rather than a roundhouse, perhaps associated with an upstanding mound, which would account for the close proximity of an early Roman burial enclosure. Alternatively it may have been contemporary with the burial. No associations of roundhouses and such burial enclosures in the Late Iron Age or Early Roman period are known to the writer from French or British excavations.

Four thin iron nails in the burial pit may indicate that the cremation urn was placed within a box of some sort. It is also possible, but less likely, that the nails came from a structure upon the surrounding postholes. The nails were, however, too slight for any substantial structure, and nails are not known from any of the Marnian burials.

The Roughground Farm cremation may be rare evidence of a Gallic immigrant in the early Roman period.

VI.5.b Later Roman burials

Fig. 69

Excluding infants 24 inhumations probably of the later Roman period were found around the settlement. It appears that burials were grouped rather than deposited at random, and this impression is supported by the occurrence of stray human bones on the site. There were few of these, but over half of the instances were in graves with other burials, suggesting that further burials had been concentrated in these same areas. Several of the recorded burials were only seen during machine scraping in the tops of ditches, or hardly penetrated the gravel; others must have been destroyed by medieval ploughing or during scraping. The extra fragments increase the number to 26, and this is probably well below the original total. In addition the cattle market group continued north and west beyond the stripped area, and this group was clearly part of a larger number.

There was a tendency to bury people at the periphery of the settlement. This was the common practice in Roman towns, where the Laws of the Twelve Tables forbade burial within the urban area, and cemeteries lined the roads outside. Nevertheless in both northern and southern enclosure groups there were burials in the middle of the enclosures as well. It may be that these were dug only when the enclosures had been abandoned, but more likely reflect the more varied practises of the later Roman period in Britain.

The parallel alignment of the graves in several of the groups suggests that the burials took place within generations rather than centuries of one another, though it is conceivable that graves were marked and venerated for very long periods. Possibly each group of burials represents the cemetery of a specific family or other unit within the farmstead, and was used for several generations, though family links have only been even tentatively suggested between two burials (see Table 64 on Fiche 2#84).

It was suggested in the RCHM volume for Gloucestershire (1976, 75) that the group of six at the south-east end of the northern enclosures constituted an enclosed cemetery. The burials, however, were not aligned upon the surrounding enclosure nor were they contemporary with its construction. It has been argued that Enclosure 825 was dug in the late 2nd century, and although the bodies were unaccompanied one was decapitated which is characteristically later Roman. The enclosure may still have been extant when the burials were made, but was most likely not dug as a cemetery enclosure. The many other burials in other parts of the site do not support the idea of a specific cemetery. Small ditched enclosures around burials are also known locally at Claydon Pike, Fairford (Miles 1984, 202), but there the burials were aligned upon the ditches of the enclosure.

The single burial found within the villa yard was probably very late in the occupation. Burials in and around villa buildings are common in the latest periods of villa life; these have been found in the area at Claydon Pike, Fairford, and Keynsham, near Bristol, to name but two. A disturbed skull fragment found in the backfill of a pit cut into the corridor of Building IV probably came from another such burial, as the corridor floor itself dated well into the 4th century.

No similar burials were found either for the pre-villa occupation or the earlier part of the villa's life; possibly burials of this date existed in the areas quarried away north and south of the villa buildings. It is unlikely that these modest later Roman burials were those of the owners of the villa; only the single earlier enclosed cremation may have been one of these. The later burials were more likely those of retainers who worked, and probably lived in, the adjacent enclosures. In the 2nd century and early 3rd century before these enclosure groups developed farmhands may not have lived close to the villa but have come in from surrounding hamlets where they were also buried. In that case the appearance of burials may reflect an influx of population to the villa environs, in effect centralisation of the work of the estate. The villa owners were probably buried in a more impressive cemetery somewhere close to the villa, as in the 3rd century at the Lower Warbank villa, Keston, Kent (Philp 1976, 11) or not on the site at all, but in a family burial enclosure in one of the neighbouring towns.

Chapter VII
The site in the landscape

The site was first occupied in the Late Neolithic, roughly contemporarily with the appearance of the Lechlade cursus. The utilisation of the 2nd gravel terrace close to junctions between the river Thames and its tributaries for ceremonial monuments is a pattern evident at Stanton Harcourt, where the Devil's Quoits, radiocarbon dated to 4010 ± 120 BP (2863–2404 cal. BC), became a focus for later henge and burial monuments, and at Dorchester, where the cursus was constructed in the later Middle Neolithic (Case in Briggs *et al* 1986, 26–32). There is similarly little evidence for earlier occupation at Stanton Harcourt, although the presence of stone and flint axes in both areas shows that some clearance was carried out earlier than this. Recent excavations of tree-throw pits at Gravelly Guy, Stanton Harcourt have shown that tree-clearance was still being carried out during the Late Neolithic, so that the landscape in which the monuments lay was only partially cleared (Lambrick in prep). Similar features were encountered at Roughground Farm containing flints but none could be more closely dated. The predominance of pig in the Grooved Ware pits, an animal usually associated with woodland and which is very helpful in clearance, would also support this.

The construction of these monuments involved considerable labour and provided a focus for numerous groups, hence perhaps the appearance of settlement sites such as Roughground Farm and The Loders (Fig. 20). The superficially dissimilar character of these two settlements may simply reflect survival of different elements of both within the pits; alternatively it may be evidence for a model of Neolithic settlement in which a number of specialised (and often seasonal) camps are utilised by transhumant groups.

In the Beaker period monuments in the Upper Thames continue in use, and are surrounded by scattered evidence of settlement, as at Roughground Farm. The few widely distributed pits are seen by Timothy Darvill as chance survivals from settlements, and thus presumably reflect a greater number of these settlements. Their more widespread distribution may also reflect a more open landscape as clearance progressed. It is also noticeable that the Late Neolithic features occur along the line of the Iron Age and Romano-British trackway (Fig. 7), and could conceivably indicate the existence of a track alongside the river Leach at this early date. If so the settlements were not randomly scattered across the landscape as it might otherwise appear.

The Neolithic cursus continued to act as a focus for burial and other monuments in the Beaker and Bronze Age periods, as is evident from the possible small henge and the ring-ditches visible as cropmarks south and south-west of the site (Fig. 110). Only one small ring-ditch has been excavated, at Butler's Field (Miles & Palmer 1986, 4); this contained a central cremation. Early Bronze Age occupation is hardly represented at Roughground Farm, but clusters of pits of the Later Bronze Age seem to indicate small encampments in an open grassland landscape, probably of semi-nomadic pastoralists. This picture is repeated elsewhere in the Upper Thames Valley, contrasting with the settled mixed farms and field systems of the Middle and Lower Thames and sites such as Fengate (Pryor 1980). It has been suggested that the Upper Thames constituted something of a cultural backwater in this period (Barrett & Bradley 1980, 249–260), and certainly at this site exploitation of the gravels was unintensive and traditional.

The Early Iron Age however sees an intensification of land use and a shift to arable agriculture, evident in the division of the landscape into fields and in the appearance of storage pits. The ring-ditch at Butler's Field was deliberately infilled, probably when this reorganisation took place; at Vicarage Field, Stanton Harcourt, where linear pit-clusters and settlements show a similar organisation into fields in the Early Iron Age, barrow-ditches were slighted and ploughed over at this time (Case 1982b, 103–117).

From the limited excavation at Roughground Farm, Butler's Field and Hambridge Lane, Lechlade and the surrounding cropmark evidence it seems that the linear pit-clusters and tightly defined settlements which accompany land-division in the Stanton Harcourt area are not present here. Pits were excavated at the Loders Field (Darvill *et al* 1986) and at Butler's Field, and a possible roundhouse associated with two four-post structures adjacent to the Lechlade Cursus (SP 212/004) (J Moore in prep). Although excavation was small-scale, neither site seemed to have a tightly organised layout. Settlement within the ditched landscape seems to have been more spread out, perhaps indicating less pressure on land. This may also be reflected in the apparent greater mobility of settlement in the Iron Age in this area; the Early Iron Age settlements so far investigated do not continue into the Middle Iron Age.

Cropmarks of small circular and oval ditched enclosures characteristic of the Middle Iron Age occur north-west (SP 217/013) and west (SP 209/006) of the Roughground Farm site (RCHM(E), Glos., 1976, 74–5), and the expansion of settlement onto the low-lying 1st terrace at Claydon Pike suggests an increase in population and pressure on grazing similar to that elsewhere in the Upper Thames, notably in the Windrush valley.

The Late Iron Age and Early Roman period sees another shift in settlement in the Upper Thames Valley. Many long-lived Iron Age settlements such as Gravelly Guy, Stanton Harcourt, Oxon are abandoned and new settlements formed alongside, some are abandoned and then reoccupied at the end of the 1st century AD, for instance Watkins Farm, Northmoor, Oxon (Allen 1990, 78–81) and new settlements such as Barton Court Farm, Abingdon (Miles 1986, 4–8) and Linch Hill, Stanton Harcourt, Site 8 (Grimes 1943 44, 47–59) appear. Continuity from the Middle Iron Age into the Roman period is rarely demonstrable. This pattern seems also to be evident in the Lechlade area; the settlement at Claydon Pike shifts to a new gravel platform in the Late Iron Age (Miles and Palmer in prep), and new settlements appear at Thornhill Farm (S Palmer pers. comm.), Langford Downs (Williams 1947, 44ff) and at Roughground Farm itself.

Despite the new siting of the settlement the Early Roman occupation at Roughground farm appears to represent a gradual transition from traditional Iron Age house types, agricultural practices and technology to Roman methods (see Ch. VI.1). Only part of the settlement was excavated, and there are hints that more Romanised occupation may have existed alongside, but the survival into the Roman period of some aspects of Iron Age settlement is also attested on other sites.

The settlement lay adjacent to a 'green' at the junction of at least two droveways. As at Appleford (Hinchcliffe & Thomas 1980, 62–3) and elsewhere in the region the droveways were first defined by ditches in the 2nd century, possibly as part of the villa reorganisaton, but the evidence suggests that they were in existence long before this (see Ch. III.B.8). The definition of an Iron Age trackway or droveway by ditches in the Roman period is well illustrated at Farmoor, Oxon (Lambrick & Robinson 1979, 136). The presence of only one focus of settlement adjacent to this open area at Roughground Farm suggests that it served a single community, though one which probably comprised several farming units. This is possibly in contrast to Appleford, where there was no one focus, enclosures spreading along several sides (Hinchcliffe & Thomas 1980, 13 Fig. 3).

The square-ditched cremation burial is unusually strong evidence of a continental burial tradition which appears in the 1st century AD in the East of England. Four-post structures surrounded by ditches and with ritual associations at Smithsfield, Hardwick (Allen in preparation) and Appleford (Hinchcliffe & Thomas 1980, 44–5 and Fig. 25) may be other examples of this continental influence in the Upper Thames region. This 2nd century burial occurs at the end of this burial tradition, perhaps further evidence of the conservatism of the settlement at Roughground Farm. The fact that it is a single burial however rather than part of a cemetery as is usual in Gaul suggests that it was the preferred burial rite of one individual rather than one adopted by the whole community.

Excavations at Claydon Pike, Fairford, Glos., and Somerford Keynes, Glos., have demonstrated that Late Iron Age settlements on the low-lying first terrace were swept away in the late 1st century and replaced by officially-fostered centres incorporating large barns, religious foci of Imperial worship and limited domestic accommodation of military type (Miles 1984, 208–9; Miles and Palmer pers. comm.). Another such site is suggested by large numbers of early Roman coins, brooches and other metalwork recovered by M Maillard in surface collection at Leaze Farm south-east of Lechlade (Fig. 4; Miles 1984, 208). It is possible that the floodplain grazing on this part of the Upper Thames Valley was under imperial control towards the end of the 1st century AD. This did not occur at Roughground Farm itself, but may have inhibited the growth of the site. The decline of the officially-fostered settlement at Claydon Pike in the mid-2nd century appears to coincide with the emergence of prosperity shown by building the villa at Roughground Farm.

The appearance of rectilinear field systems and trackways is however matched elsewhere on the gravels, for instance at Northmoor, Oxon. (Allen 1990, 83), where many Early Roman sites go out of use at this time, and perhaps indicates large-scale reorganisation of the gravels at this time. This development may be part of a wider response to the introduction of a regular money supply and the development of a market economy, as suggested by Fulford (1989, 182–190).

The apparently rapid development of the villa may imply a change of ownership towards the middle of the 2nd century, but alternatively Romanisation may already have been proceeding before this, centred upon the area destroyed without record (Chapter VI.1). The villa was clearly fitted into the existing landscape, occupying almost exactly the same area as the preceding settlement, redefining the droveways and open area and with its field system oriented on the same alignment as the ditches of the former compounds. Topographical factors cannot be invoked to explain this; part of the open area due east of the villa was thickly dotted with clay patches, and may thus have been poorly-drained, partly explaining why it was not built upon, but no such constraints existed north or west of the villa.

It is possible that the villa might have exploited most or all of the 2nd and 1st gravel terrace around it, together with the floodplains of the rivers Leach and Thames, an area of 600–800 hectares. Apart from the natural boundaries suggested by the rivers and bands of poorly-drained Oxford Clay, there is another probable villa near to Great Lemhill Farm 1.7 km upstream (Fig. 4; RCHM(E) Glos. 1976, 75).

This was dug into in 1937; the results are not published, but there were stone buildings and apparently occupation of 2nd to 4th century date (information from F Innocent). Its relationship with the villa at Roughground Farm is unknown, but the level of Romanisation perhaps implies an independent establishment, which would make the edge of the 2nd terrace a likely boundary line between them.

South of the villa there are a number of Roman sites known from fieldwalking, chance discoveries and cropmarks (for details see Miles & Palmer in prep.). Most of these are not of a size or level of sophistication comparable with Roughground Farm, and were probably subsidiary to it; good dating evidence is lacking, but it is probable that some of these were only 1st to 2nd century, and were subsumed in the villa estate in the Later Roman period when groups of enclosures grew up around the 'green' next to the villa.

At Claydon Pike itself a modest farmhouse was built in the late 3rd century, and there was another stone building salvaged c 1 km to the east at Green Farm on the 1st terrace, apparently in use from the later 2nd to the later 4th century (Miles and Palmer in prep). The building at Green Farm may have been well-appointed, as the finds included fragments of box-flue and column tiles. The Romanised occupation here could indicate that the surrounding 1st terrace and the area of second terrace west of Roughground Farm and separated from it by a band of alluvium constituted a separate holding.

The Roughground Farm villa and its neighbours form a small group at some distance from the main cluster of Cotswold villas in Gloucestershire and Oxfordshire. Although locally trackways can be traced from aerial photographs for long distances along the valley bottom, there are no major Roman roads close by; Akeman Street lies over 5 km to the north and Ermin Street 10 km to the west. Nevertheless a string of villas has now been identified S of the Thames stretching along the Corallian Ridge from Bowling Green Farm at Stanford-in-the-Vale to Barton Court Farm at Abingdon (Chambers 1989, 54–5; Miles 1982). These sites can be interpreted as estate-centres controlling the gravel terraces along the rivers Thames and Ock, and Roughground Farm can be seen as a western continuation of these.

Water-transport and water power may have been important in the development of these sites; it may have been water-transport which in part stimulated the official settlements such as Claydon Pike, with its store-building down by the river and large numbers of imported amphorae (Miles 1984, 199–202). It is not certain that the river Thames was navigable as far up as this in the Roman period, but in the Late Saxon period river transport certainly went as far upstream as Bampton (J Blair pers. comm.), and David Miles has suggested (Miles pers. comm.) that the exceptionally rich grave-goods from the 7th century Butler's Field cemetery, which are of a type commonly associated with rich burials in Kent, imply good communications between the two areas, probably by river.

In analysing the distribution of late Oxford wares Hodder (1974, 340–59) noted a wide distribution west of Oxford which was apparently unrelated to the road system, but unfortunately did not consider the possibility of river transport. Thomson (in Ralegh Radford 1972, 90) suggests that a Roman settlement further upstream at Cricklade, where Ermin Street crosses the Thames, acted as a river-port for London-Cirencester trade, but his evidence is largely circumstantial, and alternatively David Miles has argued (pers. comm.) that possibly the extreme wealth of the Butler's Field cemetery indicates that this was the furthest upstream that was navigable, and hence the controlling point for offloading and further distribution, which might also help explain the presence of villas in the valley bottom at this point.

The buildings at Roughground Farm and Great Lemhill lie close to the river, and water may have been important both for crop-processing and for transport. Most of the stone used on the former site probably came from between 3 and 10 km to the north, and would most easily have been transported down the river Leach. In the Darent valley in Kent villas are strung out all along the river, and granaries and mill-stones demonstrate the importance of water for grinding and transporting grain. The low-lying areas adjacent to the Leach alongside the villa have not been investigated for similar evidence of water-powered mills or of crop-storage, though Miles has suggested (1984, 196) that the site at Great Lemhill might have been a mill rather than a villa.

An objection to the use of the river Thames as a busy trade route is the absence of highly Romanised settlements downriver on the N bank of the Thames until below Oxford. The absence of villas between Lechlade and Oxford has been attributed to a pre-existing dense and socially complex settlement pattern (Hingley 1984, 83–6) which was not affected by official reorganisation as was settlement further upstream. The lack of gradient of the lower reaches of the rivers Windrush and Evenlode may also have hindered the development of mills along their banks. On the south side of the river however the villas along the Corallian Ridge could have exploited the river for transport.

The layout of the villa and its adjoining enclosures and trackways, though sadly incomplete, nevertheless represents an unusually clear picture of the operation of a villa as farm, and Fig. 115 is a suggested interpretation of this in its fully developed (4th century) form. Excavations at Winterton (Goodburn 1978, 93–103) and recently at Stanwick, Northants (Neal 1989) have uncovered numerous buildings of an agricultural nature in the enclosures and fields around their villas, and more probably existed in the uninvestigated areas at Roughground Farm, perhaps spread over a radius of as much as 0.3 km from its centre.

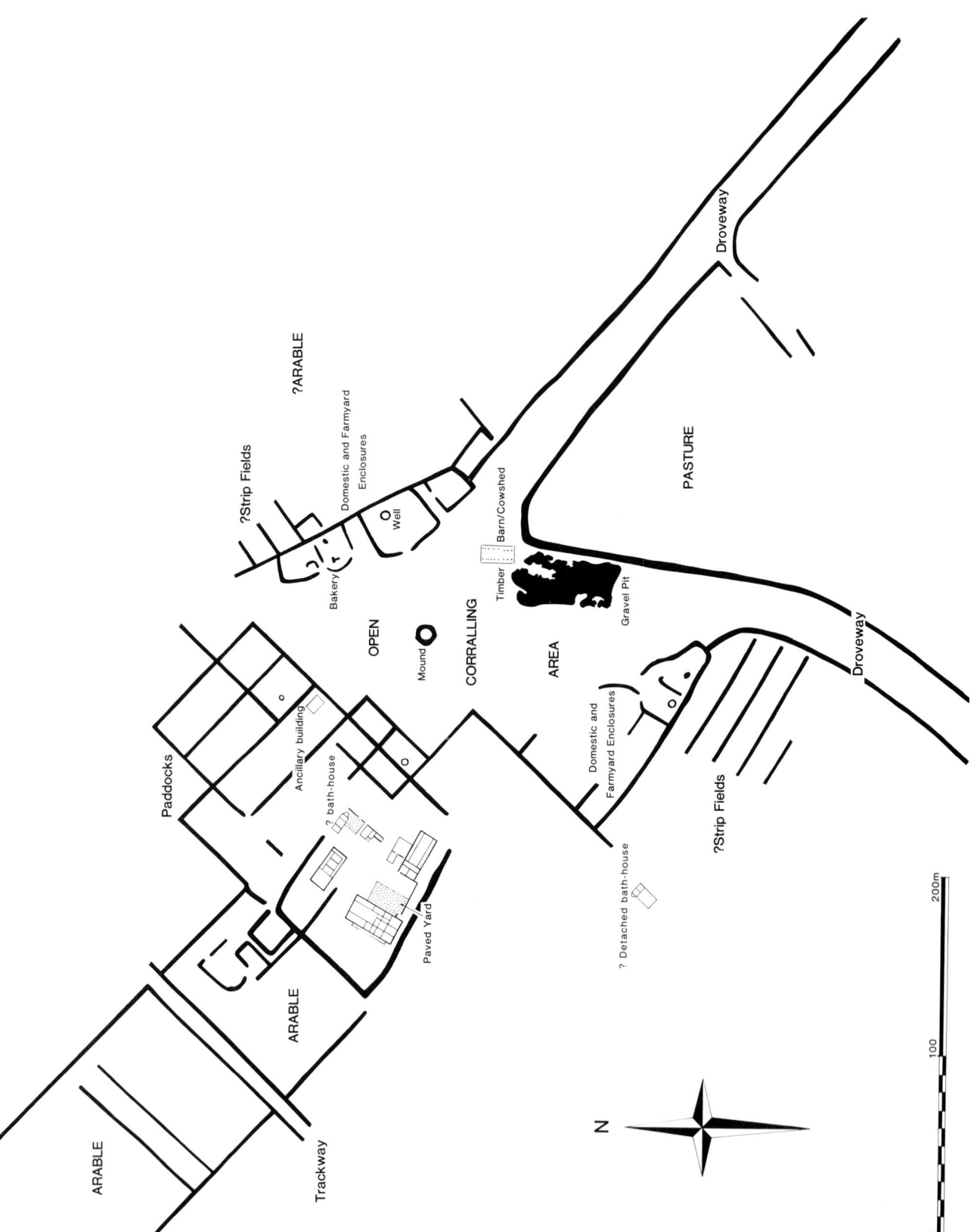

Figure 115 Interpretation of the organisation of the Late Roman villa

This was not however a planned development supplanting the pre-existing settlement. The basic elements, droveways and an open 'green' area with occupation enclosures on the north-west side, were already present in the early Roman period, and the subsequent development of the enclosure groups around the 'green' and of the gravel-pit area was gradual; the only major reorganisation undertaken all at once seems to have been the regular field system, and possibly a trackway from the south end of the 'green' north-west to the villa buildings (see Figs. 113 and 114; this is an alternative interpretation to that outlined on Fig. 74). The addition of strip-fields of standard width to the northern enclosure group in the 4th century should warn against assuming that all of the small paddocks of this width, which are only known from cropmarks, were necessarily laid out at once. Even the orientation of the field system would appear to be following that of the early Roman enclosures. The continuing use of the early Roman layout also implies, as might have been expected, that the agricultural economy was only refined, not substantially altered, with the arrival of the villa.

Although the growth of the northern and southern enclosure groups was gradual, and their origins were probably not contemporary (see Figs. 113 and 114), the periodic redefinition of a common back boundary for several enclosures in each group suggests some overall control of each enclosure group, not simply piecemeal squatting around the 'green'. The fact that the boundaries to individual enclosures, with one or two exceptions such as the 'bakery', shift back and forth, also perhaps implies common ownership of the whole, though the length of use of the enclosure groups could mean that these shifts only occurred every 15 years or so. The gradual enlargement of the enclosure groups and their encroachment upon the adjacent fields is likely to mean that ownership of both fields and enclosures was in the same hands, those of the villa owners, throughout.

The shifts in enclosure boundaries may have been in response to the villa's changing agricultural needs, but given the burials and other evidence that the enclosures were lived in, may instead reflect periodic redistribution of property between their inhabitants, possibly in accordance with the Celtic inheritance system called *tyr gwely* (Percival 1976, 139–144). However the limited skeletal evidence gives little sign of kinship groups among the inhabitants. Only an extensive survey of settlements round about will establish whether a deliberate policy of drawing in the surrounding population was practised, but the piecemeal development of the enclosures strongly suggests that the settlement process was gradual. The settlements for which there is evidence from fieldwalking or excavation, such as Leaze Farm and Claydon Pike on the first terrace, were occupied throughout the Roman period, or like Thornhill Farm were abandoned in the Early Roman period (S. Palmer pers. comm.).

The date of the end of the villa is difficult to interpret, as the latest deposits in the villa buildings had been ploughed away. The coin list includes only one issue of the house of Valentinian, coins which are relatively common on villa sites such as Claydon Pike nearby, and only one later coin, which may have been lost during robbing (see also Ravetz 1964, 28). Only 47 Roman coins were recovered from Roughground Farm, however, and the absence of late coins may simply be due to chance. Alternatively it may imply a substantial decline after 370 or thereabouts, as was suggested at some of the villas in the valley of the Bristol Avon (Branigan 1977, 96–104). The fact that there were no later coins from the enclosures on the 'green', as well as from the villa itself, perhaps suggests that the organisation that supported a money economy ceased at this time.

The postholes cut into the floor of Building IV may imply some continued use of the site, although the burials within the villa area and the scatter of silt-filled hollows across the former 'green' show that the previous organisation of the villa had largely broken down. These silt-filled hollows crammed with very late Roman pottery are very reminiscent of some of the earliest Grubenhause at Radley, Barrow Hills (Chambers in prep.), and a few objects of Anglo-Saxon type may indicate that the site remained inhabited after the arrival of the Anglo-Saxons, whose settlement is visible from cropmarks one kilometre to the south. This community was certainly established by 500 AD, but since the earliest area of the cemetery was only partly investigated it may have begun in the 5th century, as the neighbouring cemetery at Fairford did (D Miles pers. comm.). The presence of Roman stonework in relatively fresh condition in 6th century graves would suggest that villa buildings were still standing, if only as ruins, at this time.

Bibliography

Agache, R 1978. *La Somme Pré-Romaine et Romaine d'après les prospections aériennes à basse altitude.* Société des Antiquaires de Picardie, Amiens.

Allen, TG 1981. 'Hardwick with Yelford: Smith's Field', *Council for British Archaeology Group 9 Newsletter*, 11: 28–31.

Allen, TG 1988. 'Excavations at Bury Close, Fawler, Oxon.', *Oxoniensia*, 53: 293–315.

Allen, TG 1989. 'Archaeological discoveries on the Banbury East-West link road', *Oxoniensia*, 54: 25–44.

Allen, TG 1990. *An Iron Age and Romano-British Enclosed Settlement at Watkins Farm, Northmoor, Oxon*, Thames Valley Landscapes: the Windrush Valley 1. Oxford University Committee for Archaeology, Oxford.

Allen, TG, D Miles, & SL Palmer 1984. 'Iron Age buildings in the Upper Thames region', in Cunliffe, B & Miles, D (eds), *Aspects of the Iron Age in Central Southern Britain*, Monograph 2, pp. 89–101. Oxford University Committee for Archaeology, Oxford.

Allen, TG & J Moore 1987. 'Standlake: Eagle Farm', *South Midlands Archaeology*, 17: 96–7.

Allen, TG & M Robinson forthcoming. *The Prehistoric Landscape and Iron Age Enclosed Settlement at Mingies Ditch, Hardwick-with-Yelford, Oxon.*, Thames Valley Landscapes: the Windrush Valley 2. Oxford University Committee for Archaeology, Oxford.

Anderson, AS 1979. *The Roman Pottery Industry in North Wiltshire.* Report 2. Swindon Archaeological Society.

Anderson, AS 1980. *A Guide to Roman Fine Wares.* Research Series 1. Vorda, Highworth.

Anthony, IE 1958. *The Iron Age Camp at Poston, Herefordshire.* The Woolhope Club, Hereford.

Arkell, WJ 1947. *The Geology of Oxford.*

Atkinson, RJC 1941. 'A Romano-British Potters' Field at Cowley, Oxon.', *Oxoniensia*, 6: 9–21.

Atkinson, RJC 1949. 'A henge monument at Westwell, near Burford, Oxon.', *Oxoniensia*, 14: 84–7.

Atkinson, RJC, CM Piggott, & NK Sandars 1951. *Excavations at Dorchester, Oxon.* Ashmolean Museum, Oxford.

Baker, J & D Brothwell 1980. *Animal Diseases in Archaeology.* Academic Press, London.

Barrett, J 1976. 'Deverel-Rimbury: problems of chronology and interpretation', in Burgess, C & Miket, R (eds), *Settlement and economy in the third and second millenia B.C.*, British series 33, pp. 289–307. British Archaeological Reports.

Barrett, J 1980. 'The Pottery of the Later Bronze Age in Lowland Britain', *Proceedings Prehistoric Society*, 46: 297–321.

Barrett, J & R Bradley 1980. 'The Later Bronze Age in the Thames Valley', in Barrett, J & Bradley, R (eds), *The British Later Bronze Age*, British Series 83, pp. 247–269. British Archaeological Reports, Oxford.

Barrett, J, R Bradley, M Green, & B Lewis 1981. 'The Earlier Prehistoric Settlement of Cranborne Chase—The First Results of Current Fieldwork', *Antiquaries Journal*, 61: 203–227.

Bayley, J 1989. 'Metal Analyses: A. Brooches from the Iron Age cemetery', in Stead, IM & Rigby, V (eds), *Verulamium: the King Harry Lane site*, English Heritage Archaeological Report 12. London.

Bayley, J & S Butcher 1981. 'Variations in alloy composition of Roman brooches', *Revue d'Archéométrie*, Supplement: 29–36.

Benson, D & D Miles 1974. *The upper Thames Valley: An archaeological survey of the river gravels.* Survey 2. Oxford Archaeological Unit.

Boon, GC 1974. *Silchester: the Roman town of Calleva.* David and Charles, Newton Abbot.

Booth, PM & S Green 1989. 'The nature and distribution of certain pink, grog tempered vessels', *Journal of Roman Pottery Studies*, 2: 77–84.

Borrill, D 1981. 'Casket burials', in Partridge, C (ed), *Skeleton Green: A Late Iron Age and Romano-British site*, Britannia Monograph 2. Society for the Promotion of Roman Studies, London.

Bourdillon, J & J Coy 1980. 'The Animal Bones', in Holdsworth, P (ed), *Excavations at Melbourne Street, Southampton 1971–76*, Research Reports 33, pp. 79–121. Council for British Archaeology.

Bowen, HC & PJ Fowler 1978. *Early Land Allotment: A survey of recent work.* British Series 48. British Archaeological Reports, Oxford.

Boyle, A, D Miles, & S Palmer forthcoming. *The Anglo-Saxon cemetery at Butler's Field, Lechlade, Gloucestershire.* Thames Valley Landscapes: the Cotswold Water Park 2. Oxford University Committee for Archaeology, Oxford.

Bradford, JSP & RG Goodchild 1939. 'Excavations at Frilford, Berks, 1937–8', *Oxoniensia*, 4: 1–70.

Bradley, R 1986. 'The Bronze Age in the Oxford area — its local and regional significance', in Briggs, G, Cook, J, & Rowley, T (eds), *The archaeology of the Oxford region*, pp. 38–48. Oxford University Department of External Studies, Oxford.

Bradley, R, R Holgate, & S Ford 1984. 'The Neolithic sequence in the upper Thames Valley', in Bradley, R

& Gardiner, J (eds), *Neolithic studies—A review of some current research*, British Series 133, pp. 107–134. British Archaeological Reports, Oxford.

Bradley, R, S Lobb, J Richards, & M Robinson 1980. 'Two Late Bronze Age Settlements on the Kennet Gravels: Excavation at Aldermaston Wharf and Knight's Farm, Burghfield, Berkshire', *Proceedings Prehistoric Society*, 46: 217–296.

Branigan, K 1971. *Latimer: Belgic, Roman, Dark Age and Early Modern Farm*. Chess Valley Archaeological & Hist. Society.

Branigan, K 1977. *The Roman Villa in south-west England*. Moonraker Press, Bradford-on-Avon.

Briggs, G, J Cook, & T Rowley (eds) 1986. *The archaeology of the Oxford region*. Oxford University Department of External Studies, Oxford.

Brisson, A & J Hatt 1955. 'Cimetières gaulois et gallo-romains à enclos en Champagne', *Revue Archéologique de L'Est et du Centre-Est*, 6: 313–333.

Britnell, W 1982. 'The excavation of two round barrows at Trelystan, Powys', *Proceedings Prehistoric Society*, 48: 133–202.

Brodribb, ACC, AR Hands, & DR Walker 1968. *Excavations at Shakenoak Farm, near Wilcote, Oxfordshire. Part 1: Sites A and D*. Omega Press, Oxford.

Brodribb, ACC, AR Hands, & DR Walker 1971. *Excavations at Shakenoak Farm, near Wilcote, Oxfordshire. Part 2: Sites B and H*. Omega Press, Oxford.

Brodribb, ACC, AR Hands, & DR Walker 1972. *Excavations at Shakenoak Farm, near Wilcote, Oxfordshire. Part 3: Site F*. Omega Press, Oxford.

Brodribb, ACC, AR Hands, & DR Walker 1973. *Excavations at Shakenoak Farm, near Wilcote, Oxfordshire. Part 4: Site C*. Omega Press, Oxford.

Brodribb, ACC, AR Hands, & DR Walker 1978. *Excavations at Shakenoak Farm, near Wilcote, Oxfordshire. Part 5: Sites K and E*. Omega Press, Oxford.

Brothwell, DR 1981. *Digging Up Bones*. British Museum (Natural History), London.

Bushe-Fox, J 1913. *Excavations on the Roman town at Wroxeter, Shropshire in 1912*. Research Reports 1. Society Antiquaries, London.

Bushe-Fox, JP 1949. *Fourth Report on the Excavations of the Roman Fort at Richborough, Kent*. Research Reports 16. Society of Antiquaries, London.

Butler, JJ & JD Van der Waals 1966. 'Bell beakers and early metalworking in the Netherlands', *Palaeohistoria*, 12: 41–140.

Case, HJ 1956. 'Beaker pottery from the Oxford region 1939–1955', *Oxoniensia*, 21: 1–21.

Case, HJ 1963. 'Notes on some finds and on ring-ditches in Oxford region', *Oxoniensia*, 28: 19–52.

Case, HJ 1977. 'The beaker culture in Britain and Ireland', in Mercer, RJ (ed), *Beakers in Britain and Europe*, Supplementary Series 26, pp. 71–101. British Archaeological Reports, Oxford.

Case, HJ 1982a. 'Cassington 1950–2: Late Neolithic pits and the Big enclosure', in Case, HJ & Whittle, AWR (eds), *Settlement patterns in the Oxford region: Excavations at the Abingdon Causewayed enclosure and other sites*, Research Reports 44, pp. 118–151. Council for British Archaeology, London.

Case, HJ 1982b. "Pottery from the Central Pit' *in* Linnington, R. E. J. Four Ring Ditches at Stanton Harcourt', in Case, H & Whittle, A (eds), *Settlement Patterns in the Oxford Region: Excavation at the Abingdon Causewayed Enclosure and Other Sites*, Research Reports 44, pp. 81–7. Council for British Archaeology, London.

Case, HJ 1982c. 'The Vicarage Field, Stanton Harcourt', in Case, HJ & Whittle, AWR (eds), *Settlement patterns in the Oxford region: Excavations at the Abingdon Causewayed enclosure and other sites*, Research Reports 44, pp. 103–117. Council for British Archaeology, London.

Case, HJ 1986. 'The mesolithic and neolithic in the Oxford region', in Briggs, G, Cook, J, & Rowley, T (eds), *The archaeology of the Oxford region*, pp. 18–37. Department for External Studies, Oxford.

Case, HJ, N Bayne, S Steele, G Avery, & H Sutermeister 1964. 'Excavations at City Farm, Hanborough, Oxon', *Oxoniensia*, 29/30: 1–98.

Case, HJ & A Whittle (eds) 1982. *Settlement Patterns in the Oxford region: Excavations at the Abingdon causewayed enclosure and other sites*. Research Reports 44. Council for British Archaeology, London.

Chambers, RA 1982. 'Dorchester By-Pass', *Council for British Archaeology Group 9 Newsletter*, 12: 143–147.

Chambers, RA 1987. 'The Late- and Sub-Roman cemetery at Queenford Farm, Dorchester-on-Thames, Oxon', *Oxoniensia*, 52: 35–69.

Chambers, RA 1989. 'Stanford-in-the-Vale, Bowling Green Farm', *Council for British Archaeology Group 9 Newsletter*, 19: 54–55.

Chapelot, J & R Fossier 1985. *The Village and House in the Middle Ages*. Batsford, London.

Clapham, A, T Tutin, & D Moore 1989. *Flora of the British Isles*. Cambridge University Press, Cambridge, 3rd edition.

Clark, JGD 1934. 'Derivative forms of the petit tranchet in Britain', *Archaeological Journal*, 91: 32–58.

Clarke, DL 1970. *Beaker pottery of Great Britain and Ireland*. Cambridge University Press, Cambridge. 2 vols.

Clarke, DL 1976. 'The beaker network–social and economic models', in Lanting, JN & Van der Waals, JD (eds), *Glockenbechersymposion Oberried 1974*, pp. 459–477. Fibula-Van Dishoek, Bussem/Haarlem.

Clarke, G 1979. *The Roman Cemetery at Lankhills*.

Clarendon Press, Oxford.

Clifford, EM 1937. 'The beaker folk of the Cotswolds', *Proceedings of the Prehistoric Society*, 3: 159–165.

Clifford, EM 1955. 'The stamped tiles found in Gloucestershire', *Journal of Roman Studies*, 45: 68–72.

Clifford, EM 1961. *Bagendon: A Belgic Oppidum*. Heffer, Cambridge.

Courtois, L & B Velde 1978. 'Une amphore à grenat jaune du Latium à Amathonte', *Bull. Corresp. Hell.*, 103: 977–981.

Crummy, N 1983. *Roman Small Finds from Excavations in Colchester*. Monograph 2. Colchester Archaeological Society.

Cunliffe, BW 1968. *Fifth Report on the excavations of the Roman Fort at Richborough, Kent*. Research Reports 23. Society of Antiquaries, London.

Cunliffe, BW 1984. *Danebury, an iron age hillfort in Hampshire; the excavations 1969–1978*. Council for British Archaeology Research Reports 52, London.

Cunliffe, BW (ed) 1988. *The Temple of Sul Minerva at Bath, II: the Finds from the Sacred Spring*. Monograph 16. Oxford University Committee for Archaeology, Oxford.

Curle, J 1911. *A Roman frontier post and its people: the fort at Newstead in the parish of Melrose*.

Darvill, TC 1983. *The Neolithic of Wales and the midwest of England: A systemic analysis of social change through the application of action theory*. PhD thesis, University of Southampton.

Darvill, TC 1984. 'Neolithic Gloucestershire', in Saville, A (ed), *Archaeology in Gloucestershire*, pp. 80–112. Cheltenham Museum & Bristol & Glos. Archaeological Society, Cheltenham.

Darvill, TC, RC Hingley, MU Jones, & JR Timby 1986. 'A Neolithic and Iron Age site at The Loders, Lechlade, Gloucestershire', *Transactions of the Bristol & Gloucestershire Archaeological Society*, 104: 23–44.

Davey, N 1961. *A History of Building Materials*. Phoenix House, London.

Davey, N & R Ling 1982. *Wall-painting in Roman Britain*. Britannia Monograph Series 3. Society for the Promotion of Roman Studies.

De Nahlik, AJ 1959. *Wild Deer*. Faber & Faber, London.

De Roche, D 1978. 'The Iron Age Pottery', in Parrington, M (ed), *The excavation of an Iron Age Settlement, Bronze Age ring-ditches and Roman features at Ashville Trading Estate, Abingdon (Oxfordshire), 1974–76*, Research Reports 28, pp. 40–74. Council for British Archaeology, London.

Down, A 1978. *Chichester Excavations Vol. III*. Chichester.

Driesch, A 1976. *A Guide to the Measurement of Animal Bones from Archaeological Sites*. Harvard.

Driesch, A & J Boessneck 1974. 'Kritische Anmerkungen zur Widerristhohenberechnung aus Langenmassen vor- und fruh-geschichtlichen Tierknocken', *Saugetierkundliche Mitteilungen*, 22 (4): 325–48.

Dunning, G 1976. 'Salmondsbury, Bourton-on-the-Water, Gloucestershire', in Harding, DW (ed), *Hillforts—Later Prehistoric Earthworks in Britain and Ireland*, pp. 75–118. Academic Press, London.

Egan, G & F Pritchard 1991. *Dress Accessories c. 1150–c. 1450*, Medieval finds from excavations in London 3. H.M.S.O., London.

Evans, J 1897. *The ancient stone implements, weapons and ornaments of Great Britain*. Longmans Green and Co., London. 2nd Edition.

Fasham, PJ & JM Ross 1978. 'A Bronze Age flint industry from a barrow site in Micheldever Wood, Hampshire', *Proceedings of the Prehistoric Society*, 44: 47–67.

Ferembach, D, I Schwidetsky, & M Stloukal 1980. 'Recommendations for Age and Sex Diagnosis of Skeletons', *Journal of Human Evolution*, 9: 517–549.

Fowler, PJ (ed) 1975. *Recent Work in Rural Archaeology*. Moonraker Press, Bradford-on Avon.

Frere, SS 1976. *Britannia*. Routledge and Kegan Paul, London. 2nd Edition.

Frere, SS 1984. *Verulamium Excavations, III*. Monograph 1. Oxford University Committee for Archaeology, Oxford.

Frere, SS 1991. 'Roman Britain in 1990', *Britannia*, 22: 221—292.

Frere, SS & JKS St. Joseph 1983. *Roman Britain from the Air*. Cambridge Air Surveys, Cambridge.

Fulford, M 1975. *New Forest Roman Pottery: Manufacture and Distribution, with a Corpus of the Pottery Types*. British Series 17. British Archaeological Reports, Oxford.

Fulford, M 1989. 'The Economy of Roman Britain', in Todd, M (ed), *Research on Roman Britain 1960–1989*, Britannia Monograph 11, pp. 175–201. Society for the promotion of Roman Studies, London.

Gent, H 1983. 'Centralised Storage in Later Prehistoric Britain', *Proceedings of the Prehistoric Society*, 49: 243–267.

Gibson, AM 1982. *Beaker domestic sites: A study of the domestic pottery of the late third and early second millennium BC in the British Isles*. British Series 107. British Archaeological Reports, Oxford.

Gillam, J 1976. 'Coarse fumed ware in northern Britain', *Glasgow Archaeological Journal*, 4: 57–80.

Gingell, C 1980. 'The Marlborough Downs in the Bronze Age: The Results of Current Research', in Barrett, J & Bradley, R (eds), *The British Later Bronze Age*, British Series 83, pp. 209–222. British Archaeological Reports, Oxford.

Goodburn, R 1978. 'Winterton: some villa problems', in Todd, M (ed), *Studies in the Romano-British villa*, pp. 93–101. Leicester University Press, Leicester.

Grant, A 1975. 'The Animal Bones', in Cunliffe, BW (ed), *Excavations at Portchester Castle, I*, Research Reports 33, pp. 262–287. Society of Antiquaries, London.

Grant, A 1983. 'The use of toothwear as a guide to the age of domestic ungulates', in Wilson, B, Grigson, C, & Payne, S (eds), *Ageing and sexing animal bones from archaeological sites*, British Series 109, pp. 91–108. British Archaeological Reports, Oxford.

Green, HS 1980. *The flint arrowheads of the British Isles*, British Series 75. British Archaeological Reports, Oxford.

Greene, K 1978. 'Imported Fine Wares in Britain to A. D. 250: a Guide to Identification', in Arthur, P & Marsh, G (eds), *Early Fine Wares in Roman Britain*, British Series 57, pp. 15–30. British Archaeological Reports, Oxford.

Grigson, C 1982. 'Porridge and Pannage: pig husbandry in Neolithic England', in Bell, M & Limbrey, S (eds), *Archaeological Aspects of the Woodland Economy*, International Series 146, pp. 297–314. British Archaeological Reports, Oxford.

Grimes, WF 1943–44. 'Excavations at Stanton Harcourt, Oxon, 1940', *Oxoniensia*, 8 & 9: 19–63.

Guido, M 1978. *The Glass Beads of the Prehistoric and Roman Periods in Britain and Ireland*. Research Reports 35. Society of Antiquaries, London.

Hadman, J 1978. 'Aisled buildings in Roman Britain', in Todd, M (ed), *Studies in the Romano-British villa*, pp. 187–195. Leicester University Press, Leicester.

Halpin, C 1983. 'Abingdon: Ex-MG Car Factory Site', *Council for British Archaeology Group 9, Newsletter*, 13: 113–114.

Harding, DW 1972. *The Iron Age in the Upper Thames Basin*. Clarendon Press, Oxford.

Harman, M, TI Molleson, & JL Price 1981. 'Burials, Bodies and Beheadings in Romano-British and Anglo-Saxon Cemeteries', *Bulletin of the British Museum, Natural History*, 35 (3): 145–188.

Hartley, B 1972. *Notes on the Roman pottery industry in the Nene Valley*. Occasional Papers 2. Peterborough Museum Society.

Hattatt, R 1985. *Iron Age and Roman brooches*. Oxbow Books, Oxford.

Hattatt, R 1987. *Brooches of Antiquity*. Oxbow Books, Oxford.

Hawkes, C & M Hull 1947. *Camulodunum*. Research Reports 14. Society of Antiquaries, London.

Healey, E 1982. 'The flintwork', *in* Britnell 1982, pp. 133–202.

Hedges, JW & G Wait 1987. 'Cooper's Crozes', *Antiquity*, 61 No. 232: 257–259.

Hinchcliffe, J & R Thomas 1980. 'Archaeological Investigations at Appleford', *Oxoniensia*, 45: 9–111.

Hingley, R 1984. 'Towards Social Analysis in Archaeology: Celtic Society of the Upper Thames Valley (400–0BC)', in Cunliffe, B & Miles, D (eds), *Aspects of the Iron Age in Central Southern Britain*, pp. 72–88. Oxford University Committee for Archaeology.

Hodder, I 1974. 'Some marketing models for Romano-British coarse Pottery', *Britannia*, 5: 340–359.

Hoffman, M 1964. *The Warp-weighted Loom: studies in the history and technology of an ancient implement*. Studia Norvegica 14. Oslo.

Holgate, R 1984. 'Neolithic settlement in the Upper Thames Valley', *Current Archaeology*, 8: 374–6.

Howe, MD, JR Perrin, & D Mackreth 1980. *Roman Pottery from the Nene Valley: a guide*. Occasional Paper 2. Peterborough City Museum, Peterborough.

Isings, C 1957. *Roman Glass from Dated Finds*. Groningen. Djakarta, 1977.

Jackson, DA & TM Ambrose 1978. 'Excavations at Wakerley, Northants 1972–75', *Britannia*, 9: 115–242.

Jasny, N 1946. *The wheats of Classical Antiquity*. John Hopkins University Studies 62. John Hopkins University, Baltimore.

Johnston, DE 1978. 'Villas of Hampshire and the Isle of Wight', in Todd, M (ed), *Studies in the Romano-British Villa*. Leicester University Press, Leicester.

Johnston, DE 1979. *Roman Villas*. Shire Publications Ltd, Princes Risborough.

Jones, GG 1986a. "The Animal Bones' *in* D. Allen, Excavations in Bierton, 1979: late Iron Age Settlement and Evidence for a Roman Villa and a 12th-18th century Manorial Complex', *Records of Buckinghamshire*, 28: 32–39 and 74–5.

Jones, M 1986b. 'The species lists', in Miles, D (ed), *Archaeology at Barton Court Farm, Abingdon, Oxon.*, Research Reports 50, pp. Fiche F1–F4:E14. Council for British Archaeology, London.

Jones, M & G Dimbleby 1981. *The Environment of Man: the Iron Age to the Anglo-Saxon period*. British Series 87. British Archaeological Reports, Oxford.

Jones, MU 1976. 'Neolithic pottery found at Lechlade, Glos.', *Oxoniensia*, 41: 1–5.

Keevill, G 1990. 'Redlands Farm, Stanwick — The first yuppie barn conversion', *Oxford Archaeological Unit Newsletter*, 18.3: 1–7.

Kenyon, K 1953. 'Excavations at Sutton Walls, Herefordshire 1948–51', *Archaeological Journal*, 110: 1–87.

King, A 1978. *A Comparative Survey of Bone Assemblages from Roman sites in Britain*. Bulletin 15. Institute of Archaeology.

King, AC & TW Potter 1990. 'A new domestic building facade from Roman Britain', *Journal of Roman Archaeology*, 3: 195–204.

Lambrick, GH 1979. 'Berinsfield, Mount Farm', *Council for British Archaeology Group 9, Newsletter*, 9: 113–115.

Lambrick, GH 1983. 'Stanton Harcourt: Blackditch By-pass', *Council for British Archaeology Group 9, Newsletter*, 13: 144–5.

Lambrick, GH 1984. 'Pitfalls and Possibilities in Iron Age Pottery Studies—Experience in the Upper Thames Valley', in Cunliffe, BW & Miles, D (eds), *Aspects of the Iron Age in Central Southern Britain*, pp. 162–177. Oxford.

Lambrick, GH 1985. 'Stanton Harcourt, Gravelly Guy', *South Midlands Archaeology, Council for British Archaeology Group 9*, 15: 107–111.

Lambrick, GH 1986. 'Stanton Harcourt, Gravelly Guy', *South Midlands Archaeology, Council for British Archaeology Group 9*, 16.

Lambrick, GH 1988. *The Rollright Stones: megaliths, monuments, and settlement in the prehistoric landscape*. English Heritage Archaeological Reports 6. Historic Buildings and Monuments Commission for England.

Lambrick, GH & M Robinson 1979. *Iron Age and Roman Riverside Settlement at Farmoor, Oxfordshire*. Research Reports 32. Council for British Archaeology.

Lanting, JN & J Van der Waals 1971. 'British beakers as seen from the Continent', *Helinium*, pp. 20–46.

Leach, P 1982. *Ilchester Vol. I. Excavations 1974–5*. Monograph Series 3. Western Archaeological Trust.

Leech, R 1977. *An archaeological survey of the river gravels: The upper Thames Valley in Gloucestershire and Wiltshire*. Survey 4. Comm. for Rescue Archaeological Avon, Glos. and Somerset, Bristol.

Leeds, ET 1934. 'Recent Bronze Age discoveries in Berkshire and Oxfordshire', *Antiquaries Journal*, 14: 264–276.

Legge, AJ 1981. 'The Agricultural Economy', in Mercer, RJ (ed), *Grimes Graves, Norfolk, Excavations 1971–72: Vol. I*, Archaeological Reports 11. Dept. of Environment.

Linington, RE 1982. 'Four ring-ditches at Stanton Harcourt', in Case, HJ & Whittle, A (eds), *Settlement Patterns in the Oxford region: Excavations at the Abingdon causewayed enclosure and other sites*, Research Reports 44, pp. 81–7. Council for British Archaeology, London.

Liversidge, JEA 1968. *Britain in the Roman Empire*. Routledge, London.

Longworth, I, GJ Wainwright, & KE Wilson 1971. 'The Grooved Ware site at Lion Point, Clacton', in Sieveking, GDG (ed), *Prehistoric and Roman Studies*, pp. 93–124. British Museum, London.

Mackreth, D 1981. 'The Brooches', in Partridge, C (ed), *Skeleton Green: A Late Iron Age and Romano-British site*, Britannia Monograph 2. Society for the Promotion of Roman Studies, London.

Maltby, JM 1979. *Faunal Studies on Urban Sites: The Animal Bones from Exeter 1971–1975*. Sheffield University Department of Prehistory & Archaeology.

Maltby, JM 1981. 'Iron Age, Romano-British and Anglo-Saxon husbandry—A Review of the Faunal Evidence', in Jones, M & Dimbleby, G (eds), *The Environment of Man: The Iron Age to Anglo-Saxon period*, British Series 87, pp. 155–203. British Archaeological Reports, Oxford.

Manning, WH 1974. 'The Ironwork', in Neal, DS (ed), *The Roman Villa at Gadebridge Park, Hemel Hempstead*.

Manning, WH 1976. *Catalogue of Romano-British Ironwork in the Museum of Antiquities, Newcastle-upon-Tyne*. Department of Archaeology, University of Newcastle upon Tyne.

McWhirr, A 1981. *Roman Gloucestershire*. Gloucester.

Miles, AEW 1962. 'Assessment of the Ages of a Population of Anglo-Saxons from their Dentitions', *Proceedings Royal Society Medicine*, 55: 881–886.

Miles, D 1982. *The Romano-British Countryside: Studies in Rural Settlement and Economy*. British Series 103. British Archaeological Reports, Oxford.

Miles, D 1984. 'Romano-British settlement in the Gloucestershire Thames Valley', in Saville, A (ed), *Archaeology in Gloucestershire*, pp. 191–211. Cheltenham and Art Gallery and Museums, and the Bristol and Gloucestershire Archaeological Society, Cheltenham.

Miles, D 1986. *Archaeology at Barton Court Farm, Abingdon, Oxon*. Research Reports 50. Council for British Archaeology.

Miles, D & S Palmer 1983. 'Fairford/Lechlade: Claydon Pike', *Council for British Archaeology Group 9, Newsletter*, 13: 111–112.

Miles, D & S Palmer 1984. 'Fairford/Lechlade: Claydon Pike', *Council for British Archaeology Group 9, Newsletter*, 14: 93–98.

Miles, D & S Palmer 1986. *Invested in Mother Earth*. Oxford. not dated.

Millett, M 1979a. 'An approach to the functional interpretation of pottery', in Millett, M (ed), *Pottery and the Archaeologist*, pp. 35–48. Institute of Archaeology, London.

Millett, M (ed) 1979b. *Pottery and the Archaeologist*. Institute of Archaeology, London.

Moore, J 1985. 'Lechlade: Hambridge Lane', *Oxford Archaeological Unit Newsletter*, 12 (3): 2.

Moore, J & D Jennings forthcoming. *Reading Business Park: a Bronze Age landscape*. Thames Valley Landscapes: the Kennet Valley 1. Oxford University Committee for Archaeology, Oxford.

Moritz, LA 1958. *Grain Mills and Flour in Classical Antiquity*. Oxford University Press, Oxford.

Morris, P 1979. *Agricultural Buildings in Roman Britain*. British Series 70. British Archaeological Reports, Oxford.

Neal, DS 1974. *The Roman Villa at Gadebridge Park, Hemel Hempstead*. Society of Antiquaries, London.

Neal, DS 1978. 'The growth and decline of villas in the Verulamium area', in Todd, M (ed), *Studies in the Romano-British villa*, pp. 33–58. Leicester University Press, Leicester.

Neal, DS 1983. 'Gorhambury', *Current Archaeology*, 87: 115–121.

Neal, DS 1989. 'The Stanwick Villa, Northants: an interim report on the excavations of 1984–88', *Britannia*, 20: 149–168.

Neal, DS, A Wardle, & J Hunn 1990. *Excavations of the Iron Age, Roman and medieval settlement at Gorhambury, St. Albans*. English Heritage Archaeological Report 14. Historic Buildings and Monuments Commission for England, London.

Noddle, BA 1973. "Animal bones from two wells in Tripontium' *in* Cameron, H. and Lucas, J., Tripontium: second interim report', *Transactions and Proceedings of the Birmingham and Warwickshire Archaeological Society*, 85: 136–142.

Noddle, BA 1979. "The Animal Bones' *in* Gracie, H. S. and Price, E. G. Frocester Court Roman Villa', *Transactions of the Bristol and Glos. Archaeological Society*, 97: 51–60.

O'Kelly, MJ, RM Cleary, & D Lehane 1983. *Newgrange, Co. Meath, Ireland: The late neolithic/beaker period settlement*. Supplementary Series 190. British Archaeological Reports, Oxford.

O'Neil, HE 1947. 'The Roman Villa at Park Street, near St. Albans, Hertfordshire: Report on the Excavations of 1943–45', *Archaeological Journal*, 102: 21–110.

Oswald, F 1931. *Index of potter's stamps*. East Bridgeford.

Oswald, F 1936–7. *Index of figure-types on terra sigillata*. Annals of Archaeology and Anthropology, supplement volume, Liverpool.

Oswald, F & T Pryce 1920. *An Introduction to the Study of Terra Sigillata*.

Page, W (ed) 1920. *A History of the County of Hereford*. The Victoria County History of the Counties of England.

Palmer, R 1976. 'Interrupted ditch enclosures in Britain: the use of aerial photography for comparative analysis', *Proceedings of the Prehistoric Society*, 42: 161–186.

Palmer, S 1988a. 'Somerford Keynes, Neigh Bridge', *Oxford Archaeological Unit Newsletter*, 16.2.

Palmer, S 1988b. 'Somerford Keynes, Neigh Bridge', *Oxford Archaeological Unit Newsletter*, 16.2.

Parrington, M 1978. *The Excavation of an Iron Age settlement, Bronze Age ring-ditches and Roman features at Ashville Trading Estate, Abingdon (Oxfordshire) 1974–76*. Research Reports 28. Council for British Archaeology, London.

Partridge, C 1981. *Skeleton Green: A Late Iron Age and Romano-British site*, Britannia Monograph 2. Society for the Promotion of Roman Studies, London.

Peacock, D 1977a. 'Ceramics in Roman and medieval archaeology', in Peacock, D (ed), *Pottery and Early Commerce: characterisation and Trade in Roman and Later Ceramics*, pp. 21–34. Academic Press, London.

Peacock, D 1977b. 'Pompeian Red Ware', in Peacock, D (ed), *Pottery and Early Commerce: characterisation and Trade in Roman and Later Ceramics*, pp. 147–162. Academic Press, London.

Peacock, D & D Williams 1977. "The amphorae' *in* Partridge, C. Excavations at Puckeridge and Braughing 1975–79', *Hertfordshire Archaeology*, 7: 113–116.

Peacock, DPS 1971. 'Roman amphorae in pre-Roman Britain', in Jesson, M & Hill, D (eds), *The Iron Age and its Hill Forts*, pp. 161–88. Department of Archaeology, University of Southampton, Southampton.

Pearson, GW, JR Pilcher, MGL Baillie, DM Corbett, & F Qua 1986. 'High-precision 14C measurement of Irish Oaks to show the natural 14C variations from AD 1840 to 5210 BC', *Radiocarbon*, 28: 911–934.

Pearson, GW & M Stuiver 1986. 'High-precision calibration of the radiocarbon time scale, 500–2500 BC', *Radiocarbon*, 28 (2B): 839–862.

Percival, J 1976. *The Roman Villa*. Batsford, London.

Philp, BJ 1976. *A Walk through Keston. 7: The Roman Tombs at Warbank*.

Price, J 1979. "The Glass' *in* Gracie, H. S. and Price, E.G. Frocester Court Roman Villa', *Transactions of the Bristol and Glos. Archaeological Society*, 97: 9–64.

Pryor, F 1980. *Excavations at Fengate, Peterborough, England: The Third Report*. Northants. Archaeological Monographs 1 (ROM Monograph 6). Royal Ontario Museum.

Ralegh Radford, CA 1936. 'The Roman Villa at Ditchley, Oxon.', *Oxoniensia*, 1: 24–69.

Ralegh Radford, CA 1972. 'Excavations at Cricklade', *Wiltshire Archaeological Magazine*, 67: 61–111.

Ravetz, A 1964. 'The fourth-century inflation and Romano-British coin finds', *Numismatic Chronicle*, 47: 201–231.

Rawes, B 1981. 'The Romano-British site at Brockworth, Glos.', *Britannia*, pp. 45–77.

R.C.H.M.(E) 1976. *County of Gloucester. Volume 1: Iron Age and Romano-British Monuments in the Cotswolds*. H. M. S. O, London.

Reynolds, PJ 1979. *Iron Age Farm: the Butser Experiment*. Colonnade Book.

Reynolds, PJ 1981. 'New Approaches to Familiar Problems', in Jones, M & Dimbleby, G (eds), *The Environment of Man: the Iron Age to the Anglo-Saxon period*.

Richardson, L 1933. *The country around Cirencester*. Memoirs of the Geological Survey England and Wales of Sheet 235. HMSO, London.

Richmond, I 1968. *Hod Hill Vol. Two. Excavations carried out between 1951 and 1958 for the Trustees of the British Museum.* London.

Rigby, V 1982a. 'The Pottery', in Wacher, J & McWhirr, AD (eds), *Early Roman Occupation at Cirencester: Cirencester Excavations I.* Cirencester.

Rigby, V 1982b. 'The Pottery', in McWhirr, AD, Viner, L, & Wells, C (eds), *Romano-British Cemeteries at Cirencester: Cirencester Excavations II.* Cirencester.

Riley, DN 1942. 'Crop-marks in the Upper Thames Valley seen from the air during 1942', *Oxoniensia*, 7: 111–114.

Riley, DN 1943–4. 'Archaeology from the air in the Upper Thames Valley', *Oxoniensia*, 8 & 9: 64–101.

Rivet, ALF 1969. *The Roman Villa in Britain.* Routledge & Kegan Paul, London.

Rogers, GB 1974. *Poteries Sigillées de la Gaule Centrale, I, Les motifs non figurés*, 28, Supplément à. Paris.

Rowlands, MJ 1976. *The production and distribution of metalwork in the Middle Bronze Age of Southern Britain.* British Series 31. British Archaeological Reports, Oxford.

Rowley, T & L Brown 1981. 'Excavations at Beech House Hotel', *Oxoniensia*, 46: 1–55.

Royal Commission on Historical Monuments 1960. *A matter of time — an archaeological survey.* Her Majesty's Stationery Office, London.

Saville, A 1980. 'Five flint assemblages from excavated sites in Wiltshire', *Wiltshire Archaeological Magazine*, 72/3: 1–27.

Saville, A 1983. 'Excavations at Condicote Henge monument, Gloucestershire', *Transactions of the Bristol and Glos. Archaeological Society*, 101: 21–48.

Shennan, SJ, F Healey, & IF Smith 1985. 'The excavation of a ring-ditch at Tye Field, Lawford, Essex', *Archaeological Journal*, 142: 150–215.

Shepherd, J 1982. 'Appendix II. The Glass fragments from Southfield Road, in Clarke, G. The Roman Villa at Woodchester', *Britannia*, XIII: 227–228.

Silver, IA 1969. 'The ageing of domestic animals', in Brothwell, D & Higgs, E (eds), *Science in Archaeology*, pp. 283–302. Thames and Hudson, London. Revised edition.

Simpson, G 1957. 'Metallic Black Slip Vases from Central Gaul with applied and Moulded Decoration', *Antiquaries Journal*, 38: 29–42.

Smith, AG, C Grigson, G Hillman, & MJ Tooley 1981. 'The Neolithic', in Simmons, IG & Tooley, MJ (eds), *The Environment in British Prehistory*, pp. 125–209. Duckworth, Liverpool.

Smith, DJ 1978. 'Regional aspects of the winged corridor villa in Britain', in Todd, M (ed), *Studies in the Romano-British villa*, pp. 117–147. Leicester.

Smith, I 1961. 'An Essay towards the Reformation of the British Bronze Age', *Helenium*, 1: 95–118.

Smith, IF 1971. 'Ring ditches in eastern and central Gloucestershire', in Fowler, PJ (ed), *Archaeology and the landscape*, pp. 157–167. John Baker Ltd, London.

Smith, JT 1963. 'Roman-British aisled houses', *Archaeological Journal*, 120: 1–20.

Smith, JT 1978. 'Villas as a Key to social structure', in Todd, M (ed), *Studies in the Romano-British Villa*, pp. 149–186. Leicester.

Spurr, MS 1986. *Arable cultivation in Roman Italy c. 200 BC–100 AD.* Journal of Roman Studies Monograph 3. Institute of Archaeology, London.

Stanfield, J & G Simpson 1958. *Central Gaulish Potters.* Oxford University Press, Oxford.

Stanfield, JA 1929. 'Unusual forms of Terra Sigillata', *Archaeological Journal*, 86: 113–151.

Stead, I 1979. *Iron Age cemeteries in Champagne. The Third Interim Report.* Occasional Paper 6. British Museum Publications, London.

Stead, IM 1976. *Excavations at Winterton Roman Villa and other Roman sites in North Lincolnshire.* DOE Archaeological Reports 9. Her Majesty's Stationery Office, London.

Stuiver, M & GW Pearson 1986. 'High-precision calibration of the radiocarbon time scale, AD 1950–500 BC', *Radiocarbon*, 28 (2B): 805–838.

Stuiver, M & P Reimer 1986. 'A computer program for radiocarbon age calibration', *Radiocarbon*, 28 (2B): 1022–1030.

Stuiver, M & P Reimer 1989. 'Users' Guide to the programs CALIB and DISPLAY rev. 2.1', Technical report, Quaternary Isotope Lab, University of Washington.

Swan, V 1975. 'Oare reconsidered and the origins of Savernake Ware in Wiltshire', *Britannia*, 6: 39–61.

Taylor, MV 1948. 'A fragment of Romano–British sculpture from Lechlade', *Oxoniensia*, 13: 76.

Thomas, N 1955. 'Excavations at Vicarage Field, Stanton Harcourt, 1951', *Oxoniensia*, 20: 1–28.

Thomas, R 1980. 'A Bronze Age field system at Northfield Farm?', *Oxoniensia*, 45: 310–11.

Tinsley, HM & C Grigson 1981. 'The Bronze Age', in Simmons, IG & Tooley, MJ (eds), *The Environment in British Prehistory*, pp. 210–249. Duckworth, Liverpool.

Todd, M 1978. *Studies in the Romano-British Villa.* Leicester University Press.

Toynbee, JMC 1964. *Art in Britain under the Romans.* Oxford University Press.

Trow, S 1982. *Excavations at 'The Ditches' Hillfort, North Cerney, Gloucestershire (a second interim report).*

Vanvinckenroye, W 1989. *Terra sigillata uit wen Romeinse Stortplaats te Tongeren.* Province of Limburg: Hasselt, Tongeren.

Vatcher, FM 1965. 'Lechlade cursus', in *Excavations, Annual Report 5, 1965.* H.M.S.O., London.

Wacher, J & AD McWhirr (eds) 1982. *Early Roman*

Occupation at Cirencester: Cirencester Excavations I. Cirencester Excavation Committee, Cirencester.

Wainwright, GJ 1979. *Gussage All Saints: an iron age settlement in Dorset*. Archaeological Reports 10. H. M. S. O., Dept. of Environment, London.

Wainwright, GJ & IH Longworth 1971. *Durrington Walls: Excavations 1966–1968.* Research Reports 29. Society of Antiquaries, London.

Ward, GK & SR Wilson 1978. 'Procedures for comparing and combining radiocarbon age determinations: a critique', *Archaeometry*, 20: 19–31.

Warren, HS, S Piggott, JG Clark, MC Burkitt, H Godwin, & ME Godwin 1936. 'Archaeology of the submerged land-surface of the Essex coast', *Proceedings of the Prehistoric Society*, 2: 178–210.

Webster, G 1981. 'The Excavations of a Romano-British Rural Establishment at Barnsley Park', *Transactions of the Bristol and Glos. Archaeological Society*, 99: 21–78.

Webster, G, P Fowler, B Noddle, & L Smith 1985. 'The Excavation of a Romano-British Rural Establishment at Barnsley Park, Gloucestershire, 1961–1979: Part III', *Transactions of the Bristol and Glos. Archaeological Society*, 103: 73–82.

Webster, G & L Smith 1982. 'The Excavation of a Romano-British Rural Settlement at Barnsley Park: Part II', *Transactions of the Bristol and Glos. Archaeological Society*, 100: 65–189.

Webster, P 1976. 'Severn Valley Ware: a preliminary study', *Transactions of the Bristol and Glos. Archaeological Society*, 94: 18–46.

Wheeler, REM 1943. *Maiden Castle*, Research Reports 12. Society of Antiquaries, London.

Whimster, R 1981. *Burial Practices in Iron Age Britain. A Discussion and Gazetteer of the Evidence c. 700 B.C.–A.D. 43.* British Series 90. British Archaeological Reports, Oxford.

Williams, A 1947. 'Excavations at Langford Downs, Oxon (near Lechlade) in 1943', *Oxoniensia*, 11 & 12: 44–64.

Williams, D 1977. 'The Romano-British black burnished industry: an essay on characterisation by heavy mineral analysis', in Peacock, D (ed), *Pottery and Early Commerce*, pp. 163–220. Academic Press.

Williams, JH 1979. *Excavations at St Peters St, Northampton 1973–76.* Archaeological Monograph 2. Northampton Development Corporation.

Wilson, CE 1981. 'Burials within settlements in Southern Britain during the pre-Roman Iron Age', *Bulletin of the Institute of Archaeology*, 18.

Wilson, R 1978. 'The Animal Bones', in Parrington, M (ed), *The excavation of an Iron Age Settlement, Bronze Age Ring-Ditches and Roman Features at Ashville Trading Estate, Abingdon 1974–76*, pp. 110–126 and 133–139.

Wilson, R 1979. 'The vertebrates', in Lambrick, GH & Robinson, M (eds), *Iron Age and Roman riverside settlements at Farmoor, Oxfordshire*, pp. 128–133. Council for British Archaeology, London.

Wilson, R 1986. 'Faunal Remains: animal bones and marine shells', in Miles, D (ed), *Barton Court Farm Abingdon, Oxon*.

Woodfield, C & C Johnson 1989. 'A Roman site at Stanton Low on the Great Ouse, Buckinghamshire', *Archaeological Journal*, 146: 135–278.

Woods, PJ 1974. 'Types of Late Belgic and Early Romano-British Pottery Kilns in the Nene Valley', *Britannia*, 5: 262–281.

Young, CJ 1977. *The Roman Pottery Industry of the Oxford Region*. British Series 43. British Archaeological Reports, Oxford.